THE EVOLUTION OF THE ARMED FORCES
OF THE UNITED ARAB EMIRATES

Modern Military History

Series Editors

Alaric Searle, Professor of Modern European History, University of Salford, UK

Tim Bowman, Reader in Military History, University of Kent, UK

This series is dedicated to making available, at a reasonable price, quality academic military history, based on innovative and thorough scholarly research. While the main emphasis is on the publication of single-authored monographs, there will be scope for edited collections which focus primarily on new perspectives and evidence, as well as occasional translations of important foreign-language studies. *Modern Military History* will be framed in an 'inclusive' fashion, so that it encompasses armies, navies and air forces. While the traditional core concerns of military history – such as tactics, combat experience, technology, strategy and officer education – remain important fields of consideration, the encouragement of new angles and original approaches, whether methodologically, geographically or thematically, form a significant part of the editors' agenda.

Titles

The Evolution of the Armed Forces of the United Arab Emirates

Athol Yates

 Helion & Company Limited

Helion & Company Limited
Unit 8 Amherst Business Centre
Budbrooke Road
Warwick
CV34 5WE
England
Tel. 01926 499 619
Email: info@helion.co.uk
Website: www.helion.co.uk
Twitter: @helionbooks
blog.helion.co.uk

Published by Helion & Company 2020
Designed and typeset by Mach 3 Solutions (www.mach3solutions.co.uk)
Cover designed by Paul Hewitt, Battlefield Design (www.battlefield-design.co.uk)

ISBN 978-1-912866-00-7

British Library Cataloguing-in-Publication Data.
A catalogue record for this book is available from the British Library.

For details of other military history titles published by Helion & Company Limited
contact the above address or visit our website: http://www.helion.co.uk.

We always welcome receipt of book proposals from prospective authors.

Contents

List of Tables

List of Figures

Abbreviations

2IC	second-in-command
AA	anti-aircraft
ADDF	Abu Dhabi Defence Force
AFAD	Air Force and Air Defence
ALIS	Autonomic Logistics Information System
APC	armoured personnel carrier
AQAP	Al Qaeda in the Arabian Peninsula
ARAMCO	Arabian American Oil Company
Armd	armoured
Arty	artillery
AWQAF	General Authority of Islamic Affairs and Endowments
Bde	brigade
BFG	British Forces Gulf
Bn	battalion
BFAP	British Forces Arabian Peninsula
Bty	battery
CDS	Chief of Defence Staff
CICPA	Critical Infrastructure and Coastal Protection Authority
C-in-C	Commander-in-Chief
CIA	Central Intelligence Agency
CICPA	Critical Infrastructure and Coastal Protection Authority
CIWS	close-in weapon system
CMC	Central Military Command
CNIA	Critical National Infrastructure Authority
CO	Commanding Officer
CoS	Chief of Staff
CPC	Crown Prince's Court
est.	established
FAC	fast attack craft
FAF	Federal Armed Force
FCO	Foreign and Commonwealth Office
FMS	Foreign Military Sale

FO	Foreign Office
GCC	Gulf Cooperation Council
GDP	gross domestic product
GHQ	General Headquarters
GPMG	general purpose machine gun
GSO	General Staff Officer
HQ	headquarters
Inf	infantry
IRGC	Islamic Revolutionary Guard Corps
ISIS	Islamic State of Iraq and Syria
IFV	infantry fighting vehicle
JAC	Joint Aviation Command
JSF	Joint Strike Fighter
LIC	Local Intelligence Committee
LMG	light machine gun
MBT	Main battle tank
MCO	Military Contract Officer
MECA	Middle East Centre Archive
MMG	medium machine gun
MoD	Ministry of Defence
MoU	Memorandum of Agreement
MRAP	Mine-resistant ambush protected
MV	motor vessel
N/A	not applicable
NCO	Non-Commissioned Officer
OC	Officer Commanding
OPEC	Organization of the Petroleum Exporting Countries
PFLO	Popular Front for the Liberation of Oman
PFLOAG	Popular Front for the Liberation of Oman and the Arabian Gulf
PRG	Political Resident Gulf
PRPG	Political Resident Persian Gulf
r.	ruled
RAF	Royal Air Force
RAKMF	Ras Al Khaimah Mobile Force
SAM	surface-to-air missile
SAOPG	Senior Army Officer, Persian Gulf
SAS	Special Air Service
SAT	systems approach to training
SIPRI	Stockholm International Peace Research Institute
SNG	Sharjah National Guard
SNOPG	Senior Naval Officer, Persian Gulf
SO	Staff Officer
Sqn	squadron

STOL	short takeoff and landing
SWAT	special weapons and tactics
TIV	Trend Indicator Values
TNA	The National Archives
TOL	Trucial Oman Levies
TOS	Trucial Oman Scouts
UAE	United Arab Emirates
UAQNG	Umm Al Quwain National Guard
UAV	unmanned aerial vehicles
UDF	Union Defence Force
UK	United Kingdom
US	United States
VTOL	vertical take-off and landing
WAM	Emirates News Agency

Terminology

Armed forces of the Emirates versus Emirati armed forces

The term *armed forces of the Emirates* refers to all armed forces that have existed in either the Trucial States (pre-1971) or UAE (post-1971) periods, regardless of whether the force was British-controlled, ruler-controlled or federally-controlled. The term *Emirati Armed Forces* refer to militaries controlled by Emirati political leadership (i.e. ruler-controlled and federally controlled armed forces) but not British-controlled armed forces. This division is important to the narrative of this book. Table 1 lists the armed forces of the Emirates divided into these categories.

Figure 1 shows how the armed forces of the Emirates and their major formations evolved from 1951 to 2020. Part three of the book provides a detailed history of these forces.

Table 1: Armed forces of the Emirates[1]

Emirati armed forces		British-controlled armed forces
Ruler-controlled armed forces	**Federally controlled armed forces**	
Abu Dhabi Defence Force (1965-76)	Union Defence Force (1971-74)	Trucial Oman Levies (1951-56)
Dubai Defence Force (1970-76)		Trucial Oman Scouts (1956-71)
Central Military Command (1976-98)	Federal Armed Force (1974-76)	Royal Air Force (1952-71)
Sharjah National Guard (1972-76)		British Army (1955-71)
Sharjah's re-established armed force (1984-90)	UAE Armed Forces (1976-present)	Royal Navy (1800s-1971)
Ras Al Khaimah Mobile Force (1969-76)		
Ras Al Khaimah's re-established armed force (1984-mid-1990s)		
Umm Al Quwain National Guard (1975-2006)		

---

1   The establishment date of a force/formation is denoted in brackets. Minor formations and units are detailed in chapters 7 to 9.

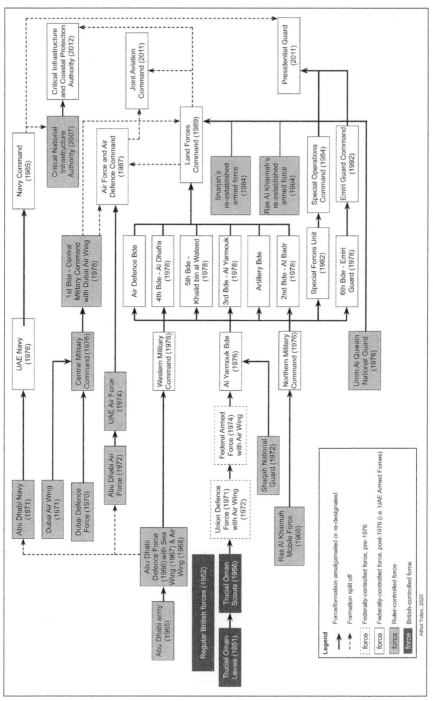

Figure 1: The evolution of armed forces and major combat formations in the Emirates, 1951-2020.

Nationals, expatriates, and residents

Following common practice in the UAE, the terms *national*s, *locals,* and *Emiratis* are interchangeable and used to mean those holding Emirati citizenship. *Expatriates* are those who have come from a foreign country to live and work in the Emirates for an extended period. The term *resident* is used to mean those who have their primary residence in the UAE regardless of nationality, that is, both expatriates and nationals.

Force, commands, formations, units and commanders

The term *force* is used to mean an armed force and has no relationship to the force's manpower numbers or the rank of its professional head. For example, the Ras Al Khaimah Mobile Force in the early 1970s consisted of just several hundred men and was commanded by a Lieutenant-Colonel, while the UAE Armed Forces today have an establishment strength of over 60,000 and are commanded by a Lieutenant-General.

A *command* is a collection of formations and units under the control of a single officer, who reports directly to a general headquarters. A command typically has several thousand personnel and covers either a geographic area or a function.

A *formation* comprises numbers of aircraft, ships or units under a single commander, and is capable of undertaking significant combat operations. Examples include divisions (land forces), brigades (land forces), wings (air force) and flotillas (navy).

A *unit* is a small organisation which is usually is made up of personnel from a single arm of service. Examples are battalions (land forces), squadrons (air force) and divisions (navy).

In this book, if the word *group* is added to a formation/unit, it indicates that the formation has additional elements attached to it. For example, a *brigade group* could be made up of an infantry brigade with engineers and logistic units attached. If the word *light* or *heavy* is added, it indicates that the unit respectively lacks or exceeds its standard complement of personnel and equipment.

Appendix 4 contains the nomenclature of formations and units used by Emirati armed forces.

This book uses the British Army naming convention for commanders as this convention has generally been used by the various armed forces of the Emirates:

- *Commander* (Lieutenant-Colonel or above) to mean a commander of a higher formation or a force (e.g. Commander Abu Dhabi Defence Force)
- *Commanding Officer* (CO) (Lieutenant-Colonel or Colonel) to mean a commander of a large formation (e.g. CO 4th Battalion)
- *Officer Commanding* (OC) (Captain or Major) to mean a commander of a unit (e.g. OC 9th Squadron)

Preface

When I took up a position at Abu Dhabi's Khalifa University to teach a Masters course in security studies to Emirati security professionals in 2013, I was surprised to find an almost complete lack of useful information on the UAE Armed Forces and its antecedent forces. The exception was coverage of the British-controlled force in the Emirates, the Trucial Oman Levies/Scouts, which existed between 1951 and 1971. While there were useful and reliable summaries of Emirati-controlled forces written in the early 1980s,[1] little has been produced since then.

This lack of attention was particularly surprising given that the UAE Armed Forces are probably the most capable Arab military in terms of its ability to undertake joint, sustained, and expeditionary operations, or more poetically a 'Little Sparta', a term attributed to General James Mattis, the recent US Secretary of Defense.[2] Over the last decade, the UAE military has been deployed operationally across the region including to Libya, Iraq, Afghanistan and Yemen. It has gone from being a recipient to a supplier of military expertise, with its training teams and advisors having supported forces in Somalia, Puntland, Yemen, and Seychelles, to name just a few states.

Its level of combat effectiveness is a considerable achievement given that the UAE became a fully sovereign nation only in 1971. It is even more so the case considering that until the early 1960s, much of the population lived as their ancestors had – in fishing, agriculture, and animal husbandry. There was little or no education, health services, roads, piped water, or electricity. And its first locally controlled armed force was formed only in 1965.

This book seeks, then, to provide an authoritative, narrative account of the evolution of the UAE Armed Forces. It is divided into three parts. The first covers the physical, social, political and historical environment as these have shaped and continue to shape the country's military development. The second part describes the defining characteristics of Emirati armed forces. It details the enduring roles of Emirati militaries over their six decades of existence, and how political control of the armed forces has

---

1   Notable examples are J.E. Peterson, *Defending Arabia* (London, 1986); J.B. Kelly, *Arabia, the Gulf and the West* (London, 1980).
2   Rajiv Chandrasekaran, 'In the UAE, the United States Has a Quiet, Potent Ally Nicknamed "Little Sparta"', *The Washington Post*, 9 November 2014.

changed over time. It also identifies the characteristics which have made the UAE Armed Forces markedly different from other armed forces in the region – notably its preference for advanced hardware, a multi-country sourcing strategy, limited domestic manpower and engagement of expatriates. The third and largest part of the book provides the most comprehensive history of the armed forces of the Emirates to date. This history focuses on the key elements that generate military capabilities, notably force structure, materiel, and personnel.

One of the primary aims of the book is to provide accurate information on the UAE Armed Forces. This is because much of what has been and continues to be written about them is incomplete, out-of-date, or incorrect. For example, the following statement appeared in a specialist military journal in 2012:

> The army of the United Arab Emirates has 49,000 men … That ground force is augmented by three separate sheikhdom forces. The 15,000 strong Abu Dhabi Defense Force has two mechanized infantry brigades, an artillery battalion, a squadron of Hawker Hunter fighters and four coastal patrol boats. The 2,000-man Dubai Defense Force is organized into a single infantry brigade called the Central Military Command, while the small sheikhdom of Ras Al Khayman [sic] fields a 900-man Defense Force Group.[3]

The errors in this extract are numerous. For instance, the so-called 'separate sheikhdom forces' had been integrated into the UAE Armed Forces decades before, the Abu Dhabi Defence Force ceased to exist in 1976, and the force's Hawker Hunters had in fact been given to Somalia in 1983.[4] Hence, a key purpose of this book is to provide, for the first time, an accurate account of the history of the armed forces of the Emirates. To enable readers to cross check this account with other writings, extensive footnotes are included which not only contain the sources of the information provided in the book but also useful contextual information.

This book has been written for several different groups of readers. One is foreign military personnel and their civilian counterparts who study, work alongside or support capacity-building in the Gulf. The book will also be of use to academics, graduate students and policy makers interested in Arab Gulf military affairs and UAE modern history. To support the reader – whether they are military, academic or an interested layperson – the book provides both detailed country and military background information, and examples of points, aiming to provide the context necessary to appreciate the meaning of significant developments.

This book only came to fruition through the support of many individuals. The most important is Jacinta Nelligan, to whom I am deeply indebted. She has not only

---

3   V. Liebl, 'Oil War: Iran and the Military Balance in the Persian Gulf', *Modern War*, Nov-Dec 2012.
4   TNA FCO 31/4053: UK Embassy in Mogadishu, 'Hawker Hunters', 11 July 1983.

provided wonderful encouragement and support, but also considerable editorial input. Without her, this work would not have come to fruition.

I am extremely grateful to my editor, Professor Alaric Searle, for his valuable contributions which have markedly improved the book. I also wish to thank my current and former colleagues for their expert guidance and valuable subject matter knowledge: these include Dr Ash Rossiter, Dr Victor Gervais, Dr Brendon Cannon, Dr Joel Hayward, and UAE historian Peter Hellyer. Many others have made valuable contributions, including those who have served in the UAE military, and both Emirati and foreign academics. While I cannot mention all those who contributed to my research for confidentiality reasons, the following individuals in particular deserve my gratitude: Major-General Sheikh Saeed bin Hamdan bin Mohammad Al Nahyan, Lt Colonel Sheikh Zayed bin Hamad bin Hamdan Al Nahyan, Major-General Andrew Pillar, Captain Mohammad Abdullah Al Abdouli, Mike Brennan, Michael Curtis, Norvell DeAtkine, Mike Edgerton, Stephen Franke, David Gregory, Steve Hay, Robin Hitchcock, Ali Iqbal, Andrew James, Ahmed Khimas, Cliff Lord, Barry McCombe, David Neild, Dr James Onley, J.E. Peterson, Kenneth Pollack, Ahmed Shubbar, Keith Steel, Miles Stockwell, Dr Kristian Coates Ulrichsen, Sir Harold 'Hooky' Walker, Tony Wallington, Zoltan Barany, Dr Nigel Warwick, Jeremy Williams, Gil Barndollar and Hugo Willis.

I would like to acknowledge the support and cooperation of the following institutions, which hold significant collections of primary source material: the National Archives of the UAE; the National Archives of the United Kingdom, Kew; the Middle East Centre Archives, St Antony's College, Oxford; and the UAE Armed Forces Museum and Military History Centre.

Finally, I wish to thank all the Emirati students I have both taught and learned much from. Of these, I am particularly indebted to Sheikh Mohammad bin Hamad bin Tahnoon Al Nahyan, Eng. Nawaf Alnuaimi, Eng. Saeed Mohammed Al Dhaheri, Mohammad Al Olama, Khalid Mohammad Al Tahsoun Al Shehhi, Brigadier Ahmed Bisho, Musabbeh Alghaithi, Ahmed Madloum, Narmeen Qambar, Fatima Al Qubaisi, Ahmed Al Khateri, Ahmed Al Yammahi, Ali Al Mazrouei, Mohamed Al Zanki, Haleema Al Hosani, Hind Al Shamsi, Huda Bamatraf, Jasim Al Shammri, Maryam Mazrouei, Mohamed Al Mesaabi, Dr Mohamed Al Kuwaiti, Brigadier Nasser Al Otaibi, Sultan Al Darmaki, Talal Faris, Abdulla Al Jallaf, Abdulla Al Tunaiji, Surour Ali Surour Al Nuaimi, Saif Al Khafili and Ahmed Alghaithi. Knowing these and the other students, I am confident that the future of the UAE is in good hands.

Athol Yates
20 September 2020

Part I

How Environment has Shaped the Military

1

Physical Environment

A nation's armed force is a distinct product of its environment – notably its geography and climate, and its peoples and their culture, and its political system and geopolitical evolution. As such, the evolution of any military cannot be understood without this context. This chapter begins by describing the Emirates' physical environment, which has enormously shaped all aspects of the country, such as its desirability for control by foreign states, its population, and its system of political control.

The UAE occupies a small land mass along the shores of the Lower Arabian Gulf[1] and Gulf of Oman (Figure 2). It is located in an area of great strategic importance. Historically this was because the area bridges the continents of Africa and Asia and sits along maritime routes connecting the Arabian Gulf with the Indian Ocean. Thus it has bordered a key route for commercial, imperial, expeditionary and religious travel. In the modern era, it has become critical because much of the world's oil supplies come from the countries along the Arabian Gulf. This has given these states great economic and financial power, making them major players in the world's globalised economy. More recently this power, coupled with the collapse of traditional Middle Eastern powers such as Iraq and Syria, has made the Gulf States key players in the politics of the Middle East and beyond.

Geography

The UAE is a small country, physically being about the size of Scotland or Austria. Its mainland area is approximately 71,000km², or around 83,600km² if its islands are included.[2]

---

1   This volume employs the term *Arabian Gulf* rather than *Persian Gulf* as the former is used by the UAE and other Arab States, and commonly by Western powers.
2   UAE Ministry of Environment and Water, *State of Environment 2015* (Abu Dhabi, 2016), p. 7; UAE National Media Council, *UAE Annual Book 2016* (Abu Dhabi, 2017), p. 6.

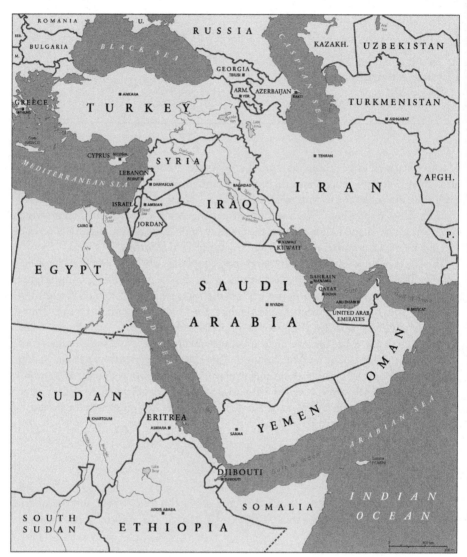

Figure 2: The Arabian Peninsula and region.

The UAE's mainland has a 734km coastline, made up of a 644km coastline along the Arabian Gulf and a 90km one along the Gulf of Oman.[3] The Arabian Gulf is a relatively shallow body of water which is rarely more than 90m deep. Historically the waters of the Emirates have been valued for their fishing and the availability of pearl oysters, as well as being a route for trade. Since the late 1950s, when oil was first discovered both onshore and offshore, the waterways of the Emirates have become essential as a key element of the country's economic and political power. Ensuring uninterrupted shipping in Gulf waters is also essential for the population's survival, as some 90 percent of all food consumed in the UAE is imported. Gulf waters are also the source of desalinated water which provides the vast bulk of the country's domestically consumed water. Thus, contamination of Gulf waters from oil, chemicals, radiation or algal blooms, or the cessation of shipping, both pose an existential threat to the Emirates.

Connecting the Arabian Gulf and the Gulf of Oman is the Strait of Hormuz. This waterway is just 54km wide at its narrowest point. It is bordered to the north by Iran, and to the south by both the UAE and the Musandam exclave of Oman. Around 30 percent of the world's seaborne-traded crude oil and other liquids passes through the Strait. It is one of the world's greatest maritime chokepoints, which means that regional powers have the ability to threaten a global economic shock by shutting down the flow of liquid fuels.

The UAE's coastline in the Gulf of Oman was historically only of importance to the local economy, except in the distant past when both Khor Fakkan and Dibba were important trading ports. However, over the last decade, it has assumed national importance, and growing regional significance. This followed the completion in 2012 of a crude oil pipeline connecting the oil fields in the UAE's west to Fujairah on the Gulf of Oman,[4] and the earlier construction of large ports at both Fujairah and Khor Fakkan. Fujairah is currently the world's second largest bunkering port. By 2022, Fujairah will become even more important. This is when the world's largest crude oil storage facility just outside the city is expected to be opened, making Fujairah a global oil storage and trading hub.[5] Nationally, the growth of Fujairah's facilities is also of great significance for they provide the UAE with an export and import route for oil and other goods which bypasses the Strait of Hormuz.

The UAE has over 200 islands, the majority of which are off the coast of Abu Dhabi Emirate. Most of these are small, often being little more than sand atolls. Nonetheless, some are of considerable size with the largest being Abu Al Abyadh Island at 306km^2.

---

3   UAE Ministry of Environment and Water, *State of Environment 2015*, p. 7.
4   The Habshan-Fujairah oil pipeline, also known as Abu Dhabi Crude Oil Pipeline (ADCOP), was commissioned in 2012 and has a capacity of 1.5 million barrels per day.
5   In early 2019, a contract was signed to construct three underground storage caverns in Fujairah, each with a capacity of 14 million barrels. WAM. 'ADNOC, SKEC to Build in UAE the World's Largest Single Underground Project Ever Awarded for Oil Storage', 27 February 2019 <wam.ae/en/details/1395302743139>

The second largest, Abu Dhabi Island (8km wide by 14.5km long), hosts the city of Abu Dhabi which is the capital of both the UAE and Abu Dhabi Emirate. This island is separated from the mainland by a channel deepened by dredging which today is about 500m wide.

While most UAE islands are close to the coastline, some are well offshore, such as Dalma, Zirku and Das Islands. A number of these are of great strategic importance because they are located near the main Gulf sea lanes, offshore oil fields, or close to the Strait of Hormuz and Iran, and, in the case of Das and Zirku islands, being major processing centres for offshore oilfields. Three of these islands have been seized by Iran – Abu Musa, Greater Tunb and Lesser Tunb. Territorial waters stretch out to 12 nautical miles from the coast, but due to the close proximity of neighbouring countries, the UAE's Exclusive Economic Zone does not extend out to the theoretical maximum of 200 nautical miles (Figure 6 shows UAE waters along with its major oil fields).[6]

The immediate littoral along the Arabian Gulf coast is very shallow and dotted with numerous reefs, shifting sandbars, islands and fast running channels which change frequently due to storms and tides. These characteristics make coastal navigation diffi-cult, and also prevent boats with deep drafts getting close to the shore along much of the coast. This means that attackers who wanted to launch an amphibious operation would either be limited to a few locations where the natural geography allows vessels with larger draughts to get close to the shore, or would have to offload equipment and personnel onto small, flat bottomed vessels to be transported ashore. Thus the littoral environment provides a significant deterrence against amphibious invasions.

The UAE has a 410km land border with Oman and a 457km land border with Saudi Arabia. Abu Dhabi Emirate has historically had a border with Qatar, but since the 1970s has been separated by a corridor of land several dozen kilometres wide which has been claimed by Saudi Arabia. Oman also has one enclave surrounded by the UAE – Madha (75km²), located half-way between Musandam and the rest of Oman.

The climate of the Emirates is harsh, as the country is in the subtropical arid zone of the Middle East. The mean annual rainfall is low (78mm), but there is consider-able variation across the country. The south-west desert areas typically receive around 40mm a year while in the north-eastern mountains it is 160mm.[7] The summers are hot, reaching 50°C with 100 percent humidity. There are no permanent rivers or lakes in the UAE, with only a few springs in the mountains.[8] Until desalination began, virtually all water came from ground sources, mainly wells and small water catch-ment systems which hold winter rainfall. Water was also brought in from elsewhere,

6   This give the UAE an Exclusive Economic Zone of 59,300km, V.L. Forbes, *The Maritime Boundaries of the Indian Ocean Region* (Singapore, 1995), p. 103.

7   K. Frenken, *Irrigation in the Middle East Region in Figures: AQUASTAT Survey – 2008*, 2009), p. 1.

8   There are or were springs at a number of places including Wadi Wurrayah and Ain Al Ghammour, both in the Hajar Mountains, plus a few small springs in the inter-tidal areas, such as on Marawah Island. P. Hellyer, email, 20 December 2018.

such as by boat from the western island of Dalma, or from Kuwait. The country has two main seasons – winter (December to March) and summer (June to September) – which are separated by two short transition periods where the average temperature changes very rapidly.

The UAE can be divided into four topographical zones: (1) the coastal plain and *sabkha* of the Arabian Gulf coast, (2) the desert, (3) the Hajar Mountains and coastal plains of the Gulf of Oman, and (4) the gravel plains. These zones are shown in Figure 3. Some 20 percent of the nation is made up of the Hajar Mountains, with the rest consisting of arid plains and deserts.[9] Figure 3 also shows places of significance in the early years of the Emirates' military history, while Figure 4 shows such places in more recent decades.

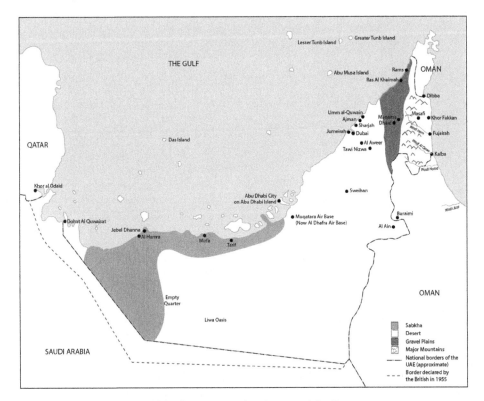

Figure 3: The four topographical zones of the Emirates.

---

9   E. O'Sullivan, *The New Gulf: How Modern Arabia Is Changing the World for Good* (Dubai, 2009), pp. 255-56.

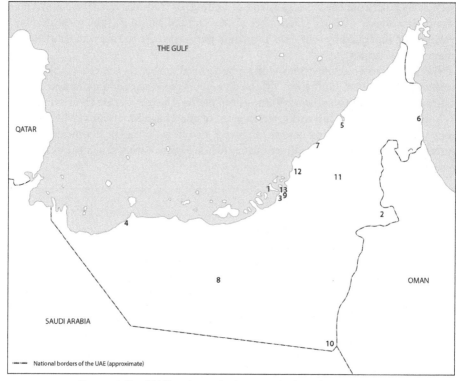

Figure 4: Key UAE military facilities marked on Google Maps.

Key

1. Abu Dhabi Island, location of GHQ, Ministry of Defence, Al Bateen Air Base and Abu Dhabi Naval Base (Zayed Port)
2. Al Ain, location of Zayed Military College, Khalifa Air College, Al Ain Air Base, Presidential Guard Institute, as well as several bases
3. Al Dhafra Air Base
4. Al Hamra, location of an air and land base
5. Al Minhad Airbase
6. Fujairah Naval Base
7. Ghantoot Naval Base
8. Liwa (Al Safran) Airbase
9. Mahawi, location of Khawla bint Al Azwar Military School plus several bases
10. Qasawera Air Base (also written as Qusaihwira)
11. Sweihan (Zayed Military City), location of Sweihan Air Base, Land Forces Institute, Air Force and Air Defence Institute, Joint Aviation Command Institute, CISPA Institute, plus several bases
12. Taweelah, location of Rashid bin Saeed Al Maktoum Naval College, Taweelah Naval Base and Coast Guard School
13. Sas Al Nakhl Air Base

The topographical zones

The coastal plain and sabkha of the Arabian Gulf coast

The UAE's 734km long Arabian Gulf coastline is characterised by sand beaches, pockets of mangroves,[10] numerous inlets, and a low, flat and featureless coastal plain. This plain includes intermittent *sabkha* which commonly extends up to 20km inland. *Sabkha* is a salt-encrusted, low-lying flatland that exists in areas where the heavily-saline water table is close to the surface. It is firm and can be crossed when dry. After rains, the crust impedes drainage and turns the *sabkha* into a quagmire, making crossing impractical.

The largest area of *sabkha* is on the western coastline of Abu Dhabi Emirate. Known as *Sabkha Matti*, it extends 150km along the coast and 150km inland. Before roads were constructed along the coast, when the *Sabkha Matti* was dry, travellers could walk across it with their camels. Although it was the shortest route between Qatar/Saudi Arabia and Abu Dhabi/Buraimi, travelling across it was unusual as there were no water wells in the area. Invariably travellers passed along an inland route which skirted around the south of *Sabkha Matti* before continuing eastward and well inland. They would then turn either north east to Abu Dhabi or south-east to Buraimi. Starting in the 1940s, cars became more frequent and they would use the sea-coast route across *Sabkha Matti* when this was possible in the dry season.[11] If vehicles from the west travelled along this route, they would commonly continue along the coast to Jebel Dhanna and eastwards via Mirfa and Tarif or southwards to Liwa.

Thus to control the eastern approaches of Abu Dhabi Emirate, control was required over both the inland and coastal route. This explains why, starting in the 1950s, the British and subsequently Abu Dhabi forces developed bases at Al Hamra (west of Jebel Dhanna), on the eastern edge of the *Sabkha Matti*, Mirfa and Tarif and from these patrolled westwards and southwards.

10   Communities of mangroves were historically located along the Arabian Gulf coast and inshore islands of Abu Dhabi, the coasts of Ras Al Khaimah and Umm Al Qaiwain. In addition, a few were in Ajman creek, and at the back of Khor Dubai and at Khor Kalba in the Gulf of Oman. In the 1970s sizeable areas of mangroves vanished due to development. However since the early 2000s, plantation and rehabilitation projects have doubled the area covered by mangroves. H. Almahasheer, *Environmental Monitoring and Assessment*, 190, 85 (2018), p. 85. In 2018, the estimated coverage of mangroves in the UAE was 155km2. Roberta Pennington, 'UAE Mangroves the Largest in the Gulf, Study Finds', *The National*, 1 February 2018.
11   Qatar Digital Library, IOR/R/15/4/3, to H.G. Jakins British Agency Sharjah, Political Agent, Bahrain, [untitled demi-official note 919-0255], 26 October 1949.

The desert

The Arabian Gulf's coastal plain merges into desert made up of rolling dunes. Sandy desert dominates most of the south and west of the UAE and extends into Saudi Arabia. This huge area is known as the Empty Quarter (*Rub Al Khali*) and is the largest sand desert in the world. Dunes in Abu Dhabi's Empty Quarter desert can reach some 300 metres in height with a slipface of up to 50 degrees. This, as well as the presence of *sabkha* in the depression between dunes,[12] made travelling very difficult in these areas before roads were constructed.

Given the lack of rain in the desert, permanent settlement was only possible in areas which had reliable groundwater. In Abu Dhabi Emirate, these mainly consisted of the significant oases at Liwa and Buraimi. The Liwa Oasis was historically always significantly smaller in terms of population than the Buraimi Oasis. In 1968, the Liwa Oasis population was 957 individuals spread over some 30 palm groves and settlements, while the population in Abu Dhabi's six villages in the Buraimi Oasis (i.e. Al Ain, Muwaiqih, Mataradh, Jimi, Qattara and Hilli) was 12,898.[13] In the pre-motor vehicle period, travelling from inland Saudi Arabia to Abu Dhabi meant reprovisioning at the Liwa Oasis. Likewise, to travel from the Omani coast (departing from Sohar) to Abu Dhabi meant stopping at the Buraimi Oasis. Thus, control of both the Liwa and Buraimi Oases was essential to protect Abu Dhabi Emirate's southern flank. This explains why starting in the 1950s, military forces were based in Buraimi, and patrolled the southern flank centred on the Liwa Oasis.

Hajar Mountains and coastal plains of the Gulf of Oman

The Hajar Mountains are a long, narrow range of barren, steep and rugged mountains that extend from Oman's Musandam exclave abutting the Strait of Hormuz, along the eastern edge of the UAE, and southwards into Oman. The UAE section of these mountains extends for some 65km and is about 25km wide. The mountains have a maximum height of nearly 2,000m, and separate the Al Batinah coast on the Gulf of Oman from the rest of the UAE. The mountains are dissected by narrow valleys and ravines.

Rainfalls in the mountains generate short-lived torrents which over time create boulder-strewn gullies known as *wadis*. The water recharges aquifers and brings down fertile sediment, which together allow agricultural activities on narrow tracts of land in some *wadis*.

Before roads were constructed, the only practical way of travelling from the Gulf of Oman to the towns of the Arabian Gulf or the Gulf hinterland was along mountain paths connected to *wadis*. The main ones were Wadi Al Qawr, Wadi Ham, Wadi

---

12   I. Al Abed and P. Hellyer, eds., *United Arab Emirates: A New Perspective* (London, 2001), p. 20.
13   Author's collection, Abu Dhabi, Dickerson files, Intelligence Section Abu Dhabi Defence Force, 'Abu Dhabi Town. Present And Expected Population to the Year 2,000', 1971. The Buraimi Oasis is shared with Oman, which historically consisted of the three villages of Hamasa, Buraimi and Sara.

Hatta and Wadi Jizi (shown in Figure 3).[14] These paths developed into the main road routes which started appearing in the 1960s.[15] Controlling these routes meant controlling access between the coast and the bulk of the Emirates. This explains the presence of military posts along these routes starting in the early 1950s.[16]

The Hajar Mountains plunge into the sea along much of the Gulf of Oman coast. There are only a few small natural harbours along this coast, notably at Khor Fakkan. In some coastal areas, there are narrow, fertile plains which have formed as outwash plains from major *wadis*, such as at Fujairah, Dibba and Kalba. These areas have historically been the site of major settlements on the Emirates' east coast, along with Khor Fakkan.

Gravel plains

Inland between the Hajar Mountains and the deserts are alluvial gravel plains. These are 150km long from north to south and are 5 to 25km wide.[17] These plains are made up of sand and gravel outwash from the Hajar Mountains. Wind-blown sand is constantly encroaching on the gravel plains from the west.[18] Movement across the plains is relatively easy.

Political geography

The UAE consists of seven Emirates, all of which existed for many decades, and some for centuries, before the formation of the UAE in 1971. The Emirates are in effect city-states, with their capitals carrying the same names as the Emirates. Each Emirate is headed by a ruler. The position of ruler is dynastically held by a male member of that Emirate's Royal Family, and while rulership is often passed from father to son, this is not always the case. Each Emirate has a different Royal Family (see Table 2) with several of these families being related. For example, the ruling families of Ras Al Khaimah and Sharjah are related. Both trace their heritage back to the Al Qasimi sheikhs who dominated the southern Gulf before the early 1800s. Another related pair are the Abu Dhabi and Dubai ruling families who both came from the Bani Yas tribe. During the

14   There were also minor routes, such as Wadi Bih across Musandam to Ras Al Khaimah, which today makes up part of the Wadi Bih – Ras Al Khaimah road.

15   The first tracks suitable for vehicles were built by 1960 and went through Wadi Ham which connected Masafi to Fujairah, and through Wadi Ayyinah connecting Masafi to Dibba. D.F. Hawley, *The Trucial States* (London, 1970), p. 176.

16   The first military post established along one of these routes was in 1952 when the TOL established one at Wadi Al Qawr. UK Foreign Office, *Historical Summary of Events in the Persian Gulf Shaikhdoms and the Sultanate of Muscat and Oman, 1928-1953* (London, 1953), p. 150.

17   Mohamed Rashed Alneaimi, 'Population Growth and Water Resources in the United Arab Emirates, 1975 to 2025: A ArcGIS Approach' (PhD thesis, University of Arkansas, 2003), p. 12.

18   Hawley, *The Trucial States*, p. 285.

early 1800s, a prominent section of the Bani Yas tribe split and moved to Dubai. This became the Al Maktoum section which has been the ruling family of Dubai since 1833. The section of the Bani Yas which rules in Abu Dhabi is the Al Nahyan.[19]

Table 2: Key characteristics of the Emirates[20]

Emirate or country	Capital city	Ruling family tribe or section (tribe)	Population, 1968 (% of Emirates population)	Population, 2015 (% of UAE population)	Mainland area km² (% of total UAE mainland area)
Abu Dhabi	Abu Dhabi	Al Nahyan (Bani Yas)	46,500 (26%)	2,784,000 (37%)	67,340 (87%)
Dubai	Dubai	Al Maktoum (Bani Yas)	59,000 (33%)	2,447,000 (32%)	3,885 (5%)
Sharjah	Sharjah	Al Qasimi	31,500 (18%)	1,461,933 (19%)	2,590 (3%)
Ras Al Khaimah	Ras Al Khaimah	Al Qasimi	24,300 (14%)	345,000 (5%)	1,684 (2%)
Fujairah	Fujairah	Al Sharqi	9,700 (5%)	213,712 (3%)	1,165 (1.5%)
Ajman	Ajman	Al Nuaimi	4,200 (2%)	262,186 (3%)	259 (0.3%)
Umm Al Quwain	Umm Al Quwain	Al Mualla (Al Ali)	3,700 (2%)	73,000 (1%)	777 (1%)
UAE	Abu Dhabi		180,200	7,586,831[a]	77,700

Notes

a. This figure is nearly 1 million less than the 2015 population figures given in Table 5. This difference reflects both the different analysis methods used by individual Emirates, and different times of measurement.

19   The Maktoums are from the Al Bu Falasah section of the Bani Yas, the Nahyans from the Al Bu Falah section of the Bani Yas.

20   The 1968 population figures are from the Exeter University, Trucial States Council, 'Trucial States Census Figures 1968', UAE 301.3295362 CEN, 1968. The census figures include 1,100 members of the TOS and are excluded from the percentage figures of each Emirate. The 2015 population figures for Abu Dhabi and Dubai are from the UAE Ministry of Economy, *Annual Economic Report 2016* (2016), p. 40. The 2015 population figures for Sharjah are from the Sharjah Census 2015 quoted in 'Sharjah's Population Crosses 1.4m, With More Than 175,000 Emiratis and 1.2 Million Expatriates', *Gulf News*, 21 January 2017. The 2015 population figures for Fujairah are from Government of Fujairah, *Statistical Yearbook Nineteen Issue 2015* (Fujairah, 2016), p. 18. The 2015 population figures for Umm Al Quwain are undated and sourced from University of Modern Sciences. 'Umm Al Quwain', n.d., <ums.ae/data.aspx?Id=1111>. The 2015 population figures for Ajman are from the census book *Ajman in Figures 2011* issued by the Secretariat General of the Executive Council of the Emirate of Ajman, and quoted at Government.ae, 'Ajman', 16 January 2018. The 2015 population figures for Ras Al Khaimah are from a census estimate by Ras Al Khaimah Center for Statistics & Studies, quoted at Government of Ras Al Khaimah. 'About RAK', n.d. <www.rak.ae/wps/portal/rak/about/ras-al-khaimah/facts> The mainland area figures exclude islands and is approximate due to several unresolved territorial claims with neighbouring countries.

There are considerable differences between the Emirates. Geographically, the largest is Abu Dhabi, accounting for 87 percent of the UAE's mainland area, and the smallest is Ajman which accounts for less than 1 percent. The topography also varies considerably which explains why there are different traditional ways of life in each Emirate. For example, in Ras Al Khaimah and Fujairah, with greater rainfall and richer soil, a substantial part of their economies were based around crops and intensive animal husbandry.[21] In desert-dominated Abu Dhabi Emirate, the economy was centred around nomadism, camels and cultivation in oases. The demographic characteristics of the populations vary considerably as discussed in the following chapter.

Each Emirate has a different history, shaped by both the environment and politics. Neighbouring rulers were always in competition and occasionally in confrontation, which ranged from localised, short-term disputes to multi-year wars. The last major inter-emirate conflict was the 1945-48 Abu Dhabi-Dubai War. A common approach used by rulers to build security against the threat from neighbouring Emirates was to seek alliances with their neighbour's neighbour. This often led to a chequerboard pattern of alliances where 'each ruler tended to be close friends with the next ruler but one, with the intermediate ruler between traditionally the opponent of both'.[22] These historic alliances, as well as long remembered insults and injuries, have been an important part of inter-emirate political dynamics since the UAE's formation.

Another element of the contemporary political dynamic has been the legacy of shift in the region's centres of power over the centuries. In the decades leading up to 1820, power in the southern Arabian Gulf was centred on Ras Al Khaimah and Sharjah which formed the base for the Al Qasimi confederation. Their influence spanned not only the areas of these Emirates today but also the lower Gulf islands, and along both the eastern Persian coast in the Arabian Gulf and the eastern coast of the Gulf of Oman. The Al Qasimi's large fleet controlled the region's maritime trade, and coupled with substantial agricultural activity, particularly in Ras Al Khaimah, the Al Qasimis were able to grow wealthy and their citizens numerous. Following Britain's 1820 destruction of the Al Qasimi fleet in order to protect its trade interests, the confederation's power diminished, and the Abu Dhabi and Dubai townships grew as they started to dominate maritime activity along the lower Gulf.[23]

The 1820 British assault introduced a new regional order in the Lower Gulf, with Britain becoming the regional maritime power. By the end of that century, through a series of treaties signed between the British and the rulers of the Emirates, Britain had become the guarantor of the Emirates' external security, and responsible for its

---

21 The economies of Ras Al Khaimah and Fujairah were also dependent on offshore fishing, plus in the case of Ras Al Khaimah, long distance maritime trade across the Gulf, to India and to East Africa.

22 G. Balfour Paul, *Bagpipes in Babylon: A Lifetime in the Arab World and Beyond* (London, 2006), p. 205.

23 The growth in maritime activity in these towns resulted in numbers of *bedu* permanently settling in both. G.H. Wilson, *Zayed, Man Who Built a Nation* (Abu Dhabi, 2013), p. 34.

external relations. The latter responsibility meant that the rulers could not sign agreements with foreign powers unless Britain agreed. The treaties theoretically gave the Rulers had internal sovereignty, but over time Britain became more involved in the internal stability and security of the Emirates.

By the mid-1800s, Abu Dhabi town had become one of the wealthiest in the Trucial States and the centre of political power.[24] Pearling was central to this rise. Along the lower Arabian Gulf coast, there are numerous pearl oyster beds, and from May to November each year, vessels would launch from coastal settlements to harvest them. The pearls would be sold locally to mostly Indian traders who would in turn sell them in Europe and beyond. The rulers would receive a percentage of pearling income as well as benefiting from the associated commercial activities that supported pearling in their townships.

By the early 1900s, however, Abu Dhabi was in decline economically and politically. This was due to a combination of shifting internal allegiances and checks imposed by the British on the plans of the ruler of Abu Dhabi, Sheikh Zayed bin Khalifa (r. 1855-1909). Britain was concerned that Sheikh Zayed's plans would negatively impact the region and Britain's interests.[25] As this was occurring, Dubai was growing, propelled by the shift in trade from the port of Lingh in Persia – which had introduced customs duty – to Dubai in the early 1900s. Economic growth further increased after 1903 when regular steamers began to stop there, and when the Ruler of Dubai abolished its 5 percent customs duty, making it a free port. The result was that Dubai became the lower Gulf's main pearl market.[26]

Commencing at the end of the 1920s, the economies of all the Emirates went into rapid decline, due to a combination of the Great Depression (1929-39) and the commercialisation of cultured pearls in Japan in the early 1930s. Cultured pearls could be produced for a much cheaper cost than the natural pearls obtained through diving. The demand for locally produced pearls plummeted, resulting in financial ruin for businesses, mass unemployment, great privation and even famine in parts of the Emirates. The economy reverted to a subsistence model and there was an exodus of people seeking employment elsewhere. In terms of the relative power of the Emirates, Abu Dhabi's influence shrank even further compared with that of Dubai.

The 1930s saw the relative power of Sharjah increase after Britain established an air station there which became an important stopover for commercial and military aircraft flying between Britain and its eastern Empire. The Ruler of Sharjah directly benefited from the facility, notably through obtaining rent for the land, and payment for providing guards to protect it. He also gained indirectly through the increased economic activity associated with the airport. Politically Sharjah had also grown in importance as it was the location of the British political representative in the Trucial

24   Ibid., p. 28.
25   M.M. Abdullah, *The United Arab Emirates: A Modern History* (London, 1978), pp. 98-103.
26   Ibid., p. 104.

States (see Appendix 8 for details on Britain's political representative system). This post had previously been run by a Native Agent but was upgraded in 1939 and since that time was manned by a British Officer, although he only served there during the winter months. In 1948, the post in Sharjah was upgraded to the level of Political Officer and was staffed all year-round.

In the early 1950s, power shifted from Sharjah to Dubai. This was due to the Dubai ruler's more supportive business attitude which saw his economy grow markedly. Reflecting this shift in power, the British political representative moved to Dubai in 1953.

The discovery of massive oil fields in Abu Dhabi Emirate in the late 1950s saw power start to shift back to Abu Dhabi, a development which accelerated when Sheikh Zayed bin Sultan Al Nahyan became Ruler of Abu Dhabi in 1966. His willingness to invest the oil income on developing his Emirate and to support financially the other Emirates gave Abu Dhabi's Ruler greater local influence. His power and prestige were reflected in the fact that the rulers of the other Emirates elected him as the first President of the UAE in 1971 and agreed that the new country's capital would initially be located in Abu Dhabi.[27]

The shifts in power over the last two-hundred years have had a legacy in the internal political dynamics of the Emirates. Specifically, some rulers of formerly powerful Emirates have been sensitive to perceived losses of sovereignty and lack of consideration for the historical importance of their Emirates. This explains why some Emirates have been resistant to Federalism at particular times, particularly if they considered they were insufficiently consulted.

An unusual feature of the UAE is the non-contiguous land owned by a number of the Emirates. Dubai is divided into two parts – one east of Abu Dhabi and the other at the borders of Oman. Sharjah is divided into three areas – one east of Dubai and the other two on the Gulf of Oman. This patchwork of borders is a legacy of the tribal past (see Figure 5).[28]

Historically, a ruler's domain was based on two 'sovereignties' – one being direct control over valuable land, and the other control over tribes.[29] Valuable land included the ruler's capital town, places of strategic importance such as hilltops overlooking

---

27   When the UAE was formed, Abu Dhabi city was only the provisional capital as there were plans to build a new capital called Al Karama on the Abu Dhabi-Dubai border. This proposal was formally dropped in 1996 when the Constitution was changed to recognise Abu Dhabi as the nation's permanent capital.

28   No UAE Government map of the country's internal borders has been located. This map was produced by the British Government in 1978. It is believed that the internal borders have since been slightly revised, but specifics are unknown. The image has been digitally altered with extraneous information removed. TNA, FCO 18/792, Cartographic Section Research Department UK Foreign and Commonwealth Office, 'Northern Emirates of the United Arab Emirates (UAE), with Internal Boundaries and Area in Active Dispute at Ras Al-Khaimah-Oman Border', 1978.

29   TNA FO 464/58: J.F. Walker, 'Report on Trucial Coast Frontier Settlement', March 1955.

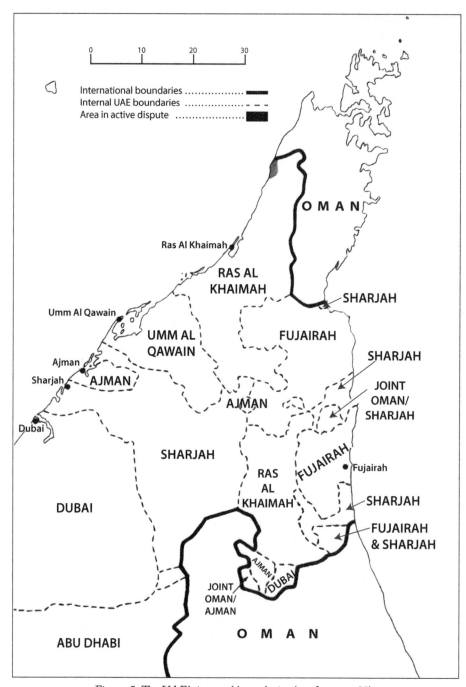

Figure 5: The UAE's internal boundaries (see footnote 28).

mountain passes, and agricultural land. The ruler exercised control over this land through direct supervision, or via the presence of his retainers and guards. Control over such land changed only when the ruler sold or gifted it. The desert was not seen as valuable, being a 'commons' in much the same way as mariners viewed the sea.[30]

The second sovereignty – control over tribes – existed when a ruler received allegiance from the sheikh of a tribe and, thus, the loyalty of the members of the tribe. This allegiance meant that the tribe's land became part of the ruler's domain, enabling him to call upon the tribe's men for defence and to levy tax (*zakat*) on crops and sometimes on livestock.[31]

Reasons for changing allegiance included dissatisfaction with the largesse a tribe received from its ruler, or with the ruler's decisions and treatment of members of the tribe. Another reason was that a neighbouring ruler was offering better inducements. Given the loss of power and income that resulted from the loss of a tribe's allegiance, a ruler placed great emphasis on retaining tribal loyalty and reacted strongly when a fellow ruler sought to win over one of his tribes.

As tribal allegiances changed, so too did the borders of a ruler's domain.[32] Defining borders grew in importance from the 1940s as: (1) the Arabian American Oil Company and Saudi Arabia more generally sought control over Abu Dhabi territory; (2) British authorities and the rulers sought to extend governmental administration over the hinterland.[33]

To settle internal borders, in 1955 the British sent one of their diplomats, Julian Walker, to make recommendations on the location of borders. Walker used two broad rules to determine land ownership. First, where a ruler exercised both 'sovereignties', this land was deemed part of the ruler's domain. Second, where the two 'sovereignties' conflicted (i.e. the ruler claiming control over a tribe but the tribe stated their allegiance lay with another), the main criteria of proof of sovereignty became the payment of *zakat* by the tribe. If the *zakat* was paid to the ruler who claimed the land, the land was deemed his. If not, it was not his.

Walker's recommendations for the internal borders of the Emirates were presented to the rulers in the mid-1950s and the majority were accepted. In a few areas, the rulers could not reach agreement and ownership remained contested. These border disputes would remain a source of tribal and inter-Emirate tension for subsequent decades, and as will be seen in Chapter 4 (Core mission 1), preventing or de-escalating these conflicts was a key role in the early decades of the armed forces of the Emirates.

---

30   Ibid.
31   Ibid.
32   M.Q. Morton, *Keepers of the Golden Shore: A History of the United Arab Emirates* (London, 2016), p. 43.
33   Aide Memoire of the United Kingdom to King Abdul Aziz bin Saud of 17 June 1949 cited in Author's collection, Abu Dhabi, Gowlett files, Abu Dhabi Defence Force, 'Tribes of Abu Dhabi', 1970.

Oil and natural resources

In the late 1950s, oil was discovered in the Emirates. This fundamentally changed the Emirates, for within a few decades they went from what were effectively subsistence economies to advanced, emerging market economies. Today the UAE has one of the world's greatest per capita incomes.

In the Gulf region, oil was first discovered in Iran in 1911. In 1932, oil was found in Bahrain and, in 1938, in Saudi Arabia. These finds encouraged oil exploration in the Emirates, with most rulers signing oil concessions with exploration companies in the 1930s. Exploration was suspended during the Second World War and, while it resumed after 1945, it progressed slowly due to territorial and political disputes. In 1958, the first commercial oil discovery was made at an offshore field near Abu Dhabi's Das Island. In 1962, the first oil exports were shipped from Das Island, and this saw a massive increase in revenues for the Abu Dhabi Ruler. Subsequently, multiple oil fields were discovered across Abu Dhabi Emirate, both onshore and offshore. Commercial quantities of oil were found in Dubai Emirate in 1966, with exports starting three years later, and in Sharjah Emirate in 1972, with exports starting two years later. No significant commercial oil or gas fields have been identified in the other Emirates.

The oil and gas reserves of the UAE are immense: it currently has around 8 percent of the proven crude oil reserves of the member states of the Organization of the Petroleum Exporting Countries (OPEC) as well as 8 percent of the natural gas reserves of OPEC members. In 2019, the UAE produced 3 million barrels of crude oil per day of which 2.4 million were exported.[34] Hydrocarbons are essential to the Emirates' economy. In the 1970s, hydrocarbons contributed about 90 percent of the UAE's gross domestic product. In 2017, they still accounted for about 22 percent.[35]

The vast majority of oil and gas reserves are in Abu Dhabi Emirate, as seen in Table 3 below. Constitutionally, the natural resources in each Emirate are the property of that Emirate rather than of the UAE as a whole.[36] Consequently, Abu Dhabi is by far the richest Emirate, which gives its ruler significant power within the UAE as it funds much of the Federal budget, as well as providing funds directly to the less wealthy Emirates. Its oil wealth is also used to financially support foreign states, groups, and causes, which gives Abu Dhabi a degree of international prestige and influence.

34   Organization of the Petroleum Exporting Countries, *2020 OPEC Annual Statistical Bulletin* (Vienna, 2020), p. 10.
35   Embassy of the UAE in Berlin, *UAE Economic Bulletin* (2018), p. 7.
36   Article 23 of the Constitution.

Table 3: Proven oil reserves by Emirate, 2015[37]

Emirate or country	Proven oil reserves billion barrels (bb) (% of total UAE reserves)
Abu Dhabi	92.2bb (94.3%)
Dubai	4bb (4.1%)
Sharjah	1.5bb (1.5%)
Ras Al Khaimah	0
Fujairah	0
Ajman	0
Umm Al Quwain	0
UAE total	97.8bb (100%)

The Emirate-based control of oil resources means that each of the three oil-endowed Emirates has sought to maximise its own oil income, regardless of any national policy. This has resulted in the rulers of Abu Dhabi, Dubai and Sharjah pursuing divergent oil policies at various times. This can be clearly seen in the various Emirates' approaches to abiding by the oil production quotas agreed through the Organization of the Petroleum Exporting Countries (OPEC). In the 1967, Abu Dhabi Emirate joined OPEC. With the formation of the UAE in 1971, the UAE became a member of OPEC, but the UAE's OPEC position only reflected that of Abu Dhabi. Consequently, only Abu Dhabi Emirate was obliged to abide by OPEC quotas. This led to the situation characterised in the 1980s where 'Dubai rarely heeded the UAE's production ceiling [which] meant that Abu Dhabi was to safeguard the OPEC quota set for the entire UAE by cutting back on its own [production]'.[38]

The uneven distribution of oil and gas reserves across the Emirates has also meant that approaches to state development have varied considerably across the Emirates. Abu Dhabi has relied more on government investment than Dubai which, with its more modest oil resources, has had to rely on its own private sector. The same applies to Sharjah. The other Emirates, lacking both natural resources and significant commercial activities, have had to rely far more on Federal (meaning Abu Dhabi-funded) support as the source of development funds, as well as direct support from both Abu Dhabi and Dubai.

A significant proportion of oil and gas fields are located offshore or in the littoral area, as can be seen in Figure 6 below. Petroleum products from these and onshore

---

37   Embassy of the UAE in Washington DC. 'The UAE and Global Oil Supply', n.d.<www. uae-embassy.org/about-uae/energy/uae-and-global-oil-supply> In late 2019, the UAE oil and gas reserves were revised. These now consist of 105 billion barrels of crude oil and 273 trillion cubic feet of conventional gas.

38   A. Ayalon and H. Shaked, eds., *Middle East Contemporary Survey, 1988*, Vol. XII (Boulder, 1990), p. 462.

fields are only exported by ship as there are no pipelines to any of the country's neighbours.

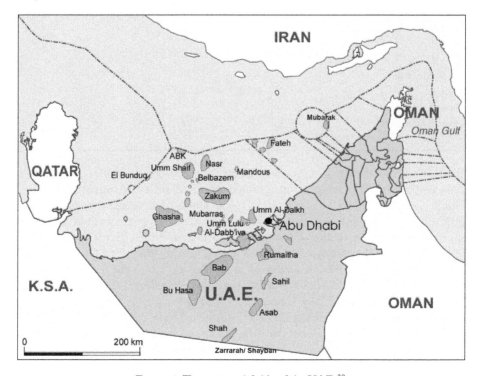

Figure 6: The major oil fields of the UAE.[39]

Looking forward

Historically, the geographic location and physical environment have determined the vulnerabilities and threats that the Emirates faced, as well as providing their rulers with the resources by which they could respond. Looking forward, how will they influence the UAE security situation in the near and mid-term future?

Being sandwiched between the region's major competing and much larger regional powers – Iran and Saudi Arabia – the UAE continues to face the prospect of being drawn into any escalating tension between the two, or being targeted by one of them as punishment for supporting the other. The close proximity of Iran means that if it is

---

39   Adapted from Bruno Granier et al., *New Insight on the Stratigraphy of the "Upper Thamama" in Offshore Abu Dhabi (UAE)* (2003), p. 2.

attacked by an external power, such as the US or Israel, the UAE risks being targeted as retribution.

As the UAE's oil resources, cities and industrial centres all lie on the Arabian Gulf coast, Iran has a plethora of targets which it could threaten, harass, or attack. Coercive activities can occur with little warning due to the geographic closeness, which also means that attackers do not need to have an expeditionary capability, as they can be supported from the mainland. Finally, this proximity also means attackers can use 'simple' capabilities, such as small, fast attack boats, rocket-assisted artillery, and sea mines. While the most likely threat at the time of writing is Iran, this would change if the UAE's current strategic alignment with Saudi Arabia were to dissolve.

Managing the threat from these two neighbours will remain first and foremost in the minds of the UAE's leadership. While possessing credible armed forces offers a deterrent and allows for sustained defensive and limited offensive operations, the UAE will want to avoid direct conflict for two reasons. Firstly, the regional powers are much larger that the UAE and have the ability to withstand significant levels of physical destruction and economic disruption, something which the much smaller UAE cannot absorb. Secondly, if the UAE was no longer seen as safe and stable, there would be a flight of capital, collapse of trade, and mass expatriate departures. This would cause enormous damage to the political economy of the UAE.

The UAE remains absolutely dependent on free and safe passage in its adjacent waters. Not only does shipping provide an economic lifeline for oil exports and trade, it is essential to its physical existence as vessels bring in everything needed for a large, modern society, such as food, raw materials and equipment. While improvements in export/import infrastructure from Fujairah and Khor Fakkan will reduce the dependency on ships transiting through the Strait of Hormuz, more states and non-state actors can now reach into the Gulf of Oman and make even this area 'high risk'. Protecting the eastern coast of the UAE will become an increasing priority as will infrastructure links with Oman so as to provide an added level of transport resilience.

The broader region in which the UAE finds itself is characterised by states with large populations, developing economies and governments which have limited ability or willingness to enforce laws. Examples are Iraq, Syria, Yemen, Somalia and Pakistan. Consequently, the UAE also faces a range of non-conventional security threats and hazards, such as piracy, smuggling of contraband, illegal fishing, people smuggling and large area pollution.

The small size of the UAE's mainland at around 400km east to west, and 350km north to south, means that the country has little strategic depth. There is simply no room for force dispersal or safe stockpiling of materiel, or to retreat out of the range of modern weapon systems.

These vulnerabilities and threats will mean that UAE leaders will continue to prioritise the country's armed forces. This may become challenging if income from both Abu Dhabi's hydrocarbon exports and returns from its sovereign wealth funds and investments continue to remain low into the 2020s.

In terms of military threats, Iran will remain the greatest concern for the foreseeable future. The UAE Armed Forces will continue to maintain a non-confrontational defence doctrine based on limited forward presence of military assets to avoid accidental escalation. By deploying the UAE's para-military coast guard, rather than the navy, to patrol maritime borders and intercept foreign small craft which illegally enter UAE waters, the use of force by the UAE to enforce its borders is framed as a law enforcement issue rather than a military responsibility. To further protect UAE territorial waters and the unhindered flow of maritime traffic in the region, the UAE also will continue to encourage friendly nations to maintain a presence in the Arabian Gulf and Gulf of Oman. Improving situational awareness over UAE land, sea and air space will grow in importance in order to identify signs of aggression, to maximise warning time, and to locate the adversary's radar, air defence and command/control systems. Defending the air/sea gap will remain far more important than preparing for land defence.

2

People and Culture

The population of the Emirates can be divided into two main groups – nationals (also known as 'locals' or 'Emiratis') and expatriates.[1] This binary categorisation hides, however, numerous important distinctions within each group. These distinctions are important to understanding both the dynamics of Emirati society and the differences in the power and prestige of various groups: they have clear parallels in military organisation and culture.

This chapter begins with a history of the UAE's demography. Since the 1960s, the Emirates have had an extremely unusual demographic makeup – expatriates have outnumbered nationals. As of the last UAE Census in 2015, the population of the UAE was 8.6 million, with nationals making up just over one million: in other words, the ratio of expatriates to nationals is roughly 8:1. Despite being in the minority, nationals have always been the 'economically and socially privileged group of UAE citizens', according to the UAE's preeminent historian, Frauke Heard-Bey.[2] Nationals

---

1   There is another significant group – *bidoons*, meaning 'without' in Arabic. In the Emirati context, *bidoon* means being stateless. *Bidoons* are those and their descendants who came to the Emirates before 1971 but by chance and circumstance were not granted citizenship when the UAE was formed. The origins of *bidoon* vary. Those in Abu Dhabi Emirate are predominantly from descendants of families that were historically nomadic pastoralists and moved between Saudi Arabia, Oman and the UAE. *Bidoons* in the northern Emirates mostly originated from the Makran coast in modern Iran and Pakistan. Since the late 2000s, many *bidoons* in the UAE have been granted passports by the Comoros Islands which is an Indian Ocean archipelago. The Comoros Islands passports allows the *bidoon* for the first time to travel internationally. Importantly, it also allows them to obtain benefits available to UAE nationals and gain employment legally. The passport does not confer Comoros citizenship nor the right to residency in that country. A. Zacharias, 'Ten years on, the UAE's Stateless People Reflect on How Life Has Improved and on the Challenges Ahead', *The National*, 5 September 2018. The numbers of *bidoons* range up to 100,000. A. Zacharias, 'The Frustration of Being a "Bidoon"', *The National*, 6 November 2008.
2   Frauke Heard-Bey, 'The United Arab Emirates: Statehood and Nation-Building in a Traditional Society', *Middle East Journal*, 59, 3 (2005), p. 357.

hold all political power, which has been true in both broader society and within the military. Despite this, the very large numbers of expatriates mean there is a 'demographic imbalance' which is seen by many nationals as a threat to the country.

It is important to note here that nationals are not homogenous and, in fact, vary considerably. One dimension is their tribal origins and another is their religious practices. Both of these are explained in details below due to their significant influence on the standing and opportunities of individuals and groups within the military.

Demographics

Historically, the population of the Emirates has been small. This is because the barren terrain, arid climate, and lack of water and other natural resources have prevented the development of large-scale agriculture and industry which is needed to support a large population. At the beginning of the 20th century, the Emirates' population was estimated to be well under 100,000, with one figure putting it as low was 40,000.[3]

It was only in the 1950s that the Emirates' population stared to grow as the economic situation started to improve, slowly at first and then more rapidly. The 1950s saw Dubai's trading-based economy expand, and agriculture, education and health projects began to pick up across the Emirates. Employment opportunities increased, which attracted those who had previously departed to seek work to return home.

The 1950s also saw numbers of expatriates arrive to take advantage of opportunities arising from the improved economic situation, as well as to support oil exploration activities. In 1958, oil was discovered in Abu Dhabi and large-scale infrastructure needed to be built to facilitate its export. Thousands of professionals, skilled tradesmen and unskilled labourers were required and, given both the small local population and the understandable lack of nationals with specialist skills, large numbers of expatriates flooded into the Emirates.

The oil growth in Abu Dhabi had knock-on benefits for Dubai and Sharjah. Dubai had good port infrastructure, Sharjah had an airport, and both were home to growing commercial sectors. Collectively, these attributes meant that these two cities became the organisational base and logistics hub for many construction projects in Abu Dhabi. Public infrastructure development in Abu Dhabi Emirate progressed in the first half of the 1960s at a much slower rate than oil-related infrastructure, which reflected the reluctance of the then Ruler of Abu Dhabi, Sheikh Shakhbut bin Sultan Al Nahyan (r. 1928-66) to seek changes to his traditional society.

A picture of Abu Dhabi in the early-1960s portrays its low level of development:

---

3   J.R. Macris, *Population and Economic Activities in the Arab Trucial States: A 1901 Accounting*, Vol. 6, 2015), p. 179. Heard-Bey quotes a figure of 80,000; she notes, however, that the source's accuracy is uncertain. Frauke Heard-Bey, *From Trucial States to United Arab Emirates: A Society in Transition* (London, 1982), p. 427.

Abu Dhabi was still a tribal society existing at the subsistence level. Its economic position in 1962 was comparable to Qatar's in 1948 ... The capital then was simply a coastal village of 4,000 inhabitants, with hardly any vegetation and no potable water other than that produced by two unreliable distillation plants of limited capacity and electricity provided by individual generators. Its *suq* [market] was uninspiring with about eight main traders ... who catered to the modest wants of a town whose inhabitants' staple diet was fish, rice and dates.[4]

When his brother, Sheikh Zayed, became ruler of Abu Dhabi in 1966, the attitude towards development changed completely. Sheikh Zayed wanted to develop his Emirate rapidly and launched a massive investment programme to build roads, electricity and water networks, hospitals, schools, and other elements of a modern infrastructure. He also made large contributions to the poorer Emirates which saw their economies also grow. To implement his massive list of projects, large numbers of foreigner workers were engaged, with many more being attracted because of follow-on economic opportunities.

From the late 1960s to the present, expatriates have made up a significant part of the Emirates' population. Table 4 shows the estimated size of ethnic groups in the Emirates as of 1969. It shows the diversity of groups, and the considerable differences in composition between the Emirates – both characteristics of today's population mix. In 1969, there were probably 20 or so nationalities in the Emirates; in 2020, there were over 200. In 1969, there were two Emirates (Abu Dhabi and Dubai) in which expatriates made up around 50 percent of the population and in all the other Emirates it was 20 percent or less.

Table 4: Population breakdown in the Emirates, 1969[5]

Population group	Abu Dhabi	Dubai	Sharjah	Ajman	Umm Al Quwain	Ras Al Khaimah	Fujairah	Total
Total population (including nationals)	46,500	60,000	31,500	4,200	3,700	24,500	9,700	180,100
Total foreignersa	24,270	28,838	8,303	543	216	1,556	180	63,906
Egyptians	43	160	102	20	4	83	4	416
Syrians	146	167	57	2	6	14	1	393
Jordanians	691	387	49	21	12	62	3	1,225
Lebanese	546	336	53			26	8	969

4   J. Maitra and A. Ḥajjī, *Qasr Al Hosn: The History of the Rulers of Abu Dhabi, 1793-1966* (Abu Dhabi, 2001), p. 248.

5   US Central Intelligence Agency, *The Persian Gulf Amirates: Economic Assets and Prospects* (Washington, DC, 1970).

Population group	Abu Dhabi	Dubai	Sharjah	Ajman	Umm Al Quwain	Ras Al Khaimah	Fujairah	Total
Iraqis	100	84	10	6	3	9		212
Other Arabs								0
Muscatis	1,338	653	102	3	4	34	1	2,135
Yemenis	433	390	125	9	3	17		977
South Yemenis[a]								0
Saudi Arabians	15	48	5			6		74
Other Arab countries	452	556	190	21	11	124	18	1,372
Iranians	11,302	11,181	4,108	308	138	627	123	27,787
Pakistanis	6,326	8,922	2,578	122	15	399	14	18,376
Indians	2,569	4,818	771	31	20	90	5	8,304
Other Asian countries	17	823	95			7	1	943
Africans	407	208	32			19		666
Other nationalities[b]	155	105	26			39	2	327

Notes
a.   No figures on Palestinians were provided.
b.   Does not include British for which a breakdown is not available. Number of British may be sizable.

Since the 1960s, the numbers of expatriates have grown continuously (Table 5). The average growth in expatriate numbers between 1971 and 2015 was 9 percent per year. In general, expatriate numbers have fluctuated depending on the state of the economy, and in particular government expenditure, which in turn has depended on oil revenue. Thus, at times when the oil price was high, government spending was high and expatriate numbers grew correspondingly. Conversely, when oil prices were low, the reverse process occurred. This explains why the expatriate population grew by an average of 15 percent per year in the decade after the 1973 oil shock which saw massive increases in Abu Dhabi's oil revenue. The 1980s saw oil income slump and the population grew at a yearly average of 5 percent as it had done during the 1990s. The 2000s saw another significant increase in both the oil price and revenue, and the population grew by an average of 10 percent per year. By the 2000s, the UAE's economy had become more diversified, with the result that oil price fluctuations have had less impact on government revenue than in the past. However, the UAE commercial and industrial sector is export dependent and heavily tied into the global economy. So, following the 2008 global recession, the UAE economy declined sharply, government revenue collapsed, and consequently the growth of the expatriate population slowed in the early 2010s. In the years immediately after the sharp drop in oil prices in 2014-15, and with the diversion of government funds to fund the UAE's involvement in the Yemen conflict, the number of expatriates has probably remained static or even declined before recovering towards the very late 2010s. The COVID-19 crisis of early 2020 saw large numbers of expatriates depart the UAE. This means that the 2020 figure in Table 5 is likely to be an over estimate of the number of expatriates in that year.

Table 5: The population of the Emirates, 1969-2020[6]

Year	Nationals	Expatriates (i.e. foreigners)	Total population	Nationals as a proportion of the total population
1968	not available	not available	180,226	–
1971 estimated	not available	not available	287,000	–
1975	201,544	356,343	557,887	36%
1980	290,544	751,555	1,042,099	28%
1985	396,114	983,189	1,379,303	29%
1990 estimated	467,000	1,306,000	1,773,000	26%
1995	587,330	1,823,711	2,411,041	24%
2000 estimated	549,000	2,446,000	2,995,000	18%
2005	825,495	3,280,932	4,106,427	20%
2010 estimated	947,997	7,316,073	8,264,070	11%
2015	1,004,000	7,577,000	8,581,000	12%
2020 estimated	1,096,000	8,204,000	9,300,000	12%

The continuous decline in the percentage of nationals as a proportion of total population is seen in Figure 7 below.[7] Today, nationals make up about 12 percent of the country's total population.

The most recently published detailed breakdown of the population by Emirate is for the year 2005. Table 6 shows that the Emirate with the largest population of nationals was Abu Dhabi at 350,000. The Emirates with the next largest population of nationals were Dubai and Sharjah, both with around 138,000 each. In terms of total population, Abu Dhabi and Dubai were similar, with some 1.4 to 1.5 million, respectively. This explains why nationals constituted just 10 percent of the population in Dubai,

6   The 1968 figures are from R. Mallakh, *The Economic Development of the United Arab Emirates (RLE Economy of Middle East)* (London, 2014), p. 10. The total population figures from 1971 to 2010 are from the UAE National Bureau of Statistics, quoted in Gulf Research Center and Migration Policy Centre. 'UAE: Estimates of Total Population by Sex, Sex Ratios and Annual Demographic Growth Rates (1970-2010)', 2014, gulfmigration.eu/uae-estimates-of-total-population-by-sex-sex-ratios-and-annual-demographic-growth-rates-1970-2010/. The national and expatriate figures for 1975, 1980, 1985, 1995 and 2005 are from UAE National Bureau of Statistics, *Census Population by Emirates 1975-2005 (excel sheet)* (Abu Dhabi, n.d.). The figures for 2015 and 2020 are from Euromonitor International, quoted in 'UAE Population and Statistical Trends', *Gulf News*, 17 November 2016.

7   The figures are from Table 5.

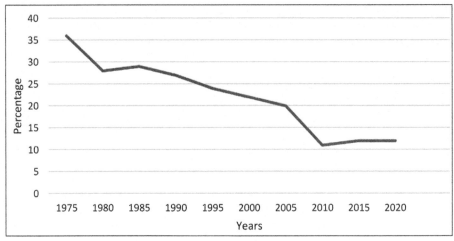

Figure 7: Nationals as a proportion of total population.

while being 25 percent of the population in Abu Dhabi. The northern Emirates of Ras Al Khaimah and Fujairah had the highest percentage of nationals at 42 percent and 45 percent respectively.

Table 6: UAE population by Emirate and nationality, 2005[8]

Emirate	Nationals	Expatriates	Total population	Nationals as a proportion of the total population
Abu Dhabi	350,277	1,049,207	1,399,484	25%
Dubai	137,573	1,183,880	1,321,453	10%
Sharjah	138,272	655,301	793,573	17%
Ajman	39,231	167,766	206,997	19%
Umm Al Quwain	15,873	33,286	49,159	32%
Ras Al Khaimah	87,848	122,215	210,063	42%
Fujairah	56,421	69,277	125,698	45%
Total	825,495	3,280,932	4,106,427	20%

While the relative proportion of nationals to expatriates is one indicator of the significance of expatriates in the country, another indicator is the labour force participation. In the UAE, this is defined as the section of the working population over the age of 15 in the economy currently employed or seeking employment. The most recently published government figures are from 2005 (Table 7). The table shows that there were just 214,000 nationals participating in the labour force, which was just 8 percent

8   UAE National Bureau of Statistics, *Census Population by Emirates 1975-2005 (excel sheet)*.

of the UAE's total labour force. The lowest percentage was in Dubai at 4 percent and the highest was in Ras Al Khaimah at 21 percent.

Table 7: Labour force participation by Emirate and nationality, 2005[9]

Emirate	Nationals (male)	Nationals (female)	Nationals (total)	Expatriates	Total labour force	Nationals as a proportion of the total labour force
Abu Dhabi	68,551	17,287	85,838	729,518	815,356	11%
Dubai	31,574	11,727	43,301	955,114	998,415	4%
Sharjah	27,684	7,640	35,324	406,681	442,005	8%
Ajman	8,035	1,796	9,831	92,944	102,775	10%
Umm Al Quwain	3,183	1,109	4,292	21,808	26,100	16%
Ras Al Khaimah	18,137	4,380	22,517	85,981	108,498	21%
Fujairah	10,620	2,717	13,337	52,055	65,392	20%
Total	167,784	46,656	214,440	2,344,101	2,558,541	8%

The number of nationals in the labour force as of 2020 is unlikely to have increased significantly over the 2005 figures. This is because there were just 152,886 nationals born between 1985 and 2000 (based on Table 5) who thus became of working age between 2005 and 2020, while during this time probably over 100,000 nationals left the workforce due to the relative early retirement age for nationals – 46 years for women and 55 for men.[10] The small growth in labour force participation by nationals is illustrated in Abu Dhabi Emirate government figures. In 2020, the number of nationals in Abu Dhabi's labour force was 90,482,[11] which is only a 5 percent increase over the 2005 figures of 85,838 (Table 6). Applying the same 5 percent growth figure to the total population of nationals of 214,440 in 2005, means that in 2020, the number of nationals in the labour force would be just 225,162.

Expatriates

Expatriates are people who live in the UAE but do not have citizenship. This group consists of those who hold foreign nationality and have either come to live temporarily in the Emirates or been born in the UAE to expatriate parents. Being born in the Emirates does not generate an entitlement to citizenship nor long-term residency. While it is technically possible for expatriates to gain citizenship, this has

9   UAE National Bureau of Statistics, *Labor force by Emirates 1975-2005 (excel sheet)* (Abu Dhabi, n.d.).
10   WAM. 'Over 40,000 Emirati women employed in Abu Dhabi's public and private sectors', 27 August 2020 <www.wam.ae/en/details/1395302865169>
11   Ibid.

rarely occurred since the 1980s. The vast majority of expatriates can only remain in the Emirates while they hold an employment visa supplied through a locally registered entity.[12] Thus, when expatriates lose their jobs, they lose their visas and must leave the country. Dependents of an employed expatriate are granted visas which are linked to the expatriate's visa, so they also need to leave the country if the expatriate loses their employment status.

Since the 1950s, the majority of expatriates in the Emirates have been low-skilled labourers and domestic workers from south Asian nations, notably Pakistan and India. At various times, other nationalities have made up a substantial proportion of low-paid workers. These include Afghani, Bangladeshi, Sudanese, Chinese, Indonesian and Malaysian nationals. Other large groups of expatriates are Arabs from non-Gulf countries and Filipinos, who mostly fill clerical and professional posts. The smallest expatriate group is Westerners and others from developed countries. These people mostly work in professional and technical roles. As workers on lower salaries are not permitted to bring their families with them, there has always been a significant imbalance between male and female expatriates in the country. Males have historically made up between 70 percent and 80 percent of the total population.

The large number of expatriates compared to nationals has long been seen by many nationals as an economic, cultural and security vulnerability for the nation. Expatriates, it is claimed, are linked to social ills such as crime rates, drug use, prostitution, the spread of diseases, and also unemployment among nationals. More recent concerns over the 'demographic imbalance' worry that expatriates are a threat to security and national cultural identity. This concern was demonstrated in both a 2007 survey of Emiratis which found that the UAE's demographic imbalance was ranked as the top current and future challenge, ahead of health-related, economic and traditional security challenges,[13] and a 2015 survey of Emiratis which reported that 77 percent believed that expatriates pose a 'moderate to extreme threat' to the UAE.[14] Kamrava notes that concern over the excessive number of expatriates was widely discussed in the UAE before 2011, but since then, discussion has been limited to private gatherings,[15] inferring that the UAE leadership accepts the need for the expatriates and to challenge this is undesirable.

Despite the concern of nationals about the large expatriate presence, it is important to note that expatriates have very limited political power. Nationals have a political voice, while expatriates do not; nationals run government, while expatriates serve

---

12   There are exceptions to this, such as wealthy expatriate retirees who can live in the Emirates without employment visas.

13   Ingo Forstenlechner and Emilie Jane Rutledge, 'The GCC's "Demographic Imbalance": Perceptions, Realities and Policy Options', *Middle East Policy*, XVIII, 4 (2011), p. 28.

14   Surour Ali Surour Al Nuaimi, 'The Relationship between Expatriates and Security in the UAE as Perceived by Emiratis and Expatriates' (Master's thesis, Khalifa University of Science and Technology, 2015), p. 84.

15   M. Kamrava, *Troubled Waters: Insecurity in the Persian Gulf* (Cornell, 2018), p. 55.

them as administrators and specialists; and nationals make up the majority of the senior business leaders, while expatriates work for them. Nor does wealth, property and company ownership provide an expatriate with access to the political system. Thus it is possible to argue that expatriates actually have little opportunity to influence government decisions, and certainly their numbers do not imply that they 'run' the country.

Nationals

Invariably, discussion about UAE nationals centres on Emiratis who are descended from one of the historic tribes associated with the Emirates. However, another important groups of nationals are the naturalised Emiratis. Both groups have played significant but different roles in the Emirati armed forces. The 1972 UAE citizenship law[16] defined paths by which nationality could be attained and this distinction is of more than merely historical relevance, for the classification of naturalised citizenship is transferred to all descendants.[17]

The first path to citizenship is through evidence of Arab ancestors who have resided in any Emirate continuously since at least 1925. Citizenship via this mechanism is known as the 'nationality-by-law' (*bi-l-qanun*).[18] Nationals-by-law are invariably descendants of the historic tribes of the Emirates, meaning those who can trace their origins back for numerous generations.

The second path to citizenship has been via naturalisation (*bi-l-tajannus*), and such nationals are known as 'naturalised nationals'. The requirements for naturalisation differ for different groups. Most nationals of Gulf Cooperation Council states are eligible after being a resident in the UAE for three years, while other Arabs must prove ten years' residence.[19] A person who 'renders marvellous deeds for the country' can also be become a citizen via naturalisation.[20]

Most naturalised nationals are descended from Omani and Yemeni families who moved to the Emirates in the decades before 1972. However, during the 1970s, and to a lesser degree in the 1980s, rulers also granted citizenship to a large number of

---

16   *UAE Federal Law No 17 of 1972 "On Nationality, Passports and Amendments thereof"* (1972).
17   Davidson characterises the benefit of being an 'original' family of the region as meaning that they are 'entitled to the state's full largesse'. C.M. Davidson, 'Government in the United Arab Emirates: Progress and pathologies', in A. Kadhim (eds.), *Governance in the Middle East and North Africa: A Handbook* (London, 2013), p. 278.
18   P. Dresch and J.P. Piscatori, *Monarchies and Nations: Globalization and Identity in the Arab States of the Gulf* (London, 2005), p. 141.
19   Ibid.
20   *UAE Federal Law No 17 of 1972 "On Nationality, Passports and Amendments thereof"* (1972).

expatriates, notably by the Ruler of Abu Dhabi to Yemenis.[21] In addition, naturalisation was given in those decades as a reward for service which explains why there are numbers of naturalised Emiratis from other countries, including Pakistan, India, Sudan, Iraq, Jordan, Egypt, Morocco and the United Kingdom. The practice of granting citizenship via naturalisation is rare today.

Determining the proportion of nationals-by-law and naturalised Emiratis is difficult as there are no official statistics that distinguish these groups. However, using 1968 figures extrapolated to 1994 (see Figure 7), and comparing these to 1995 UAE census figures, it appears that around 60 percent of nationals are descendants of the large long standing Emirati tribes. This does not mean that 40 percent of nationals are naturalised nationals or their descendants. This is because the 1968 figure probably did not include the small, long standing tribes. This would mean the figure of naturalised nationals would be well less than 40 percent.[22]

Both types of nationals can serve in the military. In a few areas, nationals-by-law have additional rights. These include permission to vote in Federal National Council elections and to hold ministerial positions. They also have additional social benefits including certain types of housing loans.[23] These additional rights reflect a desire to ensure power is maintained by the traditional inhabitants of the Emirates. Applied to the armed forces, this translates into nationals-by-law being promoted to more senior positions and serving in more influential units compared to naturalised nationals.

Tribal kinship groups

Across the Middle East, the tribe has been, and still remains, one of the defining characteristics of Arab societies. Some observers of Arab societies see the influence of tribes as all pervasive, as reflected in the oft-quoted phrase that Arab countries are

---

21   The Yemenis were granted citizenship because Sheikh Zayed naturalised tribes long connected to the Bani Yas, such as Manahil, in addition to those recruited to work in Abu Dhabi following the collapse of South Yemen, such as the Yafi and Awlaqi tribes. Dresch and Piscatori, *Monarchies and Nations*, p. 142. Some of the Yafai and Awlaqi ruling families have moved to the UAE, which has strengthened the influence between Abu Dhabi and these tribes.

22   The 1994 extrapolated figures state that there were 369,800 members of main tribes long present in the Emirates. The 1995 UAE census stated the number of nationals was 587,330. UAE National Bureau of Statistics, *Census Population by Emirates 1975-2005 (excel sheet)*.

23   The key document used to distinguish 'nationals by law' and 'nationals by naturalisation' is the Family Book (*kholasat qaid*). All Emiratis by ancestry and most by naturalisation have this document. However some do not and for details on the practical implications of not possessing a Family Book, see Sultan Al Qassemi, 'Book That Proves Some Emiratis Are More Equal Than Others', *The National*, 7 February 2010. Another important dimension of the Family Book is that it states the holder's emirate of birth which allows that holder to access those state benefits only available to their emirate's nationals.

simply 'tribes with flags'. While this somewhat overstates tribal influence, it recognises a fundamental truth that the tribe remains central to the culture, society and politics of Arab countries. The enduring influence of the tribe in the Arab world can readily be seen in Iraq post-2003. Following the invasion and the collapse of the country's government, tribal structures in the form of tribal militias and councils quickly stepped in to provide security and governance. This shows the remarkable resilience of the tribe despite Iraq's 40 years of strong, socialist and centralised government. Likewise in the UAE, the tribe remains central to the nation.

A tribe is a collection of families linked by the notion of both kinship to a common male ancestor and collective loyalty.[24] The ancestral dimension of the tribe can readily be seen in its name. A tribe's name often comes from a famous and respected progenitor. This link is easily seen in the case of the Bani Yas tribe. Bani Yas means 'family of Yas', and its claimed progenitor was Yas bin Amer, a famous leader from centuries ago. A tribal name can also come from a geographic location, the profession of an individual or family, or a characteristic or nickname of an individual.[25]

The fundamental social unit in a tribe is the family, which is hierarchical and patriarchal. The central authority figure is the father who is entitled to deference and unquestioned obedience. His role is to be the provider.[26] The oldest brother has this responsibility in the father's absence or following his demise.[27] A family is an exclusive network where membership rests solely on birth. However, qualified entry can occur through marriage and fostership.[28] The family takes precedence over all other possible

24   This definition is drawn from Hoyland who defines a tribe as a 'mutual aid group bounded together by a notion of kinship'. R.G. Hoyland, *Arabia and the Arabs: From the Bronze Age to the Coming of Islam* (London, 2002), p. 113. The word 'notion' is used as kinship may be actual perceived or claimed.

25   This is illustrated in a Sharjah-based clan of the Al Suwaidi family whose tribal name is Madloum, meaning 'oppressed'. The name was a nickname given to the tribe's progenitor, a prominent trader, who always countered any offer made by a customer with a claim that to accept it would make him a pauper. Ahmed Madloum Al Suwaidi, interview in Abu Dhabi, 2018.

26   H. Barakat, *The Arab World: Society, Culture, and State* (Berkeley, 1993), p. 101.

27   This cultural norm has real manifestations and consequence for the military, even today. For example, an only son of a family can be exempted from national service.

28   Adoption is not recognised in Islam, however fostering is allowed and encouraged. The child, who may be abandoned or an orphan, retains the family name of their biological father. It is not uncommon for ruling families to foster children. While in such cases fostered children do not have the same status as biological children, they have high status and, upon reaching adulthood, they may fill posts that are nearly as senior and influential as those of the rulering family's biological children. An example is the four children (Rasha, Razan, Khaldoon and Mohammad) of Khalifa Al Mubarak, the UAE Ambassador to France who was assassinated in 1984. These children were fostered by Sheikh Zayed bin Sultan Al Nahyan, Ruler of Abu Dhabi/UAE President. Today, Razan, Khaldoon and Mohammad all hold powerful government posts. Additionally, Mohammad heads one of the country's largest real estate companies, Aldar, and Khaldoon heads one of Abu Dhabi's key sovereign investment vehicles, Mubadala.

priorities including work, friends and personal desires. Loyalty is to the family, and this creates wide-ranging and powerful mutual obligations between family members.

These characteristics – hierarchy, patriarchy, exclusivity, and collectivism – are replicated at higher kinship levels in tribal societies. A common definition of kinship used in the UAE recognises four levels: the smallest in size is the close or extended family, followed by a clan, and then a section, with the largest group being the tribe itself. These levels are conceptual rather than practical, as the differences between them are ill-defined.[29] Some tribal sections consider themselves tribes, and some tribes are really confederations of tribes. This four-tiered classification does not automatically imply a pyramid-style power hierarchy. Some sections can have greater influence than others, and some tribes do not have a paramount sheikh as power rests with section sheikhs.

Kinship groupings have evolved over time as new groupings formed, or groups were subsumed into others. One common reason why groups separated was because an element of the group considered that the existing group's leader was weak and that greater benefits could be gained by becoming independent. Another frequent reason for separation was because an element of a larger group moved away so as to access resources, and over time it became independent. Reasons for a group being subsumed into another group included a desire to gain protection from being part of a larger or more powerful group, and to obtain benefits by self-identifying with locally important lineages. Marriage and trade relations could also be agents of transformation in kinship groups. The net result of the continual evolution of kinship groups is that the groups are rarely closed or homogenous.

The centrality of kinship in Arab society is readily seen in Arabic names. Unlike names in the Anglosphere which consist of a first, middle and surname, it is common in the Gulf for Arabic names to consist of a patronymic chain of up to five names, made up of direct ancestors (e.g. father, grandfather, great-grandfather and great-great-grandfather), followed by the name of the section/tribe.[30] For example, Sheikh Khalifa bin Zayed bin Sultan Al Nahyan, the current UAE President and Ruler of Abu Dhabi, is the son of Sheikh Zayed, who is the son of Sheikh Sultan, and they hail from the Al Nahyan family of the Al Bu Falah sub-section of the Bani Yas tribe.

The different levels of kinship groups provide the basis for identity and social order, and explain two key phenomena of tribal society. First, there is intense competition between kinship groups, with each seeking to maximise advantages for their group

29   Frauke Heard-Bey, 'The Tribal Society of the UAE and Its Traditional Economy', in I. Abed and P. Hellyer (eds.), *United Arab Emirates: A New Perspective* (London, 2001), p. 99.

30   In the recent decade, the UAE Government has introduced a new naming convention on official documents. Now a person can only list three names with the last one being the tribal or section name. This has eliminated unrecognised clans and sections. This change appears to be driven by a desire to reduce nationals identifying with small kinship groups and instead, to encourage identity built around larger tribal groupings. This in turn helps build a broader collective and national identity.

members. Second, groups may unite when faced by an external threat. These are both captured in the Arab saying, 'I against my brother; I and my brother against my cousin; I and my brother and my cousin against the world'. This phenomenon engenders a natural suspicion and closing of ranks against the 'other', and intra-group reinforcing mechanisms, such as a preference for close intermarriage and assistance or favourable treatment to those within the group.

The collectivist nature of tribal society means that there is an acceptance of the primacy of the group over the individual, and strong recognition of interdependence and reciprocity. This also leads to a suppression of individual preferences in return for security for both the individual and the collective. Within a tribal culture, the priority is on maintaining group unity which, in turn, encourages compromise, consultation and loyalty rather than initiative and unilateral action. This results in what can appear to outsiders as a slow and convoluted decision-making process.

At its extreme, the tribe's collectivist nature is reflected in collective honour where an insult to one member is an insult to all. Sir Mark Allen, an Arabist MI6 officer who served in Abu Dhabi from 1975 to 1977, described the practicality of this norm when it came to righting a wrong:

> Two individuals, if they count back from father to grandfather and meet the same forebear within five generations or less, are members of the same *ahl* [roughly translating as extended family]. This is the individual's vengeance group which is bound, if he is killed, to kill the killer or his close relatives or raise a claim against them.[31]

Bedu and hadhr

Conventionally, the traditional people in the Emirates were normally classified into two groups based on their lifestyles – nomadic (*bedu*) and those who were settled (*hadhr*). However, many groups were a mix of both. Some pastoralists who were based in one location for much of the year also travelled for extended periods with their flocks, seeking pasture, while some cultivators who lived in the mountains of the northern Emirates would also come to the coast for part of the year to trade or work.

Bedu moved constantly in search of grazing areas for their camels and herds, and in the Emirates typically moved in winter towards the coast, and in the summer to the cooler inland oases.[32] The majority of *bedu* lived in modern-day Abu Dhabi and

---

31   M. Allen, *Arabs* (New York, 2006), p. 15.
32   An exception to this were those working on pearling *dhows* who went to sea over summer. This was because from mid-May to early September, the water was sufficiently warm to allow a diver to work in the water all day. P. Lienhardt, with A. Al-Shahi (ed.), *Shaikhdoms of Eastern Arabia* (London, 2001), p. 130.

Dubai Emirates. While some travelled continuously, many were semi-nomadic in that they regularly returned to a permanent settlement, such as to the hamlets in the Liwa Oasis. The *bedu* earned income through the sale of camels and their products, by transporting people and goods, by providing security for caravans, and by undertaking seasonal employment like pearling. The land grazed by a *bedu* tribe (known the tribe's *dirah*) reflected the tribe's size and power and, as such, would vary over time as the relative prestige, number of tribal members, resources and power of the various tribes changed. Grazing in a *dirah* of another tribe would result in conflict unless explicit approval was given.[33] As *bedu* could both raid settlements and provide protection from raiders, some *bedu* tribes collected tribute in return for ensuring the security of settled groups.

Rather than being powerless in the face of the *bedu*, the *hadhr* could exert power over nomadic groups by controlling access to water and other needed resources, as well as creating rivalry between different *bedu* groups through subsidies, and by building alliances with imperial authorities who would support them against threatening *bedu* groups.[34] The prominent section/tribe of a settled group would generally seek to establish alliances with *bedu* groups for mutual advantage. These could result in a symbiotic partnership which enabled a settled group to dominate a region politically and militarily.

In the Emirates, *hadhr* can be divided into two groups. The first are those that lived on the mainland coast and islands, and whose livelihoods revolved around pearling, fishing, maritime trade and boat building. They mainly lived in settlements built around sea inlets or creeks which provided a safe harbour for fishing, trading and pearling vessels. The second group are those who lived inland, either on the plains or mountains of the northern Emirates, or in the oases of Abu Dhabi, and in inland townships like Al Dhaid in Sharjah and Khatt in Ras Al Khaimah. This group mainly depended on cultivation or animal husbandry for their livelihoods.

Hadhr have always outnumbered *bedu*. Around 1910, there were some 8,000 *bedu* and 72,000 *hadhr* in the Emirates.[35] In the 1980s, some 15 percent of UAE citizens were classified as *bedu*.[36] Despite their smaller number, the *bedu* had considerable power in premodern times because they controlled the deserts of the region, and only through negotiating with them could one cross or use their land. With the introduction of modern weapons, wireless, automobiles and aircraft into the interior of the Emirates, which started in earnest in the 1950s, the power and influence of the *bedu*

---

33   Hesam Mohammed Jalil Sultan Al-Ulama, 'The Federal Boundaries of the United Arab Emirates' (PhD thesis, University of Durham, 1994), p. 21.
34   Dale Eickelman, 'Tribes and Tribal Identity in the Arab Gulf States', in J. E. Peterson (eds.), *The Emergence of the Gulf States* (New York, 2016), p. 233.
35   Heard-Bey, *From Trucial States to United Arab Emirates*, p. 427.
36   John Duke Anthony and John A. Hearty, 'Eastern Arabian States: Kuwait, Bahrain, Qatar, the United Arab Emirates, and Oman', in D.E. Long and B. Reich (eds.), *The Government and Politics of the Middle East and North Africa* (Boulder, 1980), p. 151.

started to decline. No longer were they the gatekeepers to the desert, nor could they use it as a refuge from which to launch raids. Vehicles meant that camels had little transport value, and the work of *bedu* as guides for travellers and oil company seismic teams ended with the building of roads. By the late 1960s, the traditional *bedu* lifestyle was no longer sustainable, and they increasingly settled in new townships or on farms.

During pre-modern times when the *bedu* represented both a threat and source of protection for settlements, their importance in local politics was disproportionate to their number. In modern times, they have retained considerable status, notably in Abu Dhabi which has sought to maintain the society's historic structure.

The only published census of tribal numbers in the Emirates was undertaken in 1968. A later study extrapolated the 1968 figures to arrive at estimates of the tribal composition of the UAE in 1994 (Table 8). The figures show that in most Emirates the bulk of the tribal population is drawn from only one or a very few tribes. In a society where kinship groups form the basis of the political system,[37] the larger the tribe, the more political power it has. Thus, within each Emirate, the ruler must ensure that he maintains the support of the larger tribes at a minimum. In the case of Abu Dhabi, the key tribes are the *bedu* and *hadhr* Bani Yas which has around 20 sections and reside across the Abu Dhabi Emirate including the islands, the *bedu* Manasir of Al Dhafra, the *bedu* Awamir, the *hadhr* Dhawahir tribe based in the Buraimi region, the *bedu* and *hadhr* Naim of Buraimi, and semi *hadhr* Najadat.[38]

Table 8: Estimates of the tribal composition of the Emirates, 1994[39]

Tribal name		Abu Dhabi	Dubai	Sharjah	Ajman	Umm Al Quwain	Ras Al Khaimah	Fujairah	Total
Tribe	Common surname								
Bani Yas[a]	–	24,198	20,774	7,560	1,130	0	1,539	143	55,300
Sharqiyin[a]	Al Sharqi	421	342	610	363	131	431	44,074	46,300
Shihuh/ Habus	Al Shihhi/ Al Habsi	773	389	389	68	0	30,771	1,284	33,600
Al Ali[a]	Al Ali	315	815	2,674	447	15,067	7,607	0	26,900
Qawasim[a]	Al Qasimi	531	568	18,910	42	0	5,554	74	25,700
Manasir	Al Mansuri	16,972	1,447	257	110	0	200	0	18,900
Zaab	Al Zaabi	7,115	142	3,737	37	0	5,924	0	16,900

37   S.H. Hurriez, *Folklore and Folklife in the United Arab Emirates* (London, 2013), p. 26.
38   Author's collection, Abu Dhabi, Gowlett files, Abu Dhabi Defence Force, 'Tribes of Abu Dhabi', 1970.
39   Hendrik van der Meulen, 'The Role of Tribal and Kinship Ties in the Politics of the United Arab Emirates' (PhD thesis, Fletcher School of Law and Diplomacy, 1997), p. 84. As the table only includes significant tribes that were in the Emirates in 1968 and excludes ones which were deemed less significant, it underestimates tribal numbers.

Tribal name		Abu Dhabi	Dubai	Sharjah	Ajman	Umm Al Quwain	Ras Al Khaimah	Fujairah	Total
Tribe	Common surname								
Dhawahir	Al Dhahiri	14,972	221	573	215	0	47	300	16,300
Mazari	Al Mazrui	6,775	1,426	1,542	89	200	5,590	400	16,000
Al Bu Shamis	Al Shamsi	1,947	4,048	3,627	1,000	63	2,147	0	12,800
Bani Qitab	Al Qitbi	3,248	821	7,675	110	31	589	0	12,400
Naim[a]	Al Nuaimi	1,710	900	1,152	3,242	131	5,096	52	12,300
Naqbiyin	Al Naqbi	84	0	7,080	0	0	2,848	0	10,000
Awamir	Al Amiri	9,060	363	194	36	100	178	0	9,900
Other		12,313	9,312	11,297	1,595	1,126	18,936	1,721	56,300
TOTAL		100,444	41,400	67,222	8,481	16,893	87,450	48,107	369,800

Notes
a.   The Emirate's ruling family comes from this tribe.

In discussing the composition of the armed forces, some commentators have identified a strong *bedu* influence on the armed forces controlled by Abu Dhabi.[40] However, a more nuanced characterisation is that the Abu Dhabi rulers have a preference for filling the most senior posts and those in critical units with members of Abu Dhabi-linked *asil* tribes and other tribes historically loyal to the Abu Dhabi rulers, many of which are *bedu*.

Asil

Asil, which can be translated as 'authenticity', 'original' and 'genuine', infers that there are more and less authentic Arab tribes.[41] The most authentic are deemed to have classic genealogies, that is, those who can trace their heritage back to descendants of Ibrahim, particularly the two foundation pre-Islamic tribes of Arabia – Qahtan or Adnan.[42] Ibrahim was the common patriarch of the three Abrahamic religions.[43] In the Abu Dhabi Emirate, the Bani Yas tribal confederation has high standing and a key reason for this is due to its lineage. The tribe is named after Yas bin Amer, who is said to be descended from Adnan and who was a direct descendent of Ismail, the first son of Ibrahim.[44]

40   Duke Anthony and Hearty, 'Eastern Arabian States: Kuwait, Bahrain, Qatar, the United Arab Emirates, and Oman', p. 151.
41   N.N. Ayubi, *Over-stating the Arab State: Politics and Society in the Middle East* (London, 1996), p. 254.
42   S.B. Miles, *The Countries and Tribes of the Persian Gulf* (London, 1919), p. 2.
43   O'Sullivan, *The New Gulf*, p. 267.
44   Yas bin Amer is said to have come from the tribe of Nizar bin Mayid bin Adnan.

However, *asil* is not only judged on the basis of the connection to the original descendants of Arabia. Another important consideration is when a kinship group's ancestors arrived in the region; the further back into history a group can trace its heritage to the region, the more authentic that tribe is considered to be. Across the Emirates, some groups have ancestors who moved to the region centuries before, while the ancestors of others came just last century. Identifying ancestors living at locations associated with the tribe of the ruler's family also increases 'authenticity'. In the case of Abu Dhabi's ruling family (from the Al Nahyan/Al Bu Falah section[45] of the Bani Yas tribe), for instance, whose historic roots are in Liwa, tribes associated with the Liwa region have a particular standing. A final factor increasing *asil* is whether a kinship group has been considered an ally of a ruling family. This explains the prominence in Abu Dhabi of the Al Manasir and Al Dhawahir tribes which have allied themselves with the Bani Yas tribe for centuries. A more recent example is the small Al Ariyani tribe of Al Ain which has allied itself with the Al Nahyan section over the last half century.

In each of the Emirates, different weight is given to different aspects of *asil*. For example, in Abu Dhabi, *asil* is strongly associated with *bedu* ancestry, because the Emirate's historic population was *bedu*. The importance placed on *bedu* ancestry is reflected in today's characterisation of bedu values – freedom, self-reliance, generosity, and an enthusiasm for battle. Conversely, *hadhr* are stereotyped as soft, cowed, and lacking in the lean, hard values of the *bedu*. Other Emirates in which the rulers have descended from settled Arab tribes, do not place such significance on *bedu* ancestry.

While *asil* is a significant factor in a kinship group's social standing, it does not mean that groups which have not descended from revered lines or which lack a long-term presence in the UAE are marginalised or automatically have low standing. Certain merchant families which have geographic Persian ancestry (i.e. Arab or Persian ethnicities) or Indian roots, widely respected due to their historic and substantial ongoing contributions to the commercial life of the Emirates. These families are descended from traders who settled along the UAE's coast in the late 19th and early 20th centuries.[46] Another illustration of such a group that also has 'good' *asil* is the Al Balooshi tribe of the Buraimi region. Their ancestors came from Balochistan, a region between south-western Pakistan and south-eastern Iran. They settled in the Buraimi region in the 1800s and 1900s.[47]

45   The Al Bu Falah believe themselves to be descended from the Bani Hilal confederation, prominent in the seventeenth century.
46   About 1865, hundreds of Indian British subjects, or Banians, settled in Dubai where they became the second biggest economic class in Dubai through financing the yearly pearling expeditions, supplying the fleets with goods and taking pearls in payment. Fatma Al-Sayegh, 'Merchants' Role in a Changing Society: The Case of Dubai, 1900-90', *Middle Eastern Studies*, 34, 1 (1998), p. 88.
47   Zahlan notes that the ethnic origins of another key Emirati tribe, the Shihuh, is uncertain. However, they have lived in the northern Emirates and Oman for centuries and are considered to be very 'authentic'. Rosemarie Said Zahlan, *The Origins of the United Arab Emirates: A Political and Social History of the Trucial States* (London, 1978), p. 59.

Some Emirati leaders and organisational cultures give *asil* greater importance than others. *Asil* has always been important in the military, and in the case of Abu Dhabi-controlled armed forces, there appears to have always been a strong preference for members of tribes with higher *asil* to hold more senior and politically sensitive posts. This can be seen in a study of the tribal breakdown of senior Emiratis in defence and security organisations in Abu Dhabi published in 2011 (Figure 8). It showed that the majority of senior positions were allocated to the premier section of the Bani Yas tribe (i.e. Al Nahyan), other prominent Bani Yas sections,[48] other tribes traditionally allied to the ruling family of Abu Dhabi (i.e. Manasir and Dhawahir), tribes from the Buraimi region or other tribes which have become allied to the Bani Yas in recent decades (i.e. Awamir, Naim, Darmaki, Dhahiri, Bani Kaab, Al Bu Shamis and Bani Riyam). Less than 20 percent of senior Emiratis are from the 'other' category.

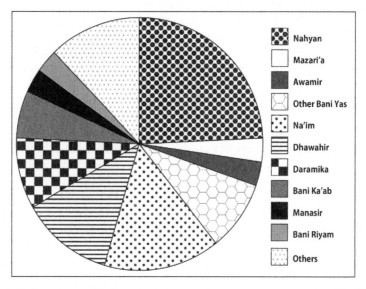

Figure 8: Tribes of senior Emiratis in defence and security organisations in Abu Dhabi.[49]

The most senior and politically sensitive posts in this context means: (1) force and significant formation commanders (e.g. Chief of Staff and Commander Air Force and Air Defence); (2) officers in charge of operations (e.g. Assistant Chief of Staff

---

48   The more prominent sections, besides the Al Bu Falah and Al Bu Falasah, are the Qubaisat, Maharibah, Hawamil, Mazari, Rumaithat, Al Bu Mahair, Qumzan and Sudan.

49   Ono Motohiro, 'Reconsideration of the Meanings of the Tribal Ties in the United Arab Emirates: Abu Dhabi Emirate in Early '90s', *Kyoto Bulletin of Islamic Area Studies*, 4, 1 & 2 (2011), pp. 29-30.

Operations, Commander Air Operations Centre, and Commander Emiri Guard); (3) front-line operators of high readiness and nationally significant critical capabilities (e.g. pilots in fighter squadrons, and special forces personnel); and (4) military intelligence (e.g. members of the Directorate of Military Intelligence, and Air Intelligence).

Religion

Islam arrived in the present-day UAE in 630AD when envoys of the Prophet Mohammed arrived. Today, virtually all nationals are Muslim, and, of these, the overwhelming majority are Sunni. Peacefully co-existing for generations alongside Sunnis are nationals who follow the Shia sect of Islam.

The UAE's Constitution recognises Islam as the official religion of the state, and Islamic law (*Sharia*) as a main (but not sole) source of its legislation.[50] Despite the centrality of Islam in the UAE, it is important to note that the country has not adopted Islam as an ideology. In other words, the religion is not seen as the sole framework for structuring the country's political, societal and economic relations. This contrasts with ideological Islamic states, such as the Islamic Republic of Iran, which consider that for society and the state to be Islamic, the state must be under the leadership of religious leaders (i.e. it must be a theocracy). That said, Islam has shaped and continues to shape UAE politics, including foreign policy. An example is the enduring concern by the UAE's leadership for protecting the holy places of Islam, including Jerusalem as the religion's third holiest site. It also explains the enduring humanitarian support given to fellow Muslim nations.

Historically in the Emirates, most of its leaders and population have been religiously moderate and pragmatic. In the Emirates, Islamic clerics (*imams*), scholars and judges (*qadi*) have never wielded significant power nor have they had excessive influence on government policy, unlike in Iran and Saudi Arabia.[51] Instead, the rulers have long advocated a pragmatic version of Islam which embraces the religion at an individual and societal level in terms of religious practice and personal behaviour, but not in terms of governing public life, politics and government institutions. In recent decades, this perspective has been formalised in the state policy of rejecting and combating Islamists and their ideology in the UAE and beyond, as it is seen as leading to sectarianism and divisions in society.

---

50   Article 7 of the Constitution. *Sharia* is not a codified law but is a set of principles derived from religious precepts of Islam and formulated by one of the schools of Islamic jurisprudence. Consequently, *Sharia* interpretation and application can differ. The 1980s UAE Penal Code introduced Sharia principles for certain crimes and punishments, and today the UAE has Sharia Courts which are concerned with personal status and family laws matters such as inheritance, marriage and divorce.
51   Butti Sultan Butti Ali Al Muhairi, 'The Islamisation of Laws in the UAE: The Case of the Penal Code', *Arab Law Quarterly*, 11, 4 (1996), p. 352.

The Emirates have avoided significant sectarian disputes, unlike the neighbouring states of Oman, Bahrain and Saudi Arabia. This does not mean the country has not or still does not face Islamist challenges from within: it does, notably from: (1) Shia adherents who are mobilised by Iran, and (2) Sunnis who are mobilised by radical jihadist and reactionary groups. The broad agenda of both Islamist forces is to ensure *Sharia* is the basis for controlling the affairs of the state and society, and hence to replace the monarchical form of government. This explains a fundamental reason for the rulers' rejection of their creeds. It is worth considering each of these two challenges in a little more detail due to their effect on the military and security.

Iranian-backed Shiaism

For decades, Shia adherents in the Emirates have made up a sizable minority of both nationals and expatriates. They come from various Shia branches, notably Imamiyyah and Zhahiri. While reliable figures on Shias in the Emirates are unavailable, some insights can be obtained through examining the demographics of Iranians and those with Persian heritage in the Emirates. However, it is important to note that numbers on Iranian Shias can be inflated. First, because they contain both Iranian nationals and people of Persian descent. There are nationals in the UAE who have descended from Arab families that originated on the Persian islands and coasts and came to the Emirates in the nineteenth century. To call these people Iranians is to mischaracterise them. Second, because many of these people are Sunni practising Arabs, not Shias.

In 1964, the Foreign Office stated that in Dubai there were some 15,000 to 20,000 Iranians out of a total population of about 60,000, that is between 25 and 33 percent of the population. In Sharjah, there were about 4,000 Iranians out of 15,000 total population (i.e. 26 percent), and 2,000 Iranians out of 10,000 in Ras Al Khaimah (i.e. 20 percent).[52] In 1995, the US Director of Political and Military Affairs Section at the US Embassy in Abu Dhabi stated that 60,000 nationals residing in the country were ethnically Iranian.[53] During the 1990s, the population of nationals was around 500,000, which means that Shias made up 12 percent of the national population.[54] In 2014, the Gulf Labour Markets, Migration and Population Program stated that there were between 400,000 and 500,000 Iranian expatriates residing in the UAE, thus making them between 4 and 5 percent of the population.[55]

---

52 National Archives of Australia, A1838, 181/1/15, Office of the High Commissioner for Australia in London to the Secretary Department of External Affairs, 'The Iranians, the Arabs and the Persian Gulf', 27 August 1964.

53 van der Meulen, 'The Role of Tribal and Kinship Ties in the Politics of the United Arab Emirates', p. 85.

54 Gulf Research Center and Migration Policy Centre, 'UAE: Estimates of Total Population by Sex, Sex Ratios and Annual Demographic Growth Rates (1970-2010)'.

55 Gulf Research Center and Migration Policy Centre. 'UAE: Estimates of Population Residing in the UAE by Country of Citizenship (Selected Countries, 2014)', n.d.,

Figures on the actual numbers of Shias were also provided in 2004 when the US Ambassador to the UAE reported that Shias made up to 15 percent of the Emirati population.[56] In 2018, the US Department of State stated that 15 percent of UAE's nationals were not Sunni Muslims. It noted that most of the remaining citizens were Shia Muslims, and these were concentrated in the Emirates of Dubai and Sharjah.[57]

The rulers have always allowed Shias (as well as Christians, Hindus, and other religious groups) to practice their religion, but proselytising is not allowed, and worship must occur in private or in sanctioned environments. The UAE acceptance of Shiaism is reflected in the presence today of Shia mosques in most Emirates, and the willingness of the UAE to provide funds to these mosques upon request. Shia mosques can broadcast their version of the call to prayer from their minarets.[58]

The rulers have never banned Shia expatriates and nationals from serving in their armed forces. For example, Shia servicemen seconded from the Pakistan armed forces have worked in the ADDF and UAE Armed Forces. This makes the UAE unlike Saudi Arabia where the rulers in the late 1980s demanded that Shias be removed from Pakistani military units deployed to Saudi Arabia.

Shia nationals have long served in the UAE Armed Forces, and continue to serve in it, as well as being called up for national service. Some Shia nationals have held very senior positions in the UAE Armed Forces. However, Barany claimed in 2019 that the UAE was increasingly eschewing Shias as potential recruits for the security sector.[59]

Despite the UAE governments' tolerance of Shiaism and lack of interference in Shia affairs within the Emirates, at various times since the late 1970s, there have been concerns over Shia adherents who sought to advance Iran's version of political Islam. This concern first arose in the late 1970s following the overthrowing of the Shah of Iran and the establishment of the Islamic Revolutionary Government. This Government sought to export its revolutionary agenda, targeting those states which were deemed to be 'un-Islamic'. From Iran's perspective, this included states which were monarchies. This was the conclusion reached in a 1981 CIA assessment which stated that 'Iranian mullahs in 1979 called on Gulf Shias to rise against the Sunni masters in these countries'.[60] The call by Iran's leaders was directed not only to the

<gulfmigration.eu/uae-estimates-of-population-residing-in-the-uae-by-country-of-citizenship-selected-countries-2014/>

56   Wikileaks, Michele J. Sison, US Ambassador to the UAE, 'UAE Minimizing Influence of Islamic Extremists', 2004.

57   US Department of State, Bureau of Democracy, Human Rights and Labor, *2018 Report on International Religious Freedom: United Arab Emirates* (Washington DC, 2019), p. 2.

58   Bureau of Democracy US Department of State, Human Rights, and Labor, *2015 Report on International Religious Freedom – United Arab Emirates* (Washington DC, 2016).

59   Z. Barany, *Military Officers in the Gulf: Career Trajectories and Determinants* (2019), p. 2.

60   US Central Intelligence Agency, *Tilting Toward Baghdad: Gulf States' Aid to Iraq* (Washington DC, 1981), p. 9.

Shia but also to the broader Persian diaspora. At that time in the UAE, there were an estimated 100,000 nationals of Iranian origin (both Persian ethnicity and Arabs who had migrated from Persia) and some 30,000 Iranian nationals (60 percent of whom were Sunni and 40 percent Shia). These large numbers and the belief that some in the UAE were 'intimately involved in the political crisis in Iran', according to the *Financial Times* in 1979, made them a threat that needed to be taken seriously.[61]

The threat of Shia extremism linked to Iran continues to the present. A particular concern is Iranian sleeper cells made up of infiltrators and collaborators who will 'wake up' and destabilise the country on orders from Iran. According to the former Iranian Consul-General in Dubai, Adel Al Assaid, who defected in 2001, Iran has maintained such a network since 1979.[62] Historical evidence to support the threat was provided in a declassified CIA report which stated that in 1985 the UAE authorities made arrests and uncovered cells of radical Shias supported by Iran.[63]

Over the last decade, to counter those who have supported Iranian-backed militant groups (e.g. Hezbollah), the UAE have removed such people from UAE government jobs and expelled them. While many of these have been Shia, the UAE has emphasised that this is not driven by discrimination against Shia but rather because of their 'ties to any suspect Islamic group'.[64]

Sunni radical jihadist and reactionary traditionalists

The second principal group of ideologically strident Islamists who represent a challenge for the UAE rulers comes from Sunni conservative and traditionalist forces. This is not a new threat as it first appeared in the 1700s with the formation of the Wahhabist movement in the Najd region of present-day Saudi Arabia. It rejected much of the then contemporary Islamic practice, claiming it was contaminated with idolatry, impurities, and unacceptable innovations. Instead it argued for what it considered a 'purer' and more traditional version of Islam. Named after the activist, Mohammed ibn Abd al-Wahhab, the Wahhabist forces of the late 1700s sought to spread their creed throughout the region. While the main tribal group of Abu Dhabi region (the Bani Yas) rejected their belief system, those in the land between Sharjah to Ras Al Khaimah (notably the ruling Qawasim tribal federation) were strongly influenced by it.[65]

---

61   M. Tingay, 'Legions Galore', *Financial Times*, 25 June 1979.
62   Duraid Al Baik, 'Iranian Spy Network Stretches Across GCC', *Gulf News*, 15 September 2008.
63   US Central Intelligence Agency, *The Terrorist Threat to the Gulf Cooperation Council States: The Next 18 Months* (Washington, DC, 1986), p. 11.
64   Margaret Coker, 'U.A.E. Vets Workers for Ties to Tehran', *The Wall Street Journal*, 16 October 2009.
65   Wilson, *Zayed, Man Who Built a Nation*, p. 30.

This development explains why there are two main Sunni schools of juris-prudence in the UAE. One is Hanbali, which is the dominant school in Sharjah, Umm Al Quwain, Ras Al Khaimah and Ajman. Hanbali was traditionally linked to Wahhabism, although Hanbali leaders have today renounced the views of the Wahhabist founder. The other is Maliki, which predominates in Abu Dhabi and Dubai.[66] Maliki, compared to Hanbali, is more accepting of innovation and considers additional sources of authority when there is ambiguity in the *Quran* and *Hadiths*.[67]

Group adherence to the different Sunni jurisprudence schools has played a small but notable role in the political dynamics of the Emirates. To be more specific, it is a contributing factor to understanding why the rulers of Ras Al Khaimah and Sharjah[68] have traditionally been more supportive of and received support from Saudi Arabia, while Abu Dhabi and Dubai have not. This has created tensions at certain times over concerns about the degree of Saudi influence in the Emirates. In terms of the general population, the presence of the Hanbali conservative school may have contributed to the receptiveness of some Emiratis to Sunni militant groups, notably the Muslim Brotherhood, and more recent groups, such as Al Qaeda and Islamic State of Iraq and Syria (ISIS). Of these, the most enduring threat from the perspective of the rulers is the Muslim Brotherhood.

The Muslim Brotherhood was formed in Egypt in the 1920s to advance *Sharia* as the driving ideology governing state and society, to unify Arab Islamic countries, and to liberate such states from imperialism. By the 1950s, it was perceived as a threat to the secular government of President Gamal Abdel Nasser. The organisation was banned, thousands of its members were imprisoned, and many more fled to foreign countries from which they sought to spread their ideology. In the case of the Emirates, the Brotherhood's presence can be traced back to the 1950s. This was when Egyptian and Syrian teachers who espoused Brotherhood views arrived. During the 1960s, they sought to mobilise students to advance the Brotherhood's agenda and, in the 1970s, their presence grew in size and influence to the point that, in 1974, a local group affili-ated to the Brotherhood, Al Islah, was officially allowed to form in Dubai.

According to Lori Plotkin Boghardt, a Gulf specialist at the Washington Institute for Near East Policy, 'Al Islah members gained considerable influence in the new

66 There are of four well accepted schools – Maliki, Hanbali, Hanafi and Shafi'I. While most nationals subscribe to either Maliki or Hanbali, Fujairah adheres to Shafi. B.M. Rubin, *Guide to Islamist Movements* (Armonk, 2010), p. 310.

67 The *Quran* is the central religious text of Islam, which Muslims believe to be a revelation from God. It was verbally revealed by God to the Prophet Mohammed through the Angel Gabriel from 609 to 632CE. *Hadiths* are the sayings, customs and actions of the Prophet Mohammad. The principal authority for Maliki jurisprudence is in the *Quran* and the trustworthy *Hadiths* (sayings, customs and actions of Mohammed); if there is ambiguity, then consideration will be given to *Istislah* (interest and welfare of Islam and Muslims), and *Urf* (custom of people).

68 Wikileaks, Sison, 'UAE Minimizing Influence of Islamic Extremists', 2004.

state during the 1970s and 1980s, with many assuming high posts in the education and justice sectors – including the cabinet-level position of education minister – and crafting the nation's curriculum'.[69] According to the scholar Kristian Coates Ulrichsen, Al Islah saw itself as a 'defender of traditional social values against the perceived encroachment of 'Western' values',[70] such as teaching English in schools, and female students being taught music and dancing.

The rise in Al Islah's influence in the UAE during the 1970s and 1980s reflected a growing Islamification across the Middle East. This was fuelled by a combination of disillusionment with the failure of secular governments to improve economic and political conditions for their populations, the perception of a loss of Arabness, and a decline in the centrality of Islam as societies modernised. Material expressions of this growing Islamification were the 1979 Iranian Islamic revolution and the 1979 siege of the Grand Mosque in Mecca. The latter involved a group of armed Sunni extremists storming the Grand Mosque and calling for the overthrow of the House of Saud. Action to dislodge the rebels not only cost hundreds of lives and took two weeks to achieve, it also resulted in a political bargain being struck between the King and the state's conservative religious leadership (*ulema*) which was sympathetic to the rebels' agenda. This resulted in the King giving more power to religious conservatives as reflected in the closing down of cinemas, banning of women in newspapers and on television, and the increased power given to the religious police.[71]

Growing Islamification across the region had its parallels in the UAE. For instance, in 1979 the Ruler of Abu Dhabi ordered that crimes of theft, fornication, adultery, murder and manslaughter be referred to courts where *Sharia* applied: the secular Abu Dhabi penal law was not to be used to judge these crimes. A further illustration from 1979 was the formation of a national committee tasked with Islamising UAE legislation. One product was the first Penal Code (1989) which included Islamic elements such as doctrinal crimes (*hadud*), financial compensation for harm (*diyah*) and retribution (*qisas*). Other signs of Islamification included the application of the *Sharia* penalty for adultery, which was stoning. In 1984, for the first time in UAE history, a judge sentenced a person to stoning. However, this[72] and all subsequent cases where this punishment was given were overturned by the UAE President. In the same year,

69   Lori Plotkin Boghardt. 'The Muslim Brotherhood on Trial in the UAE', 2013, The Washington Institute, <www.washingtoninstitute.org/policy-analysis/view/the-muslim-brotherhood-on-trial-in-the-uae>

70   K.C. Ulrichsen, *The United Arab Emirates: Power, Politics and Policy-Making* (Basingstoke, 2016), p.75.

71   R. Lacey, *Inside the Kingdom: Kings, Clerics, Modernists, Terrorists, and the Struggle for Saudi Arabia* (New York, 2009), pp. 49–52.

72   TNA FCO 8/5826: H.B. Walker, UK Ambassador in the UAE, 'United Arab Emirates: Annual Review for 1984', 20 January 1985.

in Sharjah girls' secondary schools, physical education was replaced with domestic science.[73] In 1985, alcohol was banned in Sharjah.[74]

According to Dr Butti Sultan Al Muhairi, currently the Chair of the Public Law Department at UAE University, the UAE's programme of Islamification was driven by two key factors. First, it was a defensive mechanism to pre-empt external criticism from Islamic states as it demonstrated 'loyalty and fidelity to Islam'. Second, both the rulers and the population supported a more Islamic system of justice in the belief that this would counter the rise in crime brought about by the influx of foreigners.[75]

Despite the implementation of more conservative measures in the 1980s, Al Islah argued strongly for greater stringency; and it became increasingly critical of UAE governments. This eventually led to a governmental crackdown on the group in 1994. According to Ulrichsen, this was due to 'mounting concern at Al Islah's stature as a potentially powerful alternative focus of loyalty'.[76]

A major turning point in the response to Islamist extremists was the 9/11 US terrorist attack and the threat posed by Al Qaida. Two of the 19 aircraft hijackers in the 11 September 2001 attacks were Emirati citizens.[77] In October 2002, Al Qaida's head of Gulf operations, Abdel Rahim Al Nashri, was arrested in Abu Dhabi. He was the involved in the 2000 attack on the USS *Cole* and had planned to blow up economic installations in the UAE with the aim of causing large numbers of causalities. He was also alleged to have planned suicide attacks using oil tankers as weapons.[78]

In the early 2000s, the UAE Government gave an ultimatum to Al Islah to renounce its Islamist ideology and propaganda efforts or suffer the consequences.[79] At the same time, the UAE also implemented a series of counter-radicalisation measures. These included monitoring groups and individuals deemed to be Islamist, requiring *imams* to adhere to Friday sermons with themes which had been pre-approved by the government, re-training *imams* who gave inappropriate sermons, monitoring mosques, and replacing expatriate Arab teachers in the public schools with Emirati nationals.[80] The

---

73   Ibid.
74   O'Sullivan, *The New Gulf*, p. 305.
75   Al Muhairi, 'The Islamisation of Laws in the UAE: The Case of the Penal Code', p. 352.
76   Ulrichsen, *The United Arab Emirates: Power, Politics and Policy-Making*, p.76.
77   These were Mustafa Yousef Kasem Rashid Lekrab Al Shehhi (b. 1978, Ras Al Khaimah, educated in UAE University in Al Ain and who received federally financed overseas studies and scholarships) and Fayez Rashid Ahmed Hassan Al Qadi Bani Hammad (b. 1977, Khor Fakkan). Details of Al Shehhi from C.M. Davidson, *The United Arab Emirates: A Study in Survival* (Boulder, 2005), p. 80.
78   Ibid., pp. 80, 109.
79   Ulrichsen, *The United Arab Emirates: Power, Politics and Policy-Making*, p. 76.
80   Wikileaks, Sison, 'UAE Minimizing Influence of Islamic Extremists', 2004. Organisationally, the General Authority of Islamic Affairs and Endowments (AWQAF) vets and appoints Sunni *imams* 'based on their gender, educational background and knowledge of Islam, along with security checks'. AWQAF funds public Sunni mosques and retained all Sunni *imams* as government employees. Religious affairs in Dubai are not

UAE Government enhanced border surveillance to stop the entry of extremists, and detained Al Qaida suspects.[81]

Concern over the threat of Al Islah and other political Islamist influences increased in the early 2010s after the Muslim Brotherhood came to power in Egypt during the Arab Spring. The toppling of other regimes in the Middle East, coupled with the support given to the Islamist agenda by some states, resulted in an acceleration in efforts to counter extremist movements in the UAE. In 2014 the UAE banned some 80 Islamist-linked groups, including the UAE Muslim Brotherhood, and passed a new counter-terrorism law.[82]

Efforts to contain political Islamist influences have continued. In 2018, the UAE Council of Ministers approved the formation of the UAE Fatwa Council. According to the government, it 'will be the official, reliable reference for fatwas, coordinate fatwas, unify their sources and oversees all work related to fatwas'.[83] The government has also started translating Friday sermons into English and Urdu on its website and for mobile applications.[84]

In terms of the UAE Armed Forces, there has been concern about any support of political Islam within its forces. This issue came to the fore in the immediate aftermath of the 9/11 attacks in the US. An investigation into the presence of Brotherhood members and sympathisers within the UAE Armed Forces identified some 50 to 60 Emiratis. Out of these, 40 were detained, although 39 were subsequently released as they were considered to have simply been led astray.[85] Symbolically, starting in the early 2000s, the UAE Armed Forces have required all its members to keep their facial hair short[86] as untrimmed bushy beards have become a sign of adherence to extreme Islamic beliefs.

Looking forward

For the foreseeable future, the UAE will remain a country in which expatriates will make up the majority of the population despite the global difficulties in the early 2020s. Only if the UAE's reputation as a haven for foreigners and investment is

managed through AWQAF, but through the Islamic Affairs and Charitable Activities Department (IACAD). US Department of State, *2018 Report on International Religious Freedom – United Arab Emirates*, pp. 8-9.

81   Wikileaks, Sison, 'UAE Minimizing Influence of Islamic Extremists', 2004.

82   WAM. 'UAE Cabinet Approves List of Designated Terrorist Organisations, Groups', 16 November 2014, <wam.ae/en/details/1395272478814>

83   WAM. 'Mohamed bin Zayed Highlights Role of Emirates Fatwa Council', 2018, <wam. ae/en/details/1395302698231>

84   US Department of State, *2018 Report on International Religious Freedom – United Arab Emirates*, p. 9.

85   Wikileaks, Sison, 'UAE Minimizing Influence of Islamic Extremists', 2004.

86   Ibid.

destroyed would the situation arise in which nationals constitute most of the population. If all expatriates left, then the UAE's population would have shrunk to less than 20 percent of what it is today – invariably meaning the economy would have collapsed along with the political system. Such a scenario is inconceivable unless there was a catastrophic development such as a regional nuclear war.

The next decade will see a huge increase in the number of nationals entering the labour force. These will be the nearly 400,000 nationals born between 2000 and 2010, based on Table 5. This could nearly double the number of nationals in the UAE labour force. Providing jobs for these young nationals will be a challenge and an opportunity. If they do not find employment, the likelihood of social unrest increases. On the other hand, if they have the skills and aptitude to find meaningful employment, the UAE can reduce the proportion of expatriates in the population while increasing Emirati influence in many organisations.

Despite the growing national population, nationals will remain in the minority for the foreseeable future. This means that the concern held by some Emiratis that large numbers of expatriates pose a security threat to the country will remain. This concern is likely to harden during times of uncertainty, and also if the large numbers of young nationals entering the labour force do not find employment. Political responses by the UAE's leadership to this perception could include another program of Emiratisation (i.e. replacing expatriates with nationals), and a productivity drive explicitly linked to reducing expatriate numbers. Such responses could be applied to the UAE Armed Forces.

The divisions between groups of Emiratis also have the potential to lead to tensions within society. Again, this may increase in times of economic disruption as groups become resentful over what they see as unequal burden sharing. The UAE's leadership has long sought to de-emphasise the differences between groups, but this may be undone if government entities do not reflect the leader's intentions. In other words, entities can undermine the idea that all Emiratis are equal if they do not ensure that all groups of nationals have access to similar opportunities and are treated alike. That said, Emirati society will accept some entities applying constraints to certain groups if the restrictions are seen as reasonable and justified. However, what is seen as reasonable and justified changes over time. The UAE Armed Forces runs the risk of being out of step with changes to society's norms due to the organisation's natural conservatism. Getting it wrong, such as giving incorrect weight in promotions to an individual's heritage vis-à-vis merit, means that not only is there a waste of human talent, but military members may become disenchanted, quit and potentially become hostile to the 'system'.

Turning to religion, it is highly likely that the current emphasis in the UAE on countering political Islam will continue. In terms of the UAE's foreign policy, this means that the UAE will remain opposed to states and non-state actors which are supportive of or based on political Islam, regardless of whether they come from a Shia or Sunni tradition. Possibly of greatest concern for the UAE is when political Islam becomes part of a hostile state's agenda. Militarily, the UAE does not have the capability to unilaterally oppose such states. If the hostile state is a large regional one like Turkey or Iran, the UAE's approach will be to encourage global powers and regional coalitions to take the lead, with the UAE in a supporting role. This approach aims to constrain the hostile state while minimising the UAE's exposure, both in terms of being directly targeted or being left in the frontline when partners unexpectedly depart or unilaterally make ill-considered decisions. If the hostile state or non-actor is smaller or has limited military capabilities, then there may be a willingness for the UAE to take a leadership position in military operations to counter them.

The UAE's military leadership will remain watchful for any support for political Islam within the UAE Armed Forces. This does not mean that the leadership is worried about large-scale subversion of the military but instead recognises the considerable domestic and international political damage that can be caused by isolated violent acts motivated by political Islam and undertaken by members of the UAE Armed Forces.

3

Political Control

Political control over Emirati armed forces is exercised by the rulers. The starting point in understanding how rulers obtained and institutionalised, and continue to maintain, this control to the current day is to examine the traditional Emirati system of government. This is because this system has remained at the heart of both Emirate-level and Federal governments since the first professional military was raised in the Emirates in 1951. This may seem a surprising assertion given that today's governments are unrecognisable from those of the early 1950s. Then they were organised along traditional Arab tribal lines supplemented by rudimentary administration,[1] while today they have sophisticated governance arrangements made up of multiple centres of executive, legislative and judicial power; specialised administrative organisations like ministries, departments and councils; defined budgetary cycles; and professional public services.

What explains this continuity? The answer is a combination of history, culture and oil wealth.

Historically, the British period of influence over the Emirates (early 1800s-1971) established a dynastic power structure around the ruling family of each Emirate that has continued to the present. This structure arose because of treaties signed between the British and the coastal ruling sheikhs, starting in 1820. Over time, the treaties elevated these rulers' status and enabled them to solidify their positions both in their coastal towns and in the hinterlands. Britain's treaties resulted in 'legitimizing, perpetuating and indeed fossilizing' the political order of the 1800s, according to

---

1   This was noted by the Under-Secretary of State at the Foreign Office who, following a 1952 tour of the Trucial States, wrote that 'the organisation of these States is little removed from the tribal and no administrations exist in any of them'. TNA FO 371/104268: Roger Makins, Under-Secretary of State, Foreign Office, 'Report on a Visit to the States of the Persian Gulf Under British Protection, With Some Observations on Iraq and Saudi Arabia and With Conclusions and Recommendations', 20 March 1952.

Glencairn Balfour Paul, a British Arabist and diplomat who served in Dubai and Bahrain in the 1960s.[2]

The citizenry accepted this power structure as it conformed with the cultural characteristic of Emirati society – its tribal, Arab, and Islamic nature. The structure delivered benefits to the ruled both in terms of money, gifts, hospitality, and patronage, as well as security and stability. In return, for these benefits, local leaders gave their allegiance to their respective ruler and acknowledged that sovereignty rested with him alone.

The mutually beneficial political system of the ruler providing largesse and security, and the ruled giving allegiance to the ruler continued as the Emirates' economies grew. For the last five decades, oil revenue has allowed the Emirates to provide free education, healthcare, and housing to nationals, as well as extremely generous social support, loans, grants and free land. In political science terminology, the oil-fuelled largesse has made the UAE a rentier state. Such a state is defined as one which has substantial natural resources, and these generate the majority of the state's revenue. This wealth allows the state to avoid taxing its population to pay for government-supplied goods and services. Rentier state theory asserts that a rentier government can be independent from society and is significantly insulated against pressure for change from its citizenry. The Middle Eastern scholar, Professor Louise Fawcett, notes that 'rentier states inherit a political order from history: they do not create their own political order'.[3] Thus, the oil wealth of the Emirates is the third key factor which has enabled the rulers to maintain their power over many decades.

The Emirati system of government, from the traditional to the modern, displays three main characteristics:

1. The rulers are at the centre of power/government for they are the principal source of executive, legislative and judicial power.
2. The rulers exercise close supervision over the centres of power, with the most critical activities within each power centre being directly controlled by them.
3. The rulers' decision-making style is direct and personal.

These characteristics are mirrored in the rulers' relationships with their armed forces. That is:

1. The rulers make all major executive decisions about their military, are the sole source of legislative authority over it, and can exercise judicial power over them if desired.

2   G. Balfour Paul, *The End of Empire in the Middle East: Britain's Relinquishment of Power in Her Last Three Arab Dependencies* (Cambridge, 1994), p. 102.
3   L. Fawcett, *International Relations of the Middle East* (Oxford, 2016), p. 118.

2. The rulers exercise close supervision over their military, with the most critical functions and most senior and politically sensitive posts being directly controlled by them.
3. The rulers' decision-making style with respect to the military is direct and personal.

The above characteristics can be seen across the history of the two types of Emirati armed forces – ruler-control and federally-controlled forces. Ruler-controlled forces are controlled by an individual ruler of an Emirate, and were most common up to 1976, which was when they were unified into the UAE Armed Forces. The history of ruler-controlled forces is detailed in Chapter 8. Federally controlled forces are those controlled by the UAE Government. The first of these forces was formed in 1971 and was also merged into the UAE Armed Forces in 1976. The history of federally controlled forces is covered in Chapter 9.

This chapter starts with a discussion of the traditional Emirati system of government. It introduces a model which shows how rulers have exercised control in their respective Emirates. This model is then updated to reflect Emirate-level government in the modern period. Comparing the two models shows continuity from the traditional to the modern. As part of each model, control over security and the military is described, and thus how political control is exercised over ruler-controlled armed forces.

The subsequent section describes the Federal Government. It shows how characteristics of the traditional Emirati system of government are also reflected in this level of government. It also explains how political control is exercised over federally controlled armed forces.

The final part of this chapter provides details on the mechanisms by which rulers exercise control over their armed forces.

The traditional Emirati system of government

At its core, the traditional Emirati system of government reflects the Arab tribal forms of organisation centred around kinship groups. The head of a multi-family kinship group in the Emirates is called a 'sheikh'. This word carries multiple meanings including respected elder, noble and leader. Sheikhs can be 'minor' if they head up small/minor sections of a tribe, 'significant' if they head large sections or tribes, 'paramount' (*tamimia*) if they head large tribes or a tribal confederation, or a Ruling Sheikh (*hakim*) who is acknowledged as the leader of multiple tribes.

The tribal structure is patriarchal in nature meaning decisions are centralised in the person of a sheikh. While his decisions are invariably taken after consultation, the actual decisions are the sheikh's alone. Consequently, he is held personally accountable for his decisions, and their successes, failures, and implementation. Sheikhs are traditionally appointed by a council of tribal elders and the sheikh's family members.

Historically, for ruling sheikhs, additional important actors in gaining and main-taining power were notables who included wealthy merchants and representatives of significant foreign powers as they could give or withdraw prestige, money, weapons, and security. Sheikhs remained in authority only as long as they retained the loyalty of family members etc and, indirectly, their citizens. This is commonly referred to as a tribal democracy,[4] noting that it is democracy without suffrage.

In the early 1950s, all the legislative, executive, and judicial power of the state was vested in the ruler. He was not constrained by a constitution, and thus his power was absolute. Sovereignty belonged to him and not his citizens. He was in effect the State itself. There was no separation between what the ruler personally owned and what the State owned; public revenues and property were his legal possession. Nor was there a separation between government employees and the ruler's employees. Both were directed and paid for by the ruler. This meant that the ruler saw the employees as being loyal to him and not to the state, a view also that was widespread among the employees themselves.

Edward Henderson, an Arabic-speaking Briton who played a central role in Abu Dhabi's development in the 1950s and 1960s, listed the roles of a ruling sheikh at that time as follows:

> The leader's duties in all tribes are the upholding of religion, attending the Friday prayer, the question of deciding matters of defence, of war and peace, the punish-ment of wrongdoers, the administration of justice, the collection of taxes (espe-cially the religious tax), the administration of funds and personal supervision of all the community's affairs ... He must also have *hadh* (good fortune) – priority is to make peace not war and protect without violence.[5]

The sheikh's duty of avoiding tribal conflict where possible was central to his survival. In a subsistence economy, conflict diverted resources to non-productive activities and the resulting human toll and property destruction could pose an existential threat to a tribe. Great value was placed on leaders who could maintain peace and stability, even

---

4   Monika Fatima Mühlböck, 'Rules and Regulations of the Federal National Council of the United Arab Emirates and the National Consultative Council of the Emirate of Abu Dhabi and their Functions within the Country's Socio-political Sphere', *Verfassung und Recht in Übersee / Law and Politics Overseas*, 31, 4 (1998), p. 485.

5   Henderson is recognised as an authority on Abu Dhabi and its political situation. This is because he played a major role in the 1950s Buraimi crisis and served as the British Political Agent in Abu Dhabi from 1959 to 1961. He had previously worked for the Iraq Petroleum Company, which, through a subsidiary, held the onshore oil concessions in the Emirates. This resulted in him having considerable interaction with the Trucial States' rulers. E.F. Henderson, *This Strange Eventful History: Memoirs of Earlier Days in the UAE and the Sultanate of Oman* (Dubai, 1993), pp. 39, 47.

more so due to the Arab world view that strife is endemic and hence it takes a gifted leader to avoid this natural state of affairs.[6]

Henderson also noted the difficulties of a sheikh fulfilling all the roles expected of him in pre-modern times:

> He is on his own; he has no bureaucracy to support him; he may or may not have recourse to a *qadi* [religious judge] for the trickier religious and legal problems which he has to face, he is himself on trial every minute of every day because his people have chosen him and will only continue to support him if he measures up to their requirements.[7]

Henderson's observations and those of other diplomats, academics and anthropologists[8] were used by the author to build a model to explain how the Abu Dhabi Ruler of the early 1950s controlled government (Figure 9). The starting point was a diagram produced by the political scientist Christopher Davidson in his book *The United Arab Emirates: A Study in Survival*. It sought to illustrate the relationship between the ruler and the main functions and institutions of traditional government.[9] By focusing on one Emirate, the new model provides a more comprehensive and nuanced model of one traditional government than Davidson's diagram which is more generalised for it needed to characterise the governments of all Emirates.

As can be seen Figure 9, the new model continues to situate the ruler at the centre of power and government, but it groups governmental functions and institutions into the six functional areas of:

1. Management and administration of the ruler's affairs
2. Consultation with and representations from tribal leaders, notables and the citizenry
3. Security
4. Revenue and asset management
5. Making law and upholding justice, Islam and traditions
6. Public services

The model defines two levels of ruler oversight – those functions and institutions directly controlled or closely supervised by the ruler, and those which are delegated to some degree. As can be seen Figure 9, nearly all functions and institutions were directly controlled or closely supervised by the ruler. This is not surprising given the

6   Allen, *Arabs*, p. 53.
7   Henderson, *This Strange Eventful History*, p. 30.
8   The key ones are Lienhardt, *Shaikhdoms of Eastern Arabia*; Balfour Paul, *Bagpipes in Babylon*; J. Onley, *Britain and the Gulf Shaikhdoms, 1820-1971: The Politics of Protection* (Washington DC, 2009).
9   Davidson, *The United Arab Emirates: A Study in Survival*, pp. 14-21.

small size of government at that time which allowed the ruler to oversee nearly all activities. The exception was public services, where control was significantly delegated. This observation leads to the logical proposition that if a ruler closely controls/supervises an area, it is centre of power; if he does not, then it is not a centre of power. Another way of framing this is that the more important an area is to the ruler-based political order, the higher the level of supervision given to it by the ruler.

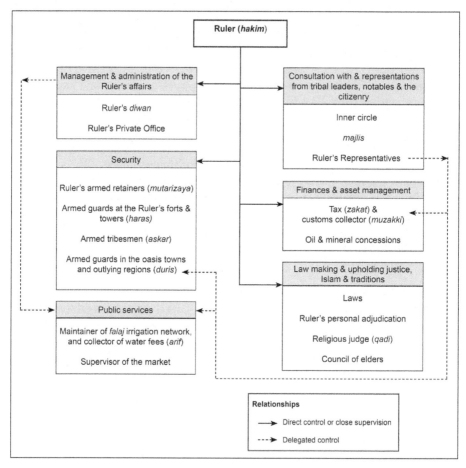

Figure 9: Model of traditional government, Abu Dhabi in the early 1950s.[10]

10   Adapted from ibid., p. 18.

The ruler

The Ruler of Abu Dhabi in the early 1950s was Sheikh Shakhbut bin Sultan Al Nahyan (r. 1928-66).[11] His decision-making style was detailed in the official biography of the rulers of Abu Dhabi: 'The internal affairs of the Shaikhdom were closely controlled by Shakhbut and his decisions were absolute … [and he did not delegate for he was] unwilling to allow government officials to act as they thought fit in the interests of his state.'[12] This perception is confirmed by an article written in 1965 by a journalist who wrote a profile of Sheikh Shakhbut and Abu Dhabi. He wrote that while the ruler 'has two sons and two brothers, all Sheiks, and a few local rulers whom he trusts, but every decision must be made by him'.[13] This centralisation meant he directed all of his subordinates' actions, and if he made no decision on an issue, his subordinates rarely took the initiative. The noted anthropologist Peter Lienhardt, who worked for Sheikh Shakhbut as his private secretary at one time, characterised the ruler's style as direct and personal.[14]

Below are details of the functions and institutions of Sheikh Shakhbut's government at that time. While this discussion may create the impression of a large bureaucratic apparatus, the footprint of his government was actually small. It was centred in the ruler's Qasr Al Hosn Palace Fort on Abu Dhabi Island, which is an ancient white-walled, coral block and stone fort. This building served as the Sheikh Shakhbut's principal residence as well as government office, law court, prison and security force barracks.

Management and administration of the ruler's affairs

Management and administration of a ruler's state were exercised through the ruler's *diwan* and the ruler's Private Office. Both were physically located in a few rooms in the palace fort.

The *diwan* consisted of a handful of functionaries. The word *diwan* is commonly translated as 'court', which can be misleading if this evokes the image of a Renaissance-era grand royal court made up of hundreds who attend on the monarch. This was not the case in the Emirates where the *diwan* was small and spartan. The *diwan* functionaries provided a small range of services, such as granting licences for pearling, fishing, and boat-owning; administering the collection of taxes; controlling

---

11   Details on the central role the Abu Dhabi ruler's palace played in dispute settlement, diplomacy etc can be found in R. Ghazal, 'Sheikha Osha Returns to Her Childhood', *The National,* 27 February 2013; N. Leech, 'Qasr Al Hosn: The Fabric of History', *The National,* 27 February 2013.
12   Maitra and Ḥajjī, *Qasr Al Hosn,* p. 237.
13   L. Crane, 'Lonely Sheik who Could Give All His People a Fortune', *Sunday Mirror,* 15 August 1965, pp. 12-13.
14   Lienhardt, *Shaikhdoms of Eastern Arabia,* p. 222.

the tax-collectors; and, granting port clearances for commercial vessels leaving any port and checking their registers.[15] The remuneration of these functionaries came either from the ruler's own money, or from a share of the payments they obtained by fulfilling their duties.[16]

The ruler's Private Office administered the ruler's private affairs but as there was little distinction between Sheikh Shakhbut's private affairs and his public affairs, the Private Office handled both. The Office was staffed by a small number of aides. The principal aide in the office was the ruler's private secretary (also known as the chamberlain) who coordinated and managed the ruler's affairs by providing advice, keeping records, managing correspondence and following up on the ruler's decisions. The private secretary was generally a literate and educated expatriate Arab and, later on in Sheikh Shabkbut's reign, occasionally a Westerner.

These organisational arrangements meant that the ruler could directly oversee all functions and institutions and could involve himself in every decision of government. Decisions, whether they were on administration, policy, legislation, or judicial issues, could be made rapidly as issues did not have to pass through a large bureaucracy. The centralisation of control also meant that the ruler could easily reverse or alter a decision and do so without reference to functionaries and aides.

Consultation with and representations from tribal leaders, notables, and the citizenry

A central element of the Arab tribal political system is consultation (*shura*) between the ruler and the ruled. Listening and taking advice was important to maintaining a ruler's authority because a ruler could not impose his will unilaterally without expecting to meet resistance. Rather, a ruler needed to seek advice and accept criticism as a way of maintaining the confidence of those providing counsel. Through demonstrating sound judgement and establishing consensus in advance, over time a ruler increasingly became the acknowledged authority with less need to seek advice as a way of ensuring support.[17]

The most important group for consultation was the ruler's inner circle, which consisted of influential people, usually ruling family members and trusted associates, but also important sheikhs, rich merchants and, occasionally, foreign representatives.

15   The register must show the size, nationality, type and quantity of arms carried, kind of cargo, name of captain, name of the port of departure and final destination. Both clearances and registers had to bear the signature of the Ruler and counter-signature of representatives before the vessels are allowed to leave port. J.B. Kelly, *Britain and the Persian Gulf: 1795-1880*, 1968, p. 155.

16   Samir Anton Carmi, 'Administrative Development of the United Arab Emirates' (PhD thesis, American University of Beirut, 1983), p. 14.

17   Henderson, *This Strange Eventful History*, p. 40.

In the case of Sheikh Shakhbut, he appears to have had a very small inner circle and only accepted advice from close ruling family members.[18]

Consultation took place in the ruler's *majlis* as well as in private discussions. A *majlis* is an open meeting where the inner circle, dignitaries and citizens would sit with the ruler and discuss public and administrative issues, as well as private matters. Armed retainers would sit close to the ruler during the *majlis*. This not only provided him with personal protection, it elevated his status, prevented unruly scenes and enabled his decisions to be enforced. A ruler's *majlis* could take place anywhere – a room in his fort, a tent or even on the ground outside the fort gates. *Diwan* staff recorded the ruler's decisions in the *majlis* and facilitated their implementation.

The ruler appointed representatives to support him in distant areas because the administration of a large sheikhdom could not be easily centralised when the principal modes of travel were camels and sailing vessels.[19] The Abu Dhabi Ruler's Representatives, known as *emirs* and *walis* in other Emirates, carried out all the ruler's responsibilities in a region, such as organising defences against attacks, collecting taxes, holding the *majlis*, adjudicating disputes, and dispensing justice. The ruler's representatives were close relatives of the ruler, a loyal supporter, or an allied local sheikh. In the early 1950s, Abu Dhabi had two main regional ruler's representatives – one in Al Ain and another in Liwa. Areas of lesser importance had minor ruler's representatives, such as in Das Island, Ruwais and Tarif. Over time, the responsibilities of the minor ruler's representatives were subsumed into those of the two main ruler's representatives.

Security

Security across the ruler's domain was provided by a combination of paid armed retainers (*mutarizaya*), armed guards at the ruler's forts (*haras*), armed tribesmen (*askari*), and armed guards in smaller settlements and outlying regions (*duris*).[20] Until the discovery of oil, the ruler's limited income prevented him from developing a modern, standing security force. This explains why in the early 1950s, there was no ruler-controlled police service nor any professional military in Abu Dhabi.

The four types of security personnel reflected in effect two different security structures. One was made up of retainers and armed guards who were paid for and directed by the ruler. In the early 1950s, the Abu Dhabi Ruler maintained over 100 armed

---

18   Maitra and Ḥajjī, *Qasr Al Hosn*, p. 237. The inner circle may have also included leading merchants.
19   Heard-Bey, *From Trucial States to United Arab Emirates*, p. 81.
20   Davidson, *The United Arab Emirates: A Study in Survival*, p. 17. The Arabic terms stated by Davidson appear to only have been used in certain parts of Abu Dhabi Emirate and at certain times. However, this book uses them to avoid providing detail which has little importance to the narrative.

retainers and guards.[21] Their roles were to protect the ruler, his family and his immediate interests. These interests included guarding forts and checkpoints, protecting public order,[22] and enforcing his decisions in his most valuable regions – Abu Dhabi Island, and the Buraimi and Liwa Oases.

The second was made up of armed tribesmen and armed guards who were raised and directed locally by a local leader or ruler's representative. If funds were available and the need for the men was of great important to the ruler, he could pay a local leader/representative who would direct them on his behalf. Their roles were to patrol the hinterland, and deter or report on unusual activity in the area, and provide security for hinterland settlements. This system allowed the ruler to provide security in his broader domain without having to raise and sustain security personnel in areas which were of secondary importance. This arrangement also allowed him to mobilise large numbers of men from his own tribe and allied tribes when faced with an imminent attack. And even then he would not necessarily have to equip nor provision them as the tribal leader and the tribesmen themselves could generally provide their own arms, food and mounts, and in the absence of payment, would receive a share of any spoils.[23]

In summary, the ruler exercised greater control over those security personnel who protected him, his family, and his immediate interests, rather than those who operated in the hinterland. He also ensured that the former group was prioritised in terms of his limited income, and only funded the latter when it was absolutely necessary.

Finances and asset management

Just as there was no difference between the public and private affairs of the ruler, there was no difference between public and private funds. All funds generated by a ruler were his, and there was no such thing as a public treasury. The ruler personally decided what to spend money on.

In the first half of the 20th century, the main sources of revenue for a ruler were: (1) profit from his own assets such as farms and pearling boats; (2) customs duties levied at a rate of a few percent of the value of goods entering his domain; and (3) taxes (*zakat*) levied on crops and livestock, collected both in cash and in kind. Rulers could also receive some revenue from licencing agreements with foreign companies which paid for the privilege to search for and exploit mineral resources. Concessions

---

21   Heard-Bey, *From Trucial States to United Arab Emirates*, p. 206. For comparison, the Ruler of Ras Al Khaimah in 1966 had three strongholds outside of his capital town – Al Shams, Al Rams and Khatt – at which were 25, 10 and 50 *mutarizaya* respectively. All *mutarizaya* were supplied from the Ruler's armourer which consisted of some light machine guns, 24 pistols in addition to .303 rifles. TNA WO 337/14: Captain A.O'B. ffrench Blake, DIO Ras Al Khaimah, 'Aladdin's Cave', 20 September 1966.

22   Lienhardt, *Shaikhdoms of Eastern Arabia*, p. 222.

23   Carmi, 'Administrative Development of the United Arab Emirates', p. 17.

related to oil exploration became a small but valued source of revenue from the 1930s onwards. During the Second World War, this exploration ceased but it resumed in Abu Dhabi in 1949.[24] This meant that, as of the early 1950s, the Abu Dhabi Ruler was starting to receive both modest concession fees as well as indirect economic benefit arising from exploration activity.[25]

Law-making and upholding justice, Islam, and traditions

The ruler, as an absolute monarch, made law by issuing decrees. This was done unilaterally without the need for any institutional approval. These decrees could be proclaimed verbally or in writing and could be handwritten or printed as circulars.[26] Decrees could relate to an immediate issue or be of enduring importance.

The community expected the ruler to uphold justice, Islam, and local traditions. However, the ruler had considerable latitude in deciding what activities needed to be punished and the nature of the punishment. For religious matters, he could ask a *qadi* who was supposed to be well-versed in both the Quran and *Sharia*. For complex non-religious issues, he could refer the issue to a council of respected elders, or a tribunal of leading merchants, but if they could not make a decision, he would have to do so. He was thus the ultimate judicial authority.

Public services

In the 1950s, the Abu Dhabi Ruler provided few of what today are considered public services. While some activities mentioned above, such as security and licensing, could theoretically be considered public services, they are better characterised as protecting the ruler's immediate interests and ensuring the stability of the ruler-based political order. In the early 1950s, the Abu Dhabi Ruler did not provide any public infrastructure such as electricity or piped water. The most notably public services the ruler provided were Al Ain's communal water channel system (*falaj*)[27] and market places (*souqs*) in Abu Dhabi and Al Ain. These services not only provided benefit to the community, they also generated revenue for the ruler either through rental or water fees. Operational responsibility for these public services was delegated to functionaries who reported to the ruler's *diwan*.

---

24   Maitra and Ḥajjī, *Qasr Al Hosn*, p. 239.
25   Shaikh Shakhbut received in 1952 £100,000 a year from oil companies for exploration rights. This would increase to £25 million in 1966. D. Holden, *Farewell to Arabia* (London, 1966).
26   R. Hay, *The Persian Gulf States* (Washington DC, 1959), p. 31.
27   A *falaj* is an underground/above ground channel which funnels ground water to irrigate crops. The crop owner pays the official (*arif*) who manages the system for the supplied water.

Two factors explain the lack of public services in Abu Dhabi at that time. Firstly, the economy was unsophisticated and, as such, government-provided services, regulation and compliance were neither necessary nor expected. Secondly, the ruler's personality made him reluctant to spend any money beyond that required to support the immediate ruling family, for he thought that to do so would lead to unwelcome societal changes. The last factor points to an important general observation about the nature of a ruler with centralised power and a direct and personal decision-making style – decisions reflect their personal preferences and they can shape the entire state.

Modern Emirate-level Government

This section describes modern Emirate-level Government which started to develop in the mid-1950s in the wealthier Emirates, and in the 1960s and 1970s in the less wealthy ones. While the functions and institutions of government have changed enormously from the mid-1950s to the present day, there has been no fundamental change in their underlying governance arrangements. That is, all Emirates have remained absolute monarchies with no written constitution; power remains centralised under the rulers; the rulers exercise close supervision over the centres of power; and the rulers' decision-making style remains direct and personal.

To illustrate the continuity with the past, the functions and institutions of modern government are overlaid onto the model of the traditional Emirati system of government (Figure 9) to create a model of the modern system of government (Figure 10). The new model has been generalised so that it is applicable to all Emirates. This model provides a tool to understand how rulers have exercised control across Emirates and as government has become more complex. In terms of the military, it not only shows how political control operates for the ruler-controlled armed forces detailed in Chapter 8, it also provides important context. Specifically, it shows the growth in security institutions of which the armed forces are just one, and illustrates that the mechanisms by which the armed forces are controlled are not fundamentally different from those used to control other centres of power.

The Emirate-level governments are often referred to as 'local governments'. This name can create a misleading impression that they are subservient to the Federal Government and have limited power and importance. They do not. The term 'Federal Government' may also lead to the assumption that responsibilities for national issues, such as external defence, security, immigration and national finances, rest entirely with this level of government. Again this is not necessarily the case, for individual Emirates have exercised, and in some cases continue to exercise, powers that commonly reside with a federal government in other countries. For example, the individual Emirates at various times maintained separate militaries, pursued oil export policies that diverged from those of the Federal Government, and pursued different foreign policy agendas.

In general, over the decades the Federal Government has assumed more powers and exercised greater influence across most of the UAE. However, this has not always occurred smoothly, for efforts towards federalisation have sometimes raised significant inter-Emirate tensions, and even resulted in constitutional crises.[28] Consequently, federalisation has occurred in fits-and-starts, and has sometimes undergone reversals.

In terms of Federal influence over the individual emirates, the seven Emirates can be divided into two categories: one made up of the less wealthy northern Emirates of Ajman, Fujairah, Umm Al Quwain, Ras Al Khaimah and Sharjah; and the far wealthier Emirates of Abu Dhabi and Dubai.

The northern Emirates did not have the funds to pay for all of their needed governmental responsibilities, so they elected to transfer some to the Federal Government. This means these services are paid for out of the Federal Budget, augmented by direct grants to the ruler from Abu Dhabi and, to a lesser extent, Dubai. The practical outcome is that Federal Government agencies provide much of the government-provided goods and services in these Emirates. Policing is a good illustration of this situation. In all of these smaller Emirates, the Federal Government's Ministry of Interior pays for a significant proportion of the police personnel working in the Emirate's police force, and it directly provides nearly all specialist policing capabilities such as the SWAT teams, forensic services and helicopters. The transfer of such responsibilities to the Federal Government obviously diminishes a ruler's power. The rulers' lack of resources also means that it has been difficult for them to fund the formation and maintenance of their own armed forces. Despite this, several rulers of the smaller Emirates have used their limited funds to have an armed force.

In the case of the wealthiest Emirates, the rulers have elected to use their own funds to pay for the vast bulk of their government's activities. This has enabled them to supervise and control not only the priority areas of government, but also the public services. This results in these two Emirates being relatively independent of the Federal Government if they wish. This autonomy can be seen clearly in the way that security is currently provided in Dubai. The Federal Ministry of Interior has little influence over Dubai, with Dubai maintaining its own police force, state security and electronic security agencies. Despite the capacity of the Abu Dhabi and Dubai Governments to remain autonomous, there are many areas in which these governments have elected to defer to the Federal Government. In summary, Abu Dhabi and Dubai's wealth make them independent of Federal Government where they want to pursue their own course. With respect to the military, their wealth has enabled their rulers to build and sustain large and expensive armed forces.

---

28   There have been two significant constitutional crises, both in the 1970s. See Mühlböck, 'Rules and Regulations of the Federal National Council of the United Arab Emirates and the National Consultative Council of the Emirate of Abu Dhabi and their Functions within the Country's Socio-political Sphere', pp. 495-7.

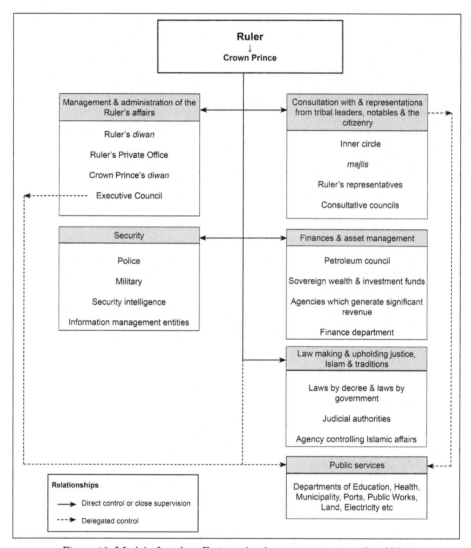

Figure 10: Model of modern Emirate-level government, since the 1970s.

The above discussion points to the complexity and variability of the power structure across Emirates. This complexity is important in understanding both the mechanisms and constraints that rulers face in forming, maintaining, and controlling their armed forces. To provide conceptual clarity in describing modern government in the Emirates, Figure 10 does not include federal functions and institutions. These are discussed in the next section. Due to the Federal Government's impact on Emirate-level government, both this and the next section should be read together.

The ruler

A key change between the traditional system of government and the modern one is the role of the crown prince. With the increasingly complexity of modern government, most rulers have tasked their crown princes with a range of formal responsibilities. These commonly include heading up or serving on the most important governmental entities. A crown prince also deputises as the ruler when the ruler is absent. In some cases, due to incapacity of a ruler, a crown prince has acted as the prince-regent for many years.

Management and administration of the ruler's affairs

As in the past, the ruler's *diwan* and his Private Office remain central to management and administration of his and his Emirate's affairs. The *diwan* and Private Office are at the apex of Emirate-level government and heading them is a high-status position.[29]

In Emirates where the ruler also holds a high Federal office, the ruler may have his *diwan* and Private Office subsumed into the ministry responsible for the ruler's Federal responsibilities, and/or may transfer some responsibilities to the Crown Prince. Using Abu Dhabi as an example, the Abu Dhabi Ruler's *diwan* is now in effect that of the Crown Prince, with certain *diwan* and Private Office functions of the ruler being undertaken by the Ministry of Presidential Affairs. The head of the ruler's *diwan* is often a close relative of the ruler, which reflects the *diwan's* importance.[30]

The growth in government has resulted in all Emirates, except Fujairah,[31] introducing a high-level governmental coordination body – the Executive Council. The Executive Council is often chaired by the ruler himself or the crown prince and is made up of the most important political and professional heads of government agencies. While referred to as a 'cabinet', the Executive Council is different from a Westminster-style cabinet. Its primary function is to aid the ruler in performing his duties and exercising his powers. The subordinate nature of the body and its mandate can be seen in the official description of Abu Dhabi's Executive Council:

> It assists the ruler to carry out his duties and powers, through regular meetings to set the Emirate's general policy, set development plans and supervise its execution, authorize projects, laws and decrees before submitting them to the ruler,

---

29   C.M. Davidson, *Abu Dhabi: Oil and Beyond* (Oxford, 2011), p. 123.
30   A current exception is Fujairah, where the ruler is Sheikh Hamad bin Mohammed Al Sharqi and the Director of the Fujairah ruler's *diwan* is Mohammed Saeed Al Dhanhani.
31   Fujairah manages its government affairs via the ruler's *diwan*, the crown prince's *diwan*, and the Municipality which has branches in Fujairah and Dibba.

supervise work flow in departments, local entities, and coordinate among them, to achieve general well-being of the country.[32]

An Executive Council generally has limited legislative functions. While it can draft laws and decrees, these must be submitted to the ruler for consideration. It also has limited budgetary power, for while it can make recommendations on projects and public finances, it is up to the ruler to accept or reject this advice. Thus, the Executive Council is better characterised as a body which both advises the ruler and oversees the implementation of the ruler's decisions.[33]

While an important institution, the mandate of the Executive Council is bounded. It generally does not consider areas and institutions which are under the ruler or crown prince's direct control. This means that the work of the Executive Council concentrates on what are in effect public service entities (i.e. those outside the power centres), as well as cross-government issues, such as human resource policies and Emirate strategic plans. Decisions relating to the power centres, including the armed forces, are made by the ruler himself and he communicates these directly to the relevant political or professional heads without reference to the Executive Council.

Consultation with and representation from tribal leaders, notables and the citizenry

In addition to the traditional consultative mechanisms of the ruler's inner circle, *majlis* and ruler's representatives, a modern institution form adopted across the Emirates is the consultative council, which can operated at issue-specific, agency, cross agency or whole-of-government level.

Two Emirates have whole-of-government consultative councils – Abu Dhabi with its (confusingly named but Abu Dhabi focused) National Consultative Council[34] and Sharjah with its Consultative Council. (The National Consultative Council has been in abeyance since the death of Sheikh Zayed in 2004, and although not formally dissolved, has not met. Its speaker, Abdulla bin Mohamed Al Masaood, died in 2019 and has not been replaced.) Members of these entities are either appointed by the ruler or elected, and invariably all are respected, representative members of local tribes or merchant families. Thus, these entities provide an organised forum by which Emiratis can offer their views to their ruler. In effect, they are a modern manifestation of two

---

32   Abu Dhabi General Secretariat of the Executive Council. 'Executive Council', n.d. <www.ecouncil.ae/en/ADGovernment/Pages/ExecutiveCouncil.aspx>

33   In the case of Abu Dhabi, due to the responsibility vested in the Crown Prince, Abu Dhabi's Executive Council advises the Crown Prince.

34   The National Consultative Council's name is a somewhat misleading given that its focus is Abu Dhabi. However, it has occasionally made statements on Federal and internal issues. Mühlböck, 'Rules and Regulations of the Federal National Council of the United Arab Emirates and the National Consultative Council of the Emirate of Abu Dhabi and their Functions within the Country's Socio-political Sphere', p. 520.

traditional mechanisms of consultation and representation – the ruler's *majlis* and the seeking of advice from influential persons.

Security

The security forces of the pre-modern era (e.g. armed retainers) had almost completely disappeared by the early 1970s and had been replaced by professionalised bodies – police, armed forces and security intelligence. Police forces were the first to be established by the Ruler of Dubai in 1956, with one formed by the Ruler of Abu Dhabi in the following year. All other Emirates formed police forces between 1967 and 1969. Emirate controlled armed forces were first established by the ruler in Abu Dhabi in 1965, in Ras al Khaimah 1969, in Dubai in 1970, in Sharjah in 1972 and in Umm Al Quwain in 1975. The first security intelligence agency formed was Abu Dhabi's Police Special Branch, which was formed by the Ruler of Abu Dhabi in 1967. All the other Emirates had established Police Special Branches by 1971; these were the precursors of today's State Security departments.[35]

Other, albeit little noticed, security-related agencies are information management entities. Most rulers started to control information and formalise the dissemination of official information from the late 1960s. They may also have established entities to manage the media policy of the rulers, ensure media laws are complied with, and prohibit material considered inappropriate – all functions seen as essential for the stability and security of both the political system and society. The names, functions and capabilities of the information management entities have changed with time.

In terms of disseminating government-related news, most Emirates today have media offices, such as the Government of Dubai Media Office (established in 2010), and the Government of Abu Dhabi Media Office (established in 2020). Media management is handled by both Emirate-level and federal entities. The most significant federal entity is the National Media Council, which formulates media bills, and is responsible for media licensing and reviewing media content in the country.

Finances and asset management

Historically, rulers derived their income from only a few sources – notably taxes and customs, and mineral/oil concessions. Today, there are far more sources, such as land sales, licencing, and profit from state-owned enterprises. For Abu Dhabi, and to a lesser extent Dubai and Sharjah, oil-related income remains very significant, and so control by the ruler over this resource is paramount. This is achieved through the ruler or the crown prince acting as the chair of the Emirate's petroleum council, which is the highest governing and executive body controlling the state's oil resources. The

---

35   A. Yates and C. Lord, *The Military and Polices Forces of the Gulf States: Trucial States & United Arab Emirates, 1951-1980* (Solihull, 2019).

wealthier Emirates store a significant proportion of their income in sovereign wealth and investment funds. Control by the ruler over these funds is again maintained by the ruler or the crown prince serving as the head of the funds' governing and/or executive body. Petroleum councils and funds do not report to Executive Councils.

The other key entity which falls within the finances/asset management centre of power is the finance department. This is the agency which coordinates government spending and releases public funds. While all Emirates have such a department, its importance varies considerably. While some finance departments have a significant influence on financial policy matters, such as setting state spending and revenue parameters, or advising on the costs-benefits of projects, in other Emirates these departments are little more than a conduit through which funds are moved. The degree of their importance to the financial decisions of the Emirate is reflected in the level of Emirati leadership that controls them.

Law-making and upholding justice, Islam and traditions

The laws that exist in today's Emirates are of two types. One type was also seen in pre-modern government – Ruler Decrees – which nowadays are generally referred to as Laws-by-Decree or Emiri Decrees. Laws-by-Decree are issued under the authority of the ruler himself. They can be issued in an extensive range of areas, but are generally more administrative in nature, such as the establishment of and changes to entities, public service appointments, and taxes and charges. The second type is known as Law-by-Government, commonly referred to as Emirate Law. Laws-by-Government are generally raised by an authorised body, primarily the Executive Council, and require approval by the ruler before they become law. This approval arrangement ensures that the ruler remains the Emirate's senior most legislative authority. Laws-by-Government covers all areas, such as civil, penal, commercial, companies, intellectual property, immigration, industrial, banking and employment law. In recent decades, as much law on these areas has been consolidated into Federal codes of law which individual Emirates can elect to adopt, the influence of the ruler over legal issues has diminished when his Emirate adopts the Federal laws.

Laws governing the ruler-controlled armed forces are invariably Laws-by-Decree. A ruler will issue a Law-by Decree to establish and change military governance arrangements, as well as to announce promotions and retirements. The use of Laws-by-Decree reflects the ruler's direct control over the military, rather than control occurring via a government agency or Executive Council.

The traditional justice system that was centred on religious judges, councils of elders and the ruler's personal adjudication has today become formalised under local judicial authorities. The three Emirates of Abu Dhabi, Dubai and Ras Al Khaimah currently maintain their own autonomous judicial departments while Sharjah, Fujairah, Umm Al Quwain and Ajman voluntarily operating under local departments of the Federal Court. The local judicial department in each Emirate has jurisdiction over all judicial matters not assigned to the Federal judicial authorities, as specified in the Constitution.[36] The rulers have significant influence over the judicial system. This is done through appointing judges, being the final authority in the Emirate's laws, and commonly appointing a close family member or trusted associate as the political head of the judicial authority. Military personnel can be processed via these judicial departments if the issue is of a non-military nature, and through the Military Court system for military issues.

Whilst, historically, the ruler's control over religion was limited to recognising religious judges and supporting religious schools, in recent decades the rulers have increased their oversight of religion. This has typically been achieved through central-ising control over Islamic affairs. In the past, all Emirates had their own entities for managing these affairs, but now most do so via a branch of the Federal Government's General Authority of Islamic Affairs and Endowments (AWQAF). AWQAF's mandate includes promoting religious awareness and preaching, developing mosques, building Quran memorisation centres, producing religious Fatwas, managing Hajj and Umrah, researching and monitoring religious publications and government *waqf* arrangements.[37] The degree to which the Federal leadership of AWQAF has influence over the individual Emirates appears to vary considerably and, hence, some rulers appear to have retained significant control over Islamic affairs in their Emirates. The increased importance given to religious issues has also been reflected in the military. Religious education has always been a component of military education, but the last decade has seen increased efforts to promote moderate Islam.

Public services

As each Emirate developed, the demand for and provision of public services increased. In general, public services in the wealthier Emirates are more comprehensive and of a higher quality than in the less wealthy ones. The institutions responsible for public services are not normally supervised directly by the ruler; instead, the heads of public service institutions report to the Executive Council.[38]

36   Articles 94 to 109 of the UAE's Constitution details the arrangements governing the local verses Federal judicial systems.
37   *Waqf* or its plural *awqaf*, refers to an inalienable charitable endowment under Islamic law for supporting religious and charitable purposes. Instances of endowment use are supporting religious institutions, providing academic scholarships, maintaining the upkeep of holy places, and support for the poor.
38   This is not the case in Fujairah which does not have an executive council. In the smaller Emirates, the rulers may be more involved in the management of public services because they have fewer competing pressures on their time, and because of the reduced scale of public service activities compared to the larger Emirates.

Federal Government

The UAE is a federation of the seven Emirates and its governance arrangements are specified in the UAE Constitution.[39] The key constitutionally-defined governance institutions of the Federal Government are the Federal Supreme Council (of rulers), the President/Vice President, the Council of Ministers, the Federal National Council, and a judiciary overseen by the Federal Supreme Court. The relationship between these elements is shown in Figure 11.[40] Attention will now be directed towards each institution, with an emphasis on illustrating how the rulers have been able to remain at the centre of politics and government, and how the rulers of Abu Dhabi and Dubai are able to wield greater influence than the others.

The Federal Supreme Council is the highest constitutional authority in the UAE and is made up of the rulers of the seven Emirates. It decides national policy, approves Federal legislation, elects the President and Vice President, and appoints judges to the Federal Supreme Court. The Constitution states that each Emirate has a single vote on the Council, but decisions on substantive matters require a majority of five votes to pass, which must include votes from Abu Dhabi and Dubai.[41] This last requirement gives the rulers of these two Emirates the power of veto on any issue one or the other does not agree with.

The President and Vice President are elected by the Federal Supreme Council for renewable five-year terms. Both officer holders must be drawn from the members of the Council. The Constitution gives the President considerable power, including representing the country both domestically and internationally, signing and issuing all Federal laws, selecting the Prime Minister in consultation with other members of the Supreme Council, and appointing the Deputy Prime Ministers and Ministers (in agreement with the Prime Minister), as well as diplomatic representatives, senior civil servants and military officials.[42] The President also assumes the powers of the Federal Supreme Council when it is not in session.[43] The scholar William Rugh (a former US ambassador to the UAE) has described the influence of the President in the following

---

39   The original constitution, known as the Provisional Constitution, was accepted by the rulers in July 1971, and came into effect on 2 December 1971. The Constitution became permanent in May 1996.

40   The terms used for these institutions are those currently in use, and not the original ones as defined in the 1971 Constitution. For instance, the Federal Supreme Council was then known as the Union Supreme Council, the Federal National Council was the Union National Assembly, and the Federal Judiciary was the Union Judiciary. Mühlböck, 'Rules and Regulations of the Federal National Council of the United Arab Emirates and the National Consultative Council of the Emirate of Abu Dhabi and their Functions within the Country's Socio-political Sphere', p. 485.

41   Article 49 of the Constitution.

42   Article 54 of the Constitution.

43   Heard-Bey, 'The United Arab Emirates: Statehood and Nation-Building in a Traditional Society', p. 364.

terms: 'the President sets policy for the country ... [while] he consults with the six other rulers on critical issues, he generally has the last word, even if they disagree with him'.[44] The Vice President theoretically exercises all the powers of the President in his absence, but otherwise has no other specific powers.

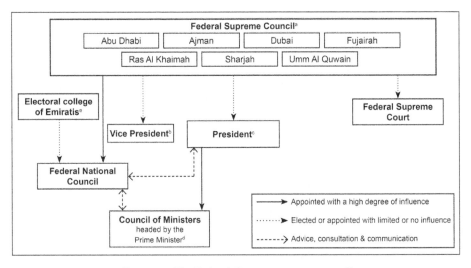

Figure 11: The Federal Government structure.[45]

Notes

a. The Federal Supreme Council elects the President and Vice President for renewable five-year terms; appoints judges to the Federal Supreme Court; and appoints half the members of Federal National Council.
b. The Vice President exercises all the powers of the President in the event of his absence.
c. The President selects the Prime Minister in consultation with other members of the Supreme Council.
d. The Prime Minister appoints the Deputy Prime Ministers and Ministers in agreement with the President.
e. The electoral college of Emiratis elects half the members of the Federal National Council.

The Council of Ministers is defined in the Constitution as the executive authority for all Federal affairs. It is headed by the Prime Minister, two Deputy Prime Ministers and over 20 senior Ministers. Thus, in theory, the Council of Ministers is the 'cabinet' of the UAE Government. However, in practice its executive powers are somewhat less encompassing than the title implies. Its role is better described as responding to the direction by the UAE's top-most leadership rather than formulating

---

44   William A. Rugh, 'The Foreign Policy of the United Arab Emirates', *Middle East Journal*, 50, 1 (1996), p. 58. Rugh's comments were specifically in relation to foreign policy but is reflective of the President's power more generally.

45   Adapted from Helen Chapin Metz, *Persian Gulf States: Country Studies* (Washington DC, 1994), p. 240.

government direction as would be expected in a Westminster-style government. The constrained role of the Council of Ministers is implied in the Constitution. It states that the Council of Ministers operates 'under the high oversight of the President of the UAE and the Federal Supreme Council', and its first defined role is to 'follow up the implementation of the general policy of the UAE Government [i.e. Federal Supreme Council]'.[46]

Since the formation of the UAE, Abu Dhabi and Dubai have maintained control over the three most important political posts – the President, Vice President and Prime Minister. The post of the President has always been filled by the Ruler of Abu Dhabi, the Vice President by the Ruler of Dubai, and the office of Prime Minister by a member of the Dubai Royal Family and, since 1979, by the Ruler of Dubai himself.[47]

Constitutionally, the Prime Minister recommends a list of ministers to the President who has the power to ratify his recommendations. In practice, the selection of ministers depends substantially on agreement between all the rulers with the Abu Dhabi and Dubai rulers holding greatest sway. Since 1971, key ministerial posts have generally been allocated to Abu Dhabi and Dubai. In the security realm, Abu Dhabi appears to have always nominated the Minister of the Interior (often a member of Abu Dhabi's ruling family), while a member of the Dubai ruling family has always held the post of Minister of Defence.[48]

The Federal National Council is a unicameral, semi-legislative body. Its main role is to debate proposed legislation forwarded to it by the Council of Ministers. Its powers are confined to consultation and making recommendations. It can neither initiate legislation nor veto bills, but it can send bills back to the Supreme Council with amendments for re-review. It has some power to scrutinise the work of the Federal Government through being able to summon and question ministers about the performance of their ministries. It is best described as a consultative body. The Council consists of 40 members, with Abu Dhabi and Dubai each having eight, Sharjah and Ras Al Khaimah having six and the remaining three Emirates having four each. The additional positions allocated to Abu Dhabi and Dubai gives them greater influence than the other Emirates. Initially, all members of the Council were appointed by the rulers of the Emirates, but today half are elected by an electoral college composed of a subset of nationals. The Council has committees which focus on particular areas.

46   Article 60 of the Constitution.
47   Between 1971 and 1979, the post of Prime Minister was held by the Dubai Crown Prince.
48   Abu Dhabi ruling family members have occupied the post of Minister of Interior between 1971 and 1990, and 2004 to the present. Sheikh Mubarak bin Mohammed Al Nahyan served as Minister of Interior from 1971 to 1990, although his illness from 1979 meant his responsibilities were assumed by the junior interior minister, Hmooda bin Ali. From 1990 to 1993, the Minister was Hmooda bin Ali, and from 1993 to 2004, it was Lieutenant General Mohammed Saeed Al Badi, former Chief of Staff. From 2004 to the present it was held by Sheikh Saif bin Zayed Al Nahyan. The position of Minister of Defence has been filled by Sheikh Mohammed bin Rashid Al Maktoum from 1971 to the present.

In the security field, the Defence, Interior and Foreign Affairs Committee is technically responsible for matters relating to the UAE Armed Forces and national security. In practice, its discussions appear to be limited to closed briefings and consultations, with public discussion limited to less sensitive dimensions of military affairs and national security.

The Federal judiciary consists of a Federal Supreme Court and several subordinate Federal courts. The Federal Supreme Court adjudicates on the constitutionality of Federal laws, and arbitrates on disputes between Emirates, or between the Federal Government and an Emirate. It also receives cases on nationally-significant issues such as trials of Federal Government Ministers and senior officials, and those affecting the country's interests, such as crimes relating to its internal or external security, forgery of official records, and counterfeiting of currency. The rulers and the President maintain control over the Federal judiciary since they appoint all judges. The President can also overrule many types of court decisions, and has the power to pardon.

Like Emirate-level laws, Federal laws are primarily of two types – Law-by-Government (known also as Federal Law or State Law) and Law-by-Decree (also known as Federal Decree or Presidential Decree).

A Law-by-Government starts as a bill drafted by the Council of Ministers, which is then submitted to the Federal National Council for consideration. The Federal National Council then forwards the bill as approved or with recommendations to the President. If the President approves the bill, he presents it to the Federal Supreme Council for ratification and, if this is given, the bill returns to the President for signature and promulgation.[49] Law-by-Government can be expedited in ways that bypass the Federal National Council; the Council of Ministers through the President and Supreme Council can develop and enact a law, although it is expected that the law will subsequently go to the Federal National Council for examination.[50]

The second type of Federal laws, Laws-by-Decree, is issued by the President together with the Council of Ministers. These laws are not examined by the Federal National Council as bills. They also do not need the ratification of the Federal Supreme Council to come into effect; however, they need to be ratified by it subsequently. Laws-by-Decree can be issued on an extensive range of issues, including the establishment of and changes to Federal entities, public servant appointments, and taxes and charges. A Law-by-Decree does not have to go to the Council of Ministers if the issue is not under the Council's responsibility, which is the case with most of the issues associated with the UAE Armed Forces.

As can be seen, the current constitutional arrangements preserve the traditional power structure of the rulers being at the centre of power and government. The rulers remain the principal source of legislative, executive, and judicial power. Traditional control via appointing relatives and trusted individuals to the most critical posts also

49   Carmi, 'Administrative Development of the United Arab Emirates', p. 37.
50   Article 110 of the Constitution.

reinforces the concentration of power. Based on who holds the more important posts and the institutional bias towards certain Emirates, it can be concluded that of all the rulers, the Rulers of Abu Dhabi and Dubai are in fact 'first among equals'. This is important in providing the broader context when it comes to understanding where controls rests over the UAE Armed Forces.

Control over the military

The UAE Constitution gives the individual Emirates jurisdiction in all matters not assigned to the exclusive jurisdiction of the Federation.[51] Its states that there are 19 areas which are the exclusive responsibility of the Federal Government. Security-related fields include: (1) foreign affairs; (2) defence and federally-controlled armed forces; (3) protection of the UAE's security against internal or external threats; and (4) matters pertaining to security, order, and government in the capital city of the UAE.[52]

The Constitution provides few actual details on the governance of the federally-controlled armed forces. It does not explicitly state who the military's supreme commander is, nor state what the role of the Council of Ministers is in relation to the military. In addition, while the Constitution identifies the posts of Minister of Defence, Commander-in-Chief, and Chief of Staff, it does not define their roles or authorities. Given the lack of details on the control of armed forces in the Constitution, the actual arrangements have had to be promulgated through both Laws-by-Government and Laws-by-Decree.

This has provided flexibility, which explains why there have been two different arrangements for political control of federally controlled forces over the history of Emirati armed forces.

The first arrangements operated between 1971-76 and covered the control of the Union Defence Force (UDF), which was renamed the Federal Armed Force (UDF) in 1974. The second was from 1976 to the present day and covers the control of the UAE Armed Forces.

The first law governing the federally controlled forces was Law No. 3 of 1971 'Regarding the Union Defence Force'. It stated that the UDF 'shall be under the supervision of the Federal Minister of Defence'. During the negotiations to form the UAE, the post of Federal Defence Minister was allocated to Dubai. The Ruler of Dubai appointed his 22-year-old, third son, Sheikh Mohammed bin Rashid Al Maktoum, to fill this post (which he continues to hold in 2020 along with the posts of Vice President and Prime Minister).

The 1971 law did not state to whom the Defence Minister was accountable, an arrangement which appears to have been a political decision to facilitate the forma-tion of the UAE. At that time, the Ruler of Dubai was concerned that Abu Dhabi's

---

51   Article 122 of the Constitution.
52   Article 120 of the Constitution.

growing military was a threat to Dubai, and by giving Dubai the defence ministerial post, that Emirate had direct command of a functioning military. This provided the Dubai Ruler with a degree of security, for while Dubai also had a ruler-controlled force at that time (the Dubai Defence Force), this force was only a year old and had extremely limited capabilities. Control over the UDF/FAF rested with the Minister of Defence until 1976, when it was merged with the various ruler-controlled forces to create the UAE Armed Forces.

New laws were introduced in 1976 which redefined the political command arrangements of the federally-controlled armed force.[53] These laws stated that the UAE Armed Forces were directly accountable to the President, with his formal title in this role being the Supreme Commander of the UAE Armed Forces. The laws also created the subordinate position of Deputy Supreme Commander. The Minister of Defence post was retained but the Minister now formally reported to the Deputy Supreme Commander. The laws stated that the professional head of the force was the Chief of Staff and that he had dual reporting lines – for a few financial and administrative issues he reported to the Minister of Defence, and for all the rest including operational command he reported directly to the Deputy Supreme Commander.

Appointments to the three posts of Deputy Supreme Commander, Minister of Defence and Chief of Staff were filled through Laws-by-Decree, effectively meaning the President could make the appointments unilaterally although there was an expectation that the other rulers would be consulted. The President appointed his son, Sheikh Khalifa bin Zayed, as the Deputy Supreme Commander in 1976, while the post of Minister of Defence continued to be filled by Sheikh Mohammed bin Rashid Al Maktoum. The President appointed a seconded Jordanian officer as the Chief of Staff. These new arrangements meant that control over the UAE Armed Forces rested squarely with the Abu Dhabi leadership. In 1978, the political command structure for the UAE Armed Forces was modified. An additional post of Commander-in-Chief was created, which sat between the Deputy Supreme Commander and Minister of Defence. The second of the President's sons, Sheikh Sultan bin Zayed, was appointed to this post. Following his departure from the post in 1982, it would never again be filled.

A case in 1980 illustrates the centralisation of power under the President, and his ability to make unilateral decisions, as the Supreme Commander, which bypassed both the Minister of Defence and the Council of Ministers. A border dispute with Oman developed, and the President was concerned that Omanis serving in the UAE Armed Forces might not be reliable. It appears that due to the strong and close relationship between the UAE President and King Hassan II of Morocco, the former asked for a loan of some 2,000 seconded Moroccan soldiers. The king willingly supplied the men who were allocated to key units across the UAE Armed Forces. According to

---

53   The main law was the *UAE Supreme Defence Council Decision No. 1 'Regarding the Unification of the Armed Forces in the United Arab Emirates'* (1976).

the British Ambassador, the President took the decision alone without consulting the Vice President (who was also the Prime Minister and Ruler of Dubai) and the Defence Minister.[54]

From 1976 until he died in 2004, Sheikh Zayed held the post of Supreme Commander, with Sheikh Khalifa holding the post of Deputy Supreme Commander. In 2004, Sheikh Khalifa became the UAE President and thus Supreme Commander. His brother, Sheikh Mohammed bin Zayed, became the Crown Prince of Abu Dhabi, and the Deputy Supreme Commander. These arrangements have continued to the present day. It should be added here that, in 2006, the laws governing military command were updated and consolidated into one law – Law No 8 of 2006 'On the Armed Forces'. This law eliminated the long-defunct post of Commander-in-Chief. The chain of command thus became Supreme Commander to the Deputy Supreme Commander and then, either directly to the Chief of Staff, or to the Minister of Defence and then to the Chief of Staff.

After the new 2006 law, the Minister of Defence continued to have little influence on military decision making. Law No 8 of 2006 stated that the Minister can only direct the Chief of Staff on a few issues, notably developing and supervising manpower policy, coordination with civil authorities, and budget issues within the allocation of the Ministry of Defence. The financial power of the Ministry of Defence was very limited as the Federal Government's allocation to the Ministry was very small compared to the amount provided directly by Abu Dhabi to the Armed Forces' General Headquarters (GHQ). As noted by the International Monetary Fund in their examination of the UAE's finances, 'defence expenditures, which are federal responsibility, ... [are in fact] managed by Abu Dhabi'.[55]

Hendrik van der Meulen, the Director of Political and Military Affairs Section at the US Embassy in Abu Dhabi from 1993-96, characterised the position of Minister of Defence during his time as 'practically only a figurehead nominally in the chain of military command'.[56] In the mid-2000s, this characterisation was repeated when the US Ambassador noted in a confidential memo that the Minister 'has no role in the decisions, staffing, or funding of the UAE Armed Forces'.[57] Most of the Minister's work was representational, such as attending international defence minister forums, military graduations and parades. The Ministry's main function from a national

---

54   TNA FCO 8/3512: D.A. Roberts, UK Ambassador, Abu Dhabi to H.D.A.C. Miers, MED, FO, 'Moroccan Troops in Abu Dhabi', 25 June 1980.
55   The IMF notes that 'Abu Dhabi also separately contributes [to the Federal budget] to cover security and defense expenditures, which are federal responsibility, but managed by Abu Dhabi'. International Monetary Fund, *United Arab Emirate Selected Issues: IMF Country Report No. 17/219* (Washington DC, 2017), p. 2.
56   van der Meulen, 'The Role of Tribal and Kinship Ties in the Politics of the United Arab Emirates', p. 96.
57   Wikileaks, Michele J. Sison, US Ambassador to the UAE, 'Points for A/USTR Novelli's FTA BILATS', 2005.

perspective was that of handling the UAE's international military regulatory and treaty matters, such as providing end-user certificates for the import of ordnance, explosives and ammunition. In other words, the Ministry had a very narrow remit compared to a Western Ministry of Defence.[58]

Since the mid-2010s, the nature of the Minister and Ministry of Defence have changed significantly. The Ministry of Defence was relocated from Dubai to Abu Dhabi with a mandate to build its ability to advise and manage capability development, international defence relations, defence procurement and defence industry development. To oversee the rebuilding of the Ministry, in 2016 a new post of Minister of State for Defence Affairs was created.[59] These developments point to an intention to transform the Ministry of Defence into a traditional defence ministry responsible for strategic issues. This would likely mean that GHQ would relinquish these responsibilities and become principally responsible for raising, training and sustaining forces, as well as the command and control of forces during operations.

The only political-military institution defined in the Constitution is the Supreme Defence Council. According to the UAE Constitution, its role is to provide 'opinion and advice on all matters pertaining to defence, maintenance of peace and security of the Federation; forming, equipping and developing the armed forces and determining the sites of their posts and camps'.[60] It is an advisory body which cannot direct military policy or decisions, and is headed by the President.[61] Legislation over the decades has provided more detail on the role of the Supreme Defence Council. The most recent was Federal Law No 8 of 2006 'On the Armed Forces'. It stated that the Council would be responsible for 'drawing of the general policy for the defence of the State … [and determining] the missions and obligations of the governmental institutions and the private sector in view of defending the State.' It also has responsibilities for managing crises affecting the defence of the state.[62] This implies that the body has a broader remit that just the armed forces, and, in effect, reaches into coordinating national security.

Despite its constitutional base and 2006 clarifying legislation, the Supreme Defence Council appears to have rarely met. The last time it was known to have made a decision was in 1978 when it promulgated a decision on the restructure of the UAE Armed Forces.

58 The Ministry at least to the mid-2000s had additional roles in Dubai, such as procurement for the military in Dubai. Wikileaks, Michele J. Sison, US Ambassador to the UAE, [untitled cable Abu Dhabi 00003851 001.2 of 006], 2 October 2006.
59 The post has been filled by Mohammed Ahmad Al Bawardi Al Falasi, the former Under-Secretary of the Ministry of Defence.
60 Article 141 of the *Constitution of the United Arab Emirates (Provisional)* (1971).
61 *UAE Federal Law No 17 of 2006 "On the Establishment of the Supreme Council for National Security"* (2006).
62 *UAE Federal Decree Law No 8 of 2006 "On the Armed Forces"* (2006).

In 2006 a new national security body was formed – the Supreme Council for National Security.[63] It appears to have become the organising entity for national security policy development and coordination and the responsibilities of the Supreme Defence Council have been folded into it. The Supreme Council for National Security has whole-of-government responsibility, and this includes formulating and implementing a national security strategic plan, and directing and coordinating the various agencies involved in security issues with the goal of improving their crisis management capabilities.[64] It also has a role in drafting national security legislation, and operational responsibilities such as providing intelligence briefings. The administrative body supporting the Supreme Council is the Secretariat of the Supreme Council for National Security, which is headed by a Secretary General. The Council is chaired by the President, and the Deputy Chairman is the Vice-President/Prime Minister. Its members are the Deputy Supreme Commander of the UAE Armed Forces, Defence Minister, Foreign Minister, Interior Minister, Minister for Presidential Affairs, Chief of State Security, Chief of Staff of the UAE Armed Forces, and the National Security Advisor. The membership of the Council is very similar to that of the defunct Supreme Defence Council, and given its whole-of-government national security elements, the Supreme Council for National Security can be considered as one of the most important bodies providing defence advice to the President. Control of the Council by the President is enhanced as he appoints the professional head of the Council's Secretariat.[65]

This section of the book has established that control over the UAE Armed Forces primarily rests with the President and the Deputy Supreme Commander, whom have always been the ruler and crown prince of Abu Dhabi, respectively. The influence of the Minister of Defence has historically been v limited, while the Prime Minister and Council of Ministers have had no formal role with respect to the UAE Armed Forces. This all points to a quite different system of governance over the UAE Armed Forces from that which would be logically inferred from examining Figure 11. A better model is presented in Figure 12. It shows that power is centralised in the President, with political control exercised via the Deputy Supreme Commander directly to the Chief of Staff. The Council of Ministers is completely absent from this model of political control, although the Minister of Defence and Minister of State for Defence Affairs are included as they have a degree of involvement.[66]

63   *UAE Federal Law No 17 of 2006 "On the Establishment of the Supreme Council for National Security"* (2006).
64   Wikileaks, US Embassy in Abu Dhabi, 'UAE Establishes National Security Council', 14 June 2006.
65   These are Saif Sultan Mubarak Al Aryani, the first Secretary-General, and currently, Ali Bin Hammad Al Shamsi, who is Deputy Secretary-General.
66   For details on how Abu Dhabi maintains control over all national security agencies, see A. Yates, 'Challenging the accepted understanding of the executive branch of the UAE's Federal Government', *Middle Eastern Studies*, September (2020).

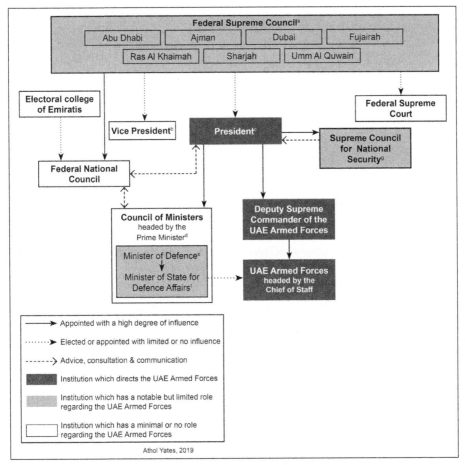

Figure 12: Political control of the UAE Armed Forces, 2020.

Notes
a. As the Federal Supreme Council meets infrequently and delegates power to the President, its influence on military matters is limited.
b. No instances in UAE history have been identified when the Vice President has acted as the Supreme Commander or made significant military decisions in the absence of the President.
c. The President appoints the Deputy Supreme Commander of the UAE Armed Forces.
d. The Prime Minister has no constitutionally defined control of the UAE Armed Forces.
e. The authority of the Minister of Defence over the UAE Armed Forces is significantly constrained by law and convention.
f. The post of the Minister of State for Defence Affairs was created in 2016; his formal power and influence over UAE Armed Forces is limited.
g. The Supreme Council for National Security was established in 2006; it is the principal body used by the President to consider and address issues of national security, defence, and foreign policy.

It is important to note that the institutional arrangements described above only tell part of the story about where political control lies and how it is exercised. In the UAE's political systems, there are informal, powerful, and often unseen lines of influence. In the case of control over the UAE Armed Forces, while the posts of Prime Minister and the Minister of Defence are structurally sidelined in the control of the military, the office holder of both (i.e. currently Sheikh Mohammed bin Rashid Al Maktoum) may have significant informal influence over military issues at times where there is a close relationship between him and the Deputy Supreme Commander. The institutional arrangements also do not show funding arrangements, which again are central to understanding power over the UAE Armed Forces.

Maintaining ruler control as forces grew

The preceding sections have shown how Emirati rulers have institutionalised political control over key power centres including the armed forces. They also demonstrated that the rulers' decision-making style can be direct and personal, and they can involve themselves in even minor decisions. This involvement can clearly be seen in the past. Illustrations from the late 1960s include the Ruler of Abu Dhabi ordering that a red stripe be added to the decorative grey sashes worn by senior NCOs, that the ADDF's Guard squadron be renamed *Al Haras Al Amiri* (Emiri Guard), and that enlisted personnel of the Emiri Guard wear the unit's shoulder flash on the right shoulder and officers on both.[67] Other examples include him designing some buildings in military camps,[68] and selecting both aircraft paint schemes[69] and the names of naval vessels.[70] The ruler's close supervision, and direct and personal engagement with his armed force was possible in past decades as the military was small, and there were fewer competing issues vying for the ruler's attention.

Despite the growing complexity of the armed forces and the rest of society today, many of the characteristics of traditional government are still at play in the UAE. This does not mean that the ruler still involves himself in minutiae. Patently he cannot, due to time limitations and the size of the modern armed forces. However, the Deputy Supreme Commander is still more involved in lower-level decisions than would be the case in most states. Specifically, the Deputy Supreme Commander is not only involved

67   *Colonel E.B. Wilson's Archives*, Vol. 1 (Abu Dhabi, n.d.), Lt Colonel E.B. Wilson, Commander ADDF to Sheikh Zayed, [untitled letter, G.1004], 1 February 1968, p. 56.
68   For example, Sheikh Zayed in the late 1960s sketched the mosque he wanted built at the Al Hamra military base. Major R. Hitchcock, OC A Squadron & subsequently founding officer 2nd Infantry Regiment, ADDF, 1967-70, interview, Cambridge, UK, 20 August 2015.
69   An illustration of this was the selection by Sheikh Zayed in the late 1960s of the red stripe between the camouflage pattern on the upper surfaces and the blue on the lower surfaces of the Hawker Hunter aircraft. R. Sheridan, ADDF Air Wing pilot, email, 21 August 2016.
70   Subject 382, Emirati Senior Naval Officer, 1980s, interview, Al Ain, 7 July 2018.

in issues that are normally the responsibility of the defence minister and the armed forces' professional head, he is also actively involved in issues which would typically be delegated to formation commanders and senior bureaucrats.

A series of recent examples illustrate his involvement in lower-level issues. In the mid-2000s, the US Embassy reported that the Deputy Supreme Commander was involved in all procurement decisions down as low as US$15 million.[71] This is a very low threshold by Western standards. In 2005, a US diplomatic report detailed that the Deputy Supreme Commander decided who should be trained to fly the new F-16 Block 60 Desert Falcon. He specified that only lieutenants and captains be assigned for training, and not older and higher-ranking officers.[72] In Western countries, such staffing decisions would normally be made by air force and manpower planning personnel. In the mid-2010s, the Deputy Supreme Commander witnessed a special forces' demonstration in the US. Impressed, he ordered that the UAE Armed Forces create a similar public spectacle. This led to the annual Union Fortress Day, starting in 2016, which sees multiple units of the Armed Forces combining to undertake a series of mock operations. Again, in Western countries, a decision to participate in public relations activities would normally be decided within the public affairs department of the armed forces in consultation with the professional head.

A natural consequence of the direct decision making by the rulers is that their personal preferences can have an enduring effect. This is seen in the situation following Iraq's invasion of Kuwait in 1990. As part of the urgent expansion of the UAE Armed Forces, the force had an immediate need for some 4,000 commercial vehicles.[73] As the UAE government did not have the funds to pay local car dealerships for their vehicles at that time, the President made a personal request to dealers to supply the needed vehicles. Only the Al Masaood family, who owned the Nissan car dealership, provided vehicles without immediate payment. As a result of this display of loyalty to the President and the country, thirty years later the UAE Armed Forces still buys mostly Nissans for its commercial fleet. In a more recent example, a number of analysts claim that the Deputy Supreme Commander's deep enmity towards political Islam and the Brotherhood has significantly shaped the foreign policy of the UAE, and where and how the UAE Armed Forces are used to support the policy.[74]

71   Wikileaks, Sison, [untitled cable Abu Dhabi 00003851 001.2 of 006], 2 October 2006.
     The control over procurement is specified in law which states that the Deputy Supreme
     Commander 'shall issue the necessary decisions for the regulation of the contracts, tenders
     and bids in the Armed Forces'. *UAE Federal Law No 8 of 2006 "On the Armed Forces"* (2006).
72   Wikileaks, Michele J. Sison, US Ambassador to the UAE, 'CENTCOM Deputy
     Commander General Smith Visits UAE', 2005.
73   G. Duncan, 'Tributes Pour in for Abdulla Mohamed Al Masaood, Former Chairman of
     the NCC', *The National*, 26 February 2019.
74   An example is Peter Salisbury, *Risk Perception and Appetite in UAE Foreign and National
     Security Policy* (London, 2020), p. 16.

Another characteristic of Emirati traditional government is that rulers exercise close supervision over their military, with the most critical functions and most senior and politically sensitive posts being directly controlled by them. Since the UAE Armed Forces were formed in 1976, the political head (i.e. the Deputy Supreme Commander) was always the senior son or brother of the President/Ruler of Abu Dhabi. The professional military head of the UAE Armed Forces, the Chief of Staff, has been highly trusted expatriate or local who has been known to the rulers for many years before their appointment, or a member of Abu Dhabi's inner royal family.

In addition, the most most critical units and functions of the military have been excised from the direct control of the professional military head. Instead, the commanders of these units reported directly to the ruler or the force's political head. Critical units in this context include the Emiri Guard which provides close personal and palace protection, high readiness conventional forces, special forces, military intelligence, and combat aviation. Critical functions include operations centres and leadership of operations (e.g. the Assistant Chief of Staff Operations and Commander Air Operations Centre,); and combat and combat support formation commanders (e.g. the Commander Air Force and Air Defence, and the Commander Joint Aviation Command).

Through these mechanisms, the rulers have continued their close supervision over the UAE Armed Forces, and ensured they remain at the centre of decision making.

Looking forward

Given that the rulers sit at the centre of government and politics, and closely supervise all centres of power, what does this mean for the military when rulership passes on?

History has shown that when a new ruler assumed power, it was common that substantial changes were made to the machinery of government and government priorities. This occurs even when the crown prince assumes the rulership. The military parallel is that if there is a change in the presidency of the UAE, then there may be significant changes to the UAE Armed Forces.

However, in the current context a major change in the direction of the UAE Armed Forces is unlikely because the person most likely to assume the presidency is Sheikh Mohammed bin Zayed Al Nahyan. For last few decades, he has been exercising almost complete authority over the military and thus shaping it as he has seen fit. Consequently, if he assumes power, the direction of the UAE Armed Forces' combat capability may not fundamentally change. However, as he will have greater influence over the Council of Ministers (i.e. Cabinet), he may seek to reform the country's governmental architecture. This could result in changes to the military if it was instructed to meet new challenges such as cyber warfare and space conflict, while shedding tasks like border security and the coast guard which could be undertaken by civil entities.

Part II

Defining Characteristics of Emirati Armed Forces

4

Missions

Armed forces are generally built around the missions they are expected to fulfil. Some missions are laid down formally, while others can only be inferred from the military's force structure, capabilities, and deployments. In the case of Emirati armed forces, the evidence points to five missions being of central importance since 1965. These are: (1) defending territorial integrity and sovereignty, (2) protecting the rulers and their families, (3) bolstering internal security, (4) contributing to nation building, and (5) supporting foreign policy. The first three are enduring roles common to all Emirati armed forces. The last two have been important to the Abu Dhabi Defence Force (ADDF) and UAE Armed Forces, but less so to the others forces. Each of these missions is described below.

Emirati armed forces have also undertaken a number of other missions, including domestic and international disaster response and recovery, aid to civil authorities, ceremonial duties, search and rescue, ambulance transport, maritime salvage, transport for island communities, and hydrographic surveys. While important, these missions have not shaped the armed forces to anywhere near the same degree as have the five missions listed above.

A number of the core missions can be seen in the founding directives of several Emirati armed forces. The purpose of the Union Defence Force (1971-74), as defined in a 1971 law, was: (1) the defence of the UAE, and (2) the protection of the Union against external and internal threats.[1] For the ADDF (1966-76) as defined in 1968 guidance, its two stated roles were: (1) guaranteeing the integrity of the State against external interference, and (2) maintaining peace and good order within the state, particularly the prevention of subversion and illegal immigration.[2]

In the UAE Constitution, security features prominently in the aims of the federation. The Constitution's first three objectives are to 'maintain the UAE's independence

---

1   *UAE Federal Law No 3 of 1971 "Regarding the Union Defence Force"* (1971).
2   MECA, St Antony's College, Oxford, Abu Dhabi Defence Force, 'Induction Booklet for New British Officers with an Introduction by Col E.B. Wilson', 1968.

and sovereignty, safeguard the UAE's security and stability, repel any aggression against the UAE's existence or the existence of its member states'.[3] These aims form the basis of, and are expanded upon, in the main law governing the military today. Federal Law No. 8 of 2006 'On the Armed Forces' states that the missions of the UAE Armed Forces are to:

1. protect the state from internal and external threats
2. defend the state and impose its authority on the waters, land and airspace thereof, and protect the resources and national interests against any aggression
3. protect and ensure constitutional legitimacy
4. help preserve security and internal stability; and,
5. carry out military engagements of the state in the Gulf, Arab region and internationally.

Only the second of the five core missions – protection the rulers and their families – is not contained in the directives and laws mentioned above. However, this role can be seen when the structure of Emirati forces is examined. All Emirati forces have had and continues to have a specialised element whose functions are to provide close personal protection for the rulers and their families, to guard the palaces of the Royal Family, and to be able to provide a rapid, well-armed response force which is personally loyal to and directed by the ruler. These elements are known as Emiri Guards.

While the five missions are common to the armed forces of most other Arab countries, there are a number of significant differences between how they are carried out in the Emirates compared with other countries. In many Arab countries, the military's role in protecting the leaders and the political regime has included suppressing internal dissent and employing coercion of the population. This has not been the case in the Emirates. Likewise, while in some Arab countries, the military has owned and managed large parts of the economy as part of their perceived role as nation builders, this has also not occurred in the Emirates. Probably the most fundamental difference between the armed forces of many other Arab states and the Emirates relates to the military's political role. While international relations scholar, Derek Lutterbeck, writes that 'practically all Arab countries can be described as military-based regimes, where the armed forces have been at the core of the political system',[4] this has not been the case in the Emirates. Never in the history of the Emirates has its military been a powerful political force. This is noted by Karen Young, a former political science professor at the University of Sharjah, who states 'in other Arab states, the military often symbolizes the mediator of order between disparate ethnic or religious rival

---

3   Article 10 of the Constitution.
4   D. Lutterbeck, 'Change and Opportunities in the Emerging Mediterranean' in Stephen Calleya and Monika Wohlfeld (eds.) (Malta, 2012), p. 160.

groups … [this is not the situation in the UAE as] the military's place in Emirati society has always been at the service of the ruler'.[5]

Core mission 1: Defending territorial integrity and sovereignty

While all countries prioritise defence of territorial integrity and sovereignty, for small states the threat of foreign incursion, land annexation and military coercion are of immense visceral importance. At various times, the Emirates have been threatened by all four neighbours who have sought their strategically important and oil-rich lands and waters. For this reason, the defence of the Emirates' integrity has been a significant driver in state development.[6] For instance, an territorial dispute with Saudi Arabia during the early 1970s and some decades before was a key driver in building up Abu Dhabi's land forces and ground attack air capability from the 1960s to the late 1970s. The threat from Iran, from the early 1970s to the present, has been a key driver in UAE air, naval, surveillance and intelligence development. Foreign states are not the only actors to have threatened the Emirates' territorial integrity and sovereignty. Non-state actors have long posed a challenge to sovereignty, notably smugglers of weapons, contraband and migrants, as well as illegal fishers. To the mid-1970s, the military was the primary government entity responsible for countering these non-state actors. In the mid-1970s, this responsibility was transferred to the Federal police, coast guard and border guard. In the 2000s, the responsibility for border security returned to the military, leading to the formation of dedicated border force formations, today the Critical Infrastructure and Coastal Protection Authority, which is a command within the UAE Armed Forces.

Border disputes with the Emirates' four neighbours

The Emirates have had border disputes with all four of its neighbours – Qatar, Oman, Saudi Arabia and Iran. The dispute with Qatar was settled in the 1960s, and the one with Oman in the late 2000s. The dispute with Saudi Arabia is in abeyance, and the one with Iran is still ongoing. The areas of dispute are shown in Figure 13.

---

5   K.E. Young, *The Political Economy of Energy, Finance and Security in the United Arab Emirates: Between the Majilis and the Market* (Houndmills, 2014), p. 106.
6   As an illustration of how defence considerations featured in the thinking of the rulers, when a town plan was developed for Abu Dhabi in the late 1960s, the Abu Dhabi Ruler chose a layout designed to counter a sea-based attack. Specifically the layout consisted of a grid-based structure with wide, straight boulevards which would allow his armed forces based at the Al Nahyan military base in the centre of the island to move quickly to the foreshore corniche road. A.R.B. Hashim, *Planning Abu Dhabi: An Urban History* (London, 2018), p. 119.

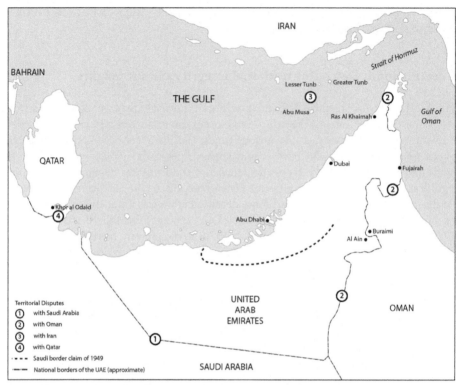

Figure 13: Settled and ongoing territorial disputes with neighbouring countries.

The dispute with Qatar revolved around the ownership of land in the western region of Abu Dhabi and southeast of Qatar, principally the Khor Al Odaid area and the islands of Halul, Dayyinah, Al Ashat and Shirauh. In the late 1950s, this disagreement escalated into shots being exchanged between the Abu Dhabi Police and Qatari forces.[7] As Britain was then responsible for the external affairs of the Trucial States and Qatar, in 1961 it unilaterally decided that Halul Island belonged to Qatar. In 1969, it similarly determined the ownership of the other islands; Dayyinah was allocated to Abu Dhabi, and Al Ashat and Shirauh to Qatar.[8] These decisions settled the dispute.

The dispute with Oman concerned the delineation of multiple stretches of the Emirates-Oman border. Two disputes in recent decades have been particularly serious.

---

7   UK Foreign Office, *Foreign Office Annual Reports from Arabia, 1930-1960: 1954-1960* (Slough, 1993), Persian Gulf Monthly Summary for December 11, 1958 to January 4, 1959, p. 775.
8   Al-Ulama, 'The Federal Boundaries of the United Arab Emirates', p. 213.

The first arose following the signing of the 1974 Treaty of Jeddah between Abu Dhabi and Saudi Arabia which included a territorial settlement over land which the Sultan of Oman considered was his. The Sultan's anger over this explains why Oman had no Embassy in Abu Dhabi until 1987, despite it being the capital of the UAE.[9]

The second Oman-UAE dispute began on 25 October 1977. It involved Oman claiming a 16km stretch of Ras Al Khaimah's northern coastline from Dawra to Rams (the area of dispute is marked in Figure 13 and in detail in Figure 5). The area encompassed a cement factory, quarry and fishmeal plant at the port of Khor Khuair, in addition to its corresponding offshore territory. Oil had just been discovered in this maritime area,[10] which may have been the impetus for Oman's claim. The dispute saw both Emirati and Omani armed forces moved to the area.[11] So significant was the dispute that the UAE National Day celebrations on 2 December 1977 were cancelled. The dispute did not escalate into a military confrontation and negotiations subsequently culminated in a reported settlement in April 1979.[12]

From the late 1970s small-scale disputes over the borders between the UAE and Oman continued to break out. The most serious dispute was when Omani tribesmen from the Madha enclave within the UAE closed traffic on the nearby Khor Fakkan-Fujairah highway for an extended period. In 2002, the UAE and Oman signed an agreement which settled outstanding areas of the roughly 1,000km long common border.[13] It was not until 2008, however, before both parties confirmed the maps and coordinates which accurately delineated the border.[14]

The Saudi-Emirates territorial dispute, which is in abeyance today, involves land along the western and southern borders of Abu Dhabi territory. The dispute dates from the 1930s which was when it became apparent that oil was likely to be found in the region (oil was discovered in 1938 in nearby areas of Saudi Arabia). Consequently,

9   Before the opening of the embassy in 1987, UAE-Oman relations were conducted via the Oman liaison office in Dubai. Fatma Al-Sayegh, 'The UAE and Oman: Opportunities and Challenges in the Twenty-First Century', *Middle East Policy*, IX, No. 3 (2002), p. 133

10 R. Litwak, *Security in the Persian Gulf: Sources of Inter-state conflict*, Vol. 2 (Farnborough, 1981), p. 60.

11 *The Times* reported this on 5 December 1977. A.H. Cordesman, *The Gulf and the Search for Strategic Stability: Saudi Arabia, the Military Balance in the Gulf, and Trends in the Arab-Israeli Military Balance* (Boulder, 1984), p. 418.

12 An unpublished agreement signed in April 1979 between Oman and Ras Al Khaimah appears to have settled the dispute. 'UAE', *Middle East Economic Digest*, December 21 (1979), p. 46.

13 This agreement was ratified by both countries in 2003. It followed a partial agreement on mutual borders in 1999 which covered a 330km stretch from Umm Al Zumul to Eastern Uqaydat in the UAE's south east. WAM. 'UAE, Oman Exchange Border Agreement Document', 2003, <wam.ae/en/details/1395226319421>; Kuwait News Agency. 'Sheikh Zayed Ratifies Border Agreement With Oman', 27 January 2003, <www.kuna.net.kw/ArticlePrintPage.aspx?id=1315340&language=en>

14 WAM. 'UAE and Oman Sign List of Final Geographical Co-ordinates and Maps – Updates', 2008, <wam.ae/en/details/1395228158935>

in 1935 Saudi Arabia's King Abdulaziz Al Saud unilaterally drew up a border between his kingdom and that of both Qatar and Abu Dhabi. In doing so, Saudi Arabia claimed land owned by Qatar and Abu Dhabi. He argued (inaccurately) that, historically, the tribes in the area had given allegiance and paid taxes to his forefathers and, hence, the land was his. This claim was rejected by Britain on Abu Dhabi's behalf and it commenced discussions with Saudi Arabia over the location of an appropriate border. In 1949, Saudi Arabia made another claim and this time it included some two thirds of the Abu Dhabi Emirate, as well as an undefined area of Oman's hinterland.[15] This again was justified on the basis of assertions that the region's tribal sheikhs owed allegiance to the Saudis and that the Abu Dhabi Ruler's authority did not extend beyond the coast.[16] The Saudi claim included Buraimi Oasis which sits at the crossroads of routes from Najd, Abu Dhabi and Muscat. Buraimi's location made it of great strategic importance to the Saudis as it would have provided them with a base from which to extend their influence into both Oman and Abu Dhabi. It was equally important for the Ruler of Abu Dhabi for protection, influence and personal reasons (it was the historic centre and a key base of his family's power). For the British, its location was also critical for if Saudi Arabia obtained control of Buraimi, British possessions along the Arabian Gulf could be undermined.

At that time, the Buraimi Oasis had a population of some 25,000 spread over eight villages, each centred in the vicinity of a water source. Six of these were governed by Abu Dhabi's Ruler and two by the Sultan of Oman. In August 1952, a small Saudi force occupied Hamasa, one of the Omani villages. The Saudis remained there until 1955 when the British forcefully evicted them; the United Kingdom with agreement of the rulers of Abu Dhabi and Muscat then declared a new border between Abu Dhabi and Saudi Arabia (for details, see the section on the Trucial Oman Levies/ Trucial Oman Scouts in Chapter 7).

Until the 1968 announcement by Britain that it was intending to withdraw its protection of the Trucial States by 1971, Saudi Arabia did not strongly prosecute its land claims. However, following that announcement, the value of the British deterrent declined and Saudi Arabia ramped up pressure on Abu Dhabi and the British to settle the territorial dispute in its favour. This Saudi pressure included making its diplomatic recognition of a union of the Emirates contingent on a 'suitable' settlement, as well as threatening to revert to its proclaimed 1949 border if such a settlement could not be reached.[17]

Recognising the political difficulties of an ongoing disagreement with its largest neighbour, in 1974 Sheikh Zayed reluctantly signed the Treaty of Jeddah. This gave Saudi Arabia ownership of land covering some 80 percent of the giant Zarrarah oil

15   Henderson, *This Strange Eventful History*, p. 95.
16   Abdullah, *The United Arab Emirates: A Modern History*, p. 204.
17   N.S. Al Mazrouei, *The UAE and Saudi Arabia: Border Disputes and International Relations in the Gulf* (London, 2016), p. 190.

field (known as Shaybah in Saudi Arabia) but 100 percent of the field's hydrocarbons rights, including the 20 percent of the field that lies under Abu Dhabi territory. Zarrarah has turned out to be one of the world's largest oil producing fields. The treaty also gave Saudi Arabia a corridor of land near Khor Al Odaid in Abu Dhabi's far west which cut the land connection between Abu Dhabi and Qatar. In return, Abu Dhabi received formal recognition that it owned the six villages in the Buraimi Oasis.[18]

Abu Dhabi's ruling family have long been dissatisfied with the 1974 border settlement process and treaty, for they consider that Sheikh Zayed signed it under duress.[19] However, Sheikh Zayed reportedly said that he did not want the treaty disputed during his lifetime.[20] According to the UAE political scientist, Noura Sabel Al Mazrouei, this was because the UAE needed to maintain its relationship with Saudi Arabia given the threats arising from the 1979 Islamic Revolution, the Iraq-Iran War (1980-88) and the Iraqi invasion of Kuwait in 1990.[21] After Sheikh Zayed's death in 2004, the UAE started pressing Saudi Arabia to revisit parts of the agreement. In 2005, the UAE Minister of Foreign Affairs stated that some parts of the 1974 treaty were not applicable and the UAE wanted 'fundamental amendments to these parts of the Agreement'.[22] Saudi Arabia refused to reconsider the treaty.

The UAE-Saudi Arabia border has remained a sensitive issue.[23] In 2004, the UAE and Qatar announced they were planning to build a causeway that would cross the Gulf from Qatar to Abu Dhabi and a gas pipeline connecting the two countries. The Saudis strongly objected, stating that the maritime boundaries in the area were

---

18   The Treaty of Jeddah also granted Saudi Arabia sovereignty over Huwaysat Island in the Arabian Gulf and UAE sovereignty over all the other islands opposite its coast in the Gulf, in addition to giving it the right to construct any general installations on the islands of Al Qaffay and Makasib. Saudi Arabia and United Arab Emirates, 'Agreement Of the Delimitation of Boundaries (With Exchange of Letters and Map.) Signed at Jeddah, Saudi Arabia on 21 August 1974.', 1974.
19   Wikileaks, Richard Olson, US Ambassador to the UAE, 'A Long Hot Summer for UAE-Saudi relations', 15 October 2009.
20   O'Sullivan, The New Gulf, p. 276.
21   Al Mazrouei, The UAE and Saudi Arabia, pp. 158-9.
22   WAM. 'Sheikh Hamdan Says Dialogue on Border Issue Will Be Completed During His Saudi Visit (corrected)', 2005, <wam.ae/en/details/1395227450777>.
23   The concern over the border reflects a broader anxiety over Saudi Arabia among the UAE leadership. This can be seen in a leaked assessment by the US Ambassador to the UAE in 2009. She noted that the UAE has long been concerned about the 'Kingdom's overbearing attitude toward smaller Gulf States'. She notes that 'while publicly expressing close ties with Riyadh, the UAE privately regards the Kingdom as its second greatest security threat after Iran (Israel is not on the list). This is based on historic enmity between the Wahabi tribes of the Najd and the Maliki Bedouin/merchants of the UAE, as well as deep seated, if rarely articulated, anxiety about what might happen if Saudi Arabia came under a more fundamentalist regime than the Sudairi/Abdullah reign'. Wikileaks, Olson, 'A Long Hot Summer for UAE-Saudi relations', 15 October 2009.

still undefined.[24] As a result, the project was halted. The continuing sensitivity over the border was reflected in the August 2009 decision by Saudi Arabia that Emirati citizens would have to use their passports to travel to Saudi Arabia rather than their national identity cards, as was standard practice for GCC nationals. [25] This was in response to the UAE issuing an identify card which showed a direct UAE-Qatar border rather than recognising Saudi Arabia's 25km-wide corridor between the UAE and Qatar. In 2010, when a Saudi patrol boat entered what the UAE considered was its waters, a UAE naval vessel fired on it and it surrendered.[26] Since the early 2010s, the issue of the border has not been visible in UAE-Saudi Arabian relations. This is because of the increasingly close relationship between the two countries, particularly over their combined efforts to counter Iran, Qatar, Turkey and political Islam, as well as to prosecute the war in Yemen.

The UAE's most serious ongoing territorial dispute is with Iran. It involves Iran's occupation of three UAE islands – Abu Musa, Greater Tunb and Lesser Tunb. Iran's annexation of the Tunb islands occurred on 30 November 1971, one day before Britain ended its protection of the Emirates. British armed forces did not respond to Iran's action as Britain had secretly agreed with Iran to allow it to take possession of the islands.[27] The small armed force of Ras Al Khaimah, which owned the Tunb islands, was incapable of defending them. No other Emirate came to the aid of Ras Al Khaimah as at that time, it had not agreed to be part of the UAE, and none of the Emirates had the forces required to dislodge the much better armed Iranians. Iran occupied part of Abu Musa, which is owned by Sharjah, in 1971 and completely occupied it in 1992.

In addition to the issue of the occupation of these islands, Iran has had a history of using its military to threaten UAE sovereignty, and it has made numerous hostile incursions into the UAE's territory. In the 1980s, it attacked oil rigs and vessels in the

24   O'Sullivan, *The New Gulf*, p. 276. So serious at the time was the UAE determination to regain the land that Sheikh Mohammed bin Zayed's Director for International Affairs, Yousef Al Otaiba, told the US Ambassador 'that the UAEG had developed a list of 27 options with which to respond to the Saudi pressure, ranging from international arbitration to military action'. Wikileaks, Michele J. Sison, US Ambassador to the UAE, 'General Abizaid Meeting with Abu Dhabi Crown Prince', 2005.

25   Wikileaks, Olson, 'A Long Hot Summer for UAE-Saudi relations', 15 October 2009. This was also claimed to be a reason why Saudi officers stopped vehicles for a time at the UAE-Saudi Arabian land border. Economist Intelligence Unit (24 August 2009), 'UAE/ Saudi Economy: Not so Neighbourly,' quoted in K.C. Ulrichsen, *Insecure Gulf: The End of Certainty and the Transition to the Post-Oil Era* (Oxford, 2015), p. 79. Another reason was that it was to signal Saudi Arabia's displeasure with the UAE over its withdrawal from the proposed GCC monetary union. Wikileaks, Olson, 'A Long Hot Summer for UAE-Saudi relations', 15 October 2009.

26   Richard Spencer, 'Naval Battle Between UAE and Saudi Arabia Raises Fears for Gulf Security', *The Telegraph*, 26 March 2010.

27   T.T. Petersen, *Richard Nixon, Great Britain and the Anglo-American Alignment in the Persian Gulf and Arabian Peninsula: Making Allies Out of Clients*, 2011), pp. 63-64.

UAE's territorial waters, and is reported to have even covertly landed Revolutionary Guard members on UAE soil.[28] This hostility has continued to this day, as witnessed by Iran's attacks in mid-2019 on tankers in UAE waters,[29] and orchestrated large-scale illegal fishing by Iranian vessels in UAE territorial waters.[30]

Use of the armed forces to protect the UAE's territorial integrity and sovereignty

The UAE is geographically a small state and has typically employed the foreign policy approaches of small states when facing more powerful neighbours – namely strategic neutrality, supporting multilateral organisations, 'band-wagoning' and 'balancing'. There follows a description of each of these four approaches, illustrated by specific examples of these types of behaviour. These show how the armed forces of the Emirates and/or partner nations have or have not been used in order to protect the country's territorial integrity and sovereignty.

Strategic neutrality involves a nation actively abstaining from siding with one party or another, so as to avoid being drawn into a struggle between powers. This was the bedrock of UAE foreign policy until 1990, and can be seen in its avoidance of taking sides in the latter parts of the Iraq-Iran War, its reluctance to establish formal protection agreements with other powers, and a determination not to provide permanent facilities for foreign forces on UAE soil.[31] Other methods the UAE has sought to preserve strategic neutrality have included freezing issues of bilateral tension, such as it did with the dispute with Iran over its annexation of islands in the 1970s, and normalising bilateral relationships even when there were tensions, for example with Iran over its aggression against the UAE during much of the Iraq-Iran War.[32] A method the UAE rulers have used to demonstrate their neutrality is through offering

---

28   A declassified 1987 CIA report notes that Iranian navel craft twice fired on UAE aircraft in 1986, Iranian ships regularly trespass in UAE waters, Iran attacked UAE oil infrastructure in 1986, and the Iranian Revolutionary Guard landed infiltrators in the UAE without detection by coastal patrols. US Central Intelligence Agency, *Iranian Threats to the Persian Gulf States* (Washington DC, 1987).

29   While the US, Saudi Arabia and several other states claim the perpetrator was Iran, Iran denies its involvement. The UAE did not accuse Iran, presumably so as to not increase tensions.

30   WAM. 'CICPA: Eight violating fishing boats spotted in UAE's territorial waters carrying out prohibited fishing activities', 17 August 2020 <https://wam.ae/en/details/1395302863059>.

31   During the 1980s, the UAE only provided port visits, ship repairs, and refuelling to US and other Western navies.

32   This improvement is reflected in an agreement to exchange ambassadors and the immediate sending of an Iranian ambassador to the UAE. Hassan Alkim, *The Foreign Policy of the United Arab Emirates* (London, 1989), p. 169. Improved links between Sharjah and Iran included the starting in January 1984 of a ferry service between Bandar Abbas and Sharjah. TNA FCO 8/5826: UK Embassy in Abu Dhabi, 'Calander of Events', 1985.

to play a brokering role between regional states facing tensions.[33] In general, the UAE's military has supported strategic neutrality by not appearing to be a source of provocation. Instances of this include the UAE's military not actively supporting one side or another in a dispute, shifting forces away from 'hot' areas so flare-ups could not accidentally occur, and not maintaining forward forces which means that only substantial penetrations of UAE air or sea space would trigger confrontation with the country's forces.

Supporting multilateral organisations is another common strategy used by small states to reduce aggressive behaviour from larger neighbours. The hope is that multilateral organisations can bring collective pressure on a transgressor. The Emirates have often been early joiners and active members of such organisations. Instances include the Organisation of Petroleum Exporting Countries (OPEC), the Arab League and the United Nations. Instances of UAE military support to these organisations include the UAE Armed Forces' 750-man contribution to the Arab Deterrent Force in Lebanon from 1977 to 1979, organised under the sponsorship of the Arab League, and its regiment-sized contribution to the humanitarian mission in Somalia from 1993 to 1994 under a United Nations mandate.

Band-wagoning and balancing are international relations concepts that are based on the understanding that relationships between states revolve around the pursuit of power. They are useful concepts for analysing the behaviour of smaller states when faced by an aggressive power, noting that while they are discrete theoretical concepts, in practice it is often difficult to identify if the behaviour of a state falls neatly into one category or another, or both.

Bandwagoning involves a smaller state aligning with a powerful state which is in an adversarial position with another similarly powerful state. Bandwagoning with the stronger state provides protection for the smaller state and may provide spoils if the partner state wins the competition. The negative of bandwagoning for the smaller state is that it forces the smaller state to adopt the positions of the larger one, which can include being coerced into participation in the partner state's wars. The UAE's security relationship with the US since 1991 has been characterised as bandwagoning,[34] as has its relationship with Saudi Arabia in recent years.[35]

Balancing involves a smaller state taking actions either to reduce the power of an adversarial powerful state, or to increase the power of states facing the adversarial

33   An example of this was Sheikh Zayed's role in the late 1983 Saudi Arabian-brokered plan to end the Iraq-Iran War. This would have involved the Gulf States paying Iran $70 billion in war reparations on behalf of Iraq. This failed as Iran wanted US$150 billion and the removal of Saddam Hussein. Wilson, *Zayed, Man Who Built a Nation*, p. 416.

34   L. Sherwood, 'Risk Diversification and the United Arab Emirates' Foreign Policy', in K.S. Almezaini and J.M. Rickli (eds.), *The Small Gulf States* (London, 2017).

35   Robert Mason, 'Breaking the Mold of Small State Classification? The Broadening Influence of United Arab Emirates Foreign Policy Through Effective Military and Bandwagoning Strategies', *Canadian Foreign Policy Journal*, 24, 1 (2018), p. 96.

power. In other words, the smaller state partners with other states to counterbalance the power of an adversary. Balancing actions can be divided into two categories – internal and external balancing.

Internal balancing involves the state building up its own military capability so as to counterbalance the adversary's force. As will be seen in later chapters, periods during which Emirati armed forces have rapidly expanded have coincided with periods of increased threat from neighbouring powers – such as in the late 1960s for both the Abu Dhabi and Ras Al Khaimah armed forces, the second half of the 1970s for the Abu Dhabi/UAE Armed Forces, and the 2000s for the UAE Armed Forces. These could be classified as internal balancing actions.

The second category of balancing – external balancing – involves a smaller state strengthening its alliances to support the security of the smaller state directly or indirectly. Below are descriptions of five cases of external balancing which have been important in the history of the armed forces of the UAE. Four of these are discrete balancing activities related to specific instances of insecurity. The final one covers the period from 1990 to the present and describes how the UAE has facilitated military cooperation with Western powers. In doing so, the UAE has sought to build a balancing force – either a regional security grouping or the presence of foreign states. The result of this activities was that their presence has acted as a balancer.

The first case arose at the start of the Iraq-Iran War in 1980 and involved the UAE seeking the informal support of major Western parties. The context for this balancing action was that Abu Dhabi believed that if Iraq attacked Iranian forces at either Bandar Abbas or on the three Emirati islands occupied by Iran, Iran would strike the UAE as retribution.[36] Such a response was considered more likely if the UAE facilitated the attack by allowing Iraqi forces to transit UAE airspace, something which occurred within a week of the war's commencement.[37] In addition, at that time there was also a fear that Iran would block the Strait of Hormuz, again drawing the UAE into the conflict.[38]

Consequently, in October 1980, Sheikh Zayed sought from the three major Western powers – France, the United Kingdom and the US – informal commitments to come to the assistance of the UAE in the event of an attack. All three indicated support. France provided the most fulsome assurances with the French President, Valéry Giscard d'Estaing, reportedly offering *carte blanche* support and signalling that

---

36   TNA, FCO 8/3908, D.A. Roberts, UK Ambassador, Abu Dhabi, 'Annual Review – United Arab Emirates', 31 December 1980.

37   The UAE did allow Iraqi Ilyushin transport helicopters to fly through its airspace on their way to Oman, although Iraq decided against a strike and withdrew its forces. TNA FCO 8/3453: D.A. Roberts, UK Ambassador, Abu Dhabi to FCO, 'Iraq/Iran', 28 September 1980. The British correspondence does not state that Sheikh Zayed opposed the strike.

38   TNA, FCO 8/3909, Lord Chalfont Alun Gwynne Jones, 'Report on a Visit to the United Arab Emirates – 5-12 January, 1981', 13 January 1981.

'whatever the UAE wanted would be sent immediately'.[39] Britain offered a range of practical assistance,[40] notably advice, training and a detailed assessment of the UAE's military capabilities and weaknesses, but avoided a definite commitment of military defence.[41] Iran was probably aware that Abu Dhabi had obtained some commitment from Western powers and uncertainty about what this entailed may have deterred it from attacking the UAE at that time.

The second case involved the creation of a collective security mechanism in the early 1980s. The context for this development was the start of the Iraq-Iran War in September 1980. As the Arab Gulf states were concerned that Iran or Iraq would attack them, Bahrain, Kuwait, Oman, Qatar, Saudi Arabia, and the UAE formed the Gulf Cooperation Council (GCC).[42] Its charter was signed in May 1981. For political reasons, the charter contained no mention of defence and security. Following the December 1981 coup attempt in Bahrain (which was perceived by the Arab Gulf states as being backed by Iran), and Iran's military gains against Iraq in 1982, security became publicly recognised as a key focus of the GCC.[43] The UAE was instrumental in establishing the GCC, as reflected in the fact that Sheikh Zayed became the first President of the GCC's Supreme Committee, and, that its first summit was held in Abu Dhabi in May 1981. The UAE was also active in promoting security activities by the GCC. For example, in October 1983, the western deserts of Abu Dhabi hosted

39   TNA FCO 8/3453: D.A. Roberts, UK Ambassador, Abu Dhabi, 'Security in the Gulf', 19 October 1980.

40   In October 1980, the Secretary of State for Defence, Francis Pym, visited the UAE, making this the first visit by a UK defence secretary for many years. He was followed by John Moberly, a senior Foreign Office diplomat specialising in Middle Eastern affairs, then a military assessment team led by Major-General Perkins, the former Commander of the Sultan of Oman's Armed Forces, at that point serving as the Director Military Assistance Office which is responsible for all British overseas foreign military assistance. TNA FCO 8/3453: Major General K. Perkins, 'Visit DMAO to the United Arab Emirates 23-30 October 1980', 3 November 1980.

41   Britain gave consideration to offering a spearhead battalion group, specialised teams such as the SAS, and anti-aircraft elements, such as a rapier detachment or a squadron of Phantoms. TNA, FCO 8/3453, Carrington, Head of Middle East Department, 'Gulf Security', 17 October 1980. What was accepted by Sheikh Zayed was a review of the UAE's present capabilities of the UAE, followed by a 'small low-profile team of experts to look into the working and the command and control for Abu Dhabi's existing Rapier system ... [and not given another advising report but] to give practical help and to put right any defects themselves'. TNA FCO 8/3453: D.A. Roberts, UK Ambassador, Abu Dhabi, 'UAE Security', 28 October 1980; TNA FCO 8/3461: R.P. Wilkin, DS11, 'Briefing for S of S's Visit to the Gulf – Secretary of State's Visit to Bahrain, Qatar, UAE and Oman: United Arab Emirates UAE/UK Defence Relations Line to Take (Draft)', 31 December 1980.

42   Another motivator was the perceived growth in Soviet power regionally.

43   Steve A Yetiv, 'The Outcomes of Operations Desert Shield and Desert Storm: Some Antecedent Causes', Political Science Quarterly, 107, 2 (1992), pp. 199-200.

the first large GCC military exercise which involved some 3,600 troops.[44] That same year, a collective GCC force was established under the name Peninsula Shield force.

The third case saw Egypt establishing military links with Arab Gulf states in 1986 and 1987. This balancing activity was also motivated by the Arab Gulf states being increasingly concerned that they would be attacked by Iran and/or Iraq as the war between them escalated. The GCC states approached Egypt to be involved militarily with the GCC states, in order to deter hostile attacks.[45]

Egypt welcomed this opportunity because, over the preceding decade, Egypt had been ostracised by the Arab Gulf states and the rest of the Arab Middle East due its relations with Israel. The isolation of Egypt resulted from secret talks held between Egyptian President Anwar Sadat and Israeli Prime Minister Menachem Begin at Camp David in 1978. These talks led to the Camp David Accords, which consisted of two framework agreements: one sought to establish a peaceful settlement of the Arab-Israeli conflict; the other led to the 1979 Egypt-Israel Peace Treaty. The Accords were strongly criticised by most Arab countries as they were considered tantamount to abandoning the cause of the Palestinians. By May 1979, all Arab countries except Oman, Somalia and the Sudan had severed diplomatic relations with Egypt. Egypt was also expelled from a number of Arab organisations, including the Arab League and OPEC. The Camp David Accords not only substantially ended diplomatic and political contact between Egypt and other Arab states, they also terminated military cooperation between them. This included a massive project to jointly develop and produce military equipment, which had commenced in 1975 when Saudi Arabia, the UAE and Qatar agreed collectively to invest over a billion dollars to create the Arab Military Industries Organisation, a defence manufacturing entity based in Egypt.[46]

For Egypt's leadership, the offer to engage militarily with the GCC states was welcomed since it would help Egypt regain its historic influence in Islamic and Arab circles.[47] Cooperation started in late 1987 with Egypt agreeing to train Arab Gulf forces, including the UAE Armed Forces, both in the Arab Gulf states and in Egypt.[48] Some Arab Gulf states also authorised an injection of a total of one billion dollars to reenergise the Arab Military Industries Organisation.

The fourth case arose as Iran pursued a more assertive role for itself across the region following the August 2005 election of the conservative Mahmoud Ahmadinejad as President of Iran. Tension increased when Iran's uranium production restarted at Natanz in 2006, and because of its increasing support for groups seeking to undermine

44 TNA FCO 8/5468: Lt Colonel J.P. Cameron, UK Defence Attaché, to UK Ambassador (UAE), 'Annual Report for 1983 on the United Arab Emirates Armed Forces', 25 January 1984.

45 Joseph P. Lorenz, 'Egypt and the New Arab Coalition', 1989.

46 Middle East Research Institute, *United Arab Emirates* (London, 1984), p. 34.

47 E. Podeh and O. Winckler, *The Boycott That Never Was: Egypt and the Arab System, 1979-1989* (Durham, 2002), p. 16.

48 Ibid., pp. 16-7.

the US-controlled Iraqi government. Further afield, Iran's support of Hezbollah during the 2006 Lebanon War was seen as indicative of its growing regional aspirations.

Ahmadinejad's continual anti-American and anti-Israeli rhetoric resonated across the Arab world, and one 2008 poll undertaken across Egypt, Jordan, Lebanon, Morocco and Saudi Arabia found he was the third most admired leader in the Arab world. A Brookings Institution scholar noted that Ahmadinejad's message of resistance was 'always combined with denunciations of Sunni Arab leaders for cowering under an American security umbrella and making humiliating deals with Israel'.[49] Ahmadinejad's appeal increased Iran's claim for global Islamic leadership and directly threatened Saudi Arabia's power as the centre of Muslim worship. In the past, Iran's attempts to build its regional influence had been curtailed by the US, but since the mid-2000s, US involvement in Iraq and Afghanistan has meant that its military has been unable to play a substantial stabilising role in the Gulf region. Concerns over Iran's intentions were amplified in 2008 when international talks to curb Iran's nuclear ambitions ended in deadlock.

The growing concern over Iran's behaviour and the increasing cross-Arab appeal of its message increased the UAE leadership's concern that the nation faced a real possibility of hostile action by Iran. Consequently, around 2009, the UAE's leadership held a series of bilateral security contingency planning meetings with the United Kingdom, the US and France, along with lesser powers.[50] At these, assurances of military protection were apparently requested. The French gave a very positive response, with the President Nicolas Sarkozy publicly proclaimed that 'an attack on the UAE was an attack on France', and that France was 'ready to shoulder its responsibilities to ensure stability in this strategic region'.[51] The US response was also positive, with commitments reportedly including the deployment of a missile shield in the region and the stationing of warships that were capable of shooting down Iranian missiles. The United Kingdom's response was considered less impressive, both in terms of what it could offer and how it was delivered.[52]

The final case covers the period from 1990 to the present day. Commencing with the 1990-91 Gulf War, the UAE created formal links with the US and other Western powers as a means of balancing the threat from both Iraq and Iran. Before the Gulf War, the UAE was not as close to the US as Saudi Arabia and Oman were.[53] Both

---

49 T.C. Wittes, *Freedom's Unsteady March: America's Role in Building Arab Democracy* (Washington DC, 2008), p. 29.
50 Subsequently, meetings are believed to have occurred with medium powers including Australia and South Korea.
51 'Sarkozy Opens UAE "Peace Camp"', *The National*, 26 May 2009.
52 The poorly-received UK response may have been a significant factor in the UAE military's doctrine, force structure and training realigning away from the UK to the US around the end of 2010s.
53 The UAE did cooperate with the US to a degree by allowing US military overflight rights in the case of 'hot pursuit' or emergencies. The US Ambassador to the UAE, David Mack,

of these countries had provided permanent facilities to the US starting in the 1980s, something which the UAE had not agreed to because of the perceived need 'to preserve the country's non-alignment', according to a 1986 editorial in the Abu Dhabi Government's newspaper.[54] The UAE feared that demonstrating such close ties to the US would generate anti-Western sentiment and be seen as a provocation by Iran or Iraq.

After the Gulf War, the US recognised that its approach of limited air and naval presence in the region, combined with rapid deployment forces located over-the-horizon, had been a failure because it had not deterred Iraq from invading Kuwait. Looking ahead, the over-the-horizon approach was also unlikely to contain Iran. Consequently, the US decided that the best approach was for it to base large naval and air forces in theatre, and also to pre-position equipment sufficient to field an armoured division once personnel were flown in.[55] To implement this strategy, the US signed agreements with the Arab Gulf states. On 23 July 1994, the US-UAE Defence Cooperation Agreement was signed,[56] which allowed the pre-positioning of US military equipment in the UAE.[57] The agreement, which has remained unpublished, is reported to include clauses which grant training facilities to US forces,[58] allow for joint training, provide the basis for US training/advisory assistance to the UAE and facilitate US arms sales to the UAE.[59] The agreement apparently did not provide an explicit security guarantee if the UAE was attacked. (In 2017, the US and UAE signed an updated bilateral defence cooperation agreement which is also unpublished.)

In 1991, the UAE also signed a defence accord with France. This appears to relate to just the provision of French military and civilian personnel to provide training, operational support and tactical advice on the Leclerc tanks, which had just been purchased by the UAE. In 1995, a more comprehensive joint defence cooperation pact

is reported to have noted that 'the hot pursuit clause essentially gave the US the right to overfly the UAE as needed'. D.B. Crist, 'Operation Earnest Will: The United States in the Persian Gulf, 1986-1989' (PhD thesis, Florida State University, 1998), p. 117.

54 'The Shield of the Nation', *Emirates News*, 2 December 1986, p. viii.

55 The key elements were an aircraft-carrier battle group (known as the 5th Fleet) with its headquarters in Bahrain, a large air presence in Dhahran, and pre-positioned equipment for a Division (15-17,000 troops) divided up with a brigade each of Kuwait, Qatar, and the UAE.

56 A.H. Cordesman, *USCENTCOM and its Area of Operations: Cooperation, Burden Sharing, Arms Sales, and Centcom's Analysis by Country and Subregion* (Washington DC, 1998), p. 10.

57 In 1995, the UAE agreed to allow the pre-positioning for a US Army armoured/mechanised brigade consisting of 120 tanks and 70 AIFVs. In addition, US Navy equipment was pre-positioned at Jebel Ali port. Ibid.

58 In 1994, 2,000 Marines of the 15th Marine Expeditionary Unit trained in the UAE. W.E. Herr, 'Operation Vigilant Warrior: Conventional Deterrence Theory, Doctrine and Practice' (Air University, Maxwell Air Force Base, 1996).

59 K. Katzman, R.F. Grimmett, *United Arab Emirates: U.S. Relations and F-16 Aircraft Sale* (Washington DC, 2000), p. 3.

was signed between France and the UAE. In 1996, the UAE also signed a Defence Cooperation Accord with the United Kingdom. At that time, the agreement represented the United Kingdom's largest defence commitment outside NATO.[60] Neither the 1991 and 1995 French accords nor the 1996 United Kingdom agreement have been published.

The strengthening of relations between the UAE and Western powers increased during the 2000s. Following the 2001 US-led invasion of Afghanistan, the UAE provided some Western nations with facilities from which they could operate. The number of foreign states accessing facilities in the UAE increased with the 2003 invasion of Iraq. Table 9 lists all the foreign states accessing facilities in the UAE between 2001 and 2020.

The late 2000s saw several nations establish facilities in the UAE, notably France and Australia, both of whom made the UAE their regional military headquarters. Following increased regional instability across the Middle East, in 2013 the British also established a permanent presence in the UAE, for the first time since 1975.[61] By the time ISIS had made significant military advances in Syria and Iraq in 2014, the countries with military facilities in the UAE had reduced to four – the US, Australia, France and the United Kingdom. For these countries, UAE facilities were important to their anti-ISIS interventions, as well as other regional security tasks such as maritime surveillance, maritime patrols and supporting activities in other theatres, such as Afghanistan. More broadly, the UAE-provided facilities serve as staging posts for transport between the foreign country and activities in the Middle East and Horn of Africa.

The UAE facilities provided to the US are the most important for providing a balancing effect. Currently, these include the Al Dhafra Air Base, which is the busiest American base in the world for surveillance flights and is home to nearly 4,000 US personnel, the UAE's Jebal Ali port, which is the busiest US Navy port of call,[62] and Fujairah Port. The UAE also makes its training facilities available to US forces.[63] The US presence in the UAE plus the UAE's participation in all US coalition actions over the last 20 years – the 1990-91 Gulf War, Bosnia-Kosovo, Somalia and Afghanistan, with the 2003 US-led invasion of Iraq the only exception – has seen the UAE become

60   UAE Ministry of Foreign Affairs and International Cooperation. 'Embassy of the UAE in London: Bilateral Relations' n.d. <www.mofa.gov.ae/EN/DiplomaticMissions/Embassies/London/AboutEmbassy/Pages/BilateralRelations.aspx>

61   The British military facility permanently staffed by British service personnel in the UAE in Sharjah at the old RAF base. It was the location of the British Military Advisory Team from 1971 to 1975. A. Yates and A. Rossiter, 'Military Assistance as Political Gimmickry? The Case of Britain and the Newly Federated UAE', *Diplomacy & Statecraft*, (2020 (in press)).

62   M. Wallin, *U.S. Military Bases and Facilities in the Middle East: Fact Sheet* (2018), p. 10.

63   The US military's first use of a UAE training facility appears to have been in October 1990 when the US Marines started training at Al Hamra. R.J. Brown, *U.S Marines in the Persian Gulf, 1990-1991: With Marine Forces Afloat in Desert Shield and Desert Storm*, 2000), pp. 50-52.

'the foremost US military partner in the Arab world', according to the Gulf scholar, Kristian Coates Ulrichsen.[64]

Table 9: Facilities used by foreign forces in the UAE, 2001-20

Country	Period of operation	Facilities used	Principal activities
Australia	2003-	Minhad Air Base	Logistics Maritime surveillance Regional command Theatre specific training Air strike
Canada	2002-10	Minhad Air Base	Logistics Maritime reconnaissance
European group made up of Belgium, Denmark, France, Germany, Greece, Italy, the Netherlands, and Portugal	2020-	Zayed Port Naval Base	Headquarters of the European Maritime Surveillance Mission in the Strait of Hormuz[65]
France	2009-	Zayed Port Naval Base	Logistics, regional command
		Al Dhafra Air Base	Air strike
		Zayed Military City	Theatre specific training
Italy[66]	2002-	Al Bateen Air Base Minhad Air Base	Logistics
Netherlands	-present[67]	Minhad Air Base	Logistics

64   Ulrichsen, *The United Arab Emirates: Power, Politics and Policy-Making*, p. 146. This has not been without cost to the UAE, as at various times there have been a backlash against the US allies. J.R. Macris, *The Politics and Security of the Gulf: Anglo-American Hegemony and the Shaping of a Region* (London, 2010), p. 236.

65   The goals of the European Maritime Awareness Mission in the Strait of Hormuz (EMASoH) are to expand participating partners' capability for autonomous situation assessment, to monitor maritime activity and to guarantee freedom of navigation in the Gulf and the Strait of Hormuz. The mission is directed from the French naval facility in Abu Dhabi port. Government of France. 'The European mission is now operational in the Arabian-Persian Gulf', 5 February 2020 <www.gouvernement.fr/en/the-european-mission-is-now-operational-in-the-arabian-persian-gulf>

66   The Italian facility was originally located at Al Bateen Air Base before moving to Minhad Air Base in 2015. When established in 2002, the Italian unit was named 'Nucleo Aeroportuale Interforze' (Joint Airport Unit). In 2003 the unit's name changed to 'Reparto Operativo Autonomo' (7th Autonomous Operational Division) then 'Reparto Distaccato della 46 Brigata Aerea' (Detached Division of the 46th Air Brigade"), and then in Task Force Air.

67   The Netherland's Forward Support Element Mirage at Minhad Air Base has two main missions: (1) providing logistics support to detachments of the Marine Corps which provide anti-piracy protection for Netherland-flagged merchant vessel; (2) providing aircraft handling for Dutch military aircraft, notably the KDC-10 transport aircraft. The Forward Support Element Mirage element is currently a four-person detachment.

Country	Period of operation	Facilities used	Principal activities
New Zealand	2004-	Minhad Air Base	Maritime reconnaissance Logistics
United Kingdom	2013-	Minhad Air Base	Air strike Maritime reconnaissance Theatre specific training
United States	2001-	Al Dhafra Air Base	Reconnaissance, air strike
		Al Bateen Air Base	Support
		Jebal Ali Port Fujairah Port	Logistics, port visits
		Fujairah International Airport	Logistics

Core mission 2: Protecting the rulers and their families

Threats to a ruler have historically come from his own family, typically in the form of assassination, or in the form of a collective decision by the family to replace him with another family member.[68] Historically, the rulers have mitigated this threat by surrounding themselves with loyal armed retainers, commonly members of tribes closely allied with the ruler, or foreigners including manumitted slaves. Foreigners have the advantage over tribesmen of not being swayed by loyalty to their tribe and hence not being influenced by tribal politics. Another advantage is that foreigners are generally unable to build a support base among the population from which to overthrow the ruler. The latter factor probably explains why Britons and Pakistanis, rather than non-Gulf Arabs, were often appointed to leadership posts in the early years of the Emirati armed forces. The concern with foreign Arab officers was that they could use their shared language and religion with nationals and other Arabs in the military as a basis for spreading revolutionary ideologies and, thus, create a power base from which to mount a coup.

From the 1960s onwards, the rulers replaced their armed retainers with military personnel because military-quality training and weaponry were needed to counter increasingly better armed and trained adversaries. These personnel were grouped into

---

68   Assassination had not been an uncommon mechanism for accession in previous centuries. In the early 1900s, the following Abu Dhabi rulers were assassinated by their family members: Hamdan bin Zayed (ruled 1912-22), Sultan bin Zayed bin Khalifa Al Nahyan (ruled 1922-26), and Saqr bin Zayed Al Nahyan (ruled 1926-28). The last family-related murder of a ruler in the UAE was in 1972 when the Ruler of Sharjah, Sheikh Khalid bin Mohammed Al Qasimi, was killed by his cousin, Sheikh Saqr bin Sultan Al Qasimi. Another family-related mechanism for removing a ruler is through the ruling family reaching a consensus that change is required. Examples of this are the 1965 replacement of the Ruler of Sharjah, and the 1966 replacement of the Ruler of Abu Dhabi.

a unit known as the Emiri Guard which is described in detail in Chapter 9. Emiri Guard forces have historically received the most up-to-date equipment in an armed force.

Very rarely has the military been used overtly in a family dispute. In recent decades, this has only occurred twice. Once was in 1987 when the Commander of Sharjah's armed force and brother of the Ruler used the military to claim the rulership of Sharjah (see Chapter 8 for details). The other was in in 2003 in Ras Al Khaimah, when its Ruler removed his eldest son as crown prince, a post he had held since 1963, and replaced him with another son. The eldest son claimed this action was illegal and demonstrations broke out in Ras Al Khaimah. Military units from Abu Dhabi Emirate were deployed to facilitate a peaceful transition.[69]

Core mission 3: Bolstering internal security

The internal security role of Emirati armed forces can be divided into two missions – preventing and defusing tribal disputes and maintaining public order.

The armed force's part in the first role has involved it interceding between disputing tribal groups and establishing an initial truce which would then allow negotiations and arbitration to occur. If the military representative on the scene could not broker a settlement, a senior political leader would become involved. Before 1971, this leader would typically have been a ruler or the local British political representative. After 1971, it was the Ruler, President, Vice President, or, in some rare cases, a regional head of state. To prevent the resurgence of a dispute, the military would actively patrol in the affected area, and sometimes establish a military base. This explains the presence of bases at places which have no strategic importance from a national defence perspective. Such bases were established at Ham Ham, Masafi and Khor Fakkan. The importance of the military in dealing with tribal disputes was noted by a visiting US military officer who had studied the Trucial Oman Scouts/Union Defence Force in the late 1960s and early 1970s. He observed that 'had it not been for the Scouts' almost constant presence along the unsettled boundaries [between tribes] they undoubtedly would have erupted into tribal clashes, and there was the strong possibility that those boundaries which were settled would have erupted as well'.[70]

Tribal disputes commonly arose due to disagreements over ownership and access to land, water and other resources. These could, and occasionally did, escalate into inter-Emirate conflict. A key reason for these disputes was a lack of defined borders

---

69   Khalid Al-Dhaheri, 'An Arabian Approach To Politics: Environment, Tradition and Leadership in the United Arab Emirates' (PhD thesis, University of Exeter, 2007), p. 246; C.M. Davidson, *After the Sheikhs: The Coming Collapse of the Gulf Monarchies* (Oxford, 2015), p. 184.

70   R.H. Barratt, 'British Influence on Arab Military Forces in the Gulf: The Trucial Oman Scouts' (MA thesis, American University of Beirut, 1972), p. 110.

between the Emirates. As detailed in Chapter 3, these were primarily addressed by the 1955 border survey by a British Foreign Office diplomat, Julian Walker. However, a number of areas remained contested and this led to sporadic protests and violence up to at least the 1990s.[71] Long-standing grievances and blood feuds are another cause of tribal disputes and these have continued up to relatively recent times. In March 1983 a dispute over the allocation of low-cost housing in the Masafi area triggered the re-emergence of a long-standing feud between the Fujairah and Ras Al Khaimah tribes. This reportedly resulted in several deaths. Armoured units and police had to close roads in the area for three days in order to prevent an escalation of the violence.[72]

The second internal security role of Emirati armed forces is to maintain public order. From the 1950s and, depending on the Emirate, up to as late as the mid-1970s, the military had the prime responsibility for containing strikes, protests, and riots. This was because they had the ability to deploy large numbers of personnel rapidly, while the police (where it existed) generally did not have a mobile force. Consequently, the military was trained in riot control and internal security plans were developed and practiced.[73] Currently, police forces have the primary responsibility for maintaining public order but, when their capabilities are overwhelmed, the military will provide support to the civil authorities. The most serious incident of public disorder in which the military was involved was in 1992. In December of that year, a large crowd of Hindus in the city of Ayodhya, India, demolished the 16th-century Babri Mosque. Muslims, particularly those from Pakistan and India, protested around the world, including in Sharjah, Dubai and Al Ain. The only violent protest in the UAE was in Al Ain,[74] and according to newspapers in Pakistan which published a statement from WAM quoting Mohammed Ahmed Al Mahmoud, the then UAE Ambassador to Pakistan, the Ambassador stated that in Al Ain 'Christians and Hindus and their places of worship were attacked and that policemen who tried to control the riots without use of force were killed or injured'. Many of the Al Ain protestors came from an informal settlement on the outskirts of Al Ain, known locally as Pathan town. It was home to over 40,000 mostly devout Muslim Pathans who came from the border areas between Pakistan and Afghanistan. Many of these were illegal migrants. A large military operation commenced in Al Ain and during their search for perpetrators, a

---

71   Al-Ulama, 'The Federal Boundaries of the United Arab Emirates', p. 21.
72   TNA FCO 8/3909: Haskell, UK Embassy in Dubai, 'UAE Internal Security', 22 March 1982; TNA, FCO 8/3909, Haskell, UK Embassy in Dubai, 'My Tel No 55: UAE Internal Security', 23 March 1982.
73   The heritage of anti-riot plans dates to the time when British-controlled forces operated in the Emirates. Probably the first one developed for Abu Dhabi Emirate was in 1958 and concerned Das Island where oil extraction and export infrastructure was being built by a large, expatriate work force. The plan was developed by the Trucial Oman Scouts and followed the May 1958 strike on the island. TNA FO 1016/624: Maj C.M. Rouse, GSO 2, Land Forces Persian Gulf, 'Trucial States Internal Security Scheme – Das Island', 15 July 1958.
74   There were also scuffles at Umm Al Nar.

number of weapons were discovered. The consequences of this incident included at least 1,300 Pakistanis being deported for rioting, the Pathan town being demolished, and much tighter immigration procedures being introduced in the UAE.[75]

In more recent decades, the UAE Armed Forces have been used to support police in combating worker riots. An example was in Ras Al Khaimah in 2008 when several thousand workers 'went on a rampage at their labour camp on Friday night to protest against the poor quality of food being served', according to an Indian media report. Some 3,000 were arrested and the UAE Armed Forces provided transport assistance.[76]

Following the 2011 Arab Spring uprisings which brought down or threatened a number of governments across the Middle East, the UAE Armed Forces' focus on internal security has increased. Some military units are prepared, trained and equipped to undertake internal security missions including riot control, operating vehicle checkpoints, searching people and places, and transporting/holding detainees.

Core mission 4: Nation building

Emirati armed forces have been and continue to support nation building. Their involvement has taken many forms over the decades. One of the first such uses was to generate support for the proposed federation of the Emirates in the late 1960s. Sheikh Zayed, as the key proponent of a federation, recognised that he needed to attract other rulers and their populations to this project. This required him to build up his prestige; a key method of doing this was to demonstrate his wealth, influence and ability to protect the other rulers and their citizens. The ruler's armed forces offered him a vehicle to achieve this. By purchasing the most modern military equipment and building an impressively large force, he could use it to impress others. He did this by inviting his fellow rulers to watch impressive firepower demonstrations and military parades, as well as dispatching his military to tour the other Emirates and Lower Gulf States to impress the public.

Once the UAE was formed, developing a new national identity which saw citizens giving their allegiance to the nation rather than to their tribe and respective ruler was critical. The armed forces have been important in helping to foster this national identity. This is illustrated perfectly in the following 2012 editorial in the *Nation Shield*, the UAE Armed Forces' military professional magazine:

75   'Many Killed in UAE violence Over Demolition', *The News International*, 21 December 1992; 'Muslim Expatriates in Al Ain Rioted on 6 December 1992 – Pakistani Deportation', *APS Diplomat Recorder – Arab Press Service Organization (ASPR)*, 26 December, 37: 26 1992.

76   D.P. George, 'UAE Arrests 3,000 Indian Workers for Rioting', *The Times of India*, 8 July 2008.

> Since the declaration of the UAE Federation our forces have played a key role in strengthening national identity ... and it is no wonder they are described as the 'incubator for men', not only in terms of training and military rehabilitation, but also in deepening loyalty and allegiance to our beloved land.[77]

A valuable mechanism in building this national allegiance in the early decades of the federation was to appoint senior members of the various Emirates' ruling families and tribes as officers in the military. This helped bind them to the success of the federation via a system of rewards and benefits. It also helped to reduce apprehension about the military and the federation more broadly as the officers' relatives now had both information on and some influence over the military. An early illustration of this was the 1971 appointment of the son of the Ruler of Dubai as the Minister of Defence, for at that time the Ruler of Dubai had significant reservations about the federation. Another was to appoint the sons of the rulers of key Emirates as regional commanders following the 1976 unification of Emirati armed forces, thus continuing the system of local influence in the, by now, national armed forces.

To build allegiance to the federation among the broader population, a strategy of recruiting military members from all the Emirates was actively pursued from the late 1960s. For those in the northern Emirates, employment in the armed forces was highly valued due to limited local job opportunities. Employment in the military offered not only valuable income and thus, brought wealth to the poorer Emirates, but it has also provided upward social mobility as members are promoted, gain skills, built connections and gain status. The loyalty-generating benefit of employment needs to be seen in terms of Emirati political tradition. Specifically, just as in pre-modern times, a ruler would buy loyalty by providing largesse to the tribe, thus employment in the armed force of a ruler was seen as a continuation of the traditional approach.

The military has also been a key socialisation mechanism by instilling national values and a sense of patriotism. This can be readily seen in the justification given for national service, introduced in 2014. A military spokesperson for its implementation noted at that time that national service makes 'a genuine step towards raising the awareness of Emirati youth to national principles, preserving the country's achievements and strengthening patriotism, as well as boosting discipline'.[78]

In recent years, the military has become even more important and is arguably central to building an Emirati national identity. The introduction of national service and operations undertaken in Syria, Libya and Yemen have resulted in increased reference to and reverence for the nation's armed forces. This became particularly apparent after the September 2015 attack in Yemen which resulted in the deaths of 52 Emirati

---

77   'The Armed Forces: An Active Role in Strengthening UAE', *Nation Shield*, 486, July (2012), p. 39.
78   Samir Salama, 'UAE National Service Draft Strategy Announced', *Gulf News*, 5 January 2015.

soldiers, leaving the nation in shock. According to the political scientist Kristian Ulrichsen, this led to a noticeable change in public discourse about the military. As he put it: 'dead soldiers were referred to as "martyrs" and the idea of a "blood sacrifice" rapidly gained common currency'.[79]

The military has also contributed to national pride through its use symbolically to demonstrate sovereignty and foster a more martial national identity. By participating in public celebrations, the military with its large size and modern weaponry makes a public statement that the state has the power to protect its interests and people and is not beholden to other states.

Use of ruler-controlled armed forces in public displays dates to the late 1960s when the Abu Dhabi military formed the centrepiece of the ruler's yearly accession day parades. The presence of the military in parades and celebrations has become far more prominent over the last decade. An example of this is the newly established annual Union Fortress Day. Starting in 2016, this is the nation's largest public military spectacle and is structured around a scenario in which elements from multiple services work together to defeat an enemy. Such activity reflects a desire to build public pride in the military as well as public support for military operations.[80]

The military has also contributed to nation building through exposing military members to 'modern' values and skills, such as rationality, facts-based decision making and strategic planning. In general, serving in a modern military engenders a positive outlook towards modernisation and, in the case of the Emirates, military service may have led to such values spreading to the broader community. This, in turn, may have helped to mute ongoing concerns over modernity and the loss of traditional values resulting from massive societal transformation since the 1960s. In some ways, the military has come to provide an important psychological bedrock for nationals as it is one of the few constants that has always been there ready to provide assistance and protection when other structures, such as tribal cohesion, have changed dramatically. In terms of education and skills development of nationals, the military has long played a major role. This has primarily occurred through large-scale training which has ranged from basic literacy to highly specialised skills, and from administration to leadership (see Chapter 6). Former military members are an important source of

---

79   Ulrichsen, *The United Arab Emirates: Power, Politics and Policy-Making*, p. 210.

80   This more recent use of the military in building national identity is not unique to the UAE. It has become common across the Arab Gulf states and is part of government effort to promote national identity based around preserving traditions, language, popular lore and dress code. Imad K. Harb, 'Arab Gulf Military Institutions: Professionalism and National Development', in D.B.D. Roches and D. Thafer (eds.), *The Arms Trade, Military Services and the Security Market in the Gulf States: Trends and Implications* (Berlin & London, 2016), p. 161.

skilled Emiratis for both government and business and are often used by the rulers to fill senior government posts.[81]

Core mission 5: Supporting foreign policy

Military activities in support of foreign policy range along a continuum from of soft (co-optive) to hard (coercive) power, with an intermediate point being incentive (economic) power. As defined by Joseph Nye who popularised the concepts of soft/hard power, soft power involves getting 'others to want the outcomes that you want' and, more particularly, 'the ability to achieve goals through attraction rather than coercion'.[82] Hard power involves using coercion through threats and inducements so as to get 'others to act in ways that are contrary to their initial preferences and strategies'.[83] Incentive power involves rewards in return for support.[84] Figure 14 lists activities undertaken by Emirati armed forces along the soft-hard power spectrum, with Table 10 providing examples of each.

Over their history, Emirati armed forces have supported their respective rulers' foreign policy through undertaking soft and incentive power activities. Starting with the 1990-91 Gulf War, UAE forces have been used for hard power. Subsequent use of hard power includes the 1994 deployment for the protection of Kuwait;[85] the 2002 to 2014 involvement in Afghanistan;[86] as part of the NATO-led Operation Unified Protector in Libya (2011); in the Libyan civil war;[87] the anti-ISIS missions in Iraq and Syria (2014-15); and in Yemen as part of the Saudi-led coalition (2015 onwards) (see Appendix 7 for the full list).

The increasing use of the UAE Armed Forces in hard power activities in the 2010s reflects the UAE becoming 'far more hawkish in the politics of the Middle East', and its adoption 'a more muscular posture both regionally and internationally', according to the Middle Eastern scholar, Kristian Ulrichsen.[88] This view is echoed by a policy analyst at the Arab Gulf States Institute in Washington, Hussein Ibish, who has

---

81   For example, the last two Commanders-in-Chief of the Abu Police were former military officers. These were Major-General Mohammed Khalfan Mater Al Rumaithi (2014-19) and Major-General Faris Khalaf Khalfan Al Mazrouei (2019-).

82   J.S. Nye, *Soft Power: The Means To Success In World Politics* (New York, 2004), p. 5.

83   J.S. Nye, *The Future of Power* (New York, 2011), p. 11.

84   Gregory Winger, 'The Velvet Gauntlet: A Theory of Defense Diplomacy' (Institute for Human Services, 2014).

85   The UAE sent a squadron of fighter aircraft to Kuwait as part of the US Operation Vigilant Warrior. Cordesman, *USCENTCOM and its Area of Operations*, p. 10.

86   Ulrichsen, *The United Arab Emirates: Power, Politics and Policy-Making*, pp. 148-50.

87   J.M. Rickli, 'The Political Rationale and Implications of the United Arab Emirates' Military Involvement in Libya', in D. Henriksen and A.K. Larssen (eds.), *Political Rationale and International Consequences of the War in Libya* (Oxford, 2016).

88   Ulrichsen, *The United Arab Emirates: Power, Politics and Policy-Making*, p. 137.

described the UAE, along with Saudi Arabia, as assuming the position of the de facto leaders of the Arab world.[89]

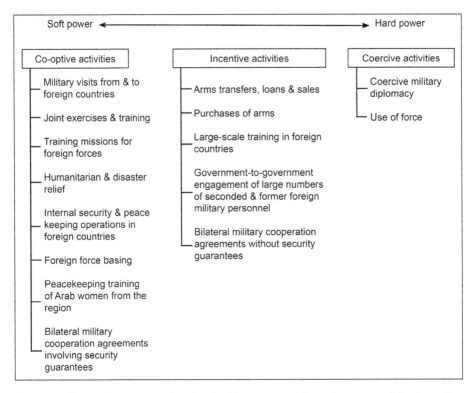

Figure 14: Types of activities undertaken by Emirati armed forces in support of foreign policy along the soft-hard power spectrum.[90]

89   Hussein Ibish, *The UAE's Evolving National Security Strategy* (Washington DC, 2017), pp. 47-48.
90   Heavily adapted from Winger, 'The Velvet Gauntlet: A Theory of Defense Diplomacy'.

Table 10: Activities undertaken by Emirati armed forces in support of foreign policy, 1965-2020

Military statecraft activity	Historical and more recent examples
Military visits from and to foreign countries	• In the years immediately preceding 1971, Abu Dhabi's navy undertook 'showing the flag' operations in the other Emirates, Bahrain and Qatar.[91] • In 2018, the UAE military participated for the first time in a Pakistan National Day parade in Islamabad.[92]
Joint exercises and training	• In 1983, UAE participated with the other five Arab Gulf states in the first GCC exercise held in Abu Dhabi Emirate.[93] • Commencing in 2011, some 2,000 Afghan army personnel and 70 air force pilots were trained in the UAE.[94] • In 2018, the UAE hosted the fifth Desert Tiger exercise which involved UAE and Malaysian land forces.
Training missions for foreign forces	• In 1969, Abu Dhabi offered to train Qatari naval personnel on its patrol boats.[95] • From 2015 to 2020, the UAE trained and equipped some 90,000 Yemeni fighters.[96]
Humanitarian and disaster relief	• In 1970, the first Emirates' military-supported humanitarian relief effort occurred when an ADDF Air Wing aircraft flew to Amman to provide medical support to King Hussein during the Black September conflict when Jordanian Armed Forces fought with the Palestine Liberation Organisation.[97] • In 2007, the UAE military aided the eastern Emirates following Tropical Cyclonic Storm Gonu.
Internal security and peace keeping operations in foreign countries	• In 1973, Abu Dhabi's military deployed infantry squadrons to Sohar in Oman, so as to allow the Omani police unit in Sohar to be sent to Dhofar as part of the counter-insurgency campaign.[98]

91   D.J. Gregory, ADDF Sea Wing Officer, 1969-75, interview, Woodstock, UK, 30 May 2016.
92   Ashfaq Ahmed, 'UAE Military Contingent to Participate in Pakistan National Day Parade', *Gulf News*, 19 March 2018.
93   The GCC joint military exercise 'Peninsula Shield' was held at Al Hamra in October 1983. It was the first GCC military exercise and involved a total of 3,600 GCC troops. TNA FCO 8/5468: Cameron, 'Annual Report for 1983 on the United Arab Emirates Armed Forces', 25 January 1984.
94   Carol Huang, 'Afghanistan's New Armed Forces Receive Training in the UAE', *The National*, 20 October 2011.
95   Local Intelligence Committee, Abu Dhabi. 'Record of the Abu Dhabi Local Intelligence Committee meeting held on 29 October 1969' in A. Burdett, ed. *Records of the Emirates 1966-1971: 1969* (Slough, 2002), p. 294.
96   Thomas Juneau, 'The UAE and the War in Yemen: From Surge to Recalibration', *Survival*, 62, 4 (2020), p. 193.
97   P. Horniblow, *Oil, Sand and Politics: Memoirs of a Middle East Doctor, Mercenary and Mountaineer* (Cumbria, 2003), pp. 218-28.
98   TNA FCO 8/2371: Colonel J.S. Agar, UK Defence Attaché, 'Intelligence Report No 10', 4 April 1974.

Military statecraft activity	Historical and more recent examples
Foreign force basing	• From 1971 to 1975, the British Military Advisory Team was based in Sharjah. • Since 1990, the US has based forces and equipment at several locations in the UAE.
Peacekeeping training of Arab women	• In 2018, UAE announced it had partnered with the United Nations to provide women from Arab region with three months basic military training followed by two weeks of peacekeeping instruction at Khawla Bint Al Azwar Military School for Women in Abu Dhabi. The initiative was designed to prepare female military officers for UN peacekeeping operations.[99]
Bilateral military cooperation agreements involving security guarantees	• Between the late 1850s and 1971, rulers of the Emirates signed treaties with Britain which gave it responsibility for the Emirates' external defence. • In 2017, US and UAE signed an updated bilateral defence cooperation agreement.[100]
Arms transfers, loans and sales	• In 1974, Abu Dhabi loaned armoured cars to Oman to support its counter-insurgency efforts.[101] • In 2012, the UAE supplied armoured vehicles to Libya.[102]
Purchases of arms	• In 1965, the Abu Dhabi Ruler placed his first significant order with Britain. It was for infantry weapons, armoured cars, munitions, and stores. • In 2016, the UAE bought some $773 million worth of weapons from the US.
Large-scale training in foreign countries	• In the mid-1960s, officer cadets from Abu Dhabi's military started attending officer education in the United Kingdom and Jordan. • Between 2012-13 and 2018-19, some 781 Emiratis per year undertook military courses in the US.[103]

99   WAM. 'Mohammed bin Rashid Forms the Central Military Grievance Committee of Dubai, Names Board Members', 25 September 2018 <wam.ae/en/details/1395302710146>

100 Phil Stewart, 'U.S. Signs New Defense Accord With Gulf Ally UAE', *Reuters*, 16 May 2017.

101 Six Saladins, complete with first line ammunition and 20 percent spares, were loaned with crew to the Sultan's Armed Forces. TNA FCO 8/2371: Agar, 'Intelligence Report No 10', 4 April 1974.

102 These were Cougar, Spartan and Cobra models made by Streit Group in Ras Al Khaimah. Panther T6 armoured vehicles produced by the UAE's Minerva Special Purpose Vehicles (MSPV) were also supplied. United Nations Security Council, *Letter Dated 4 March 2016 From the Panel of Experts on Libya Established Pursuant to Resolution 1973 (2011) Addressed to the President of the Security Council* (2016).

103 The figures were for financial year for 2012-13 was 1,041 students, for 2013-14 was 800, 2014-15 was 943, 2015-16 was 802, for 2016-17 was 743 students, for 2017-18 was 425 students, for 2018-19 was 715 students, and 2019-20 was 394 (provisional figure). US Department of Defense, *Foreign Military Training Fiscal Year: Joint Report to Congress* (Washington DC, 2012-13 to 2019-20 inclusive).

Military statecraft activity	Historical and more recent examples
Government-to-government engagement of large numbers of seconded and former foreign military personnel	• From 1965 to the mid-1970s, Abu Dhabi's military engaged large numbers of seconded British military officers. • Since 2011, the UAE Armed Forces have engaged a training team from the US Marine Corps. • Since 2011, a South Korean Army and Navy contingent, known as the Akh unit, has been based in Al Ain to provide military training in special warfare.[104]
Bilateral military cooperation agreements without security guarantees	• In the mid-1970s, the French and Abu Dhabi governments signed agreement for technical military support. • In 2017, UAE and Russia signed an MoU to develop jointly a fifth-generation light fighter.[105]
Coercive military diplomacy	• From 2 August 1990 to 17 January 1991, the UAE Armed Forces participated in Operation Desert Shield to convince Iraq to withdraw from Kuwait. • In 2010, a UAE Navy vessel fired warning shots, then detained a Saudi Arabian patrol boat's crew to enforce the UAE's territorial claim over waters off western Abu Dhabi Emirate.[106]
Use of force	• From 17 January 1991 to 28 February 1991, the UAE Armed Forces participated in Operation Desert Storm to evict Iraqi forces from Kuwait. • Since 2015, the UAE Armed Forces have been involved in Saudi Arabian-led intervention in Yemen.

Looking forward

Protecting sovereignty and territorial integrity is invariably the foremost priority of all armed forces. This has been and will remain the case for the UAE Armed Forces. Since the early 1990s, the UAE has achieved this through building up its own military and sheltering under the US security umbrella. Up until the late 2000s, the defence focus was squarely on protecting the country's land and territorial waters. Since that point, the UAE has pushed out its security boundaries as it has sought to reshape regional security and, along with its economic and political muscle, the UAE Armed Forces have been deployed outside the country to assist in this mission.

Looking forward, it is likely that the UAE's reliance on the US will decline for three main reasons – a perceived reduction in the level of interest in the Middle East by the US, the US's lack of thoughtfulness in, and commitment to, its own policy

---

104 Jeongmin Seo, 'South Korea–Gulf relations and the Iran factor', in J. Fulton and L.C. Sim (eds.), *External Powers and the Gulf Monarchies* (London, 2019), pp. 159-60; Jung Da-min, 'Service members stationed overseas celebrate Chuseok', *The Korea Times*, 13 September 2019.

105 S. Cronin, 'Idex 2017: UAE and Russia to Develop Fighter Jet', *The National*, 20 February 2017.

106 Spencer, 'Naval Battle Between UAE and Saudi Arabia Raises Fears for Gulf Security'; Al Mazrouei, *The UAE and Saudi Arabia*, pp. 167-69.

decisions, and the US's inconsistent approach to providing advanced military systems and munitions to allies. That said, the US will still remain an important security partner simply because there are no other nations that can realistically provide the balancing presence needed to counter Iran.

This means that increasingly the UAE's defence policy will be concentred around building greater self-reliance. However, partners will still play an essential role, and this role will vary depending on circumstances. For land defence, defence strategy will rely on the UAE Armed Forces providing the first line of defence, with the expectation that assistance will be rapidly provided by the USA, other major Western powers and Saudi Arabia. For maritime defence, defence strategy will involve avoiding direct confrontation and will instead encourage regional and global powers to provide a security buffer. The UAE military will only become involved in action in this buffer zone in extreme circumstances. Outside the Gulf, the UAE's defence strategy will be to build political alliances with other countries and actors so as to improve stability and security, as well as to advance its other interests. The UAE Armed Forces will support these alliances using the same means typically employed by middle to large powers, including training and education for foreign military and security personnel; joint exercises with foreign forces; ship visits; equipment provision; knowledge transfer; train, advising and accompanying missions; intelligence and combat support assistance; and operational deployments.

Regarding the military's second mission of protecting the rulers and their families, the period after the Arab Spring uprisings demonstrated categorically that the loyalty of nationals to the UAE's key rulers is both genuine and strong. This relationship appears not to have been damaged even following considerable Emirati casualties in Yemen. This can be taken to mean that the emphasis given to this mission will decline. This could see a reduction of the forces responsible for ruler protection.

Evidence over the last few decades has indicated that internal security threats from expatriates and domestic sources are decreasing. This is because the key cause of large-scale expatriate protests – late wages – has been substantially addressed by a new electronic wage payment system. The likelihood of violence arising from imported anger over a foreign religious outrage has also decreased as there is now greater awareness among expatriates that such action is unacceptable and will lead to deportation. Given also that the police forces have become more effective in handling riots, the military's role in bolstering internal security may reduce and become limited to logistic support, such as transport and detainee processing in the rare event of mass rioting.

Without doubt, the UAE Armed Forces will remain an important element in building national identity and demonstrating the sovereignty of the state domestically. It can be concluded that the use of the UAE military in this context is not about building a martial culture but about increasing national pride, cohesion, and shared values among Emiratis.

5

Equipping

Emirati forces have been equipped for several decades with the most advanced military systems. They have been extremely well funded due to the wealth of Abu Dhabi and Dubai. One unusual aspect of their arms purchases has been that they have been sourced from a range of countries, in contrast to other nations in the region. As a result, in recent decades, the UAE Armed Forces have been able to deploy forces of a quality which is normally only fielded by larger powers and, very unusually, show a blend of equipment from both Western countries and those which have traditionally been their adversaries, such as the Soviet Union/Russia and China.

An example of the UAE's arms purchasing policy is its multi-layered missile defence system. The system is designed to counter everything from unmanned aerial vehicles (UAVs) to missiles fired from air platforms, and from surface-to-surface missiles to intermediate range ballistic missiles. The UAE's air defence system is based on short-range air defence being provided by both shoulder-launched man-portable missiles and Russia's Pantsir-S1 combined missile and cannon system (ceiling of 15km, range of 20km); medium to long-range defence by both the US's MIM 23-Hawk missile system (ceiling of 20km, range of 50km) and the MIM-104 Patriot PAC-3 (ceiling of 24km, range of 20km); and, high-altitude area defence which is provided by the US's THAAD system (ceiling greater than 200km).

There are three main tendencies in the equipment purchasing policies of the Emirati armed forces: (1) substantial defence expenditure, (2) preference for advanced systems, and (3) multi-country sourcing of weaponry. These approaches can be seen in relation to three forces – the Abu Dhabi Defence Force, the Dubai Defence Force/Central Military Command and the UAE Armed Forces. These policies are not generally observable in the other forces, i.e. Ras Al Khaimah Mobile Force, Sharjah National Guard, Umm Al Quwain National Guard, and the Union Defence Force/Federal Armed Force. This is because the rulers of these forces did not have the necessary funds.

Substantial defence expenditure

Emirati governments have never published accurate and comprehensive expenditure figures for their armed forces. This is illustrated in the figures given in the Federal Budget on monies spent on the federally-controlled armed forces. The figures, which are under the category of defence and security, do not separate the two. In addition, the figures only include a portion of what is actually spent on defence and security. Specifically, they do not include monies provided by Abu Dhabi as the nation's capital to support military and internal security.[1]

What is known is that capital-provided funds make up the bulk of the funds spent on the armed forces. This is shown in the last reliable figures on federal expenditure, which are from 2007 and were produced by the IMF. It reported that UAE income for federal operations consisted of three sources: (1) profit generated from federal enterprises, plus fees and charges, (2) grants from Abu Dhabi and Dubai Emirates, and (3) Abu Dhabi funding of federal services in its role as the UAE's Capital. In 2007, (1) was 20.1 billion dirhams, (2) was 14.4 billion of which Abu Dhabi Emirate provided 13.2 billion (i.e. 92 percent) and Dubai Emirate 1.2 billion (i.e. 8 percent), and (3) was 31.3 billion. The first two income sources were reported in federal accounts and totalled 34.5 billion. The last source was not included in the federal accounts. This off-account 31.3 billion contribution was 'mainly defence and security outlays', according to the IMF.[2] The official federal expenditure on salaries, goods and services for 2007 was 25.5 billion.[3] Only a small part of this would have been defence expenditure as the federal government provides a range of other functions, such as education, infrastructure and health care. Comparing the Capital's off-account 31.3 billion contribution to federal defence/security services with the total official federal expenditure of 25.5 billion means that the Capital is highly likely to pay for the vast bulk of the UAE Armed Forces.

Given the lack of defence expenditure figures provided by Emirati governments, alternative sources of information need to be relied upon. The most commonly used data available is that provided by Stockholm International Peace Research Institute (SIPRI). SIPRI notes that military expenditure figures are 'uncertain and lacking in transparency' and, consequently, they can only make educated guesses.[4] While SIPRI figures may not be definitive, they do provide the best approximate estimate of the scale of defence spending in the UAE. SIPRI's military expenditure figures are only available for the period 1997 to 2014 (as of August 2019); these are shown in Table 11.

1   For a discussion of funding from Abu Dhabi in its role as the nation's capital verses
      funding from the Federal Government, see Yates, 'Challenging the accepted understanding
      of the executive branch of the UAE's Federal Government'.
2   International Monetary Fund, *United Arab Emirates: IMF Country Report No. 09/120*
      (Washington DC, 2009), Statistical Appendix, p. 13.
3   Ibid., Statistical Appendix, p. 12.
4   SIPRI. 'Military Expenditure Data: 1988–2018' <www.sipri.org/databases/milex>

Table 11: UAE military expenditure figures, 1997-2014[5]

Year	Military expenditure as percentage of gross domestic product	Military expenditure as percentage of government spending
1997	6.80%	19.20%
1998	8.60%	20.60%
1999	7.70%	20.70%
2000	8.30%	26.20%
2001	5.60%	22.20%
2002	4.90%	22.90%
2003	4.70%	23.40%
2004	4.60%	26.00%
2005	3.70%	23.20%
2006	3.20%	20.60%
2007	3.30%	18.60%
2008	3.70%	16.70%
2009	5.50%	15.60%
2010	6.00%	18.70%
2011	5.50%	17.50%
2012	5.10%	17.40%
2013	6.00%	19.90%
2014	5.60%	17.00%

These figures show large expenditure in recent decades as a proportion of both gross domestic product (GDP) and total government spending. Specifically, during the period 1997 to 2015, the UAE's defence budget averaged 5.5 percent of GDP.[6] This places the UAE in the top five countries globally for defence spending. Over this period, the UAE's average military expenditure as a percentage of government spending was 20.36 percent, again placing it in the top five globally. Other sources suggest that these figures are probably reliable. A leaked 2006 report by the US Ambassador to the UAE, for instance, stated that between 2000 and 2006 defence spending accounted for 41 percent of federal-level expenditure.[7] Other sources would seem to indicate that this high level of spending has not been restricted to this time period, either. In 1982 the CIA considered that the UAE was sixth in the world in terms of the ratio of military expenditure to central government expenditure.[8] A

5   Ibid.
6   Ibid.
7   Wikileaks, Sison, [untitled cable Abu Dhabi 00003851 001.2 of 006], 2 October 2006.
8   US Arms Control and Disarmament Agency, *World Military Expenditures and Arms Transfers 1972-1982* (Washington DC, 1984), pp. 1, 5.

1983 report by the United Kingdom Defence Attaché to the UAE stated that defence spending accounted for 51 percent of federal-level expenditure.[9]

In terms of defence equipment, the UAE has long been one of the world's largest importers. Between 2006 and 2010, the UAE was the world's sixth largest conventional arms importer, accounting for 4 percent of the world's total major arms imports.[10] Between 2012 and 2016, the UAE was the third largest importer, accounting for 4.6 percent of the world's total.[11] The Emirates' total arms imports since 1968 are shown in Figure 15. The figures show that there was a steady rise in imports between the 1970s and late 1980s, with a large jump in the late 1980s to late 1990s, and another in the mid-2000s and early 2010s. These correlate with increases in perceived insecurity on the part of the UAE's leadership.

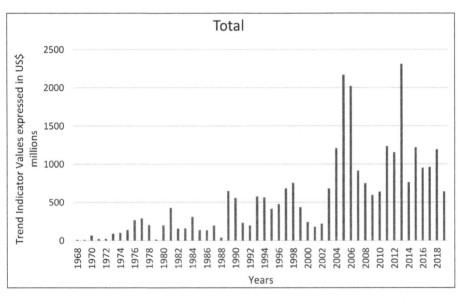

Figure 15: Arms imports to the Emirates in US $ millions, 1968-2019.[12]

9   TNA FCO 8/5468: Cameron, 'Annual Report for 1983 on the United Arab Emirates Armed Forces', 25 January 1984.
10   SIPRI, *Trends in International Arms Transfers*, 2011), pp. 3, 7.
11   Ibid., pp. 5, 7.
12   Arms imports are attributed to the year when the equipment is delivered not ordered. These deliveries are typically one to three years after a contract is signed, but in some cases have been up to a decade later. SIPRI. 'Arms Transfers Database (recipient/supplier)', 2018, <www.sipri.org/databases/armstransfers>. The value of arms imports is given as SIPRI Trend Indicator Values (TIVs) expressed in US$ million at constant (1990) prices. The TIV was developed as a measure to calculate the volume of international transfers of major weapons. The figures used are based on the known unit production costs of weapons and is intended to represent the transfer of military resources rather than the financial

Table 12 provides an overview of arms imports broken down by weapons category. It reveals that aircraft and missiles are the two largest weapons categories, followed by armoured vehicles and ships. Peaks in expenditure correlate with one or two significant orders. For example, the purchase of aircraft fleets accounted for part of the peak in the mid-1980s to mid-1990s, as well as from the early 2000s to the mid-2010s. Armoured vehicle purchases were significant in the 1990s, as were ship and air defence systems in the early 2010s.

Since 1971, the largest proportion of the defence acquisition budget has been directed towards air and air-defence forces, followed by land forces and, finally, naval forces. Over the last decade, in descending order, the greatest expenditure has been on Air Force and Air Defence, followed by Joint Aviation Command, Land Forces, Presidential Guard and finally Navy.[13]

Table 12: Arms imports to the UAE by weapons category in US$ million, 1971-2018[14]

Category	1971-75	1976-80	1981-85	1986-90	1991-95	1996-2000	2001-05	2006-10	2011-15	2016-18	Total
Aircraft	302	385	526	804	699	699	3,243	3,158	2,373	239	12,428
Air defence systems	0	199	23	198	10	10	0	352	943	250	1,985
Armoured vehicles	14	126	227	12	722	722	343	112	226	547	3,051
Artillery	0	48	19	28	141	141	7	25	44	14	467
Engines	0	4	16	6	7	7	31	28	113	65	277
Missiles	54	88	87	188	305	305	828	962	1,715	1,729	6,261
Naval weapons	0	10	20	8	3	3	0	0	12	11	67
Other	0	0	0	0	0	0	0	0	30	0	30
Sensors	0	36	85	140	35	35	22	162	138	138	791
Ships	25	100	191	205	76	76	0	62	931	376	2042
Total	393	992	1,193	1,589	2,000	2,000	4,473	4,861	6,525	3,368	27,394

value of the transfer. Consequently, the figures may be different from the recorded official value of the transfers. SIPRI. 'SIPRI Arms Transfers Database – Methodology', 2018, <www.sipri.org/databases/armstransfers/background>.

13   International Trade Administration US Department of Commerce, *2016 Defense Markets Report Regional and Country Case Study: Middle East* (Washington DC, 2016).

14   Figures are SIPRI Trend Indicator Values (TIVs) expressed in US$ million at constant (1990) prices. SIPRI. 'Arms Transfers Database (weapons category)', 2019 <www.sipri.org/databases/armstransfers>

Preference for advanced systems

A dominant driver of military equipment procurement has always been a desire to obtain the most advanced systems. The most obvious reason for this is to develop a force with a qualitative edge over potential adversaries in order to deter aggression, and should a conflict break out, achieve a quick solution with minimal damage to the UAE while inflicting unacceptable losses on the enemy. However, other important reasons for the purchase of advanced systems have been to demonstrate political power in the region and to use the prestige of possessing advanced armed forces as a way of attracting allies (see Chapter 4, Core mission 4).[15] More recently, it has been seen as a route to reducing manpower. There are, of course, other acquisition objectives. These include obtaining value for money through equipment life extension, such as occurred in the 2016 upgrade of the 1980s-designed Leclerc main battle tanks through the fitting of reactive armour.[16] Another is to build an interim capability. An example of this was the 1990s purchase of two old Dutch *Kortenaer* class frigates, which was partially justified as a way of building up the expertise needed for the advanced *Baynunah* missile frigates the UAE Navy was planning to introduce in the 2000s.[17]

The preference for advanced systems dates to the early days of the Emirati armed forces. In 1968, when the Ruler of Abu Dhabi, Sheikh Zayed, was considering which fighter aircraft to buy, he expressed interest in obtaining the Electric Lightning supersonic fighter. This was remarkably ambitious given that his air force at that time consisted of a handful of propeller-driven light transport planes flown by expatriates. There were no Emirati pilots, nor were any under training.

While in the case of the Electric Lightning, the British Government convinced Sheikh Zayed to settle for a less modern aircraft, he was more successful in obtaining other advanced systems. This included equipment which had not entered service with its home force. In the late 1960s, he ordered British Ferret Mark 2/6 scout cars to carry Vigilant wire-guided anti-tank missiles. At that time, this combination had not been fielded by the British Army. Similarly, the UAE obtained the British 105mm towed L118 light gun in the mid-1970s before it entered service with the British Army.

Obtaining foreign equipment before it entered home service has continued to the present day. The UAE's F-16 E/F Block 60 Desert Falcons, which started arriving in

---

15   Saab notes the importance of prestige in defence procurement decisions by all Arab Gulf States and that understanding this is essential to putting procurement decisions in context. Bilal Y. Saab, 'The Gulf Rising: Defense Industrialization in Saudi Arabia and the UAE', 2014.

16   Below The Turret Ring. 'Up-Armored Leclerc Operational with UAE Army', 16 December 2017 <below-the-turret-ring.blogspot.ae/2017/12/up-armored-leclerc-operational-with-uae.html>.

17   Ian Davis and Steve Schofield, *Upgrades and Surplus Weapons: Lessons From the UK Disposal Sales Agency* (1997), p. 14.

2005, were a half-generation ahead of the F-16 C/D Block 50/52+ aircraft which then formed the backbone of the US Air Force. The UAE funded the F-16's development cost was because it was not able to get the far more capable Joint Strike Fighter F-35 Lightning II and needed to upgrade the aging F-16 to meet the mission requirements of the UAE. Another instance was the Russian Pantsir-S1 mobile short-range air-defence system which the UAE received around 2009,[18] three years before it entered Russian military service.[19]

To obtain advanced equipment which met local requirements, the UAE sometimes had to invest directly in its development. One reason for this was to obtain a capability that did not then exist, as occurred with the UAE's US$100 million plus investment in the development of the Pantsir-S1 system,[20] and the almost US$3 billion contribution to support the development and production of the F-16 E/F Block 60 Desert Falcons.[21] A second reason why the UAE invests in system development is to obtain a capability that, while currently available, cannot legally be sold to the UAE due to restrictions imposed by the manufacturer's government. As an illustration, the UAE funded the Al Hakim family precision-guided munitions for the Mirage fighter jets because the US was unwilling to sell existing and comparable weapons, or to integrate them into Arab aircraft, due to Israeli objections.[22]

The manpower-saving advantages of advanced equipment has also been a major rationale for this policy. This has been explicitly acknowledged; in 2012, the Navy Commander, Major-General Ibrahim Salem Al Musharakh, in explaining the vision for his force's future, stated: 'The Navy has to operate with a limited number of men, so we need to operate ships with advanced technological capabilities to compensate [for this limitation].[23]

The labour-saving value of such projects can also be seen in the UAE-built, Jobaria portable, multiple-cradle rocket launcher. This piece of equipment consists of just one vehicle which is manned by a crew of three, but can generate the same firepower as the UAE's traditional rocket battery made up of six vehicles manned by 30 operators.[24]

18   'APID-55 VTOL Minature UAV'. n.d., Airforce Technology

19   V. Shcherbakov, 'Pantsir: Guarding the Skies', *Army & Navy Review (Russia)*, 2017, pp. 54-55.

20   The contract signed in 2000 was reported to be valued at US$734 million which was for the supply of 50 Pantsir S1s. Shehab Al Makahleh, 'Moscow had Signed a $734m Contract to Supply 50 Pantsir-S1s to the UAE in 2000', *Gulf News*, 19 February 2013.

21   TNA WO 337/15: Trucial Oman Scouts, 'Trucial Oman Scouts Intelligence Summary No 61', December 1965.

22   B. Thomas and J. Lake, 'Innovation for and From the UAE', *Military Technology*, 2 (2017), p. 66.

23   Awad Mustafa, 'UAE Navy Goes High-tech to Thwart Pirates', *The National*, 11 December 2012.

24   Army Recognition, 'IDEX 2013 Jobaria Defense Systems Multiple Cradle Launcher' (2013).

Another example was the procurement in the mid-2010s of around 40 Volat MZKT-741351 off-road tank transporters. These 8×8 all-wheel drive vehicles consist of a prime mover, semi-trailer, and trailer. A single vehicle can carry three tracked and wheeled combat vehicles (Leclerc, BMP-3, Howitzer G6) which offers significant capacity improvements over tank transporters which can carry just one vehicle.[25]

While the strategy of obtaining advanced technology has obvious benefits, it also has significant disadvantages. One is that funding development of systems can lead to unique platforms being produced. These are invariably far more expensive to support and upgrade as the manufacturer cannot spread development costs across multiple buyers. This is the seen with the F-16 E/F Block 60 Desert Falcons which have become hugely expensive and difficult to sustain, as they have never been purchased by other forces.

Another problem is that sophisticated systems require better skilled personnel. This means that the time taken to develop the skilled operators is longer, which in effect means more people in the training cycle at any one time. More advanced systems also require more support and maintenance, so increasing the number and skill level of the required technicians. Generating these technicians not only means substantially longer training times but also demands recruits with a higher level of secondary schooling, notably in science, technology, engineering, and mathematics. Finally, many of these technicians need to have English, as foreign suppliers of sophisticated equipment rarely provide training or supporting documentation in Arabic. Foreign language ability is particularly important for those needing advanced skills, as these are often only taught in the equipment supplier's home country. The limited numbers of Emiratis with the required educational background and skills are prioritised as operators and deployable technicians, with expatriates being relied upon to provide support such as training, doctrine-development and depot level maintenance.

Multi-country sourcing of weaponry

Emirati armed forces have sourced their equipment from dozens of different countries (see Table 13). In addition to buying from the globally dominant defence exporting countries, the UAE has also purchased from numerous smaller nations, such as Austria, Brazil, Bulgaria, Finland, Indonesia, New Zealand, and North Korea. The top six exporting countries to the UAE have been France, US, United Kingdom, Germany, Italy, and Russia. No one country has dominated sales for more than a decade or so. In the 1960s, Britain was virtually the sole supplier of military

---

25   Belarus Government. 'UAE Testing Belarusian Combat Tank Transporters', 15 December 2016, <www.belarus.by/en/business/business-news/uae-testing-belarusian-combat-tank-transporters_i_50298.html>; Military-Today. 'MZKT-74135 Tank Transporter', n.d., <www.military-today.com/trucks/mzkt_74135.htm>.

equipment to the UAE, but in the 1970s it sold little to the UAE as France became the UAE's foremost supplier. In the 1990s, France was still a major supplier, yet so too were Russia, the US and the United Kingdom. Since the 2000s, the US has replaced France as the dominant seller. Israel is not included in the list although it has been a specialist equipment supplier for several decades.[26]

Table 13: Countries supplying arms to the UAE in US$ million, 1971-2016[27]

Country	1971-75	1976-80	1981-85	1986-90	1991-95	1996-2000	2001-05	2006-10	2011-15	2016	Total
Austria								12			12
Brazil		12									13
Bulgaria							18				18
Canada	4	53	23	5				2	54	7	148
China					14			6			20
Denmark									4	2	6
Finland								5	4	12	20
France	267	573	230	881	282	1,189	2,676	1,419	548	336	8,397
Germany	5	88	186	164	83	76	31	92	117	21	861
Indonesia					57						57
Italy		42	131	62	49			42	419	11	756
Libya								54			54
Netherlands				10	10	488	2				509
New Zealand									1		1
North Korea				44							44
Romania					40			40			79
Russia						652	380		402	270	1,703
Singapore			15	41				2	6		62
South Africa					117	1	1	19	41	20	199
Soviet Union				6							6
Spain			15	0					294		309
Sweden		16	10	20	7	24	0	60	241	17	394
Switzerland			114	10					122		246
Turkey						36	9	24	130	80	279
Ukraine							22				22
United Kingdom	49	206	264	57	357	207	4		66		1208
United States	69	13	196	291	331	211	1,712	2,690	4,205	773	10,490
Total	394	991	1,196	1,591	1,999	2,612	4,475	4,863	6,528	1,279	25,913

26   Aluf Benn, 'Israel Selling Military Wares to Mideast Countries, Britain Says', *Haaretz*, 11 June 2013.
27   Figures are SIPRI Trend Indicator Values (TIVs) expressed in US$ million at constant (1990) prices. SIPRI, 'Arms Transfers Database (recipient/supplier)'.

Four main reasons explain why the UAE's rulers have sourced weaponry from multiple countries.

The first reason – the best package of offerings based on capability, price, delivery times, support and sales effort – has been shown to be critical during the 1970s and 1980s by Simon C. Smith in his analysis of British archival sources. It is highly likely that this motivation continues to remain unaltered, although there are no accessible sources currently available which can confirm this. Smith has identified numerous examples where British officials had anticipated sales which subsequently were lost to competitors due to a better package being offered. Among the reasons for the successful sales were lower costs; much quicker delivery times; closer government-industry coordination in support of sales; equipment designed specifically for export; far greater and more assertive sales efforts; coordination and representation in the Gulf States; more flexible credit arrangements; regular visits to the Gulf States by the supplying countries' political leaders in support of sales; a greater range of products; and, superior after-sales support.[28]

The French were particularly successful in providing better packages. The British attributed France's success for the reasons just cited, as can be seen in the quote below. In addition, France manufactured equipment specifically for exports and it had a willingness to take equipment from their own armed forces for overseas sales. The French also appeared able to create the impression that they supported Arab aspirations.[29] Smith quotes a senior British Foreign Office official in 1981 lamenting the poor British effort in the Gulf:

> While the French offer the Arabs participation in building a whole generation of aircraft, marrying Pakistani and other technically qualified manpower with Saudi money and French design/manufacturing capability, we potter from Gulf State to Gulf State offering a single type, off the shelf, with no element of local manufacture/transfer of technology, and without imagination to find out, let along offer, what the customers really want.[30]

The second reason for 'multiple sourcing' has been that as buying a foreign country's equipment helps build interest and support from that country's elite, the more countries the UAE buys from, the more foreign support it can potentially create. This interpretation appears confirmed by the leaked assessment of the UAE military's procurement approach written by the US Ambassador to the UAE in 2006:

---

28   S.C. Smith, *Britain and the Arab Gulf after Empire: Kuwait, Bahrain, Qatar, and the United Arab Emirates, 1971-1981* (Oxon, UK, 2019), pp. 89, 91, 92, 133, 134, 138, 140, 151.
29   Ibid., p. 127, 133, 140, 151.
30   Ibid., p. 150-51.

Keeping multiple allies in the procurement game boosts economic ties as well as military cooperation with a broader range of potential partners. The UAE is strategically disinclined from consolidating its purchases ... The operating principle is that the UAE must have 'tentacles' in multiple international arenas ... 'defensive' procurement strategy goes well beyond 'defense spending' and includes commercial contracts of all sorts. Playing host to a significant U.S. investment in the oil sector can, for example, 'keep the attention of the White House' and ensure increased U.S. interest in UAE security. A diverse investment portfolio can therefore be a core strategic asset. You've got to shop around.[31]

Given that the most important countries in the field of arms exports are the five permanent members of the UN Security Council, this explains why the UAE places very large defence orders with all but one of them. The exception is China, although since the mid-2010s it has slowly been increasing its tally of purchasers; in fact, small volumes of Chinese military equipment had been purchased by the UAE before the 2010s.[32] The reasons for China receiving few defence orders from the UAE up to the late 2000s were characterised by the US Ambassador to the UAE as 'possibly due to China's generally inferior offerings in the defense arena, or the UAE may see other commercial avenues as more effective in bolstering ties with Beijing'.[33] Since 2010, the volume of Chinese military hardware procured by the UAE has increased, and has included UAVs, artillery systems and missiles.[34]

This defence spending pattern has been characterised as the 'security council procurement policy'. According to one US Ambassador to the US, this is because the 'UAE wants to show that it is a meaningful global player by engaging with the "big five" and spreading its wealth around within this influential group'.[35]

A third reason for the UAE's multi-country purchasing approach is that the rulers do not want to be viewed by other Arab leaders as being beholden to any one country, nor for their purchases to be viewed as indicating approval of a political position by the supplying country. This explains why the UAE purchased little military equipment from the US before the 1990s. As a CIA report from 1982 stated, while the 'UAE have expressed strong interest in obtaining US fighter aircraft ... differences over the Palestinian issue and growing Arab frustration over US support for Israel are creating

31   Wikileaks, Sison, '[untitled cable Abu Dhabi 00003851 001.2 of 006], 2 October 2006.
32   These included the Hongjian-8 (Red Arrow-8) anti-tank guided missile in the 1990s.
33   Wikileaks, Sison, [untitled cable Abu Dhabi 00003851 001.2 of 006], 2 October 2006.
34   Key purchases included the (1) 25 Wing Loong-1 Medium-Altitude Long-Endurance UAV (arriving 2013-17), (2) 15 Wing Loong-2 UAV (2017-18), 500 air-to-surface Blue Arrow-7 anti-armour missile (2017-19), (3) Norinco AH4 155 mm/39 calibre lightweight gun-howitzers (6 arrived in 2019), (4) GP6 laser-guided 155 mm projectiles, and (5) Norinco SR5 multiple rocket launchers (arrived in 2019) which fires 220 mm artillery rockets or King Dragon 60 laser and GPS-guided surface-to-surface missiles.
35   Wikileaks, Sison, [untitled cable Abu Dhabi 00003851 001.2 of 006], 2 October 2006.

internal pressure on the Saudis and other Gulf Arabs to put greater distance between themselves and the US'.[36] The report continued, noting that 'none of these regimes can afford to ignore Arab public opinion without undermining their credibility at home and leaving themselves vulnerable to Arab radical as well as Iranian-inspired subversion'.[37] This said, these statements require qualification in that the UAE has purchased some expensive US equipment, notably transport aircraft and helicopters. But these were bought via direct commercial sales arrangements, which do not have the political connotations of those sales which have gone through the Foreign Military Sales process.

A final reason for multi-country sourcing is that the rulers want to avoid the possibility of a supplying country being able to pressure the Emirates by threatening to withhold supply. Statements by rulers over the decades have emphasised this point. In the early 1970s, for example, Sheikh Zayed stated that to purchase weapons from one country alone would weaken a military, 'since it would place them under the control of a monopoly'.[38] In the mid-1980s, Sheikh Mohammed bin Rashid, Minister of Defence, in referring to the need to diversify sources of weapons stated, 'this way we can guarantee the independence of our political decisions'.[39] Or, to put it another way, as Sheikh Mohammed bin Zayed reportedly said in 2006, buying from multiple countries avoided putting all the country's eggs in one basket.[40]

The risk of an arms seller refusing to supply equipment was vividly illustrated in late 2017 when Norway suspended all exports of munitions and arms to the UAE due to its involvement in Yemen.[41] In this context, it can be seen that the US, due to its long history of restricting sales, presents a degree of risk to the UAE in its arms purchasing strategy. Not only has it occasionally refused to sell equipment, it has sometimes only agreed to provide downgraded export versions and/or added restrictive conditions in order to protect its own interests.[42] An early articulation of the US's restrictive

36   This report excludes an important reason for the limited interest in engaging with the US from the perspective of Sheikh Zayed. During the 1950s confrontation over Buraimi, the US supported the Saudis against Abu Dhabi. This issue continued to remain important decades later, as reflected in Sheikh Zayed's explanation of why the UAE had deep ties with the UK but not with the USA. The importance of this history was noted in TNA, FCO 8/3453, J.C. Moberly, 'My Tel No 352: UAE Security', 27 October 1980.

37   US Central Intelligence Agency, *Persian Gulf Security: The Iranian Threat* (Washington DC, 1982), p. 8.

38   I. Al Abed, P. Vine, and A. Al Jabali, *Chronicle of Progress: 25 Years of Development in the United Arab Emirates* (London, 1996), p. 94.

39   TNA FCO 8/6170: Michael Tait, UK Ambassador, Abu Dhabi to FCO, 'First Calls on the Rulers of the Northern Emirates', 19 May 1986.

40   Wikileaks, Sison, [untitled cable Abu Dhabi 00003851 001.2 of 006], 2 October 2006.

41   Norway had not allowed class A sales since 2010, and these and other military equipment exports were worth US$112.3 million. J.M. Olsen, 'Norway Suspends Arms Exports to UAE Amid War in Yemen', *AP*, 3 January 2018.

42   There are two main reasons for Washington denying requests to purchase US equipment. They are strict export controls and the Qualitative Military Edge policy. Saab, 'The Gulf Rising: Defense Industrialization in Saudi Arabia and the UAE', 2014.

approach occurred in 1978. The then US Ambassador to the UAE described this in his report on his country's approach to defence sales: 'we seek to avoid – and to encourage others to avoid – sale to UAE or to individual Emirates within the UAE of weapons and other types of equipment which because of their quantity, sophistication, or offensive nature would (1) create a destabilizing factor in the region or within the UAE itself, and (2) further tax already severely limited UAE military manpower capabilities'.[43]

An early illustration of the US refusal to sell the UAE equipment occurred in 1986. Following an attack on Abu Dhabi's Abu Al Bukhoosh offshore oil platforms by Iranian aircraft, the UAE expressed interest in purchasing Stinger man-portable surface-to-air missiles (SAMs).[44] The US declined to permit the sale, justified on the implausible grounds that the flames produced by the burning off of natural gas at the platform meant that the missile would become confused and crash into the oil platforms.[45] Subsequently, the UAE bought Russian portable SAM systems from 1986 which was the start of Soviet/Russian defence equipment penetration into the UAE.[46] The development of UAVs in the mid-2000s is yet another case of American sales conditions driving the UAE to partner with other countries. According to the UAE's Air Force and Air Defence Commander, Major-General Khalid bin Abdullah, the reason why the UAE worked with Austrian, South African and Swedish companies to develop and build UAVs rather than the US was because the Americans were sensitive about sharing UAV technology with the UAE.[47]

The F-16s the US sold to the UAE provide an example of the US imposing restrictions in the 1990s and 2000s which have had repercussions during the 2010s. A condition of that sale was that the weapons the aircraft carried could not conflict with the US State Department's Missile Technology Control Regime. This meant that the aircraft were forbidden to carry the non-US Black Shaheen cruise missile (a variant of

---

43   Wikileaks, F. Dickman, US Ambassador Extraordinary in Abu Dhabi, 'Security Assistance Reporting – First Annual Integrated Assessment – UAE', 25 July 1978.
44   TNA FCO 8/6177: Lt Colonel A.D. Defence Attaché Pratt, to MoD, 'Call on Sh Mohammed bin Zaid – 10 Dec 1986', 16 December 1986.
45   The real reason was Congressional opposition to selling military hardware. Crist, 'Operation Earnest Will: The United States in the Persian Gulf, 1986-1989', pp. 51-52. This was despite the weapon being the most appropriate and the fact that the US was then supplying the UAE with I-Hawk air defence system. The I-Hawk's utility for defending offshore oil and gas installations was limited. This was because it was designed for aircraft flying at higher altitudes rather than low flying aircraft attacking across the Gulf, as was the case in the Abu Bakhoush raid. Association for Diplomatic Studies and Training, *Country Reader: United Arab Emirates* (Arlington, 2019), pp. 80, 82.
46   These consisted of some 100 Strela-3/SA-14 (delivered 1986-87, 24 Mistral (delivered 1990), 500 Mistral (delivered 1993-94) and 400 Igla-1/SA-16 (delivered 1998-99).
47   'APID-55 VTOL Minature UAV'.

the British Storm Shadow).[48] This restriction continued at least to 2011 when it was a factor in the UAE's election of aircraft to be deployed in NATO's Operation Unified Protector in Libya.

Even when the US has been willing to sell its most sophisticated technology to the UAE, the conditions it applies can make the purchase unattractive. This is likely to be the case with the fifth-generation fighter aircraft, the F-35 Joint Strike Fighter (JSF). The UAE has long expressed an interest in obtaining the JSF, but the Obama administration refused to consider this due to the American commitment to preserving Israel's 'Qualitative Military Edge'.[49] This is a policy designed to ensure Israel maintains a military advantage in the region, in order that it is able to deter and defeat numerically superior adversaries. Israel has purchased JSFs which started to become operational in 2017.

In 2017, the Trump administration agreed to discuss the possibility of JSF sales to the UAE.[50] However, it is likely that the US will apply conditions to the UAE to maintain Israel's Qualitative Military Edge, despite the growing UAE-Israel relationship. A key condition will be that the UAE can only operate its JSFs through the JSF's cloud-based centralised computer management system, known as the Autonomic Logistics Information System (ALIS). Currently, Israel is the only country able to operate their aircraft unconnected to the ALIS. The ALIS is the gateway through which all data to the aircraft is transferred, including software updates, serviceability condition and mission planning packages. While ALIS offers great efficiency benefits, it allows the US to wield enormous control over JSFs. According to the military journalist, Joseph Trevithick, 'if the geopolitical environment in the Middle East were to change dramatically, pitting Israel and the UAE against each other for some reason, it would likely be far easier for the US to limit the latter country's ability to use its F-35s. The US government could quickly halt access to vital software updates and logistics support or even launch an active cyber-attack on the ALIS terminals in the Emirates to try and disable the aircraft or certain core functions.'[51]

The US imposes a condition of sale for certain equipment that require only approved nationalities to work on their equipment. This restriction is designed to limit the spread of information and technology. While Emiratis are generally allowed to work on US equipment, due to a lack of Emiratis with the required skills, expatriates

48   Karl P. Mueller, *Precision and Purpose: Airpower in the Libyan Civil War* (Santa Monica, 2015), p. 357. This explains why during the 2011 Operational Unified Protector mission in Libya, the UAE had to deploy alongside its five F-16E/F, six Mirage 2000-9DAD as these could carry Black Shaheen.

49   K. Katzman, *The United Arab Emirates (UAE): Issues for U.S. Policy* (Washington DC, 2019), p. 20.

50   B. Opall-Rome, 'Trump Could Let the UAE Buy F-35 jets', *Defense News*, 4 November 2017.

51   J. Trevithick, 'UAE Could Become the First Middle Eastern Country After Israel to Get the F-35', *The Drive*, 6 November 2017.

are needed. This requirement often means that only nationals from the equipment's supplying country, or from nations allied to the supplying country which already have the equipment, can work on a particular type of weapons system. This allows a further degree of control by the US over equipment it supplies to the UAE.

Looking forward

As defence expenditure invariably increases in times of insecurity, and this will be the situation in the UAE's region for the foreseeable future, it is logical to expect that the current substantial level of spending on defence will continue. There appears to be no great internal pressure challenging the policy of maintaining a large and costly military organisation; nor is there any notable financial pressure to reduce defence spending given that Abu Dhabi can call upon its enormous sovereign wealth funds to compensate for any shortfall in government revenue arising from oil price volatility.[52] Finally, large defence spending is recognised by the UAE leadership as being important to creating interest in, and support for, the UAE by global powers.

The demand for advanced systems is also likely to continue as the UAE Armed Forces seek to maintain a qualitative edge over potential adversaries. Recent tensions and conflicts have highlighted areas of particular importance in the improvement of capabilities. Some are obvious, such as improved awareness of the air and maritime domain to allow the identification of hostile preparations and defeat attacks out to at least 1,000km (i.e. as far as Yemen). Others are less visible but equally important, such as building effective and robust systems to ensure a high-level of equipment and munitions availability. Future acquisition is expected to follow a more strategically orientated capability development process driven by the Ministry of Defence.

In terms of sourcing, the US appears likely to remain the main supplier of imported military equipment in both the near and medium term. However, over time other countries will inevitably obtain an increasing percentage of foreign orders due to concerns about the reliability of the US commitment to the UAE, America's willingness to provide its advanced technology, and the increasing influence of other major powers in the region – notably Russia and China. Increasing defence purchases from these countries would allow the UAE to reinforce its bilateral relations as well as improve diversity of supply. Finally, the UAE will not hesitate to buy from any country which has the best solution to a specific need.

---

52   The disconnect between defence spending and oil income has been noted by the Arab Gulf States Institute in Washington when it reported that, as of late 2017, despite the decline in government revenue since the 2015 oil price drop, defence expenditure has been largely quarantined. However, while there has been 'some reduction in military spending … [it is] not as sharp as the oil price decline'. K.E. Young and M Elleman, *Unlocking Growth: How the Gulf Security Sector Can Lead Economic Diversification* (Washington DC, 2017), p. 3.

The small proportion of the UAE Armed Force's equipment that is obtained locally at present will almost certainly increase. This trend is being driven by a recent consolidation of the UAE defence industry, as well as a politically-endorsed strategy to grow defence exports. Partnerships with Saudi Arabia and Egypt will see a growing regional defence industry, which will not only supply equipment for the UAE Armed Forces but provide political leverage with neighbouring countries.

6

Manpower

An enduring and significant challenge which all Emirati armed forces have faced has been recruiting and retaining sufficient numbers of nationals with the requisite skills. This challenge has arisen because of the small size of the population of nationals compared to the large size of the forces required by the rulers; the mismatch between the education and skills of the population versus what is needed to support advanced military systems; and certain military policies and practices which have aggravated manpower shortages.

This chapter considers the three solutions which have been pursued to overcome the challenge: (1) improving education and training for nationals; (2) engaging foreigners; and (3) the recruitment and retention of nationals.

Manpower challenges

Over the last five decades, the size of the Emirati armed forces has generally been large compared to the total population, and extremely large if only compared to the number of nationals.

The exact ratio of armed forces to population cannot be calculated as Emirati governments have never published comprehensive figures on the strength and composition of their armed forces. Typical is the 2011 statement by Major-General Juma Ali Khalaf Al Hamiri, Head of Human Resources, and Administration at the General Headquarters of the UAE Armed Forces. He stated the UAE has 'over 40,000 Emirati personnel at a high state of readiness'.[1] This statement lacks essential detail to make the figures meaningful, such as whether this figure constitute the total establishment strength, or just those military members that serve in combat formations. While figures can be derived based on official UAE statistics, these are often approximate as necessary information is missing. For example, a 2009 report by the

---

1   'UAE Armed Forces Have Developed Extensively Since Their Establishment 40 Years Ago – Official', *Gulf News*, 16 May 2011.

UAE's National Bureau of Statistics stated that 2.3 percent of all employed citizens work in the Armed Forces.[2] However, the report does not state how many citizens are employed, so converting this percentage to a number is not possible.

As a result of the lack of official UAE statistics, other figures need to be employed to estimate the forces' size. The most widely cited public sources are *The Military Balance* published by the International Institute for Strategic Studies (IISS) and publications of the Center for Strategic and International Studies (CSIS). Other sources are the US Arms Control and Disarmament Agency which was absorbed into the Department of State in 1999, and declassified or leaked US and UK government estimates. Of these sources, the only ones which contain detailed information down to unit strengths are the declassified British diplomatic reports which are available up to 1983. The precise nature of the figures given implies a reasonable degree of accuracy. The source of information is rarely stated, but it is reasonable to assume that the sources in most cases were the rulers themselves, their senior staff, other diplomats, or expatriates serving in Emirati armed forces.

Table 14 lists the manpower figures from the various sources mentioned above. It does not include national service personnel, of which around 70,000 have been trained since 2015 (see Chapter 9).

Table 14: Reported manpower figures for Emirati armed forces, 1965-2016

Year	Cordesman[3]	IISS[4]	US Arms Control and Disarmament Agency/ Department of State[5]	Declassified or leaked government figures
1965				158[6]
1969				2,190[7]
1972			10,000	

2   UAE National Bureau of Statistics, *UAE in Figures, 2009* (Abu Dhabi, 2009), pp. 19, 41.
3   A.H. Cordesman and A. Wilner, *The Gulf Military Balance in 2012* (Washington DC, 2012), pp. 17-18.
4   The World Bank. 'Armed Forces Personnel, Total 1985-2015', n.d. <data.worldbank.org/indicator/MS.MIL.TOTL.P1?end=2015&start=1985>
5   Except where noted, figures for 1972 to 1982 are taken from US Arms Control and Disarmament Agency, *World Military Expenditures and Arms Transfers 1972-1982*, p. 48. Figures for 1995 to 2005 are taken from Bureau of Arms Control US Department of State, Verification and Compliance, *World Military Expenditures and Arms Transfers, 2005* (Washington DC, 2005). Figures for 2006 to 2016 are taken from Bureau of Arms Control US Department of State, Verification and Compliance, *World Military Expenditures and Arms Transfers, 2018* (Washington DC, 2018).
6   This was for the ADDF in June 1966. TNA FO 371/185551: A.T. Lamb, Political Agent Abu Dhabi to P. Gent FO, [untitled letter], 7 June 1966.
7   Author's collection, Records Office Force Headquarters Abu Dhabi Defence Force, 'A Statistical Survey of Records Office Information Covering the Period 1 April 1968 to 31 March 1969', 1969.

Year	Cordesman[3]	IISS[4]	US Arms Control and Disarmament Agency/ Department of State[5]	Declassified or leaked government figures
1973			11,000	16,655[8]
1974			19,000	
1975			21,000	
1976			27,000	24,800[9]
1977			25,000	
1978			25,000	
1979	25,150		25,000	
1980	25,150		44,000	
1981	42,500		44,000	50,600[10]
1982	48,500		44,000	
1983	49,000			52,900,[11] 40,000[12]
1984	43,000			
1985	43,000	43,000		
1986	43,000			
1987	43,000			
1988	43,000			45,500[13]
1989	43,000	43,000		
1990	44,000	66,000		
1991	44,000	66,000		
1992	54,500	55,000		
1993	57,500	55,000		
1994	61,500	60,000		
1995	70,000	71,000	60,000	

8   This consisted of 12,332 in the ADDF, 2,623 in the UDF, 1,130 in the DDF, and 270 in SNG (plus 300 in the RAKMF who were not included in Attaché report). TNA FCO 8/2371: Colonel J.S. Agar, UK Defence Attaché, 'Annual Report for 1973 by Defence Attaché United Arab Emirates', January 1974.

9   This consisted of 15,000 in the Western Military Command, 2,600 in the Central Military Command, 700 in the Northern Military Command, 4,600 in the Al Yarmouk Brigade, 400 in the UAE Navy, and 550 in the UAE Air Force. TNA FCO 8/2897: Colonel T.N. Bromage, UK Defence Attaché, 'Annual Report for 1976 on the United Arab Emirates Armed Forces', 30 January 1977.

10 TNA FCO 8/4385: Lt Colonel J.P. Cameron, UK Defence Attaché, 'Annual Report for 1981 on the United Arab Emirates Armed Forces', 31 January 1982.

11 TNA FCO 8/5468: Cameron, 'Annual Report for 1983 on the United Arab Emirates Armed Forces', 25 January 1984.

12 Office of Near East and South Asian Analysis US Central Intelligence Agency, *Military Capabilities of the Smaller Persian Gulf States* (Washington DC, 1984).

13 Committee on Armed Services US Senate, *Department of Defense Authorization for Appropriations for Fiscal Year 1989: Hearings Before the Committee on Armed Services, United States Senate, One Hundredth Congress, Second Session, on S. 2355* (Washington DC, 1988), p. 239.

Year	Cordesman[3]	IISS[4]	US Arms Control and Disarmament Agency/ Department of State[5]	Declassified or leaked government figures
1996	70,000	65,500	60,000	
1997	70,000	65,500	60,000	
1998	70,000	65,500	65,000	
1999	64,500	65,500	65,000	
2000	64,500	66,000	62,000	
2001	65,000	66,000	70,000	
2002	65,000	41,500	60,000	
2003	41,500	50,500	45,000	
2004	50,500	50,000	45,000	
2005	50,500	51,000	45,000	
2006	50,500	51,000	65,000	
2007	51,000	51,000	65,000	
2008	51,000	51,000	65,000	60,000[14]
2009	51,000	51,000	65,000	
2010	51,000	51,000	65,000	
2011	51,000	51,000	65,000	
2012	51,000	51,000	65,000	
2013		63,000	65,000	
2014	51,000	63,000	65,000	
2015		63,000	65,000	
2016	62,300[15]		65,000	

Figures from different sources for the same year show considerable variation. For example, for 1973, the British figures are 16,655, while the US ones are 11,000. This translates to the British numbers being 51 percent higher than the US. This gap is less in 1981 where the British figures were 15 percent higher. In 2012 the IISS figures were 51,000 and the US ones were 65,000, making the US figures 27 percent higher than the IISS ones.

The point of highlighting the variation in figures is to remind the reader that military personnel numbers should be treated with caution. They also need to be read in context, such as whether the figures are actual or the establishment strength. Anecdotal reports across the decades point to Emirati military units being consistently under-strength, so if the figures are based on establishment strength, they may significantly over estimate the size of the force. In addition, if the figures are based on actual strength, it still may mean that personnel are not actually in their assigned

14   Wikileaks, Michele J. Sison, US Ambassador to the UAE, 'U/S Burns' January 22 Meeting with Abu Dhabi Crown Prince and UAE Foreign Minister', 2007.
15   A.H. Cordesman and A. Toukan, *Iran and the Gulf Military Balance* (Washington DC, 2016), p. 61.

unit because they are detached to other units, on missions, undertaking fatigues, or on official and unofficial leave due to the need to attend to family demands, such as crises and supporting chronically ill family members.

Another factor compounding the difficulty in interpreting manpower figures is differentiating between military personnel and non-military personnel. In the case of the Emirati forces, historically a significant proportion of personnel have been non-military. These consist of two types – defence civilians and enlisted followers. Defence civilians undertake technical and professional activities, notably in the areas of administration, procurement, legal, finance, medical, health, planning, training and supply. Defence civilians can be both nationals and expatriates, with the latter being mostly from Islamic countries. Enlisted followers undertake unskilled or manual tasks, such as cooking, cleaning and establishing field camps. They are mostly south Asians, i.e. Indians, Pakistanis and Bangladeshis.[16]

The scale of the non-military workforce can be significant. In 1982, the British Defence Attaché wrote that the UAE Armed Forces' establishment strength 'of 50,550 does not represent the true strength of the Armed Forces as these figures include waiters, cleaners, civilians etc. A more realistic figure for the fighting strength would be estimated at about 25,000.'[17] Thus, nearly 50 percent of the force at that time was non-military personnel. Other reliable assessments of non-military personnel numbers identified that it was 13 percent for the Abu Dhabi Defence Force in 1966[18] and 30 percent for the Dubai Defence Force in 1975.[19] In 1967, when the Commander of British Land Forces in the Gulf questioned the Commander of the Abu Dhabi Defence Force about what appeared to be an excessive number of enlisted followers, he noted that 'soldiers will not do manual tasks'.[20] While at present numbers of locally

---

16   Historically, civilians were divided into three sub-groups – non-industrial (e.g. clerk, shorthand typist, works supervisor and draughtsman), artisans (e.g. carpenter, fitter, plant operator, boiler attendant, chlorinator and ice plant mechanic), and miscellaneous (e.g. *barusti* palm hut maker and attendant, driver, greaser and oiler, well digger, nursing orderly, fireman and storeman). Enlisted followers included cook, kitchen hand waiter, *syce* (horse groom), watchman, wet sweeper, dry sweeper, water carrier, messenger, dining room orderly, barber and *muttawa* (policeman). Enlisted followers were sometimes collectively referred to as *farash*, a Hindi word meaning a menial servant who pitched tents, etc. TNA FO 1016/736: Major for General Officer Commanding, Middle East Land Forces to Ministry of Defence, 'Proposed Pay Increases for the Arab Element of the Trucial Oman Scouts', 7 October 1966.

17   TNA FCO 8/4385: Cameron, 'Annual Report for 1981 on the United Arab Emirates Armed Forces', 31 January 1982.

18   As of June 1966, some 7 percent of the force was enlisted followers and 6 percent civilian staff. TNA FO 371/185551: Lamb, [untitled letter], 7 June 1966.

19   The DDF's 1975 total force strength was 1,733, made up of 537 civilians, 61 commissioned officers and 1,135 enlisted personnel. TNA FCO 8/2371: Colonel J.S. Agar, UK Defence Attaché, 'Intelligence Report No 12', 3 June 1974.

20   *Colonel E.B. Wilson's Archives*, Vol. 5 (Abu Dhabi, n.d.), Lt Col E.B. Wilson, Commander ADDF, to Brig I.R.R. Holyer, Commander Land Forces Gulf, 'Expansion of A.D.D.F.', 20 December 1967, p. 6.

engaged civilians still remain in the military, the number of enlisted followers directly engaged appears to have fallen dramatically. This is because this work is now down by contracting companies.

In short, the actual strength of the UAE Armed Forces has in recent decades not been known to any degree of accuracy; even so, ball-park figures indicate the military was always large in comparison to the population.

The military burden

A commonly used metric to compare the military burden on a nation's labour resources across countries and time is the ratio of military members per 1,000 people in the population. This can be calculated for active military, reserve military and paramilitary forces. As the UAE has only recently formed a reserve force, this section only uses active military numbers in the discussion of the military burden.

Table 15 lists the UAE's military burden in the years for which more reliable figures are known. The figures are calculated in two ways. The first is the ratio of military members per 1000 of total population, which is the standard measure used globally to allow comparisons between countries. However, this measure is not relevant to the UAE because of the very large percentage of the population is expatriates, and over time, there has been an emphasis on restricting service in the armed forces to nationals. This means that a more appropriate method to measure the UAE's military burden is to calculate it based on military members per 1000 of population of nationals. When calculated this way, the figures reveal that while the UAE's ratio of military members per 1000 of total population was historically high but now is low, it has always been extraordinarily high when only nationals are considered.

Table 15 shows that the military burden ratio based on the entire population was in the 40s during the 1970s and 1980s. This was globally quite high at the time. In 1981, the ratio was 46 which at that time was one of the highest rates in the world. Israel's ratio was 46.2 per 1000 population, followed by North Korea at 38, with the highest Arab states being Iraq at 32.1 and Syria at 30.9.[21] In the 2000s and 2010s, the ratio in the UAE was comparatively small.

However, the military burden ratio based on just nationals has been and still remains high. In the 2000s and 2010s, it was by far the largest in the world. It reached a peak in the 1980s, at 163, and was still 63 in 2016. By comparison, in 2016, the country with the next highest ratio was North Korea at 47, the highest Western country was Singapore at 12.5, and the highest Arab country was Jordan at 12.3.

---

21   US Arms Control and Disarmament Agency, *World Military Expenditures and Arms Transfers 1972-1982*, p. 4.

Saudi Arabia's ratio was 8.1, Iran's was 6.3, the US's was 4.2, Australia's was 2.5 and the UK's was 2.4.[22]

The assertion that the UAE military burden based on nationals is extremely high is supported by figures in the 2009 Labour Force Survey published by the UAE Government. The survey stated that 19.6 percent of employed Emiratis worked in the Armed Forces.[23] To put this into context, in the US less than 1.4 percent of the working population currently serve in its military.

Table 15: The UAE's military burden[24]

Year	Military manpower	Total population	Ratio of military members per 1000 of total population	Number of nationals	Ratio of military members per 1000 if only nationals served
1973	16,655	400,000	42	170,000	97
1976	24,800	600,000	41	218,000	113
1981	50,600	1,100,000	46	310,000	163
1983	52,900	1,200,000	44	360,000	146
2008	60,000	7,800,000	8	880,000	68
2016	64,000	8,724,800	7	1,022,400	63

Education and health

Manpower challenges facing Emirati armed forces not only relate to the number of nationals, but also relate to quality, specifically enlisting Emiratis with the required education upon which to build the leaders, operators, specialists and technicians needed for a modern military. Up to the late 1960s, the majority of the Emirates' population was illiterate. The consequence for military training was highlighted in a 1968 British military report, commissioned by Sheikh Zayed, on expanding the Abu Dhabi Defence Force (ADDF). The report identified that 95-98 percent of all recruits were illiterate, which posed a significant challenge for any tasks beyond basic infantry skills. It noted that 'while the simple skills of driving and small arms weapons training are relatively easy to achieve, the training of illiterates in the more complex techniques of map reading, range-taking, surveying, gun laying and compass work make the training of specialist … teams much more difficult and lengthy.' The report highlighted that the only way to overcome this challenge was a high quality and lengthy basic training

22   The International Institute of Strategic Studies, *The Military Balance 2017* (London, 2017).
23   UAE National Bureau of Statistics, *UAE in Figures, 2009*, p. 19.
24   The sources of the figures for military manpower are listed in Table 12 with the 2008 figure coming from Wikileaks, Sison, 'U/S Burns' January 22 Meeting with Abu Dhabi Crown Prince and UAE Foreign Minister', 2007. The figures for total population and the number of nationals were produced from a linear extrapolation from figures in Table 5.

before specialist and technical training could be undertaken. It noted that even with solid basic training there was a risk that if complicated weapon systems were introduced, 'the skills required to operate the weapons effectively may never be fully assimilated ... and be beyond the capacity of the present standard of solider in the force'.[25]

Illiteracy in the military remained a problem in the early years of Emirati forces. A 1975 report by the British Defence Attaché, noted that the Abu Dhabi military was experiencing a 'severe shortage of literate local officers and soldiers – one Commanding Officer [of a Regiment] is said to be illiterate'.[26] Literacy among nationals has risen enormously over the subsequent decades. Figures for 2005 state that only 5.9 percent of male nationals are illiterate, with another 9.1 percent being able to just read and write, and 17.2 percent only having completed primary education.[27] Illiteracy rates in the northern Emirates are higher than in Abu Dhabi, however. As the northern Emirates are a significant source of military manpower, there remain small numbers of illiterate and semi-illiterate military members in the enlisted ranks.[28]

Just as literacy has improved over the decades, so too has the general level of education in the Emirates. This can be seen in the rate of secondary school completion. In 1984-85, some 50 percent of boys dropped out of secondary school before completion.[29] By 2007-08, which is the last year for which figures are available, the rate had dropped to around 10 percent.[30] However, completing schooling does not tell the full story about education in the UAE as the quality of secondary education can vary. This is reflected in a 2012 study which identified that about 80 percent of students enrolled in local universities have to take one or two years of remedial education before commencing their studies.[31] These findings point to ongoing difficulties for the military in recruiting members with a sound secondary education.[32]

25   TNA FCO 8/1241: UK Land Forces Gulf Headquarters, 'Report on Abu Dhabi Defence Force', 1968.
26   TNA FCO 8/2371: Agar, 'Annual Report for 1973 by Defence Attaché United Arab Emirates', January 1974.
27   The corresponding figures for females are 11.7 percent, 9.9 percent and 15.2 percent. UAE National Bureau of Statistics, *UAE in Figures, 2009*, p. 11.
28   This is supported by field observations. Subject 699, expatriate serving in a training institute from the late 2000s to mid-2010s, interview, 2017. It is also supported by inference. A 2014 Federal Government study on its employees, excluding those in security agencies, found that around 3 percent of Emirati employees were illiterate or their education had ended at primary school. UAE Government, *Study on the Educational Level of the Staff of the Federal Government in 2014* (Abu Dhabi, 2014), p. 6.
29   TNA FCO 8/6181: J. Jenkins, UK Embassy in Abu Dhabi to SP Day, FCO, 'Women in the UAE', 7 April 1986.
30   N. Ridge, S. Farah, and S. Shami, *Patterns and Perceptions in Male Secondary School Dropouts in the United Arab Emirates* (2013), p. 20.
31   R. Soto, *Education in Dubai from Quantity to Quality* (Dubai, 2012), p. 26.
32   Boys have been able to able to join the military without completing secondary schooling. N. Ridge, S. Kippels, and B.J. Chung, *The Challenges and Implications of a Global Decline in the Educational Attainment and Retention of Boys*, Vol. RR 2.2017 (Qatar, 2017), p. 43.

Problems also exist in recruiting sufficient nationals with tertiary education. Around 1971, there were less than forty nationals in the entire country with university degrees.[33] The UAE's first university was established in 1977. By 2012, 57 percent of nationals aged between 18 and 23 had been enrolled in higher education. The rate is 68 percent for females and 45 percent for males.[34] While tertiary qualified nationals accounted for nearly 66 percent of the Emiratis employed in non-security Federal Government agencies in 2014,[35] the percentage in the military is likely to be far less. This is because UAE officer cadet colleges did not offer academic qualifications until the 2010s. Now, all UAE military colleges have partnered with local universities so that officers have gained a Bachelor's degree by graduation. This is expected to increase the number of military members with higher education qualifications.

A final constraint on recruiting sufficient nationals for the military is health. This problem was noted as long ago as the early 1950s. During efforts to recruit locals for the Trucial Oman Scouts, many were found to have poor health due to a lack of both healthy diet and medical care.[36] Today population ill-health remains a significant problem; however, it is now more due to poor dietary choices and a sedentary lifestyle. This has resulted in obesity and early-onset diabetes affecting a significant proportion of the population. The consequence of this is seen in the fact that some 20 percent of nationals called up for national service between 2014 and 2017 (i.e. those aged between 18 and 30) were deemed not fit for military service even after a major health intervention to enable them to be ready for the military training.[37]

Policies compounding manpower shortages

Certain military policies and practices have aggravated manpower shortages in the UAE military, with many of these being common to all armed forces. A particular issue is the military allowance and promotion system. When a service member gains a skills qualification, undertakes hazardous work, or serves in a more 'prestigious' unit, he is entitled to an additional allowance; however, service personnel can also lose an allowance. An example where this occurs is when a member of an 'important unit' undertakes extended training in another unit to obtain a skill such as truck driving, he may lose his 'important

33   S. Chubin, *Security in the Persian Gulf: Domestic Political Factors*, Vol. 1 (Farnborough, 1981), p. 24.
34   Center for Higher Education Data and Statistics, *Indicators of the UAE Higher Education Sector Students and the Learning Environment 2012-13* (Abu Dhabi, 2012), p. 6.
35   UAE Government, *Study on the Educational Level of the Staff of the Federal Government in 2014*, p. 6.
36   TNA DEFE 68/397: G.G. Arthur, Political Residency, Bahrain to the Secretary of State for Foreign and Commonwealth Affairs, 'The Trucial Oman Scouts', Diplomatic Report No 115/72, 21 January 1972.
37   J.B. Alterman and M. Balboni, *Citizens in Training: Conscription and Nation-Building in the United Arab Emirates* (Washington DC, 2017), p. 16.

unit' allowance. The consequence is that this member is 'incentivised' to avoid gaining a truck driving licence, and hence a driver must be allocated to the unit. Another case of a policy which increases manpower requirements is forcing all officers seeking a promotion to undertake mandatory courses, regardless of their relevance. When this occurs, additional personnel are needed to backfill the post of the officer under training.

In addition to the above, there are factors that have compounded manpower shortages which are particularly pronounced or unique to the UAE. One is the duplication of forces. It was particularly pronounced before the 1976 unification of the armed forces when there were five separate armed forces. Even following the unification, duplication existed and, like all armed services, it has continued. For example, from the early 2010s, both the Emiri Guard and Special Operations Command maintained explosive ordnance disposal and sniper capabilities, each with different equipment and training arrangements. Reasons for duplication can be legitimate, such as when two units do the same task but in a different context. However, at times, having duplicated capability is wasteful.

A second factor which compounds manpower shortages is the impact of *asil*. As noted in Chapter 2, usually only members with high *asil* can hold senior and sensitive posts, which means the pool of potential candidates from which these posts can draw is significantly reduced. A final factor is the practice of buying large volumes of sophisticated systems from multiple countries. This creates a rapid demand for significant numbers of better educated and higher skilled personnel.

Solutions to the manpower challenge

Three solutions have been pursued over the last five decades to overcome the shortages in nationals serving in the Emirati armed forces. They are: (1) improving education and training for nationals, (2) engaging foreigners, and (3) increasing national recruitment and retention. Each of these three policies requires examination in depth, given what each can tell the observer about how successfully the Emirati armed forces have dealt with some of the significant challenges they face.

Improving education and training for nationals

The larger Emirati armed forces have always put considerable effort into both education and military-specific training for their military members. An early educational initiative was the establishment of military schools for boys. The first was established by the ADDF in the late 1960s and, by the early 1970s, the armed forces of Dubai and Sharjah had also introduced them.[38] These were based on the success of the British

---

38   The first Emirati military school was the Abu Obaida Military School in 1968 in Abu Dhabi, which had just a single classroom with only 15 pupils when it opened. Other

boys' military school formed in the 1950s by the Trucial Oman Scouts. Its aim was to generate a supply of literate and school-educated recruits who could be trained for technical roles such as signallers and as a leadership cadre.[39] The UAE Armed Forces' boys' schools operated for several decades, although all but a handful had been closed by the early 2000s. Since the mid-2000s, boys' military schools have undergone a revival; as of 2019, three are in existence in Abu Dhabi alone.[40] In addition, Emirati armed forces also put considerable effort into encouraging illiterate serving members to gain basic education. In the early 1970s, the ADDF offered financial incentives to its members to attend civilian adult learning centres,[41] of which, by the mid-1980s, there were 115 nationwide.[42]

The beginning of military-specific training in an Emirati armed force dates back to September 1966 when the ADDF opened its Recruit Depot in Al Ain.[43] Within a few years, specialist schools had been established; by the early 1980s, these included an armoured school in Abu Dhabi, an artillery school in Al Ain, an infantry school in Manama,[44] a parachute and special forces school in Al Ain, and apprentice and language schools in Sweihan.[45] After 1980, other schools were established, including the pilot training school, Joint Services NCO School, Chemical Defence School, Military Intelligence School, the Naval School, and the Administrative Affairs School.

In recent decades, these schools have been grouped together to form institutes. At present, most commands have dedicated institutes. The main ones are the Naval Forces Institute in Al Taweelah; the Presidential Guard Institute in Al Ain; and, at

schools established in the following decades were the Bida Zayed Military School (opened 1972), Khaled bin Al Waleed Military School in Sharjah; Ghayathi Military School in Ghayathi City; Al Ain Military School in Al Ain City; Al Wagan Military School in Abu Dhabi City; Manama Military School in Al Manama City; Sweihan Military School in Sweihan City; and Rashid Military School in the central military region. Nasser Al Dhaheri, *Roll of Honour: the Armed Forces of the United Arab Emirates* (Abu Dhabi, ca. 2006), p. 110.

39   The low literacy rates in the Trucial States was a justification for establishing the TOS boys' school. 'Military Justification for Boys' School Trucial Oman Scouts', Annex A to QQ 0618/1B, 5 October 1961, in A. Burdett, ed. *Records of the Emirates 1961-1965: 1962* (Slough, 1997).

40   These are the Military High School Al Dhaid (est. 2015), Military High School Al Ain (formerly the Air Force High School) and Western Military High School Madinat Zayed (est. 2013).

41   Al Abed, Vine, and Al Jabali, *Chronicle of Progress*, p. 36.

42   TNA FCO 8/6181: Jenkins, 'Women in the UAE', 7 April 1986.

43   TNA WO 337/15: Trucial Oman Scouts, 'Trucial Oman Scouts Intelligence Summary No 105', 20 September 1967.

44   Al Dhaheri, *Roll of Honour: the Armed Forces of the United Arab Emirates*, pp. 98-99.

45   There were a number of others. One was the military Nursing School established in 1970 to run basic nursing courses, which in 1985 had become the School of Medical Services of the UAE Armed Forces. Another one was the Navy's school for ratings established in 1977.

Zayed Military City in Sweihan, the Land Forces Institute, Joint Aviation Command Institute, Joint Logistics Institute, Air Force and Air Defence Institute, and the Critical Infrastructure and Coastal Protection Authority Institute. The constituent elements of these institutes are typically named 'schools', which may have detached 'wings' at bases across the UAE. Smaller commands, branches and other entities also have dedicated training facilities. Among these are the Military Police, which has a school in Al Mahawi, and the Chemical Defence Command, which has a school in Sweihan. The institutes and schools are mostly for individual training. There are also collective training facilities, such as the combat training centres.

In terms of officer training, the first specific officer cadet college established was the Zayed II Military College, established in 1972 in Al Ain. The Air Force opened its own college in 1982 at the Al Dhafra Air Base, which has since been named the Khalifa bin Zayed Air College and moved to Al Ain. The Navy opened its college in 1999, now named the Rashid bin Saeed Al Maktoum Naval College at Al Taweelah. Today, officer education is generally two years and four months. Generally, an officer cadet graduates as a lieutenant with a bachelor's degree in Military Science from Abu Dhabi University. They will then undertake basic officer training at their respective service school. For example, if they are joining a manoeuvre branch of Land Forces, they will undertake the 12-week Junior Officer Course which provides them with the basic army knowledge needed to undertake their second course – the 8-week Basic Officer Leader Course relevant to their respective branch (e.g. armour, field engineering). Upon completion of the Basic Officer Leader Course, the lieutenant will serve in one of the manoeuvre brigades as a platoon commander.

Local training of mid-level officers for command and staff positions started in 1991 with the establishment of a staff college, now known as the Joint Command and Staff College, located on Abu Dhabi Island. Its courses are focused on military art and practice, and are taught in Arabic.

To provide more strategically focused education for both service personnel and civilians who would be assuming senior posts in the armed forces and national security, the National Defence College was established in 2013, also on Abu Dhabi Island. It offers a combined civil and military curriculum which emphasises a whole-of-government approach to national security. The National Defence College's current education offering is a full time 43 to 45-week long course. This leads to a master's degree in security and strategic Studies, or if the student lacks the relevant educational prerequisites, a Diploma.[46]

While the majority of individual training is done within the UAE, Emirati armed forces have also sent personnel to foreign countries for training. In the 1960s and 1970s, the primary destinations for training were the United Kingdom, Egypt, Jordan, Sudan and Pakistan, with France joining the list in the latter-half of the 1970s and the US in

---

46   N.W. Toronto, *How Militaries Learn: Human Capital, Military Education, and Battlefield Effectiveness* (Lanham, Maryland, 2018), p. 64.

the early 1980s.[47] Since the mid-1980s, the number of countries has increased significantly, which probably reflects diplomatic decisions, opportunities and a broadening of the countries from which the UAE purchases equipment and, hence, to which the UAE sends its personnel for specialist training. As well as attending course, another form of individual training was attaching Emiratis to a foreign military service: as one example, a number of UAE officers were attached to British Army units in the United Kingdom and the British Army of the Rhine in the 1980s.[48]

Over the last two decades, the number of UAE military members sent to foreign training facilities has increased markedly. Between 2012-13 and 2018-19, some 781 Emiratis per year trained in the US on military courses.[49] This training appears to fall into two categories – individual training on new equipment and collective training. An example of the former is advanced pilot training. Around 2005, the UAE had between 150 and 190 military pilots but, by 2007, it needed 400 pilots to man its new fleets of fighters and helicopters which were scheduled to arrive at the end of the 2000s.[50] While the UAE's training facilities had provided all basic pilot training since the early 1980s, as well as some advanced training, the UAE did not have the ability to train the required numbers of pilots on the new aircraft. Consequently, some 600 UAE personnel per year were sent to undertake training in the US.[51]

Even where local training facilities existed the UAE has continued to send its personnel to foreign training establishments. Thus, although the Zayed II Military College was established in 1972 for officer cadet training, for the last 50 years, the UAE has continued to send Emiratis to Royal Military Academy Sandhurst. As seen in Table 16, an average of three to five Emiratis per year have passed out from Sandhurst. These cadets were sourced from the best students at Zayed Military Academy, as well as well-connected Emiratis. Around 36 sons of the various UAE Royal Families have attended Sandhurst since the early 1970s.[52] It should be noted that Sandhurst is just one foreign destination for UAE officer cadets. During the 2000s and 2020, other key ones in the Commando Training Centre Royal Marines (UK), École Spéciale Militaire de Saint-Cyr (France), Australian Defence Force Academy, US Military

---

47   TNA FCO 8/5468: Cameron, 'Annual Report for 1983 on the United Arab Emirates Armed Forces', 25 January 1984.
48   TNA FCO 8/3461: UK Ministry of Defence, 'Secretary of State's Visit to Bahrain, Qatar, UAE and Oman: United Arab Emirates UAE/UK Defence Relations Line to Take', ca. December 1980.
49   See footnote 99, Chapter 4.
50   Apache helicopter crews were trained at the US Army Aviation Centre at Fort Rucker, Alabama, while the F-16 crews were trained at centres in Tucson, Arizona. US training programmes are often included as part of an equipment procurement contract. In the case of the F-16s, when the UAE purchased 80 Block 60 F-16s at a cost of US$6 billion, the training included six to 25-month pilot training and 12-month crew training. M. Knights, *Troubled Waters: Future U.S. Security Assistance in the Persian Gulf* (Washington DC, 2006), p. 138.
51   Ibid.
52   The number comes from a list maintained by the author.

Academy West Point, the Annapolis Naval Academy (US), Air Force Academy (US) and Coast Guard Academy (US).

Table 16: Emirati officer cadets passing out from the Royal Military Academy Sandhurst[53]

Year	Graduates
1973-77	33
1978-81	27
1982-86	14
1987-91	19
1992-95	17
1996-2000	17
2001-05	40
2006-09	27
2010-15	30

In terms of collective training, the vast majority of this has occurred within the UAE; occasionally it has been provided in a foreign country. For instance, in 1999 UAE forces undertook collective training in southern France, in preparation for their deployment to Kosovo as part of an international peace-keeping force.[54] Since the early 2010s, UAE Presidential Guard and Land Forces units have undertaken collective training at the US Marines' base 29 Palms in California.

In general, specialised training for new equipment is initially done in the supplying country. Over time, this training is gradually transferred to the UAE. To illustrate this point, UAE personnel first attended courses in the US on the Patriot surface-to-air missile system which was introduced into the UAE around 2012. Currently, the 16-week Patriot operators' course is taught at the Air Force and Air Defence Institute at Zayed Military City. For more complex systems, a providing country may maintain a support cell in the UAE. This has been the case with the Patriot missile systems. The UAE purchased 13 Patriot systems and since 2012, a small team of US personnel have continued to work in the UAE to support these. Known as the US Patriot Security Assistance Team, the team provides to the UAE Air Force and Air Defence 'training in march order and emplacement, launcher reload, missile selectability, preventive checks and services, and Patriot radar operations, as well as initial Patriot certification

---

53 Data before 1973 is unavailable. The data from 1973 to 2009 is based on annual figures while those from 2010 to 2015 are based on the financial years, commencing with 2010/2011. The figures from 1973 to 2009 were obtained from Brigadier A. Pillar, Senior Military Contract Officer, UAE Armed Forces, 2002-11, interview, UK, 2016. The figures from 2010 to 2015 are from UK Ministry of Defence, *Freedom of Information Request Ref: 05/04/79426/FOI2017/09220* (London, 2017).
54 WAM. 'Special Report: UAE-France Relations', 2006, <wam.ae/en/details/1395227687080>.

training or refresher training for UAE personnel transitioning into different roles within Patriot'. In 2019, the team consisted of seven US military members.[55]

Engaging foreigners

In the early years of Emirati armed forces, large numbers of foreigners were recruited to make up for a shortage of nationals. Over the last five decades, expatriates have served in every rank from soldier to a force's most senior officer; they have filled all roles including command, staff, operational, training and technical posts. They have been engaged as uniformed members, defence civilians and enlisted followers, and worked under employment contracts, as well as under secondment arrangements negotiated by their home country's armed services.

In the early years of some Emirati armed forces, expatriates made up the majority of members. This can be seen in the ADDF in 1974 (Table 17) when 70 percent of officers and 81 percent of enlisted ranks were expatriates. Nationals only formed a majority of enlisted tradesmen. The proportion of expatriates was lower in other forces, but still high. In the Dubai Defence Force (DDF), in 1975, 45 percent of its officers and 27 percent of the enlisted ranks were expatriates.[56]

Table 17: ADDF personnel, March 1974[57]

Nationality	Officer	Enlisted ranks	Enlisted tradesmen	Civilians	Total
Omani	54	5,578	502	120	6,524
Abu Dhabian	139	909	483	28	1,559
UAE, (excluding Abu Dhabi)	42	871	316	50	1,279
Pakistani	115 (78 seconded, 37 contract)	808	59	862	1,834
Jordanian	97 (60 seconded, 37 contracted)	179	–	124	403

55   Continual improvement is also provided by the cooperation between the US and UAE through multinational training events. In the case of the Patriot system, the two UAE Patriot battalions, and the deployed US Patriot 1-43 Air Defense Artillery Battalion out of Al Dhafra Air Base have monthly activities which include seminars, leader engagements, professional working groups and social gatherings. Debra Valine, US Army. 'United Arab Emirates gets air defense boost from U.S.', 2019 <www.army.mil/article/218898/united_arab_emirates_gets_air_defense_boost_from_u_s_>

56   Of the total strength of 1,335 officers and men, 46 percent were from Dubai, 37 percent from other Emirates, 13 percent from Oman and 4 percent from other nations. TNA FCO 8/2371: Agar, 'Intelligence Report No 12', 3 June 1974.

57   TNA FCO 8/2371: Agar, 'Intelligence Report No 10', 4 April 1974.

Nationality	Officer	Enlisted ranks	Enlisted tradesmen	Civilians	Total
Sudanese	47 (46 seconded, 1 contracted)	35	–	18	93
Indian	1	847	40	341	1,229
Gulf States (excluding UAE)	2	13	–	13	28
Other Arabs	7	15	5	62	89
British	96 (12 seconded, 84 contracted)	–	–	2	98
Others		97	160	2	259
Totals	600	9,352	1,565	1,622	13,395–13,3959[a]
Percentage who were Abu Dhabi nationals	23%	10%	31%	2%	6%
Percentage who were UAE nationals	30%	19%	51%	5%	21%

Note
a.   Numbers do not add up in the original table.

Over time as more Emiratis were recruited and trained, the percentage of expatriates declined in all the armed forces. The rate of decline was faster in some areas, notably for officers in combat units, and in more sensitive units, such as military intelligence and the Emiri Guard. Enlisted personnel was the area with the slowest rate of Emiratisation.

The UAE Armed Forces have never published figures on numbers of foreigners. Like the overall UAE military manpower figures, there is also uncertainty about the accuracy of publicly available figures for foreigners after the mid-1980s. Reliable early figures identify the proportion of expatriates as 79 percent for the ADDF in 1974,[58] 80 percent for the entire UAE military in 1978[59] and around 66 percent in 1983.[60] The 1990 edition of *The Military Balance* claimed that around 30 percent of the military were expatriates.[61] This 30 percent figure continued to be quoted in the 2004 edition which does not seem plausible given the trend towards reducing the number of expatriates.[62]

58   Ibid.
59   Wikileaks, Dickman, 'Security Assistance Reporting – First Annual Integrated Assessment – UAE', 25 July 1978.
60   TNA FCO 8/5468: Cameron, 'Annual Report for 1983 on the United Arab Emirates Armed Forces', 25 January 1984.
61   Metz notes that other (unstated) authors suggest a much higher proportion. Metz, *Persian Gulf States: Country Studies*, pp. 362-4.
62   A.H. Cordesman, *The Military Balance in the Middle East – An Analytic Overview* (Washington DC, 2004), p. 274.

A 2009 National Bureau of Statistics' report stated that 0.2 percent of employed non-nationals and 19.6 percent of employed Emiratis worked in the armed services. Statistics on the actual number of employed in the UAE are not available, but using estimates of the 2009 population[63] and assuming that 70 percent of non-nationals work and 30 percent of nationals work,[64] this equates to about 52,900 nationals and 9,100 non-nationals worked in the UAE Armed Forces at that time.[65] Based on this figure, this means some 15 percent of the military in 2009 was expatriate.

In 2013, the *Financial Times* reported that 'foreigners are estimated by people close to the government to account for 2,000-3,000 of the UAE's more than 40,000 military personnel.'[66] The *Financial Times'* figure, which equates to 5-7 percent of personnel being expatriates, aligns with both anecdotal evidence collected by the author, and one limited data point from the 2010 Statistical Yearbook of Dubai. The Yearbook stated that the Headquarters of the 4th Squadron of the Coast Guard had reported that 4 percent of its 244 members were expatriates.[67]

Today, there are two distinct groups of professional military expatriates who work for the UAE Armed Forces. One is made up of expatriates who serve as advisors, trainers, administrators, and specialists. These can be either directly hired by the UAE Armed Forces or provided through manpower companies and management consultants. The second group are expatriates who serve in a guards and infantry light force – popularly but incorrectly known as the Colombians. The first of these arrived in the summer of 2010 and were former Columbian military personnel who had been employed by a commercial contractor to build an 800-man foreign-manned battalion by early 2011.[68] Other South American nationals, notably El Salvadorian, Panamanian and Chilean personnel, and South Africans, were subsequently hired. The unit grew to some 1,400 by 2013,[69] then 1,800 by 2015,[70] with plans for it to

---

63   The estimated population, extrapolated from Table 5 for 2009, was 900,000 nationals and 6,500,000 non-nationals.
64   The working rate figures for Abu Dhabi is based on the 2005 Abu Dhabi Census which was 22 percent for nationals and 68 percent for non-nationals. These figures are lower than national figures and were 30 percent for nationals and 70 percent to non-nationals in 2008. Abu Dhabi Government, *The Abu Dhabi Economic Vision 2030* (Abu Dhabi, 2008), pp. 92-93.
65   UAE National Bureau of Statistics, *UAE in Figures, 2009*, p. 18.
66   M. Peel and Andres Schipani, 'Bogotá Alarmed by Exodus of Colombian Soldiers to UAE', *Financial Times*, 3 June 2013.
67   Dubai Statistics Center Government of Dubai, *Statistical Yearbook – Emirate of Dubai 2010* (Dubai, 2011), p. 69.
68   M. Mazzetti and E.B. Hager, 'Secret Desert Force Set Up by Blackwater's Founder', *The New York Times*, 14 May 2011.
69   Peel and Schipani, 'Bogotá Alarmed by Exodus of Colombian Soldiers to UAE'.
70   E.B. Hager and M. Mazzetti, 'Emirates Secretly Sends Colombian Mercenaries to Yemen Fight', *The New York Times*, 25 November 2015.

expand to around 3,000.[71] Various reasons have been advanced for this unit. These range from the 'suppression of possible uprising inside the country's numerous and sprawling labour camps, securing of radioactive and nuclear materials, … [and even] to take over the disputed islands' in the Gulf.[72] They have also been suggested as being a response to the Arab Spring which started in December 2010,[73] however this is illogical as the contract for their formation was awarded before this. The unit was most likely established as part of the UAE's ongoing efforts, initiated in the mid-2000s, to accelerate the modernisation and expansion of UAE military capabilities.

The end of the 2010s and start of the 2020s saw significant cuts to the number of professional military expatriates in the UAE Armed Forces. This may be in response to the need to reduce expenditure, a concerted effort to cut dependence on expatriates, and a reduced need for the knowledge transfer from expatriates to nationals as Emirati operational experience has been built up.

The number of nationalities serving in Emirati armed forces varied over time. In the ADDF in 1974, there were over eight nationalities (see Table 17) while in 1984, 21 different nationalities were reported serving in the UAE Armed Forces. Several times in the UAE's history, the rulers have made abrupt changes in the composition of the nationalities in their forces. Four examples illustrate this.

The first was in 1972 when Dhofaris from Oman's southernmost province were dismissed en masse from the UDF and ADDF, with some arrested and sent to prison.[74] This was because all became suspect following the discovery that some 50 Dhofaris in these forces were supporters of a Marxist and Arab revolutionary group known as the Popular Front for the Liberation of Oman and the Arab Gulf (PFLOAG) which was fighting against the Sultan of Oman.[75] The second was in 1980 when the

---

71 Peel and Schipani, 'Bogotá Alarmed by Exodus of Colombian Soldiers to UAE'. The force's establishment was contracted to the US company, Reflex Responses under a $529 million contract. According to the *New York Times*, which first reported the development of the force, documents from Reflex Responses stated the force's roles were to 'conduct special operations missions inside and outside the country, defend oil pipelines and skyscrapers from terrorist attacks and put down internal revolts.' Mazzetti and Hager, 'Secret Desert Force Set Up by Blackwater's Founder'.

72 Kamrava, *Troubled Waters: Insecurity in the Persian Gulf*, p. 101-102.

73 Mazzetti and Hager, 'Secret Desert Force Set Up by Blackwater's Founder'.

74 Author's collection, Abu Dhabi, TOS files, Trucial Oman Scouts HQ, 'Arab Officers TOS', 1969-70, amended September 1973.

75 TNA FCO 8/2371: Agar, 'Annual Report for 1973 by Defence Attaché United Arab Emirates', January 1974. According to Abu Dhabi Special Branch Officer, Michael Butler, in 1968 Dhofaris served in both the ADDF and TOS (X Squadron), with most being Other Ranks and NCOs, with one or two junior officers, and 'to a greater or lesser degree all these people sympathized with the rebels fighting against Sultan's Armed Forces in the south of Oman, and some while at home on leave from the TOS took an active part in various skirmishes between SAF and the dissidents'. Butler considers little was done until the leadership of the Dhofar Liberation Front was seized by a small group of extreme Marxist radicals, and it was renamed the PFLOAG with the new goal of overthrowing

first of around 5,000 Moroccan serving soldiers started arriving in the UAE,[76] and simultaneously, the recruitment of Omanis was sharply curtailed.[77] This development was sparked by a border dispute between Ras Al Khaimah and Oman (see Chapter 4, Core Mission 1). Sheikh Zayed was concerned that the Omanis in the UAE military, who then made up 50 percent of the entire force, might not remain loyal to the UAE if a conflict ensued.[78]

A third example resulted from Saddam Hussein's occupation of Kuwait in 1990. While the UAE and other GCC countries opposed Saddam, other Middle Eastern states and groups did not, notably Jordan, Algeria, Sudan, Yemen, Tunisia, and the Palestinian Liberation Organisation. Having soldiers from these countries in the UAE military posed an unacceptable risk and, consequently, they were dismissed. A fourth example is the engagement of large numbers of personnel to fill specialist gaps. In 1998, the UAE recruited large numbers of retired Pakistan Air Force personnel to maintain its growing fleet of aircraft. It selected 693 technicians, with the first batch of 78 arriving later that year.[79]

The heritage of having large numbers of expatriates serving in Emirati armed forces is that it is common to read in recent years that a large part of the UAE Armed Forces is still made up of expatriates. In 2011, Davidson wrote that 'the majority of lower ranks ... are Arab expatriates ... [and] the UAE has one of the world's largest mercenary armies [due to the presence of large numbers of expatriates]'.[80] Almezaini in 2011 stated that UAE nationals constitute 70 percent of the total forces, the 'other 30 percent being mostly from Egypt, Oman and Sudan'.[81] In 2019, Barany wrote that the UAE has a 'massive reliance on mercenaries'.[82] These claims are simply not true. The UAE Armed Forces have not had significant numbers of foreigners serving in their units since the early 1990s.

not just the Sultan of Oman, but also all the traditional rulers in the Gulf. This concern took several years to materialise and culminated in 1972 decision to remove all Dhofaris from the ADDF and the UDF. M. Butler, ADDF 1968, & Special Branch Al Ain, 1968-70, email, 8 August 2019.

76   I. Rabinovich and H. Shaked, eds., *Middle East Contemporary Survey, 1986*, Vol. X (New York, 1988), p. 106.

77   TNA FCO 8/5468: Cameron, 'Annual Report for 1983 on the United Arab Emirates Armed Forces', 25 January 1984.

78   TNA FCO 8/3512: Lt Colonel R. Jury, Defence Attaché to the UAE, 'Moroccans', 10 July 1980.

79   A.R. Shaikh, *The Story of the Pakistan Air Force, 1988-1998: A Battle Against Odds* (Islamabad, 2000), p. 234.

80   Davidson, *Abu Dhabi: Oil and Beyond*, p. 144.

81   K.S. Almezaini, *The UAE and Foreign Policy: Foreign Aid, Identities and Interests* (London, 2012), p. 27.

82   Barany, *Military Officers in the Gulf: Career Trajectories and Determinants*, p. 14.

Increasing the recruitment and retention of nationals

Recruiting more nationals and retaining those already in the force has been another approach adopted to address manpower challenges. Increased recruitment has often relied on providing additional financial incentives such as improved salaries, allowances and conditions. In 1973-74, when the ADDF sought to expand rapidly, the accommodation allowance of its members was raised by 45 percent for married men and 30 percent for single men.[83] In that same year, the ADDF also announced that its pension scheme would recognise any time served in the TOS/UDF,[84] thus encouraging TOS/UDF members to join the ADDF.

Another method used to increase recruitment was to broaden the recruitment pool of nationals: from around the mid-1970s, nationals from the northern Emirates were targeted for the military.[85] Since then, and to the present, northern Emiratis have made up a sizeable proportion of UAE military personnel. This can be seen in military death statistics. Between 1976 and late 2015, 39 percent of nationals killed in the UAE Armed Forces were from the northern Emirates, while the entire northern Emirates' population makes up just 25 percent of the UAE's national population. Between July and October 2015 alone, which included an attack in Yemen in which over 50 Emirati soldiers died, northern Emiratis made up 51 percent of military deaths.[86] These statistics demonstrate a clear over-representation of northern Emiratis compared with the lower proportion they represent in the UAE population.

To increase the recruitment pool, women have also been permitted to join the military. Following Saddam Hussein's invasion of Kuwait in 1990, the demand for more Emirati personnel, and the enthusiasm of female nationals, led the UAE military to create the Women's Military Service. The UAE was the first Arab Gulf country to allow women to join the military beyond serving medical and other specialist areas. Today, women serve in all the major commands. While most appear to be engaged in administrative work, some serve in active roles, including close personal protection and as pilots. The highest profile woman in the armed forces today is Major Mariam Al Mansouri, the first female UAE fighter pilot. She participated in the coalition bombing campaign against ISIS in Syria. The number of women in the UAE Armed Forces is currently unknown, but limited evidence indicates that they constitute just a few percent. Specifically, a 2009 National Bureau of Statistics document stated that

83   TNA, FCO 8/2371, Agar, 'Intelligence Report No 10', 4 April 1974.
84   Ibid.
85   Tingay, 'Legions Galore'.
86   Between 1971 and October 2015, 190 nationals in the UAE Armed Forces were reported killed. 139 of these had a place of birth listed, and this group was the basis for identifying that 39 percent of those killed were from the northern Emirates. Between July and October 2015, 68 nationals with an identified place of birth were killed. Data from Gulf News. 'Roll of Honour', ca. 2015 <imedia.gulfnews.com/GN_Interactive/martyrs/phone/index.html>

0.4 percent of females in the UAE's labour force served in the military, meaning some 1,700 females.[87] Thus, it is likely that some 3 percent of the UAE Armed Forces are female.

The most recent mechanism used to increase the size of the military manpower pool has been the establishment of national service in 2014. Further details are provided in the section on the National Service and Reserve Authority in Chapter 9.

Methods for increasing retention have included offering incentives such as increased pay, allowances and re-enlistment bonuses. Another is to not accept a member's request to resign, which has been common when the armed forces suffered from a major manpower shortage. For example in 1973, when the ADDF was rapidly expanding, it forbade the 'discharge of soldiers for any reason unless their contract expires'.[88] Anecdotal reports indicate that over the last decade with the increased operational tempo, the military has again made it difficult for service personnel to resign. Numerous instances have been identified of personnel only being permitted to resign after several attempts over many months, or even years. A final retention approach used in the 1970s and 1980s was to offer naturalisation to select foreigners serving in an Emirati armed service if they agreed to stay on. This offer was mainly made to Omanis and Yemenis.[89]

Looking forward

The current size of the UAE Armed Forces places a considerable military burden on the state. Assuming that the current force consists of 65,000 Emiratis and that the number of nationals in the labour force is around 225,000 (see Chapter 2), this means that around 28 percent of all Emiratis in the labour force serve in the military. Will this drain both the country's human resources and finances and lead to a drive to reduce the size of the UAE Armed Forces? For the foreseeable future, the answer appears to be no. Firstly, there is a large labour pool from which to recruit; as noted in Chapter 2, nearly 400,000 nationals will be entering the labour force during the 2020s. This number is nearly double the 2020 national labour force of 225,000. Secondly, the benefits of having a sizeable percentage of Emiratis serving under arms outweigh the costs. Among the benefits, from a security and foreign affairs perspective, are offering a credible deterrent, providing additional ways of advancing foreign policy interests and demonstrating a commitment to self-defence, which is critical to the support of the UAE's Western allies. The main domestic benefits are providing a valued and

87   UAE National Bureau of Statistics, *UAE in Figures, 2009*, pp. 19, 41.
88   TNA FCO 8/2134: Colonel J.S. Agar, UK Defence Attaché, 'Intelligence Report No 3', 14 April 1973.
89   Tingay, 'Legions Galore'.

respected employer for Emiratis, soaking up excess labour, reinforcing UAE national identity, and helping to build an educated and skilled national workforce.

In terms of costs, the financial impact is considerable, estimated at around 40 percent of Abu Dhabi expenditure in its role as the nation's capital. In the context of Abu Dhabi's huge revenue, however, it is not crushing, as the government can still provide the high and closely woven social safety net expected by Emiratis, as well as fund economic and social development. Possibly the greatest cost of a large military structure is the opportunity cost which arises from Emiratis in the military not being able to work elsewhere. More specifically, this reduces the pool of Emiratis who can take leadership positions in government, business and civil society, which results in a greater reliance on expatriates in these areas.

However, the impact of the manpower drain that can result from having a large military is somewhat mitigated by two practices – one involving retired officers taking up new roles elsewhere, and the other the seconding of serving officers. The first sees high-ranking officers, who have retired from the military, being appointed to senior civilian posts. These posts are often in the police, Ministry of Interior and entities of the Supreme Council for National Security. The second is the practice of seconding mid-level officers (i.e. Lt. Colonels and Colonels) to government agencies, including many to non-security agencies. This practice appears to be more common for military officers who have decided not to seek promotion, or those who have been identified as not being candidates for further promotion but who can still make a significant contribution. Together, these two practices have meant that other parts of the economy have benefited from having so many nationals in uniform.

Part III

History of the Emirates Armed Forces

7

British-Controlled Armed Forces

The year 1951 can be considered the beginning of the modern era in military affairs in the Emirates; this was the year when the first permanent, professional armed force was formed on Emirati soil – the Trucial Oman Levies.[1] This should not be taken to imply that that there was no military history before this date. The first half of the 20th Century saw the Abu Dhabi-Dubai War (1945-48) and Sharjah hosting military camps and the Royal Air Force during Second World War. The 19th Century saw Great Britain undertaking punitive military expeditions against the Qawasim Sheikhs in Ras Al Khaimah and elsewhere around the Gulf (1809 to 1819). And a millennium earlier in 632 AD, three armies clashed in the Battle of Dibba which allegedly claimed 10,000 lives.

The period from 1951-71 saw two types of British-controlled forces operating in the land, air and water of the Emirates. These were:

1. The British officered, locally raised force known as the Trucial Oman Levies (TOL), renamed the Trucial Oman Scouts (TOS) in 1956
2. Regular British forces – the Royal Navy, the Royal Air Force (RAF) at Sharjah, and the British Army in the Trucial States.

The policy and military command of all British forces in the Emirates was a shared responsibility between the British foreign affairs and military establishments. These arrangements and how they changed from 1951-71 are detailed in Appendix 8.

Of the two types of forces, the TOL/TOS was the most important in terms of the actual development of the Emirates and the Emirati armed forces. Over its twenty

---

1   It should be mentioned that there was a small British and US military presence at RAF Sharjah and Dubai during the Second World War. This was primarily to support military transit flights, and after 1942, anti-submarine duties. N. Stanley-Price, *Imperial Outpost in the Gulf: The Airfield at Sharjah (UAE) 1932-1952* (Sussex, 2012). The forces had no off-airfield security role and as such, they are of peripheral relevance to the development of military forces in the Emirates.

years of existence, the force made the Emirates safe through patrolling and intervention both to prevent and end violent tribal disputes. Its presence rapidly 'encouraged the rulers to eschew force as a means of settling their internal disputes and removed the fear of outside aggression', according to the British Political Resident in 1955.[2] This reduction in conflict created the essential conditions to initiate economic development, in addition to assisting in the building of trust between the rulers.

This impact of the force has been described by Lieutenant-Colonel C. (Colin) Barnes, who was attached to the TOL during the Buraimi Crisis in the 1950s.[3] He noted that the force brought about:

> peace to the area by the settlement of many long standing inter-tribal disputes over boundaries, wells, grazing, land ownership etc, all of which had previously caused many outbreaks of tribal fighting and much loss of life. As the Force expanded more and more, men from the indigenous tribes enlisted and therefore the tribes who over the centuries had, by tradition, been fighting each other were slowly drawing more closely together. This did a great deal to make the area peaceful.[4]

In addition to providing a safe and secure environment, the TOL/TOS also made a direct and significant contribution to all of the ruler-controlled armed forces as well as the first federally-controlled force. This contribution took multiple forms. First, its personnel were loaned to rulers to help establish their armed forces, and to provide training and advice. Second, rulers could request the release of serving members who were from tribes aligned with them, thus providing each ruler with a core of trained personnel around which to build their own force. Third, retired and separated TOL/TOS personnel, including British officers, were also recruited to build the various rulers' forces. And, fourth, rulers could also send their new recruits to TOL/TOS facilities for training.[5] Another significant contribution made by the TOL/TOS was

2   UK Foreign Office, *Foreign Office Annual Reports from Arabia, 1930-1960: 1954-1960*, 1955, p. 172.

3   N. van der Bijl, *Sharing the Secret: The History of the Intelligence Corps 1940-2010* (Havertown, 2013), p. 234.

4   Royal Society for Asian Affairs, Colin Barnes, 'A Short History of the Trucial Oman Levies, Trucial Oman Scouts and the Union Defence Force of the Trucial States (later United Arab Emirates) of the Arabian Gulf, 1951 to 1972', ca. 1976.

5   The first members of the armed forces from Abu Dhabi and Ras Al Khaimah were trained by the TOS. However, in the case of Abu Dhabi, while its recruits started training at the TOS Training Depot in Manama, in March 1966 they were withdrawn part way through their course on orders of the Abu Dhabi Ruler. He only wanted them to be trained on Abu Dhabi soil and negotiated to have TOS instructors come to Abu Dhabi to finish their training. TNA WO 337/15: Colonel F.M. de Butts, Commander TOS, 'Trucial Oman Scouts Intelligence Summary No 72', 6 April 1966.

in helping to establish the rulers' non-military security institutions, including their police and special branches.[6]

The importance of the TOL/TOS in the new armed forces can be seen in the fact that several of its service personnel would go on to hold very senior posts in various ruler-controlled and Federal forces. An example was Mohammed Said Al Badi who was a Corporal in the TOS, before undertaking officer training in England. In 1982, he became a Brigadier and the first Emirati to hold the post of Chief of Staff of the UAE Armed Forces. He was subsequently promoted to Lt. General and appointed the Minister of Interior.

The Trucial Oman Levies (1951-56) and Trucial Oman Scouts (1956-71)

The Trucial Oman Levies was formed in 1951[7] and over its two decades in existence, until it was disbanded in December 1971, the force was a combination of a *gendarmerie* (i.e. soldiers trained for police and military duties) and motorised light infantry. It operated across the Emirates with its headquarters located permanently in Sharjah. Its core elements were rifle squadrons and squadron detachments which were dotted around the Emirates, with their location dictated by both internal security and external defence needs. The force was primarily a land force, although it did use motorised *dhows* (traditional boats) for coastal patrols and transport. It had no organic aircraft and relied, instead, on the RAF's fixed wing and helicopters for observation and transport.

Origins

Discussions in London to form a force in the Trucial States commenced around 1948, prompted by the Foreign Office becoming directly responsible for fulfilling Britain's treaty obligations with the Gulf rulers. Previously, British India had administered Britain's responsibilities on behalf of London, but this ended when India gained independence. Control up to this point had been based on having a Royal Navy presence in the Gulf and sending in British troops as needed. This reflected the approach of British India which 'adopted a model of low-cost imperial control in the region,

---

6   For details on their broader contribution to security institutions see Tancred Bradshaw, 'Security forces and the end of empire in the Trucial States, 1960–1971', *Middle Eastern Studies,* (2020). For an example on how the TOS assisted in the development of the Abu Dhabi Police, see Athol Yates and Ash Rossiter, 'Forging a force: rulers, professional expatriates, and the creation of Abu Dhabi's Police', *Middle Eastern Studies,* 56, 6 (2020).

7   The TOS was formed on 19 March 1951 by the authority of a King's Regulation (British orders and regulations governing British forces). TNA DEFE 68/397: Arthur, 'The Trucial Oman Scouts', Diplomatic Report No 115/72, 21 January 1972.

and they only intervened if their interests were impinged', according to the historian Tancred Bradshaw.[8]

By the late 1940s, there was recognition in London that this approach was no longer the most suitable mechanism to ensure that British national interests were being protected and advanced.[9] From London's perspective, the Emirates were becoming more important due to: (1) their oil potential, (2) their location as an essential air transport link between Britain and its eastern empire, and (3), as part of the regional buffer to Soviet expansion. Of immediate concern was the possible annexation of the potentially oil-rich Abu Dhabi Emirate by Saudi Arabia, which in 1949 had made a claim for some four-fifths of the Emirate.[10] Having a permanent on-the-ground British military presence was seen as essential to addressing these strategic concerns. Other justifications for an armed force based in the Trucial States were that it could provide assistance to regular British forces in the region in the event of an emergency, prevent slave-trading which was politically damaging to Britain's reputation,[11] and could act as a way to establish a secure and stable environment essential for economic, social and political development.[12]

In the late 1940s, the Foreign Office investigated various options for the force's structure, such as establishing an Imperial Arab army for the Gulf, and basing British Army units in the Trucial States.[13] The option selected was a structure used by the Arab Legion in Jordan, i.e. a British officered, locally raised Arab force. As the rationale for the formation of the force was to advance British foreign political interests rather than military ones, the Foreign Office decided it would pay for the force entirely from its own budget. Consequently, the Foreign Office determined the force's structure and composition and would, in its first few years, direct and administer it, rather than the War Office.[14] The heads of the British military services recognised the political nature of the force as seen in a brief prepared for the Secretary of State for Air in 1954. This stated that 'the Trucial Oman Levies have been organised and trained primarily to meet a political

8   T. Bradshaw, 'Book Review – British Policy in the Persian Gulf, 1961-1968: Conceptions of Informal Empire, Helene von Bismarck', *Britain & the World*, 9, 1 (2016), p. 147.
9   T. Bradshaw, 'The Hand of Glubb: the Origins of the Trucial Oman Scouts, 1948-1956', *Middle Eastern Studies*, 53, 4 (2017), p. 660.
10 Saudi Arabia claimed the whole of Abu Dhabi's coast west of Mirfa, as well as the western desert including Liwa and the region around Buraimi.
11 TNA FO 371/75018: B.A.B. Burrows, FO, to Captain H.E. Butler Bowden, Chiefs of Staff Committee, [untitled letter], 6 September 1949.
12 Tom Walcot, 'The Trucial Oman Scouts 1955 to 1971: An Overview', *Asian Affairs*, 37, 1 (2006), p. 19.
13 For a discussion of the options to establish the force, see Bradshaw, 'The Hand of Glubb: the Origins of the Trucial Oman Scouts, 1948-1956'.
14 R. Porter, 'The Trucial Oman Scouts (TOS) 1951-1971', *The Bulletin: Journal of the Military Historical Society*, 41, 163 (1991), p. 135.

commitment'.[15] With the exception of the Ruler of Sharjah, who entered into an agreement for the force to be based in his Emirate, the other Trucial States' rulers were not consulted about the formation of this new force. They were simply notified that it was being established.[16]

Establishment

In 1950, the British Government requested that the Arab Legion provide a training team to form the TOL. In February 1951, a 35-man team from the Legion arrived in Sharjah, led by Major J.M. (Michael) Hankin-Turvin, a contract British officer serving in the Legion and a former Palestine Mandate Police Force officer. The rest of the team consisted of two Arab officers and 30 enlisted Legionaries.[17] The War Office provided the force with its military equipment, notably 30 rifles, two Bren light machine guns, 2-inch mortars and radio sets, as well as six Land Rovers and four 3-ton trucks.[18] The force was based in the Second World War-era and now vacant RAF levies lines,[19] located beside the Sharjah airfield.[20]

The duties of the TOL as of 1951 were to: (1) maintain peace and good order in the Trucial States, (2) prevent or suppress any traffic in slaves, and (3) provide an escort for any British political representative travelling in the Trucial States.[21] This resulted in the force being structured, trained and equipped as a *gendarmerie* rather than an infantry force. To assist it in its policing duties, it was given the power of arrest. At this time, the force was solely directed by the Political Resident Persian Gulf and his delegate, the Political Officer for the Trucial States who was based in Sharjah. The Political Officer would decide on a particular objective and the Commander TOL would determine the most appropriate method of operation.[22] This control is clearly seen in the *Directive for the Trucial Oman Levies* given to the Commander TOL, on 22 April 1951:

15   TNA AIR 8/1888: S.6 to Secretary of State for Air, 'British Troops in Sharjah', 15
     February 1954.
16   TNA FO 1016/193: C.M. Rose, Foreign Office, 'Record of Discussion with Sir Rupert
     Hay on 30 June 1950, Trucial Oman Levies', 3 July 1950.
17   UK Foreign Office, *Foreign Office Annual Reports from Arabia, 1930-1960: 1938-1953*
     (Slough, 1993), 1951, p. 448.
18   M. Mann, *The Trucial Oman Scouts: The Story of a Bedouin Force* (Wilby, Norwich, 1994),
     pp. 22-24.
19   UK Foreign Office, *Historical Summary of Events in the Persian Gulf Shaikhdoms and the
     Sultanate of Muscat and Oman, 1928-1953*, PG 53, p. 149.
20   Stanley-Price, *Imperial Outpost in the Gulf*, p. 96.
21   TNA FO 371/82175: Political Resident Persian Gulf, 'Draft Directive to the
     Commandant of the Trucial Oman Levies from the Political Resident in the Persian
     Gulf', ca. 1950.
22   Ibid.

Except in an emergency, the Levies will only undertake an operation at the request of the Political Officer, Trucial Coast ... The Political Officer will define the particular object of each operation, and the Commandant will decide the method to be employed. The areas of the Trucial Coast Shaikhdoms within which the Levies may operate will be defined in directives issued from time to time by the Political Resident in the Persian Gulf. Except in an emergency the Levies shall not operate within a town which is the capital of a Trucial State Ruler or within the Palace of a Ruler without the specific instructions of the Political Officer or his representative.[23]

The Foreign Office's initial plan for the TOL was for it to grow to some 80 members.[24] While some recruits from local tribes were forthcoming,[25] other nationalities had to be recruited to increase the numbers. Recruiting enough locals was always going to be a challenge, which explains the presence in the force of significant numbers of Omanis (both Arab and Baluchi ethnicity), Baluchis from Pakistan, Dhofaris and Adenese over the decades.[26] As noted by the TOL's Commanding Officer who assumed control in mid-1953, the low number of locals was also encouraged by policy which 'dictated that emphasis should not be placed on recruiting the local Arab as doubt existed apparently as to his reaction to local situation'.[27]

Within a few months of the TOL's establishment, the Arab Legionaries collectively protested as many wanted to return home.[28] This would be the first of many 'mutinous' incidents during the force's history and provides a glimpse into fundamental differences between it and British Army forces. In British military parlance, this collective protest would be deemed to be a mutiny. However, to use this word would give an incorrect characterisation, for it was not a rebellion against authority per se. Rather it was an action common in tribal society where the group does not accept a unilateral decision made by its leader and, instead, seeks consultation and intervention by a superior leader or outside party. Over the force's two decades, such incidents mostly took the form of sit downs, refusals to obey orders, or leave without permission, but sometimes they were violent. In this particular instance, the protest was non-violent and resulted in two Arab officers and some men being sent back to Jordan.

23 UK Foreign Office, *Historical Summary of Events in the Persian Gulf Shaikhdoms and the Sultanate of Muscat and Oman, 1928-1953, Appendices, Genealogical Tables* (London, 1953), p. 274.
24 TNA FO 371/75018: Burrows, [untitled letter], 6 September 1949.
25 UK Foreign Office, *Foreign Office Annual Reports from Arabia, 1930-1960: 1938-1953*, 1951, p. 448.
26 Even by 1968, some 20% of the Other Ranks were not from tribes domiciled in the Trucial States or on the periphery (i.e. 275 out of 1,345). TNA WO 337/13: K.C.P. Ive, Commander TOS, 'Trucial Oman Scouts Security Report, July-Dec 1967', 1968.
27 Imperial War Museum, Documents.4105 Private Papers of Lieutenant Colonel W J Martin, W.J. Martin, 'Just a British Soldier [unpublished autobiography], c.a. 1986.
28 Mann, *The Trucial Oman Scouts: The Story of a Bedouin Force*, p. 29.

In 1951, the security situation outside of the coastal cities where the rulers exercised direct authority was described by one historian as 'little more than a battlefield for warring tribes, a haven for brigands and a profitable hunting ground for slave traders'.[29] Following the commencement of active patrolling by the TOL in March 1951,[30] the situation improved rapidly.[31] By the end of the year, the Political Resident reported that 'no cases of abduction into slavery had occurred during the year and that the decrease in highway robbery was marked'.[32] This was a considerable achievement given that the TOL numbered just 60 at the end of 1951.[33]

Early evolution

1952 and 1953 saw major changes to the mission, force structure and command of the force. By mid-1952, the force's strength had reached one hundred. TOL posts had been established at Rams where there had been a challenge to the Ruler of Ras Al Khaimah, and in the Wadi Al Qawr,[34] which was the only practical motor vehicle route between the Trucial Coast and the Gulf of Oman, and an area contested by local tribal groups.[35] In August 1952, a Saudi Arabian armed constabulary force led by Turki bin Abdullah Al Ataishan, the Saudi Emir of the oil-rich province of Ras Tanura, travelled from the west through Abu Dhabi land and occupied the Buraimi Oasis village of Hamasa (Hamasa was one of three Omani oasis villages, with the other six villages that made up the Buraimi Oasis belonging to Abu Dhabi). Saudi Arabia justified this action by claiming that the land in western Abu Dhabi historically belonged to it. The occupation appears to have been motivated primarily by Saudi Arabia's desire not only to seek influence over Abu Dhabi and Omani tribes in the region, but also to put pressure on Abu Dhabi as part of a much larger land

29   A. Ajjaj, 'Social Development of the Pirate Coast', *Middle East Forum*, XXXVIII Summer (1962), p. 76, cited in Barratt, 'British Influence on Arab Military Forces in the Gulf', p. 109.

30   UK Foreign Office, *Historical Summary of Events in the Persian Gulf Shaikhdoms and the Sultanate of Muscat and Oman, 1928-1953*, PG 53, p. 149.

31   A. Cawston and M. Curtis, *Arabian Days: Memoirs of Two Trucial Oman Scouts* (Hampshire, 2010), p. 184.

32   Hawley, *The Trucial States*, p. 174.

33   The figure of 60 comes from Barratt, 'British Influence on Arab Military Forces in the Gulf', p. 51. However there is uncertainty over the force's numbers in its first year. In October 1951, the TOL reportedly consisted of one British Office, 30 Jordanians and 50 local Other Ranks. P. Clayton, *Two Alpha Lima: The First Ten Years of the Trucial Oman Levies and Trucial Oman Scouts (1950 to 1960)* (London, 1999), p. 27. After the protest action, the force's numbers were given as 50 locals, 30 of who were *bedu* and the rest civilians (e.g. drivers and menial staff). UK Foreign Office, *Historical Summary of Events in the Persian Gulf Shaikhdoms and the Sultanate of Muscat and Oman, 1928-1953*, PG 53, p. 149.

34   UK Foreign Office, *Historical Summary of Events in the Persian Gulf Shaikhdoms and the Sultanate of Muscat and Oman, 1928-1953*, PG 53, p. 150.

35   Ibid., p. 146.

claim (see Chapter 4) in order to access the potential oil resources of Abu Dhabi and the region.[36]

Britain chose not to respond militarily to the Saudi occupation and convinced both the Ruler of Abu Dhabi and the Sultan of Oman likewise. Instead, Britain sought to resolve the situation peacefully. In November 1952, a standstill agreement was reached with Saudi Arabia which allowed Saudi and British forces to remain in their positions in the Oasis while negotiations for a peaceful settlement were undertaken.[37] Both sides agreed not to reinforce their forces or to subvert local tribes via bribes and coercion.

Recognising that the existing TOL was not an infantry force capable of assaulting occupied positions, or effectively guarding the Trucial States' borders against further Saudi encroachments, in early 1953 the British Government decided to increase the TOL to 500 men.[38] As it would take many months to recruit and train this enlarged force, the British brought in reinforcements as a stopgap measure. In January 1953, a detachment of RAF armoured cars arrived[39] and, starting in February 1953, the first of over 300 RAF-controlled Aden Protectorate Levies arrived.[40] While this was occurring, the TOL started recruiting several hundred discharged Adeni solders on two-year contracts.[41] By August 1953, the desired strength of the TOL had been achieved which allowed the Aden Protectorate Levies to return to Aden.[42] The structure of the TOL in mid-1953 consisted of three rifle squadrons – one squadron recruited from the Emirates and manned mostly by Abu Dhabians, and two squadrons of Adenese – plus a regimental headquarters squadron which included signal, mortar/transport and administrative troops.[43]

Many of the former Adeni soldiers who had been recruited turned out to be unreliable and frequently engaged in criminal behaviour. Around May 1953, it was agreed that these men needed to be removed, and with the help of Sheikh Zayed bin Sultan

---

36   The importance of the oil potential of Abu Dhabi's land was reflected in the fact that the US-backed Arabian American Oil Company (ARAMCO) provided encouragement for the Saudi land claim, logistical support for the Saudi incursion in Buraimi and Abu Dhabi's western region, and formulation of the legal argument for Saudi Arabia to use in subsequent negotiations over the territory. H. Phillips, *Envoy Extraordinary: A Most Unlikely Ambassador* (London, 1995), p. 38.

37   UK Foreign Office, *Historical Summary of Events in the Persian Gulf Shaikhdoms and the Sultanate of Muscat and Oman, 1928-1953*, PG 53, p. 160.

38   Ibid., p. 150.

39   Ibid., p. 161.

40   N.W.M. Warwick, *In Every Place: The RAF Armoured Cars in the Middle East 1921-1953* (Rushden, 2014), pp. 573, 583.

41   UK Foreign Office, *Foreign Office Annual Reports from Arabia, 1930-1960: 1938-1953*, 1953, p. 718.

42   UK Foreign Office, *Historical Summary of Events in the Persian Gulf Shaikhdoms and the Sultanate of Muscat and Oman, 1928-1953*, PG 53, p. 150.

43   Imperial War Museum, Documents.4105 Private Papers of Lieutenant Colonel W J Martin, Martin, 'Just a British Soldier [unpublished autobiography], ca. 1986.

Al Nahyan, the governor of Al Ain and brother of the Abu Dhabi Ruler, Sheikh Shakhbut, locals were recruited to replace them.[44] The removal of the Adenese was accelerated following the November 1953 mutiny by one of the Adeni-manned TOL squadrons. Soldiers in the squadron in Buraimi murdered two British officers and an NCO. Immediately all but 12 of the 90-man Adenese-manned squadron were dismissed.[45]

Despite the standstill agreement, Saudi Arabia encouraged activities against the rulers of Abu Dhabi and Oman. In January 1953, a party of Bani Kaab tribesmen 'carrying a Saudi flag attacked a Levy Post at the Wadi Al Qawr ... [although in this case] the attack was easily beaten off'.[46] In March 1953, a Saudi tax collector and a party of 38 armed men arrived in Buraimi seeking to collect *zakat*.[47] This act was to bolster Saudi Arabia's land claim, for in the Arabian Peninsula, the payment of tax to someone indicates that the recipient has sovereignty over the taxed person and his land.

The breaches of the standstill agreement by the Saudis resulted in additional TOL troops being sent to Buraimi and in November 1953, the TOL Commander issued a directive for his force 'to prevent arms, ammunition, supplies and reinforcements from entering the Trucial States and to blockade the Saudis in Hamasa'.[48] To do this, one squadron was based at Kahil to the north of Hamasa on blockade duties.[49] To prevent Saudi from also pushing into the western side of Abu Dhabi Emirate, the TOL also established additional posts there. The most westerly TOL post was at Nakhla, a point west of Al Sila and in present-day Saudi Arabian territory. It was supported by the TOL squadron based at Tarif, which also supported a post in the Liwa Oasis.[50]

44   Ibid., p. 124.
45   UK Foreign Office, *Foreign Office Annual Reports from Arabia, 1930-1960: 1938-1953*, 1953, p. 718; Royal Society for Asian Affairs, Barnes, 'A Short History of the Trucial Oman Levies, Trucial Oman Scouts and the Union Defence Force of the Trucial States (later United Arab Emirates) of the Arabian Gulf, 1951 to 1972', ca. 1976. This event did not end all Adenese in the TOS. Some 70 were serving in the TOS when the force was handed over to the UAE in 1971. TNA DEFE 68/397, GG Arthur, Political Resident at Bahrain to the Secretary of State for Foreign and Commonwealth Affairs, 'The Trucial Oman Scouts', Diplomatic Report No 115/72, 21 January 1972. For a first-hand account of the munity, see Imperial War Museum, Documents.4105 Private Papers of Lieutenant Colonel W J Martin, Martin, 'Just a British Soldier [unpublished autobiography]', c.a. 1986.
46   UK Foreign Office, *Historical Summary of Events in the Persian Gulf Shaikhdoms and the Sultanate of Muscat and Oman, 1928-1953*, PG 53, p. 161.
47   Ibid.
48   M.Q. Morton, *Buraimi: The Struggle for Power, Influence and Oil in Arabia* (London, 2013), p. 123.
49   Royal Society for Asian Affairs, Barnes, 'A Short History of the Trucial Oman Levies, Trucial Oman Scouts and the Union Defence Force of the Trucial States (later United Arab Emirates) of the Arabian Gulf, 1951 to 1972', ca. 1976.
50   Imperial War Museum, Documents.4105 Private Papers of Lieutenant Colonel W.J. Martin, Martin, 'Just a British Soldier [unpublished autobiography]', c.a. 1986.

While initially the War Office had minimal involvement with the TOL, the Saudi activity led to a request for greater British Army engagement. In early 1952, the first British Army officer arrived to serve in the TOL. He was followed by several others, and their training and leadership accelerated the force's professionalism.[51] With the return to Jordan of Major Hankin-Turvin in August 1953, the first serving British Army officer, Lieutenant-Colonel W.J. (William) Martin, became Commander TOL.

In 1953, operational and administrative control of the TOL became the responsibility of the War Office through the Commander-in-Chief's Committee, Middle East.[52] To provide regional British Army control over the TOL, the post of Senior Army Officer Persian Gulf (SAOPG) was established and co-located with the British Political Residency in Bahrain.[53] With the transfer of administrative control, stores, weapons and equipment were ordered in the same way and through the same channels as for other British Army units. Despite the fact that operational and administrative control of the TOL now rested with the British Army, the Foreign Office, through the Political Resident, retained policy command of the force. This would continue until the force was disbanded in 1971. This is seen in the Chiefs of Staff Committee's 1967 Directive which stated that the TOS is 'controlled by the Political Resident and their employment is subject to his authority, exercised where appropriate through the Political Agent, Dubai and Abu Dhabi'.[54] The influence of the Foreign Office over an armed force was unusual; the Political Resident, 1961-66, William Luce, commented that it was the only recorded instance of a British diplomat commanding a private army.[55]

From 1952 onwards, British Army officers would fill most officer posts in the TOL/TOS's units, and they commanded the force from 1953. Arab officers only filled junior posts. British Army NCOs also served in the force with the majority filling training and specialist roles. The language of the force's headquarters, as well as signals and technical training, was English, while in the rifle squadrons it was Arabic. This meant that British officers in these squadrons required Arabic language skills; they would generally attend an Arabic language course before joining the force.[56] British NCOs did not need Arabic and would not attend such courses.

51 This was Major P. (Peter) MacDonald who, following the Saudi occupation of part of Buraimi Oasis, was sent with his squadron to Buraimi to provide security. J.F. Walker, *Tyro on the Trucial Coast* (Durham, UK, 1999), p. 33.
52 R. Trench, ed. *Arab Gulf Cities* (Slough, 1994), A.R. Walmsley, FO, to F.B. Richards, British Residency Bahrain, 1 February 1957, pp. 336-7.
53 UK Foreign Office, *Historical Summary of Events in the Persian Gulf Shaikhdoms and the Sultanate of Muscat and Oman, 1928-1953*, PG 53, p. 150.
54 TNA CAB 163/116: Major General J.H. Gibbon, Secretary, Chiefs of Staff Committee, 'Directive for the Commander, British Forces Gulf', 20 November 1967.
55 Balfour Paul, *The End of Empire in the Middle East*, p. 110.
56 Barratt, 'British Influence on Arab Military Forces in the Gulf', p. 87.

By the end of 1954, the TOL was constituted as an HQ squadron at Sharjah and three 100-man rifle squadrons. The force's total strength was just over 500 men, 14 of whom were British.[57] The OCs and 2ICs of the rifle squadrons were British officers, as were the HQ staff. At this time, one rifle squadron was based in the Al Ain region watching the Buraimi Oasis, another at Sharjah to provide patrols across the Emirates and security for the HQ TOL, with the third at Tarif where continuation training was done.[58] The location of Tarif, on the western coast of Abu Dhabi, was chosen to deter Saudi subversive activities in the region; it also provided protection for local oil exploration activities. Each squadron was mounted in its own transport, allowing it to move at short notice and operate independently. By this time, recruits signed up for two years, with the possibility of their enlistment being renewed. Recruits undertook an eight-week basic course, including drill and weapons training.[59]

In July 1954, Saudi Arabia and Britain signed the Jeddah Agreement which referred the Buraimi issue to an impartial international tribunal headed by a Belgian judge of the International Court. Despite a commitment by Saudi Arabia not to subvert the loyalty of Omani and Abu Dhabi tribes in the Buraimi region, it continued to do so through bribery and intimidation.[60] By 1955, Saudi Arabia's behaviour had become so egregious that Britain abandoned the tribunal's dispute settlement process and ordered a military operation to expel the Saudi forces from Buraimi by force. On 26 October 1955, two TOL squadrons, supported to a degree by Abu Dhabi tribesmen, Omani forces and regular British forces, assaulted the positions of the Saudi and their allied tribesmen. The operation was successful, although two TOL soldiers were killed and three wounded.[61] Up to 11 dissident tribesmen were also killed, but no Saudis died.[62] All the Saudis were deported, while a number of allied tribesmen went into exile.

Despite the success of the operation, it revealed significant weaknesses in the TOL, including that it could not effectively operate as an infantry force due to a lack of manpower, combat training and infantry heavy weapons.[63] Consequently, the force was up-armed, expanded and formally given the mission of defending the Trucial State borders.[64] In doing so, it became seen as fulfilling an 'Imperial Defence' role in

57   Walcot, 'The Trucial Oman Scouts 1955 to 1971: An Overview'.
58   M. Type, 'TOL', *Soldier Magazine*, January (1956), p. 23.
59   Ibid.
60   J. Priestland, ed. *The Buraimi Dispute: Contemporary Documents 1950-1961, Volume 5: 1954-1955* (Slough, 1992), Foreign Office to Jedda, 'Addressed to Jedda telegram No 692 of October 25', 25 October 1955, p. 735.
61   Ibid., BAB Burrows, Bahrain, to Foreign Office, Telegram no 765 of October 26, 26 October 1955, p. 737.
62   Ibid., BAB Burrows, Bahrain, to Foreign Office, Telegram no 784 of October 30, 26 October 1955, p. 757.
63   Mann, *The Trucial Oman Scouts: The Story of a Bedouin Force*, p. 61.
64   TNA WO 32/16413: DSD UK Government, War Office, 'Title – Trucial Oman Levies', Loose Minute to 29/55, 14 September 1955.

addition to advancing Foreign Office interests.[65] A consequence of this was that the War Office was told to pay for half the costs of the force from August 1956.[66] The expansion saw a fifth rifle squadron formed, and all rifle squadrons increasing from 94 to 150 men; both a training wing and a mortar platoon were also formed. This resulted in the force doubling in size.[67]

To build this new force, a substantial increase in British personnel was needed. To encourage more British serving personnel to volunteer, the force's name was changed in 1956, substituting the word 'scout' for 'levies'. This was to eliminate the impression that the force was conscripted, as well as making the force sound more exotic and alluring.[68] The regulations which promulgated the name change also gave the Political Resident the power to deploy the force outside the Trucial States.[69] Over the following few years, the number of British personnel in the force increased, and by 1960-61, there were of around 40 British officers and 100 NCOs.[70]

By the end of the 1950s, the TOS was structured into five 120-man rifle squadrons, named as 'A', 'B', 'C', 'D' and 'X' squadrons,[71] under a single force HQ. It also had a substantial HQ Squadron which included a workshop, a transport troop, a signals centre, a small hospital, a pipe band and a training squadron at Manama.[72] The TOS's disposition in the late 1950s also changed, with squadrons redeployed to protect the rapidly expanding oil exploration in the west of Abu Dhabi Emirate, in addition to the northern Emirates to enhance internal security.

Involvement in the Sultanate of Muscat and Oman

The TOS's conventional infantry capabilities grew in the late 1950s as it became involved in operations in the neighbouring Sultanate of Muscat and Oman. In the

65   A. Rossiter, *Security in the Gulf: Local Militaries before British Withdrawal* (Cambridge, 2020), p. 99.
66   TNA FO 371/120627: H.W. Minshull, FO, 'Financial Responsibility for the Trucial Oman Scouts', 14 September 1956.
67   TNA FO 371/114680: GHQ Middle East Land Forces to MoD, 'Trucial Oman Levies', 24 October 1955.
68   The new name was one of two suggested for 'psychological effect on would-be officer volunteers' by Field Marshal Sir Gerald Walter Robert Templer, Chief of the Imperial General Staff during his visit to Bahrain in 1955. The other was the Trucial Oman Regiment, which was rejected by the Foreign Office, as this would have required a complicated procedure of changing the Order in Council which had established the force. TNA, WO 32/16413, UK Government, 'Title – Trucial Oman Levies', Loose Minute to 29/55, 14 September 1955.
69   Ibid.
70   Mann, *The Trucial Oman Scouts: The Story of a Bedouin Force*, p. 124.
71   In Arabic, and sometimes in English, the squadrons were referred to by numbers (i.e. '1', '2', '3', '4' squadrons) rather than letters, except for 'X' Squadron which kept its letter. Lt. Colonel N.C.F. Weekes, UDF/FAF, 1974-76, telephone interview, 25 January 2017.
72   Walcot, 'The Trucial Oman Scouts 1955 to 1971: An Overview', p. 21.

mid-1950s, a separatist movement in the Sultanate's interior began to grow. Headed by the Imam of the Islamic Ibadi sect, the movement sought to establish an independent state in the interior of Oman. In mid-1957, the separatists defeated the Sultan's forces in the interior, and the TOS was tasked with supporting British and Omani forces to reassert the Sultan's authority. In July, elements of the TOS moved to Oman and were engaged in combat operations. They re-established the Sultan's rule within a month, and so in August, the TOS returned to the Trucial States. After a lull in the hostilities, however, the insurrection reignited and, consequently, the TOS returned to the Sultanate in November 1957. Following the decisive defeat of the separatists in the Jebel Akhdar assault in January 1959 (which was supported by RAF aircraft flown out of Sharjah), most TOS elements returned to the Trucial States in the following month.

The experience of the first short TOS campaign in Oman (July-August 1957) highlighted inadequacies in the force and, in October 1957, Britain's Military Co-ordination Committee recommended a major re-organisation and expansion of the TOS.[73] This saw the force split into two regiments by 1960 – the Desert and Trucial State Regiments. The Desert Regiment focused on conventional infantry combat, such as that which the TOS had recently undertaken in the Sultanate. The Desert Regiment initially consisted of two squadrons (X Squadron in addition to C Squadron at Buraimi), commanded by a mobile regimental headquarters headed by a Lieutenant-Colonel. It was initially based in Buraimi. However, due to political sensitivities in having the force concentrated there, it was moved to Idhen, just north of Manama. The squadrons in the Desert Regiment were subsequently increased to three – X, A and D Squadrons. In addition, it gained a heavy weapons support group equipped with 3-inch mortars and medium machine guns. The Trucial States Regiment started out as four rifle squadrons and ended up as two (B Squadron at Mirfa and C Squadron at Buraimi), as well as the Training Squadron at Manama.[74] The Trucial States Regiment focused on the traditional TOS internal security mission.

The HQ structure of the force now consisted of the HQ Desert Regiment located with that regiment, and a combined HQ for both the TOS overall and the Trucial States Regiment based in Sharjah. The Sharjah HQ was staffed as a brigade-level force, with the expectation that other British units would flesh out the brigade in times of conflict. In May 1960, the TOS's establishment strength was nearly 1,300. Locals from the Trucial States still formed a minority of the force, accounting for 450

73   TNA FO 371/126951: Military Co-ordination Committee (Persian Gulf), 'The Organisation and Deployment of Land Forces in the Persian Gulf, Muscat and Oman', 3 October 1957. In September 1958, the War Office approved the enlargement and re-organisation of the TOS. Clayton, *Two Alpha Lima*, p. 124; Mann, *The Trucial Oman Scouts: The Story of a Bedouin Force*, p. 131; Barratt, 'British Influence on Arab Military Forces in the Gulf', p. 57.

74   Mann, *The Trucial Oman Scouts: The Story of a Bedouin Force*, p. 131; Barratt, 'British Influence on Arab Military Forces in the Gulf', p. 57.

of the 1,150 non-British enlisted personnel. The 1,150 enlisted personnel consisted of some 600 soldiers from Oman, 450 from the Trucial States and 100 in total from Pakistan, Aden, Somalia and of Baluch origin.[75] The expansion did not see an increase in the number of rifle squadrons however, the strength of each squadron increased. In that same month, the Political Resident, through the Military Co-ordination Committee, issued a directive to the Commander TOS which redefined the force's duties. The TOS's primary duty was now 'to prevent or repel any armed incursion into or attack on the Trucial States', with the traditional task of ensuring law and order in the Trucial States being the second duty.[76]

The TOS in the 1960s

By mid-1961, the improved capabilities of the Sultan of Oman's armed forces meant it was very unlikely that the TOS would return to the Sultanate. In addition to the cumbersome[77] nature of the two-regiment structure meant that the twin-HQ/regiment structure was no longer appropriate. Consequently, in September 1961, the Desert Regiment was disbanded,[78] with the force returning to its earlier structure – five rifle squadrons under a single HQ supported. This structure (see Figure 16) would continue virtually unchanged until the TOS was disbanded in 1971.

The TOS remained structured as a lightly armed, mobile force with distributed rifle squadron bases around the Emirates. The role of the TOS in the face of an attack from Saudi Arabia was to slow a Saudi advance so to buy time for the arrival of regular British forces.[79]

A system of regular rotation for the rifle squadrons had by then been introduced. Known as the 'squadron roundabout', this involved the rifle squadrons moving roughly every four to six months through each outstation in turn, as well as Sharjah, where one squadron was co-located with the HQ TOS. In 1962, the outstations were at Masafi in the Hajar Mountains,[80] Manama near Sharjah, Jahili Fort at Al Ain, and Mirfa on Abu Dhabi's western coast. The rotation was designed both to prevent relationships developing between the troops and the locals, which was seen as potentially inhibiting the force's impartiality, and to provide respite from the more uncomfortable camps.[81]

---

75   TNA FO 371/149048: J.F. Walker, 'Composition of Trucial Oman Scouts', 25 May 1960.
76   Clayton, *Two Alpha Lima*, p. 142.
77   Burdett, *Records of the Emirates 1961–1965: 1962*, 'Revised Establishment Proposal for the Trucial Oman Scouts', 20 June 1962, pp. 313-27.
78   Author's collection, Abu Dhabi, Ash files, Captain Tim Ash, 'The Trucial Oman Scouts', n.d.
79   TNA FO 371/157038: Sir William Luce, PRPG to FO, [untitled letter], 5 August 1961.
80   This squadron camp was established following an outbreak of violence between tribesmen of Ras Al Khaimah and Fujairah in the area north of Masafi in May 1959. Barratt, 'British Influence on Arab Military Forces in the Gulf', p. 56.
81   Mann, *The Trucial Oman Scouts: The Story of a Bedouin Force*, p. 132.

Outstations would sometimes maintain subordinate posts where a detachment from a squadron would be based. Both outstations and posts moved locations from time to time which reflected changing security needs, such as new flashpoints of tribal disputes, countering Saudi subversion efforts, and where oil drilling parties operated and needed security.

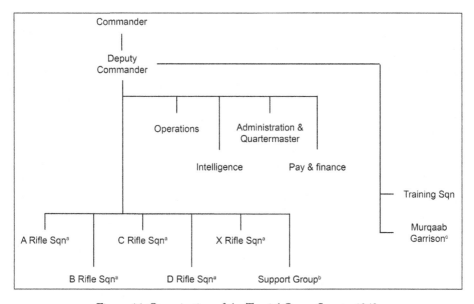

Figure 16: Organisation of the Trucial Oman Scouts, 1969.

Notes

a. A rifle squadron in 1966 was made up of a Squadron HQ, and three troops of approximately 30 men. It was normally commanded by a major, with a captain as 2IC. It typically had between 80 and 100 men. The Squadron HQ was mounted in two Fitted for Radio (FFR) Land Rovers and was responsible for command and administration (e.g. rations, petrol oil and lubricants, medical, signals and vehicle operations). Each troop was commanded by an Arab officer supported by a troop sergeant. A troop was divided into three sections of 8 men, each led by a corporal. The section was armed with No.4 .303 rifles and a two-man Bren Gun team. Each troop also included a signaller, a runner and driver. One troop was mounted in Land Rovers, while the other two troops were mounted in Bedford 4-ton vehicles.[82]

b. The Support Group consisted of a Reconnaissance Group made up of two machine gun sections, equipped with two GPMG SF, and a mortar troop consisting of three sections, each with two 81mm mortars.

c. The Murqaab Garrison consisted of an HQ Squadron, Signals Squadron, Transport Squadron, Quartermasters, Workshops, Stores, Work SVC organisation, Education Unit, Medical Squadron (consisting of Medical Reception Station Murqaab and Medical Centre Manama), Pipes and Drums Band, Regimental Police, Cooks, Transit Wing and Stables.

82 M. Curtis, 'On Secondment with the Trucial Oman Scouts 1966-1968', *Liwa: Journal of the National Center for Documentation & Research*, December 2:4 (2010), p. 50.

The internal security functions of the TOS in the early 1960s continued as before – intervening in and de-escalating tribal disputes, deterring crime and apprehending criminals in the hinterland (including gun-smugglers who were supplying separatist and revolutionary groups in Oman), and protecting the movements of the Political Residency staff and British oil operations. The TOS was also involved in maintaining public order in settlements. For example in April 1963, a mob of dissatisfied labourers and unemployed trouble-makers attempted to storm the airfield at Sharjah but were deterred by the TOS's presence.[83] The TOS also settled labour protests due to their presence, such as in late 1963 on Abu Dhabi's key oil exporting facility at Das Island.[84]

Infrequently, the force was called upon to help re-establish or reinforce the authority of a ruler or intervene in disputes within a ruling family. One such instance was in 1955, when the force assisted the Ruler of Dubai in preventing his overthrow by relatives.[85]

The force was involved in two operations to replace rulers.[86] The first such operation was in 1965 when the TOS supported the deposition of the Ruler of Sharjah, Sheikh Saqr bin Sultan Al Qasimi. Sheikh Saqr was an outspoken nationalist and supporter of pan-Arabism, who was seen by the British as seeking to undermine Britain's position in the region. The deposition operation involved the British Political Agent inviting Sheikh Saqr to the Dubai Political Agency and then informing him that he had lost the support of his family and was to be exiled. The TOS provided security for the operation, and a RAF aircraft flew the Ruler into exile. The Ruler of Ras Al Khaimah, Sheikh Saqr bin Mohammad Al Qasimi, wanted the deposed ruler to be reinstated and mobilised a force of tribesmen to remove the new ruler, Sheikh Khalid. However, the TOS blocked the routes from Ras Al Khaimah to Sharjah and the tribesmen dispersed.[87] The second operation occurred in 1966 when the TOS facilitated the replacement of the Ruler of Abu Dhabi, Sheikh Shakhbut bin Sultan Al Nahyan, due to concerns held by the British and Abu Dhabi ruling family that he was impeding state development.[88]

83   Ibid., p. 139.
84   TNA FO 371/179929: T.F. Brenchley, FO to H. Phillips, PRPG, [untitled letter], 10 August 1965.
85   This involved Sheikh Juma bin Maktoum, brother of the Ruler, and his three eldest sons, Obaid, Maktoum and Hamed. TNA FO 371/114589: B.A.B. Burrows, PRPG, to H. Macmillan, Secretary of State for Foreign Affairs, [untitled letter], Despatch No. 69, 31 May 1955.
86   For details on the political background of replacing the rulers of Sharjah and Abu Dhabi, see H. von Bismarck, *British Policy in the Persian Gulf, 1961–1968: Conceptions of Informal Empire* (Basingstoke, 2013), pp. 148-53, 181-85.
87   Mann, *The Trucial Oman Scouts: The Story of a Bedouin Force*, p. 153.
88   For details on the TOS involvement in Sheikh Shakhbut's disposition, see ibid., pp. 161-63; Cawston and Curtis, *Arabian Days*, pp. 121-27; Balfour Paul, *Bagpipes in Babylon*, pp. 203-05.

The TOS in the early 1960s continued to grow and by February 1964 had an establishment strength of 1,235.[89] The force's expansion at that time was unusual as Britain's global defence policy was then one of force reduction. This reduction was driven by the 1957 Defence White Paper which radically changed Britan's defence strategy, capabilities and force structure. It announced a reduction in the three military services from appoximately 700,000 men to half that over the following four years, as well as a downgrading of British overseas military commitments.[90] However, this downsizing did not apply to the TOS as the White Paper noted that the 'territories on the Persian Gulf for whose defence Britain is responsible' would not be earmarked for force reduction.[91] This was due to the region's oil and its importance to British strategic interests. By mid-1960, however, the TOS was no longer being protected from the reduction in global commitments; hence, plans were drawn up to reduce the force. These included the proposal in 1965 to eliminate up to two rifle squadrons within a few years as Abu Dhabi's embryonic armed force was expected to take over some of the TOS's responsbilities.[92] As a result, one goal was to cut the number of British Army personnel by 38%, which would take it from around 130 to 80.[93]

However, these plans were shelved due to three major political and military developments in the region – the 1966 decision by the British Government to withdraw forces from Aden, the increasing regional security challenges facing Britain, and then in early 1968, the annoucement that British forces would be withdrawn from the Gulf by 1971.

In mid-1965, the British Government decided to withdraw its forces from Aden following years of anti-British, pan-Arabic, and revolutionary political agitation and revolt.[94] The decision was made public in February 1966 as part of the 1966 Defence White Paper.[95] This change was part of Britain's policy to reduce overseas military commitments in countries 'East of Suez'. In late 1966, the British Government decided that the date of withdrawl from Aden would be 1 January 1968. One of the Government's objectives as it withdrew was to 'leave behind a stable and viable government on independence, preferably covering the whole of South Arabia'.[96] However, the security situation rapidly deteriorated in Aden, and subsequently the

---

89   TNA FO 371/174718: M04 UK, War Office, [untitled letter], 26 February 1964.
90   UK Ministry of Defence, *Defence: Outline of Future Policy* (London, 1957), p. 9.
91   Ibid., p. 6.
92   TNA FO 1016/736: Brigadier I.R.R. Hollyer, HQ Land Forces Persian Gulf, 'Trucial Oman Scouts Arabisation', 28 June 1966.
93   TNA FO 1016/736: Major for General Officer Commanding, 'Proposed Pay Increases for the Arab Element of the Trucial Oman Scouts', 7 October 1966.
94   TNA DEFE 68/397: Arthur, 'The Trucial Oman Scouts', Diplomatic Report No 115/72, 21 January 1972.
95   S. Mawby, *British Policy in Aden and the Protectorates 1955-67: Last Outpost of a Middle East Empire* (London, 2006), p. 143.
96   Cabinet Defence and Oversea Policy Committee, 'South Arabia: problems of preparing for independence', TNA CAB 148/31: IPD (67) 19, memorandum, in W.R. Louis and S.R. Ashton, *East of Suez and the Commonwealth 1964-1971* (London, 2004), p. 214.

British Government decided to bring forward the date of departure to the end of November 1967. Following the accelerated British withdrawal and the failure to establish a functioning state, violence increased in Aden and its economy collapsed.

The Gulf Arab rulers watched the developments in Aden with mounting anxiety, for they demonstrated that Britain's presence in the Gulf was not open-ended despite promises made by British leaders. Events in Aden also showed that withdrawal commitments could be enacted at short notice which meant that the British pledges to leave behind a stable state were more aspirational than real commitments.

The British Government recognised that the withdrawal from Aden raised concerns among the Gulf Arab rulers so the British Foreign Minister, Goronwy Roberts, toured the Gulf in late October and early November 1967 to reassure the rulers that Britain would not withdraw its forces in the near future.[97] A Foreign Office report of the visit described the visit in the following way: 'Mr Roberts gave an official assurance to each of the rulers that Her Majesty's Government would maintain the British political and military presence in the Gulf so long as it was necessary to maintain peace and stability in the area and that no time-limit was set to this presence.'[98]

The withdrawal

However, on 16 January 1968, the British Prime Minister, Harold Wilson, announced a reversal of the policy of just two months before. This was primarily motivated by cost cutting due to significant problems with the British economy, including a 14% devaluation of the pound. Wilson's January 1968 announcement stated that British forces would withdraw from the Gulf by the end of 1971. The unilateral announcement left the Gulf Arab rulers in dismay, and to mollify them, again Minister Roberts was dispatched to the Gulf. His role was to reassure the rulers that the withdrawal would be more orderly than in Aden.

The 1966 announcement by Britain that it would withdraw from Aden emboldened groups hostile to Britain's presence in the Gulf. Consequently, in 1966, British military planners recognised that due to the 'increased threat to the Trucial States, on operational and political grounds the strength and role for the TOS must remain as at present.'[99] Not only were the planned force reductions for the TOS halted, plans were also made to base some 2,400 regular British forces personnel in Sharjah[100] as

---

97   Uzi Rabi, 'Britain's "Special Position" in the Gulf: Its Origins, Dynamics and Legacy', *Middle Eastern Studies*, 42, 3 (2006), pp. 359-60.

98   National Archives of Australia, A1838, 181/1/15: UK Foreign Office, 'Visit of Minister of State, Foreign Office, to Southern Gulf States, 31 October-8 November 1967', 22 November 1967.

99   TNA, FO 1016/736, Hollyer, 'Trucial Oman Scouts Arabisation', 28 June 1966.

100   TNA FO 371/185548: Political Resident Persian Gulf, 'Record of Salient Points Arising from a Conference between PRPG and Service Staffs at Bahrain 22 February 1966', February 1966.

part of Britain's efforts to enhance security in Gulf. The British personnel moved into the TOS facilities beside RAF Station Sharjah which was upgraded to include battalion-sized air-conditioned barracks,[101] with the TOS moving in September 1967 to a new camp at Murqaab, a few miles north-west of Sharjah.[102] The separation of the TOS from British troops had a number of benefits including preventing locals and the rulers seeing the TOS as 'mere British auxiliaries'.[103] Likewise, TOS members were not exposed to the better conditions and benefits received by British regular forces, and hence prevented agitation for improvements.[104]

Most of the wealthier Arab Gulf rulers wanted to see Britain retain its military presence in the Gulf at least in the short-term after 1971, and offered to pay the United Kingdom Government to do so.[105] In an interview a few days after the offer was made, the British Secretary of Defence, Denis Healey, stated 'Well I don't very much like the idea of being a sort of white slaver for the Arab sheikhs ... And I think it would be a very great mistake if we allowed ourselves to become mercenaries for people who would like to have a few British troops around.' In addition to being offensive to the rulers, the statement ran counter to UK practice. Foreign governments have had a long tradition of contributing to the cost of British forces on their territory. Indian taxpayers financially supported the British Army regiments stationed in British India, West Germany contributed to the costs of the British Army of the Rhine, and the people of Hong Kong underwrote the British protecting them.[106]

While Britain did not want its military to remain in the region after 1971, it wanted to ensure that the TOS would continue to provide security and stability for the Emirates as they transitioned from Protected States to a fully sovereign federation of states. Britain advanced the idea that the TOS could become the nucleus of a collective force for the federation. It offered to transfer the force to the proposed federal state, as well as to continue to allow British personnel to serve in this force, and to sell or gift the TOS's weapons, equipment and facilities to the new state.

During the discussions from early 1968 to the end of 1971 over the establishment of some form of federation, the British worked to ensure that the TOS remained a viable and capable force. In 1969, Britain re-equipped the TOS with modern British

101 Vice-Admiral Sir John Martin, 'The Last Year in Aden – The Royal Navy', *Journal of the Royal Air Force Historical Society*, 18 (1998), p. 98.
102 TNA DEFE 68/397: Artur, 'The Trucial Oman Scouts', Diplomatic Report No 115/72, 21 January 1972.
103 TNA FO 371/185548: Trucial Oman Scouts HQ, 'Redeployment and the Trucial Oman Scouts', May 1966.
104 TNA FO 371/185548: Brigadier M.W. Holme, Commander LFPG, to Major General J.E.F. Willoughby, General Officer Commanding Middle East Land Forces, [untitled note], February 1966.
105 The force cost Britain around £1.5 million per year. TNA, DEFE 68/397, Arthur, 'The Trucial Oman Scouts', Diplomatic Report No 115/72, 21 January 1972.
106 Onley, *Britain and the Gulf Shaikhdoms, 1820-1971*, p. 22.

infantry weapons.[107] The force continued to operate as before, despite its uncertain future. In early 1968, a squadron defused a tribal rebellion in Ras Al Khaimah. This tension resulted in a new base in Ras Al Khaimah – at Ham Ham – being built.[108]

In addition to ensuring the TOS remained an operational force, the British assisted in the development of the Abu Dhabi military in order to allow it to take over the TOS's security commitments in that Emirate. By 1968, the Abu Dhabi force had grown sufficiently, so the TOS squadron at Mirfa in Abu Dhabi Emirate was withdrawn. This left only one squadron in Abu Dhabi Emirate, at Al Ain.[109] This in effect made the TOS a 'security force for the Northern Trucial States'.[110]

By the second half of 1971, the rulers of the Trucial States (except for Ras Al Khaimah) had agreed to form a federated state. At midnight on 1 December 1971, the Treaties of Protection were annulled; thus, the UAE came into being. Control of the TOS remained with the British until 21 December 1971. The handover date three weeks after Britain's withdrawal was an essential part of Britain's Gulf run-down plan. Specifically, Britain wanted a fully operational and full-strength TOS so that it could guarantee internal security as British forces were extracted.[111] This would then avoid damage to British prestige and loss of life as forces withdrew under fire – as was the case in the 1967 withdrawal from Aden.

The day before the ending of the Treaties, Iranian forces seized the two Tunb islands owned by Ras Al Khaimah, and landed forces on Abu Musa Island, which was owned by Sharjah. Britain did not intervene, despite its treaty obligations. Anti-British riots broke out in a number of Emirates. The TOS helped maintain public order in the following days by supporting local police forces, notably in Ras Al Khaimah and Sharjah. The TOS did not intervene in protests in Dubai and Abu Dhabi which were handled by local security forces.[112]

At a ceremonial level, the end of the TOS was marked at the passing out parade of TOS recruits on 29 November 1971. This was to be the TOS's largest batch of recruits to pass out at one time.[113] The size of the parade sent a strong political message that the force was still operational and growing, thus remaining a force for security and stability despite Britain's departure.

107 This included L1A1 Self-Loading Rifles and the L7 GPMGs. Mann, *The Trucial Oman Scouts: The Story of a Bedouin Force*, p. 173.
108 Ibid., p. 174.
109 TNA FCO 8/900: E.F. Henderson, Political Agent, Abu Dhabi, 'Minutes of the Abu Dhabi LIC Meeting on 17 April 1968', 21 April 1968.
110 TNA FCO 8/1779: Joseph Godber, Minister of State for Foreign and Commonwealth Affairs, 'The Trucial Oman Scouts', 4 August 1971.
111 TNA FCO 8/1779: R.F.D. Sibbring, Defence Secretariat 6a to Lt Colonel W.M.L. Adler, Arabian Department, FCO, 'Trucial Oman Scouts', 6 July 1971.
112 Mann, *The Trucial Oman Scouts: The Story of a Bedouin Force*, p. 188.
113 Ibid., p. 190.

At midnight on 22 December 1971, the TOS was officially disbanded and all its local members discharged;[114] at this point, it had 35 British officers,[115] 33 Arab officers and a total strength of around 1,500.[116] However, to ensure the Emirates retained an effective armed force, all TOS members, along with its British officers and NCO, in the weeks leading up to the disbandment had been invited to join to a new force, the UAE's federally-controlled Union Defence Force (UDF). Virtually all took up this offer. Britain transferred the bulk of the TOS's equipment and facilities to the UDF. This meant that on the first day of the UDF's existence, it was a fully functioning armed unit.

Regular British forces

Royal Navy

The Royal Navy had guaranteed maritime security in the Gulf since the 1800s. From 1935, the Royal Navy's presence in the Gulf was based at HMS *Jufair* in Bahrain. HMS *Jufair* was home to the Gulf Squadron, which consisted in the 1950s of a handful of sloops or frigates. With the 1961 Kuwait Crisis, the Royal Navy's presence in the Gulf expanded to include mine-countermeasures and amphibious warfare squadrons. The Royal Navy's vessels patrolled the waters of the Gulf so as to deter aggressors as well as intercepting vessels carrying illegal immigrants, drugs, rebels or arms.

The Royal Navy would also occasionally take action to support British interests. For example, the Royal Navy was used 'to stabilise the situation' at the oil exploration site of Ras Sadr, east of Abu Dhabi in 1950, following a strike by local employees.[117] A later example, which involved the TOL, occurred in July 1952, when the former *wali* (governor) of Rams, Salim bin Salih, defied the authority of the Ruler of Ras Al Khaimah, Sheikh Saqr bin Mohammed Al Qasimi. The former governor and around 100 supporters occupied positions in the mountains around Rams and in the palm groves at Dhayah. On the request of the Ruler of Ras Al Khaimah and authorised by the Political Agent, a TOL detachment of 20 men went to the area. To provide an intimidating show of force, the Royal Navy's sloop HMS *Flamingo* anchored off Rams, and sent a 50-man landing party ashore to support the TOL. The British presence had the desired effect and when the landing party and the TOL advanced,

---

114 TNA DEFE 68/397: Arthur, 'The Trucial Oman Scouts', Diplomatic Report No 115/72, 21 January 1972.
115 The majority of these were serving British Army officers; however, a handful were contract officers.
116 TNA DEFE 68/397: Arthur, 'The Trucial Oman Scouts', Diplomatic Report No 115/72, 21 January 1972.
117 UK Foreign Office, *Historical Summary of Events in the Persian Gulf Shaikhdoms and the Sultanate of Muscat and Oman, 1928-1953*, PG 53, p. 155.

they found the area deserted.[118] The intervention restored the sovereignty of Ras Al Khaimah over Rams.

Other than occasionally supporting operations and undertaking military exercises on Sir Bani Yas island, Royal Navy involvement in the Trucial States was limited. Hence, the discussion below of regular British forces necessarily focuses on the RAF and the British Army, both of which made a substantial contribution.

Royal Air Force

The origins of the RAF in the Trucial States can be traced back to a 1928 decision by the British Cabinet to develop a strategic air route linking the United Kingdom with India and beyond. The RAF surveyed the route along the southern shores of the Gulf, and identified major landing sites, emergency landing sites, and refuelling locations. In the Trucial States, an air station was established in Sharjah in 1932, and it served as an overnight stop for Imperial Airways as well as for occasional use by the RAF.[119] Other air infrastructure built in the Trucial States consisted of natural surface landing grounds (e.g. on Sir Bani Yas island in 1935 and at Kalba on the Gulf of Oman coast in 1936), petrol stores (e.g. in Dubai in 1934), and beacons (e.g. on Halul and Sir Bu Nair islands in 1936).[120]

Following the start of the Second World War, the RAF established a permanent facility alongside the Sharjah's civil air station. From 1942 to 1944, this facility was home to the RAF's 244 Squadron, which carried out maritime patrols and convoy escorts, primarily of tankers carrying oil from the Gulf.[121] American aviation forces were also based there during the war, and it became an important stop for aircraft being flown out to the far east theatre.[122] Protection of the Sharjah air facilities was initially provided by the guards of the Ruler of Sharjah, but, in 1942, protection became the responsibility of the Bahrain-controlled and locally raised Persian Gulf Levies. These were subsequently replaced by RAF-controlled levies.[123] At the end of

---

118   The TOL detachment was headed by the TOL's Acting Commandant, Captain Nasir Al Nif. A. Burdett, ed. *Defence 1920-1960*, Vol. 10, The GCC States: National Development Records (Slough, 1994), M.S. Buckmaster, Acting Political Officer, Trucial States to Political Resident, Bahrain, 26 July 1952, pp. 513-25.

119   Shirley Kay, *Wings Over the Gulf* (Dubai, 1995); Stanley-Price, *Imperial Outpost in the Gulf*.

120   UK Foreign Office, *Historical Summary of Events in the Persian Gulf Shaikhdoms and the Sultanate of Muscat and Oman, 1928-1953*, PG 53, p. 163.

121   A. Iqbal and P. Hellyer, 'The UAE in World War Two: The War at Sea', *Tribulus*, 25 (2017), p. 34.

122   There were up to 53 US Army Transport Corps personnel in Sharjah, with another 270 men in Bahrain. The US Air Force had established a system of wireless communication and direction finding at both of these stations. Shaikh Abdullah bin Khalid Al-Khalifa and M. Rice, eds., *Bahrain Through The Ages – The History* (London, 1993; repr., 2014), p. 582.

123   Levies were based in both Dubai and Sharjah, and remained there until a few months after the end of the war. A. Iqbal, P. Hellyer, and L. Garey, 'The UAE in World War Two: A Forgotten Fatal Air Crash in Sharjah', *Tribulus*, 25 (2017), pp. 28-29.

the war, the US completely withdrew from Sharjah, while the RAF retained a small maintenance party even though no aircraft were based there.[124] The civilian air station continued to operate.

In 1952, the RAF became substantially more involved in the Trucial States when it deployed both aircraft and ground troops. This involvement arose following Saudi Arabia's occupation of parts of the Buraimi Oasis in August 1952. To deter further Saudi aggression and encourage the occupying forces to leave, the RAF initially deployed a flight of three Vampire jet fighters and a Vickers Valetta transport plane to Sharjah.[125] The Vampires made low-level, intimidatory sweeps over the oases and the Valetta dropped leaflets, encouraging the inhabitants to remain loyal to the Sultan and to reject the blandishments of the Saudis. By mid-February 1953, the Vampires of No 6 Squadron had returned to the RAF Air Station at Habbaniya, west of Baghdad.

In January 1953, it became clear that the Saudi detachment was not leaving Buraimi and that additional ground forces were needed to help the TOL deal with the Saudis. This led to the deployment of RAF ground forces. At that time, Britain's military security in that part of the Middle East was the responsibility of the RAF. This had arisen because the RAF had, since the First World War, successfully applied the doctrine known as 'Aerial Policing' or 'Air-and-Armour Control' in the region. This approach allowed the RAF to control significant areas without a large network of bases at which substantial numbers of ground troops were located, as would have occurred if the British Army had had this responsibility. The doctrine involved the RAF having a small number of bases at which were concentrated aircraft and mobile ground forces. The latter consisted of British officered but locally raised field (rifle) squadrons,[126] and British-led and manned armoured car units.

From these bases, the RAF would fly British and local leaders around to govern and to mediate disputes. If a peaceful resolution could not be achieved, RAF aircraft would be sent to intimidate and, as a last resort, attack the belligerent villages or aggressors. The latter action would generally be preceded by warnings to evacuate and was predominantly aimed at inflicting economic or agricultural disruption. If this did not result in an acceptable outcome, RAF armoured cars would be sent in supported by field squadrons.[127] Aerial Policing depended on a combination of British prestige,

124 In 1948, RAF Sharjah consisted of just one officer and a small ground staff. The RAF ran a weekly flight between Bahrain and Sharjah. Henderson, *This Strange Eventful History*, pp. 14, 57.

125 Warwick, *In Every Place*, p. 573. Other RAF aircraft deployed during the dispute included Meteors, Ansons, and Lancasters. Ibid., p. 582.

126 The RAF field (or rifle) squadron is an infantry-like organisation of 100 to 150 men. It was established primarily for the local defence of RAF airfields and installations, but in areas which applied Aerial Policing, the field squadron could be used for expeditionary tasks. TNA, AIR 8/1888, Air Marshal Sir Claude Pelly, Middle East Air Force, [untitled, MEAF/TS.312889/SGDSO], 18 November 1954.

127 For a detailed history of Aerial Policing, see Warwick, *In Every Place*.

a tribally organised society where the tribe followed the decisions of its leader, and overwhelming military power. By the time of the deployment in the Trucial States, the Middle East had changed considerably, and these three conditions were increasingly no longer applicable. However, the RAF's Aerial Policing force structure in Iraq and the Arabian Peninsula still existed, which meant that when ground forces were required in the Trucial States in 1953, the RAF provided them.

In January 1953, RAF No 2 Armoured Car Squadron arrived in the Trucial States from Iraq.[128] The force was headquartered in Sharjah Air Station. Its wheeled light reconnaissance armoured cars were sent to support TOL operations, both to counter Saudi subversive efforts in the east of the Emirates,[129] and to stop the flow of Saudi men and materiel into Abu Dhabi Emirate western region. This saw a detachment of the squadron being located at Tarif. In February 1953, the Armoured Car Squadron was augmented by a field squadron of the RAF's Aden Protectorate Levies. At that time, Aden Protectorate Levies were led and staffed by RAF Regiment personnel.[130] Further detachments would arrive over the next several months, with the peak strength of the Aden Protectorate Levies' around 300.[131] The Aden Protectorate Levies allowed the TOL to concentrate on blockading Saudi forces in Buraimi, and so relieved the RAF's armoured car forces, which then departed around mid-May 1953.

During 1953, the TOL expanded significantly and, by August 1953, the Aden Protectorate Levies were also no longer needed. They then returned to Aden. However, a significant number of the personnel recruited by the TOL turned out to be unreliable, with violence erupting in Al Ain. Fearing their mutinous behaviour would spread to Sharjah and so threaten the RAF Air Station there, RAF ground forces returned in November 1953. They withdrew shortly afterwards when the situation stabilised.[132] RAF ground forces would not return to the Trucial States after this; shortly afterwards these forces were restructured and were directed to only focus on what they do today – protecting RAF air facilities.[133]

128 No 2 Armoured Car Squadron, equipped with Humber armoured cars and Land Rovers, arrived on Jebal Ali beach via a Royal Army Service Corps' landing ship tank on 18 January 1953. Ibid., pp. 573-86.
129 This included the operation at Wadi Al Qawr as described in the TOL/TOS history above.
130 K.M. Oliver, *Through Adversity: The History of the Royal Air Force Regiment, 1942-1992* (Rushden, 1997), p. 194.
131 The first detachment arrived over 15 to 18 February 1953. Warwick, *In Every Place*, p. 581. The last detachment appears to have arrived in early May 1953. F. Edwards, *The Gaysh: A History of the Aden Protectorate Levies 1927-61 and the Federal Regular Army of South Arabia 1961-67* (Solihull, 2004), pp. 116-17.
132 Burdett, *Defence 1920-1960*, L.A.C. Fry, 'Note for the Securetary of State's use at the Cabinet Meeting, March 10th', 9 March 1954, pp. 537-38.
133 This explains why No. 2 Armoured Car Squadron left the majority of their ageing Humber cars behind, most of which were scrapped and apparently not used by the Aden Protectorate Levies or other forces. Warwick, *In Every Place*, pp. 586-87.

Unlike the RAF's ground forces, the RAF's aircraft remained in Sharjah and would do so until 1971. These aircraft had three key roles. The first was to support the TOL/TOS in the defence of the external borders of the Trucial States. The concept of operations was that the TOL/TOS would first encounter the enemy and if overwhelmed would retreat in good order while harassing the enemy's advance. This would provide both the trigger and the time for RAF forces to respond. The RAF was in effect the second line of defence, with the British Army the third. This was because RAF aircraft could respond very rapidly to an incursion, while the British Army would require weeks to bring in large numbers of troops and heavy equipment, by which time an invading force could have overrun the defenders.[134] In this function, the key assets brought by the RAF would be its ground-attack aircraft, notably the the De Havilland Vampire and Hawker Hunter. To practice the ground support role, RAF's forward control officers would occasionally deploy with TOL/TOS patrols.

The second role of the RAF was to provide non-combat support to the TOL/TOS and regular British forces in the Trucial States and region. This included reconnaissance, logistic and medical evacuation missions.[135] This role increased in importance in the late 1960s with the build-up of British forces in the Gulf. Consequently, additional support aircraft were based in Sharjah, such as the No 78 Squadron equipped with Wessex helicopters. This capability was aided by British Army Air Corps aircraft which also were deployed to Sharjah; British Army Air Corps aircraft regularly based at RAF Air Station Sharjah included the Beaver light plane, Scout general purpose military helicopter, and Sioux light observation helicopter. This role saw the RAF and the TOL/TOS construct natural surface landing grounds in the Emirates, particularly in the Abu Dhabi zone of Buraimi and near the Qatar-Abu Dhabi frontier.

The third role was to provide support to Britain's regional security operations. An example of this was in mid-1958, when the number of Shackleton bombers based in Sharjah was increased to four as a precautionary measure owing to the anti-British situation in Iraq.[136] Later, in mid-1961, RAF Station Sharjah became home to a squadron of Canberra medium bombers which could be called upon if Iraq attempted to invade Kuwait.[137] The RAF also undertook combat and non-combat operations in Oman to counter the various separatist and revolutionary movements. Possibly the last

---

134 Sir William Luce to A.R. Walmsley, FO. [untitled letter], in A. Burdett, ed. *Annual Records of the Gulf: 1961*, Volume 4: United Arab Emirates and Oman (Slough, 1991), p. 275.

135 UK Foreign Office, *Historical Summary of Events in the Persian Gulf Shaikhdoms and the Sultanate of Muscat and Oman, 1928-1953*, PG 53, p. 164. At least for the 1950s, the RAF did not permit single-engine aircraft to fly by themselves. This was because of the difficulty in locating lost aircraft. In the case of the single-engine Pioneer aircraft, this meant that two of these needed for fly for each mission. A. Shepherd, *Arabian Adventure* (London, 1961), p. 100.

136 D. Hawley, *The Emirates: Witness to a Metamorphosis*, 2007), p. 67.

137 Air Vice-Marshal John Herrington, 'Operation Vantage – Kuwait 1961', *Journal of the Royal Air Force Historical Society*, 21 (2000), p. 96.

RAF combat operation was in December 1970. Called Operation Intragon, this was a ten-day internal security operation in the mountains of the Musandam Peninsula. Another mechanism by which the RAF supported Britain's regional security operations out of Sharjah was the use of Shackleton maritime surveillance aircraft for aerial search and rescue (SAR).

RAF Sharjah was formally closed in October 1971,[138] whereupon regional RAF routing moved to the RAF's facilities on Masirah Island, off the coast of Oman.

British Army at Sharjah (1955-71)

The first sizable British Army presence in the Trucial States was a company from the King's Royal Rifle Corps. It was deployed from October 1955 to May 1956 as a support element for the TOL's operation to evict Saudi forces from Buraimi Oasis. It had been flown in from Libya. It was not, in fact, required, but did subsequently garrison Tarif to support the local security efforts to ensure Saudi Arabia respected the border (called the modified Riyadh line), declared on 26 October 1955. From there, it provided support to the tribal posts established by the Ruler of Abu Dhabi in Liwa in November 1955 and patrolled the border by both the TOL and Abu Dhabi tribesmen.[139]

The King's Royal Rifle Corps unit was replaced by another regiment, and rotations continued until 1971. Numerous other British units deployed to the Trucial States between 1955 and 1971 with the main ones being the Royal Armoured Corps, Royal Artillery, Royal Engineers, Royal Electrical and Mechanical Engineers, Royal Signals, Royal Corps of Transport, Royal Army Ordnance Corps and the Special Air Service.

The principal activities of these British Army combat units were training, acclimatisation, desert familiarisation and exercises. From Sharjah, some British Army elements detached or were deployed to operations in Aden and Oman. On a few occasions, the British Army would support the TOS in internal security operations, but only in a support role. In 1957, an infantry company sent platoons to Buraimi Oasis to free up the TOS unit there so it could deploy to combat in Oman;[140] and, during the 1967 Arab-Israeli War, the British Army participated in a limited fashion to support the TOS and local security forces to quell unrest in Sharjah and Dubai. British Army forces based in Sharjah were also used in regional security activities such as the Kuwait deterrence operation against Iraq in the early 1960s.

---

138 TNA DEFE 11/880: HQ British Forces Gulf, 'Gulf Withdrawal Plan 1/69 (Provisional First Revise)', 29 August 1969.
139 UK Foreign Office, *Foreign Office Annual Reports from Arabia, 1930-1960: 1954-1960,* 1955, p. 175.
140 This was the Cameronians (Scottish Rifles). Mann, *The Trucial Oman Scouts: The Story of a Bedouin Force,* p. 88.

British Army forces also helped in state building activities. For example, the Royal Engineers undertook surveys along Abu Dhabi's borders with Oman and Saudi Arabia, as well as large scale surveys in key coastal areas across the Emirates. They also built bridges and roads.[141] Another example was the Desert Intelligence Officers who operated between 1961 and 1971. These were British Army personnel who were loosely attached to the TOS, but focused on political intelligence collection and worked for Local Intelligence Committees headed by the British Political Agents.[142]

Another reason for the presence of British Army units was to 'show the flag' in order to demonstrate the British presence in the region.[143] This became more important following the British withdrawal from Aden in 1967. The British priority was to enhance security in the Gulf and in 1967 substantial numbers of army personnel were relocated to Sharjah. British Army numbers peaked at around 2,000 in 1967-68.[144] Collectively known as British Troops Sharjah, its main elements were a garrison HQ, infantry battalion, armoured reconnaissance squadron, light battery Royal Artillery, field squadron Royal Engineers, signals squadron, transport troop and port unit from the Royal Corps of Transport, medical reception station, field ambulance detachment, a forward ordnance depot, workshops, and an Army Air Corps flight.[145] Following the January 1968 announcement that British forces would leave the Gulf by 1971, the British Troops Sharjah started its run down. In early 1970, local British Army training ended, as did second line support by the Royal Electrical and Mechanical Engineers.[146] Combat formations had mostly been withdrawn by mid-1971, with the last significant element to leave being an infantry company assigned guard duties.

141 M.C. Ziolkowski, Ziolkowski, L.T., 'The Bridges of Wadi Ham, Fujairah, U.A.E.', *Liwa: Journal of the National Archives*, 7, 16 (2016), pp. 43-80.
142 A. Yates, 'The Formation of Military Intelligence in the United Arab Emirates: 1965-1974', *Journal of Intelligence History*, (October 2020).
143 An illustration of the activities undertaken by a British Army force can be found in M. Naylor, *Among Friends: The Scots Guards 1956-1993* (Havertown, 1995), pp. 69-82.
144 The number of British Army personnel based in Sharjah is not known. The plan from early 1966 was for a maximum of 2,437 British tri-service personnel to be based in Sharjah. TNA, FO 371/185548, Political Resident Persian Gulf, 'Record of Salient Points Arising from a Conference between PRPG and Service Staffs at Bahrain 22 February 1966', February 1966. The planned rundown of British forces in the Gulf as of August 1969 stated that there were to be 1,921 British Army troops to remain in Sharjah by March 1970, in addition to 963 RAF personnel and 50 defence civilians, given a total size of Sharjah's military personnel of 2,934. TNA, DEFE 11/880, HQ British Forces Gulf, 'Gulf Withdrawal Plan 1/69 (Provisional First Revise)', 29 August 1969.
145 'A Report by the Working Party on the Arabisation of the Trucial Oman Scouts', in A. Burdett, ed. *Records of the Emirates 1966-1971: 1966* (Slough, 2002), p. 498.
146 TNA, DEFE 11/880, HQ British Forces Gulf, 'Gulf Withdrawal Plan 1/69 (Provisional First Revise)', 29 August 1969.

British military involvement after 1971

The handover of the TOS to the UAE, and the withdrawal of British military units from the Gulf in 1971 did not end British military involvement in the Emirates completely. In late 1971, a group of 90 regular British Army officers and Other Ranks arrived in Sharjah. Known as the Military Advisory Team, this group was tasked with four missions: (1) specialised training assistance to local forces; (2) planning, co-ordination and execution of military assistance projects and other indirect measures; (3) assistance to visiting Britain units and to loan personnel; and (4) keeping alive techniques on desert warfare and conducting trials of equipment in desert conditions. The Military Advisory Team continued to function until 1975 when it was disbanded.[147]Moreover, from 1971 to the present, the British military has continued to assist the UAE. This has included seconded military personnel to the Emirati militaries, training teams, capability reviews, capacity building through joint exercises, intelligence, and direct military assistance.[148]

---

147 Yates and Rossiter, 'Military Assistance as Political Gimmickry? The Case of Britain and the Newly Federated UAE'.
148 For an overview of Britain's post-1971 involvement, see G. Stansfield, and S. Kelly, *A Return to East of Suez? UK Military Deployment to the Gulf* (London, 2013); A. Yates, 'The Use of British Seconded and Contracted Military Personnel to Advance Britain's Interests: A Case Study from the United Arab Emirates from 1965-2010', in G. Kennedy (eds.), *Defense Engagement since 1900: Global Lessons in Soft Power* (Kansas, 2020).

8

Ruler-Controlled Armed Forces

Ruler-controlled forces, as the name implies, are those which are directly accountable to the ruler of an Emirate. They are the rulers' personal armed forces. Between 1965 when the first was formed and 1976 when Emirati forces were unified, there were four ruler-controlled forces. These were the Abu Dhabi Defence Force (1965-76), the Ras Al Khaimah Mobile Force (1968-76), the Dubai Defence Force (1971-76) and the Sharjah National Guard (1972-76).

In May 1976, the Supreme Defence Council issued a directive to unify the armed forces of the UAE. This involved integrating the four ruler-controlled forces, in addition to the sole federally controlled force (i.e. the Federal Armed Force) under a General Headquarters (GHQ), to form the federally controlled UAE Armed Forces. However, this unification was only partial. Not only was control over all the forces not transferred to the headquarters of the UAE Armed Forces for many years, some rulers went on to form new armed forces. Over the subsequent decades, four other ruler-controlled forces were raised and maintained, before being integrated into the UAE Armed Forces. These were Dubai's Central Military Command (1976-98), the Umm Al Quwain National Guard (1976-2006), Ras Al Khaimah's armed forces (1984-mid-1990s), and Sharjah's armed forces (1984-90).[1] By 2006, the last remaining ruler-controlled force had been formally integrated into the UAE Armed Forces.

This irregular military development can be, at times hard to follow and confusing. As such, this chapter provides a detailed survey of all of the ruler-controlled forces. This is important because it provides an understanding of the historical lineage of the UAE Armed Forces and highlights the internal tensions between the rulers of the Emirates and their desire to retain sovereignty.

Ruler-controlled forces fall into two categories. The first was a regular force structured to deter threats and defeat aggression. The armed forces of Abu Dhabi and Dubai were

---

1   It could be argued that the Critical National Infrastructure Authority (CNIA) formed
     by Abu Dhabi in 2007 was also a ruler-controlled force. It was absorbed into the UAE
     Armed Forces in 2012. See Chapter 9 for details on the CNIA.

of this type. Abu Dhabi's force had three military services (army, air force and navy) while Dubai's force had only two (army and air force). In addition, both had a separate force whose role was to protect the ruler and his family, known as the Emiri Guard.

The second category was forces which were primarily Emiri Guard in nature. The armed forces of Ras Al Khaimah, Sharjah and Umm Al Quwain were of this type. In some cases, their purpose is reflected in their name as seen in the forces of both Sharjah and Umm Al Quwain – the National Guard. This name echoes the Emirati political and cultural perception that the ruler is the embodiment of the state, and hence guarding the ruler is the same as guarding the nation. The naming exception is the Ras Al Khaimah Mobile Force which reflects its original operational concept, not its purpose.

Abu Dhabi Defence Force (1965-76)

Establishment

The first ruler-controlled armed force was established by the Abu Dhabi Ruler, Sheikh Shakhbut bin Sultan Al Nahyan. It was formed in 1965 when weapons were first ordered and recruitment of personnel started. The Ruler had long wanted his own military but was stymied both by a lack of funds and British reluctance to support such a venture, as they wanted to see all rulers rely on the TOS. However, by 1964, Sheikh Shakhbut had the funds, created by oil revenue, and the British had reluctantly come round to supporting the establishment of an Abu Dhabi army. This turnaround was due to recognition that such a force would reduce British military expenditure as a TOS squadron could be withdrawn from Abu Dhabi. The expectation was that it would take three or four years for the Abu Dhabi force to be in a position to take over TOS commitments.[2] The ruler had agreed to have serving British officers run his force which gave the British confidence that their interests would be protected.

The envisaged roles of this new military were for it to act as a bodyguard for the ruler and guard the Al Maqta causeway.[3] The latter was the only crossing point from the mainland to Abu Dhabi Island, which housed the ruler's fort and Abu Dhabi town.[4] Another role mentioned was for it to provide internal security in the form of

---

2   TNA FO 371/179929: J.E.H. Boustead, Political Agent Abu Dhabi to Sir William Luce, PRPG, [untitled letter], 27 March 1965.
3   The regime protection rationale was reflected in the following note by Colonel de Butts. The Ruler wanted a force of his own as he was 'doubtful of his own position and wishes to ensure his position'. TNA, WO 337/11, Colonel F.M. de Butts, Commander TOS, 'Trucial Oman Scouts Intelligence Summary No 8', 11 July 1964.
4   J.E.H. Boustead, Abu Dhabi Political Agency, to Sir William Luce, Bahrain Political Residency, [untitled letter], 17 June 1964, cited in A. Burdett, ed. *Records of the Emirates 1961-1965: 1965* (Slough, 1997), p. 212.

'quelling riots' in the oil fields or in Abu Dhabi township.[5] Another probable motivating factor for the decision to form the force was to counter political pressure from
other countries, notably Iraq and Kuwait, which wanted to see an Arab-controlled
force in Abu Dhabi rather than a British-controlled one.[6]

In the latter half of 1965, two British officers arrived to run the force. Both were
TOS officers who were temporarily attached to the new force. These were Major
E.B. (Tug) Wilson and Captain C.W. (Charles) Wontner, who filled the posts of
Commander and Deputy Commander, respectively. The plan at this stage was to
build a force consisting of just these two British officers, one Arab warrant officer and
213 Other Ranks.[7]

The force was modelled on the TOS as it was a locally recruited Arab force, led by
British officers. The difference between it and the TOS was that the new force was
accountable to the ruler rather than the British, although as the officers were serving
British officers, they also needed to follow the British military chain of command.
The roles of the British officers were to 'organise, train and command the force', as
well as to advise the ruler's son, Sheikh Sultan,[8] who at that time was expected to
be the force's Commander-in-Chief. The command role of Sheikh Sultan is unclear
during the years 1965 and 1966. In February 1966, Sheikh Shakhbut said that his son
was not the Commander of the Army and Sheikh Sultan should be left out of Army
matters. However, in June 1966, Sheikh Sultan still held the title of Chairman of the
Department of Defence. No records of Sheikh Sultan have been located which indicate he had any substantive influence on military matters.

The original plan for the force was developed by Major-General E.S. Lindsay of the
UK Ministry of Defence and submitted to Sheikh Shakhbut in October 1964.[9] He
proposed that the force should consist of nine British officers and 245 Other Ranks.
The force's proposed structure was an HQ, two rifle troops, one armoured car troop,
a transport troop, and an administrative group. Transport was to be 38 Land Rovers
(11 armoured) and seven Bedford trucks.[10]

5   F.D.W. Brown to T.F. Brenchley, FO, [letter], 29 July 1964 cited in A. Burdett, ed. *Records
    of the Emirates 1961-1965: 1964* (Slough, 1997), p. 213. This was also noted by Wilson,
    who later that year would command the Abu Dhabi force, when he wrote that Shakhbut
    wanted a force because of his 'desire for an army of his own arose from the trouble in the
    oilfields in 1963 and his dependence then on the [Trucial Oman] Scouts which he found
    humiliating'. TNA FO 371/179929: Brenchley, [untitled letter], 10 August 1965.
6   TNA WO 337/11: Trucial Oman Scouts, 'Trucial Oman Scouts Intelligence Summary
    No 13', August 1964.
7   TNA FO 371/179929: MoD Sheikh Sultan bin Shakhbut to Major General E.S. Lindsay,
    [untitled letter], 8 March 1965.
8   TNA FO 371/185551: Lamb, [untitled letter], 7 June 1966.
9   TNA FO 371/179929: Boustead, [untitled letter], 27 March 1965.
10 TNA WO 337/11: Trucial Oman Scouts, 'Trucial Oman Scouts Intelligence Summary
    No. 27', 12 December 1964.

Following discussions between Sheikh Shakhbut, Wilson and the Political Residency at the end of 1965, a new force structure was agreed upon. The force would continue to be a motorised light infantry force, mounted on Land Rovers and Bedford trucks, but now augmented by two Ferret scout car troops, in addition to a troop of medium mortars.[11] Over the following year, the force's roles were formalised to include deterring attacks and defending Abu Dhabi Emirate. This resulted in the force being organised into two rifle squadrons. Their missions were to counter any Saudi Arabian encroachment and protect oil infrastructure. The deployment concept as of April 1966 was for one rifle squadron to be based at Al Hamra on the coastal route between Qatar and Abu Dhabi,[12] supported by one troop of armoured cars; and the second rifle squadron with an armoured squadron located on Abu Dhabi Island. Training establishments were set up in both Abu Dhabi and Al Ain.[13]

By June 1966, the Abu Dhabi Defence Force had reached a strength of 158, consisting of two British and four Arab officers, and 59 trained soldiers, with the remainder consisting of recruits under training, and support personnel. Simultaneously, recruiting was underway to increase the number of British officers from two to nine, and to expand the force to 250 men.[14] Despite the plans, development was slower than hoped for and the force was nowhere near operational by mid-1966. This was mainly due to the failure of the ruler to release funds for the force.[15] In particular, soldiers were not paid for months, which resulted in them leaving; at the same time, stores and equipment could not be purchased.

First expansion

On 6 August 1966, after years of dissatisfaction with the rule of Sheikh Shakhbut, because of his unwillingness to spend his considerable oil revenues on development and his capricious ways, the ruling family transferred their support from Sheikh Shakhbut to his brother, Sheikh Zayed. The British facilitated this transition by

11   MECA, St Antony's College, Oxford, Abu Dhabi Defence Force, 'Induction Booklet for New British Officers with an Introduction by Col E.B. Wilson', 1968.
12   The ADDF's Al Hamra base was sited to the west of the TOS's Mirfa base. The TOS squadron at Mirfa was withdrawn in June 1968. TNA, FCO 8/900, Henderson, 'Minutes of the Abu Dhabi LIC Meeting on 17 April 1968', 21 April 1968. This occurred after an ADDF unit (A Squadron) arrived at the Al Hamra base. The location of Al Hamra was chosen as it protected the oil hub of Jebal Dhana, enabled a rapid response to Das Island in the case of civil unrest, as well as being a deterrent to Saudi Arabia. Major R. Hitchcock, OC A Squadron & subsequently founding officer 2nd Infantry Regiment, ADDF, 1967-70, email, 15 September 2018.
13   *Colonel E.B. Wilson's Archives*, Vol. 2 (Abu Dhabi, n.d.), Lt Colonel E.B. Wilson, CO ADDF, to Brigadier M.W. Holme, Commanding LFPG Bahrain, 26 April 1966, G.1004, p. 170.
14   TNA FO 371/185551: Lamb, [untitled letter], 7 June 1966.
15   Ibid.

using the TOS to close the Al Maqta causeway to prevent the arrival of tribesmen loyal to Sheikh Shakhbut, and by surrounding the ruler's fort on Abu Dhabi Island. Sheikh Shakhbut initially refused to step aside and remained in his fort protected by his personal retainers. While the role of the Abu Dhabi military was to protect Sheikh Shakhbut, the troops remained in their barracks on the orders of their Commander.[16] Recognising his lack of support, Sheikh Shakhbut surrendered peacefully and was escorted to the Abu Dhabi airstrip and flown into exile on a RAF aircraft.

One of the first decisions made by Sheikh Zayed upon his accession was to expand his armed force significantly. He also issued a decree formalising its name to be the Abu Dhabi Defence Force (ADDF). As of September 1966, Sheikh Zayed's plan was for the ADDF to expand to between 800 and 1,000 men over the following two to three years.[17] This number was subsequently increased the following year to some 1,500 men.[18] The operational concept of the force was that it would work in coopera-tion with friendly forces, notably the TOS, the British Army and RAF, 'in resisting any threat to the integrity of the State as well as performing its internal security role'.[19] Its force structure was to be one infantry battalion, an armoured squadron and an artillery battery, in addition to support companies.[20] The primary armoured elements were Saladin and Ferret wheeled armoured cars, which had enough fire power to destroy any vehicles likely to penetrate into Abu Dhabi territory; tanks were extremely unlikely to be used given the challenges of deploying and supporting tanks in the region's sandy deserts.[21]

The expansion plans included forming an air wing of four light aircraft and a sea wing of five patrol launches.[22] Such an expansion required additional experienced officers and NCOs to be engaged, as well as increased entry-level recruitment. The former led to the engagement of more British and former TOS personnel, and the latter to the establishment of the ADDF's Recruit Depot in Al Ain by the end of 1966.

---

16   Despite serving as the Commander of the ruler's armed force, Lt Colonel Wilson was a seconded British Army officer and ultimately took orders from the Commander TOS. Thus on 6 August 1966, when Captain J.M. (Michael) Curtis, 2IC of A Squadron, TOS, met with Wilson on Abu Dhabi Island and informed him verbally of the Commander TOS's request that he order the ADDF to return to their barracks and not support Sheikh Shakhbut, Wilson did so. Captain J.M. Curtis, A Squadron, TOS, 1966–68, email, 15 July 2020.

17   TNA, FO 1016/736, Brigadier I.R.R. Hollyer, HQ Land Forces Persian Gulf, 'Future Organisation and Administration of the Trucial Oman Scouts', 1 September 1966.

18   MECA, St Antony's College, Oxford, Abu Dhabi Defence Force, 'Induction Booklet for New British Officers with an Introduction by Col E.B. Wilson', 1968.

19   Ibid.

20   UAE Armed Forces, *The UAE Armed Forces History and Missions* (Abu Dhabi, 2011), p. 13.

21   TNA FCO 8/1241: UK Land Forces Gulf Headquarters, 'Report on Abu Dhabi Defence Force', 1968.

22   MECA, St Antony's College, Oxford, Abu Dhabi Defence Force, 'Induction Booklet for New British Officers with an Introduction by Col E.B. Wilson', 1968.

The planned expansion of 1966 was of concern to the British as reflected in the comment by the British Resident that it would create 'the fashion for private armies [which was feared] would inevitably spread up the coast'.[23] The British wanted Sheikh Zayed to agree to place the ADDF under the political direction of the Political Resident and operational control of the TOS Commander.[24] Sheikh Zayed rejected this proposal, but did mollify Britain's concerns by stating that he would commit to the fullest cooperation with the TOS.[25]

In January 1968, the British Government unexpectedly announced that it would withdraw its forces from the Gulf by 1971. This had two key implications from Abu Dhabi's perspective. First, it was now unlikely that the British would come to the aid of Abu Dhabi in the event of aggression from outside. Second, the region would become more unpredictable with the loss of Britain's stabilising influence.[26] This perception resulted in major changes being made to both the role of and capability of the ADDF.

The missions of the ADDF were redefined as: (1) guaranteeing the integrity of the State against external interference, and (2) maintaining peace and good order within the State, particularly the prevention of subversion and illegal immigration.[27] The ADDF's size and structure changed, with the goal now being to establish a brigade-sized force (expected to be about 3-4,000 men)[28] that was highly mobile, and which would be supported by ground attack aircraft before Britain's 1971 departure. The force would also need an enhanced sea patrol capability for border security.[29] The organisation being built as of early 1969 is shown in Figure 17. The force was integrated under one single commander who controlled the land forces, the Sea Wing and the Air Wing. This was because the Commander ADDF considered that a single Service force was the 'only way to effectively control the development of the Force and to give it the necessary flexibility ... [and because] separate services are outmoded and expensive; they also lead to inter-service rivalry, which in a Force of this size cannot be tolerated.' He also considered that this would be the most economical structure as it would minimise administration costs, which would release more manpower for the force's fighting elements.[30]

23   TNA FO 371/185551: G. Balfour Paul, PRPG to A.T. Lamb Political Agent Abu Dhab, [untitled letter], 28 August 1966.
24   TNA FO 1016/736: Hollyer, 'Future Organisation and Administration of the Trucial Oman Scouts', 1 September 1966.
25   J. Maitra, *Zayed: From Challenges to Union* (Abu Dhabi, 2007), pp. 147-48.
26   MECA, St Antony's College, Oxford, Abu Dhabi Defence Force, 'Induction Booklet for New British Officers with an Introduction by Col E.B. Wilson', 1968.
27   Ibid.
28   TNA FCO 8/1255: Defence Intelligence Staff UK Ministry of Defence, 'Intelligence Briefing Memorandum-Trucial States', 3 December 1968.
29   MECA, St Antony's College, Oxford, Abu Dhabi Defence Force, 'Induction Booklet for New British Officers with an Introduction by Col E.B. Wilson', 1968.
30   *Colonel E.B. Wilson's Archives*, Vol. 7 (Abu Dhabi, n.d.), Colonel E.B. Wilson to Ruler of Abu Dhabi, 'Future of ADDF', 2 February 1969.

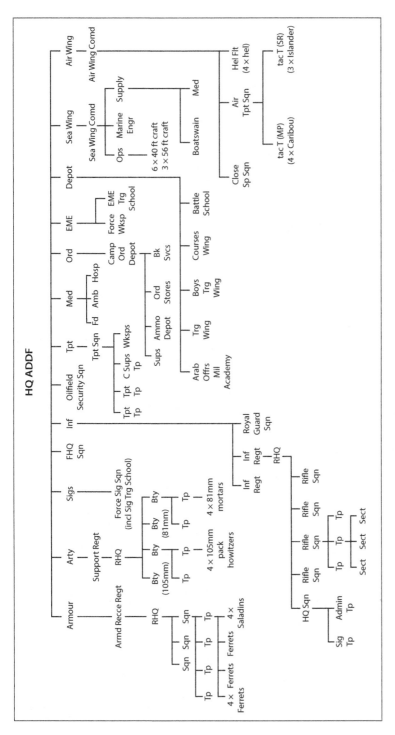

Figure 17: Organisation of the Abu Dhabi Defence Force, early 1969.[31]

31 Ibid, Proposed organisation of the ADDF, ca. early 1969.

While the Political Resident recognised that Abu Dhabi needed an effective defence force, he was concerned that 'it must not expand too much or have weapons which would make it look provocative' to the neighbouring rulers and states. In addition, there was concern that a strong Abu Dhabi force would undermine efforts to form a federation of Lower Gulf Emirates and, in particular, would end the idea of building a federally-controlled armed force around the TOS which was the preferred British position.[32] As well as trying to convince Sheikh Zayed to reduce the planned force's expansion, the Political Resident made efforts to impede the ADDF from obtaining sophisticated equipment.[33]

Second expansion

Despite British efforts, Sheikh Zayed instructed the armed force to expand and buy advanced weaponry. Between April 1968 and March 1969, the force's manpower increased by 200 percent to 125 officers and 2,065 enlisted personnel. Given the lack of trained officers, numbers of former British officers were hired on contract and were augmented by British, Pakistani and Jordanian seconded officers.[34]

By December 1968, the ADDF's land forces were made up of an HQ, an infantry regiment of four rifle squadrons, an armoured car squadron, and a mortar support troop.[35] A second infantry regiment (Sultan bin Zayed Regiment) started to form in 1969, as well as the first armoured regiment (Salah ad-Din Regiment) and an artillery regiment (Hamdan bin Zayed Regiment).[36] Significant volumes of new army equipment started to arrive around mid-1970, including nearly 200 armoured personnel carriers (allowing the infantry to become mechanised), armoured cars, towed artillery guns and surface-to-air missiles.[37]

The Emiri Guard was also established in 1968.[38] The ADDF Air Wing was formed in May 1968 with its key roles being to provide both a transport service for ADDF personnel and equipment, and a ground attack capability to support ADDF's land forces. Its first aircraft, consisting of transport and communication fixed wing and rotary aircraft arrived in late 1968. Over the course of 1970-71, 12 Hawker Hunter jets arrived, and through the engagement of experienced, mostly British Hunter

---

32   Maitra, *Zayed: From Challenges to Union*, pp. 247-48.
33   Ibid., p. 248.
34   Author's collection, Abu Dhabi Defence Force, 'A Statistical Survey of Records Office Information Covering the Period 1 April 1968 to 31 March 1969', 1969.
35   TNA FCO 8/1255: UK Ministry of Defence, 'Intelligence Briefing Memorandum-Trucial States', 3 December 1968.
36   UAE Armed Forces, *The UAE Armed Forces History and Missions*, p. 13.
37   These were around 198 Panhard M3 VTT armoured personnel carriers, 90 Panhard AML 60/90 armoured cars, 59 L-118 105mm, and 12 Rapier SAM systems, some of which started being delivered around 1975/76 and others around 1978.
38   UAE Armed Forces, *The UAE Armed Forces History and Missions*, p. 13.

pilots, the ADDF Air Wing rapidly developed effective ground attack and air-to-air defence (albeit limited) capabilities.

The Sea Wing of the ADDF was the smallest of the three military services. Formed in 1967, the Sea Wing's initial assets were three royal yachts[39] which were used for training in preparation of the arrival in the second half of 1968 of six lightly armed 40ft/12m small patrol boats (*Dhafeer* class).[40] These boats were augmented by three 56ft/17m patrol boats (*Kawkab* class), which arrived in 1969.[41] This fleet gave Abu Dhabi a limited brown-water patrolling capability in the waters of the Arabian Gulf and in the littoral region of the northern Emirates in the Gulf of Oman. These vessels were in effect day patrol craft as their limited water, food and fuel supplies prevented them from staying on station or patrolling for more than a day without either returning to base or being resupplied by other ships.[42]

The command structure of the ADDF in 1966 consisted of the Commander ADDF, reporting directly to the Ruler of Abu Dhabi. Under the Commander was the Deputy Commander, supported by a small staff. In February 1969, the Abu Dhabi Department of Defence was established.[43] Its head was Sheikh Zayed's oldest son, Sheikh Khalifa bin Zayed, who was given the rank of Lieutenant-General.[44] In 1971, the Abu Dhabi Government was restructured, and one change involved the creation of ministries. The Ministry of Defence (MoD-Abu Dhabi) was formed and Sheikh Khalifa bin Zayed became the Minister of Defence. The executive head of MoD-Abu Dhabi was Undersecretary Colonel Sheikh Faisal bin Sultan Al Qasimi, a former TOS officer. He was the son of a deposed Ruler of Ras Al Khaimah, and, since mid-1968, the private secretary to Sheikh Khalifa bin Zayed.[45]

The growth in the ADDF's capabilities also meant that increasingly the ADDF's Sea and Air Wings were given service-specific roles, rather than just acting as support

---

39   These were Al Shuja, Al Shaheen and Al Aqab, which were handed over to the ADDF in May 1968. A. Yates and C. Lord, *The Naval Force of Abu Dhabi 1967-1976* (Canberra, 2019), p. 17.

40   *Colonel E.B. Wilson's Archives*, 1, Letter from Colonel Wilson to His Highness Shaikh Zayid bin Sultan Al-Nahyaan, 4 July 1968, p. 41. The *Dhafeer* class vessels were P401 Dhafeer, P402 Ghadunfar, P403 Hazza, P404 Durgham, P405 Timsah and P406 Murayjib. Their armament was a .5 calibre machine gun and two .303 Bren guns on the flying bridge. They had a crew of one officer and five men, and a range 350 miles at 15 knots.

41   The *Kawkab* class boats (also known as the Keith Nelson 32 tons vessels) were P561 Kawkab, P562 Thoaban and P563 Bani Yas. Their armament was two Hispano-Suiza 20mm cannons and two 7.62mm machine guns. They had a crew of two officers and nine men, and a range of 445 miles at 15 knots.

42   Yates and Lord, *The Naval Force of Abu Dhabi*.

43   *Abu Dhabi Emiri Decree No 8 of 1969 "Establishment of a Department of Defense to Be Responsible of Abu Dhabi Defense Force Matters at the Borders"* (1969).

44   G.H. Wilson, *Khalifa: Journey Into the Future* (Abu Dhabi, 2015), p. 18.

45   TNA FCO 8/900: A. Reeve, Assistant Political Agent, Abu Dhabi, 'Minutes of the Abu Dhabi LIC Meeting Held on Thursday, 11 July 1968', 15 July 1968.

to the ADDF's land forces. Reflecting this, the Sea Wing was renamed the Abu Dhabi Navy in 1971, and the Air Wing became the ADDF Air Force in 1972.[46]

Force restructure

In December 1973, all Abu Dhabi Ministries and Ministers were replaced by Departments and Chairmen, who were to work within the now established Federal Government structure. Consequently, the MoD-Abu Dhabi was renamed the Command of the General Headquarters (GHQ) of Abu Dhabi,[47] once again headed by Sheikh Faisal bin Sultan Al Qasimi, who now carried the title of ADDF Chief of Staff and who was promoted to Brigadier. With the abolition of the Minister of Defence (Abu Dhabi), a new position of Commander-in-Chief of the ADDF was established. This position was filled by Sheikh Khalifa.

In early December 1973, the ADDF was also restructured into four commands – Land Forces, Air Force, Navy and Emiri Guard, and the posts of Commander and Deputy-Commander ADDF were abolished.[48] Each of the commands had their own headquarters. While technically all reported to GHQ headed by the Chief of Staff, the actual arrangements appear to have varied with the command, time, and situation. In the advent of war, it was expected that the Commander Land Forces would assume command of all Abu Dhabi forces, with the Chief of Staff moving to the field.[49] The new structure is shown in Figure 18.

The early 1970s also saw a significant enlargement of the ADDF's training infrastructure. Key new establishments included the 1971 founding of the Zayed Military Academy for officer cadets in Al Ain, and, in 1974, the establishment of the Armoured Centre which included an armoured school. Other training facilities were also expanding such as the Recruit Depot in Al Ain, which was turned into a base for a training regiment. The School of Infantry had also been established and by 1974 it offered courses for NCOs, Troop Commanders and Squadron Commanders.[50] New camps were built and existing ones upgraded.[51] Support facilities were also developed, such as the Military Hospital (established 1974) and firing ranges.

---

46   UAE Armed Forces, *The UAE Armed Forces History and Missions*, pp. 39, 41; TNA FCO 8/2371: Agar, 'Annual Report for 1973 by Defence Attaché United Arab Emirates', January 1974.
47   UAE Armed Forces, *The UAE Armed Forces History and Missions*, p. 13.
48   TNA FCO 8/2371: Agar, 'Intelligence Report No 10', 4 April 1974.
49   TNA DEFE 68/397: C.J. Treadwell, Abu Dhabi Political Agent, 'Your Telno 15: British Loaned Officers in UDF and ADDF', 18 January 1972.
50   Ibid., Annex B to DA/INT/51.
51   Key ones included camps at Al Hamra, Umm Al Ishtan (est. 1974), Masafi, Khor Fakkan, Sweihan, Mafraq, Radoom, Kalba, and Bada Zayed (Madinat Zayed). In addition, the ADDF HQ/GHQ moved several times before 1976. It was initially based at the Al Nahyan Military Camp before moving to Al Hesn Camp, and finally to the Al Maqta area.

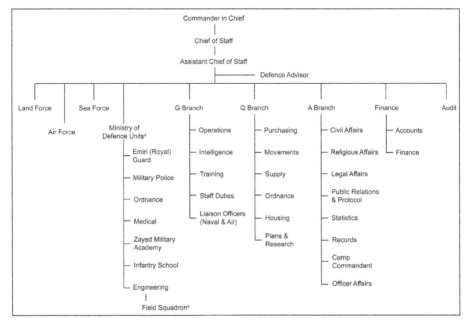

Figure 18: Organisation of the Abu Dhabi Defence Force, April 1974.[52]

Notes

a. This is Abu Dhabi's Ministry of Defence and not the Federal Government's Ministry of Defence. Its units appear to be a combination of joint capabilities and those needed for regime security.

b. In 1974, there were plans to form a Field Squadron of two troops if personnel were available.

In early 1973, the ADDF had a strength of around 12,000 personnel.[53] By early 1974, it was around 13,000,[54] and by the 1976 unification of Emirati armed forces, it was probably about 15,000.

The air force

Like Abu Dhabi's Land Forces, its Air Force had similarly expanded in both capabilities and size in the first half of the 1970s. With the delivery of the first batch of Mirage jets starting in 1973 (piloted by seconded Pakistani officers), the Abu Dhabi air combat and strike force grew considerably. These supersonic strike fighters caused congestion at the shared military and civil Al Bateen airport on Abu Dhabi Island. In 1973, the Hawker Hunters moved to Sharjah airport and then, in 1974-75, the

52   TNA FCO 8/2371: Agar, 'Intelligence Report No 10', 4 April 1974.
53   Author's collection, Abu Dhabi, US Ambassador in Tehran to General Brent Scowcroft Helms, White House, 'Paragraph 4 of WH 31209, May 16, 1973', 16 May 1973.
54   TNA FCO 8/2371: Agar, 'Intelligence Report No 10', 4 April 1974.

Mirages moved to the newly built Mugatara Air Base (today known as Al Dhafra Air Base). The inventory of transport and army liaison aircraft also continued to grow substantially in the mid-1970s. These included tactical fixed-wing transports, and light and medium transport/utility helicopters.[55]

While in the late 1960s the overwhelming majority of pilots and other air officers were British, this changed in the early 1970s. Increasing numbers of pilot posts were filled by seconded Sudanese, Jordanian and Pakistani officers and, by late 1973, the majority of Air Wing officers were Pakistanis. Up until 1972, the commander of Abu Dhabi's air forces was a British contract officer.[56] He was replaced by a seconded Pakistan Air Force officer; Pakistanis would continue to command the nation's air force until the mid-1980s.

The navy

In 1975-76, the Abu Dhabi Navy received six 110ft/33m large patrol craft (*Ardhana* class). As well as being more heavily armed, the *Ardhana* vessels' range was four times that of the *Kawkab* class vessels, allowing them to traverse UAE waters without continual refuelling.[57] In 1974 and 1975, Abu Dhabi's close inshore capabilities increased with the arrival of five 9m (*Fairey Marine Spear* class) coastal patrol craft.[58] In 1975, the Navy also received two 40-ton (*Cheverton* class) coastal patrol boats.[59] Abu Dhabi's naval base was initially in a bay near the Al Nahyan Military Camp on Abu Dhabi Island, but was shifted to the newly-completed port in Abu Dhabi in 1975. Naval facilities were built at the far west of Abu Dhabi Emirate[60] and on the eastern coast of Fujairah to provide patrol coverage throughout UAE waters.[61] When first formed, Abu Dhabi's naval force was staffed with British contract officers. Pakistani seconded officers started to serve in the naval force by the late 1960s, as did a few other foreign nationalities. A British contract officer commanded the force until 1975, when the post was filled by a seconded Egyptian officer.

---

55   These included ten SA-316B Alouette-3 (delivered 1972-74), around five SA-330 Puma (delivered 1972-74), and two C130H Hercules tactical long-range transports (delivered 1975).
56   This was Lt. Col. G.J. (Twinkle) Storey (1968-72).
57   The *Ardhana* (also written as the *Arzhana*) class patrol boats (also known as the Vosper Thornycroft 110ft/33m vessels) were P131/1101 Ardhana, P132/1102 Ziraru, P133/1103 Murbah, P134/1104 Al Ghulian, P135/1105 Al Sila/Radoom (now sitting in storage at the Abu Dhabi Ship Building yard in Musafah, Abu Dhabi) and P136/1106 Ghanadhah. Their armament was two 30mm A32 Oerlikon twin cannons and one 20mm A41A. They had a crew of 26, and a range of 1,800 miles at 14 knots.
58   The *Fairey Marine Spear* class vessels were armed with two medium machine guns. They had a crew of three.
59   The Cheverton craft were Al Shaheen and Al Aqab. They carried one machine gun.
60   This was at Dohat Al Quwaisat, which became an advance base for operations in August 1973.
61   This was at Khor Fakkan.

Foreign operations

The first half of the 1970s also saw some participation by the ADDF in foreign operations. Following a request from the Sultan of Oman in 1973, Abu Dhabi sent two ADDF infantry squadrons to the city of Sohar in northern Oman, which allowed Sohar's Omani *gendarmerie* unit to deploy to fight rebels in Dhofar in southern Oman. These squadrons were based in Sohar from October 1973 to January 1974 and, again, from November 1974 to April 1975. During the 1973 Arab-Israel War (6-25 October 1973), the ADDF Air Wing's Caribous served as air ambulances in Jordan.[62]

Ras Al Khaimah Mobile Force (1968-76)

The Ras Al Khaimah Mobile Force (RAKMF) was a ruler-controlled military organisation formed in 1968. It was established by the Ruler of Ras Al Khaimah, Sheikh Saqr bin Moḥammad Al Qasimi, to provide increased security and stability in the face of tribal-linked protest against his rule, as well as to protect the Emirate in the light of Britain's withdrawal announcement in January 1968. The RAKMF was a motorised light infantry unit, supported by machine guns, mortars and armoured cars.[63] In May 1968, the first recruits began training at the TOS training facility in Manama.[64] However, the force lacked qualified officers which constrained its capabilities. To rectify this, a TOS officer known to the ruler, Major D. (David) Neild, was offered command of the force if he resigned from the TOS. In mid-1969, Neild was appointed Commander RAKMF with the rank of Lieutenant-Colonel. His 2IC was the former Ras Al Khaimah Police officer, Major Mifta bin Abdulla Al Khatiri.

Under Lieutenant-Colonel Neild, the force initially consisted of 120 men, structured into four mobile platoons and a medium mortar troop.[65] By early 1972, the force's strength had increased to 300. The RAKMF's key task was patrolling outside of Ras Al Khaimah town, with security within the town being the responsibility of the Ras Al Khaimah Police. In early 1972, Neild resigned, and command passed for a short period to his 2IC before the ruler's second son, 25-year old Sheikh Sultan, became its commander. The force was supported by Saudi Arabia which provided funds to buy equipment, as well as seconding a handful of officers from the early to mid-1970s.

62   Sheridan, email, 21 August 2016.
63   TNA FCO 8/1245: A.J. Coles, Political Agency Dubai to T.J. Everard, PRPG, 'Ras Al Khaimah Mobile Force', 31 July 1969.
64   TNA FCO 8/910: K.C.P. Ive, Commander TOS to D.A. Roberts, Political Agent, Dubai, [untitled, 12053],18 May 1968.
65   TNA CAB 163/116: Col M.C. Thursby-Pelham, British Forces Gulf, 'Present and Projected Develop of Local Forces in the Gulf', 28 March 1969.

By June 1974, the RAKMF had a total of 365 personnel. Its Table of Organisation consisted of: an HQ; an infantry squadron made up of four infantry troops, one mortar troop of eleven 81mm mortars and a GPMG troop; a reconnaissance troop of six Ferret scout cars; and a training centre. The HQ and the infantry squadron minus two infantry troops were based at Manaourah with two infantry troops north of Al Shams. The training centre was at Breirat.[66] Unlike other ruler-controlled forces which had a separate Emiri Guard, ruler protection and palace guarding was provided by infantry troops. Due to the Emirate's very limited financial means, the RAKMF changed little in size or equipment between 1974 and 1976 when it and other Emirati forces were unified into the UAE Armed Forces.

Dubai Defence Force (1970-76)

From the mid-1960s, the Ruler of Dubai, Sheikh Rashid bin Saeed Al Maktoum, had discussed forming his own armed force. In 1967, Sheikh Rashid seriously considered taking this step in the aftermath of riots in Dubai against the British after a false rumour spread that British forces in Sharjah were intervening on Israel's side during what became known as the Six-Day War.[67] The ruler deferred a decision and instead increased efforts to build a more capable Dubai police force instead.

In early 1970, Sheikh Rashid finally ordered the formation of the Dubai Defence Force (DDF).[68] The rationale behind the force's formation was to protect the Emirate in case the union of the Emirates failed and to deter aggressive acts from other emirates.

Sheikh Rashid asked the TOS to assist in the DDF's formation and, in February 1971, the TOS temporarily attached a British officer Captain K. (Keith) Steel to the DDF, as well as an Arab officer and several NCOs. A short time later Steel was promoted and became Britain's first Seconded Officer to the DDF. Major Steel was instructed by Sheikh Mohammed bin Rashid, the third son of the Dubai Ruler and head of Dubai Police and Security, to build a force of between 400 and 500 soldiers.[69] Operationally, Major Steel worked closely with the Dubai Police Commander, the Briton Jack Briggs, who had, with Sheikh Mohammed bin Rashid's agreement, already ordered the necessary weapons, radios, vehicles and stores to stand up the force. The TOS personnel were augmented around mid-1971 by a small Jordanian military team, tasked to help with recruit training. However, the team was dismissed a few months later due to perceived poor-quality outcomes. A key source of early

---

66   TNA FCO 8/2371: Agar, 'Intelligence Report No 12', 3 June 1974.
67   H.G. Balfour-Paul, Political Agency Dubai to A.J.D. Stirling, PRPG, [untitled letter], 14 September 1967 in A. Burdett, ed. *Records of the Emirates 1966-1971: 1967* (Slough, 2002), pp. 173-74.
68   Ibid.
69   Captain K. Steel, Commander DDF, 1971-72, telephone interview, 4 August 2015.

recruits were Dubaians who were either serving or former members of the TOS, as well as armed retainers and guards of the Royal Family.[70]

The DDF quickly established its own 12-week recruit training programme based on that of the TOS.[71] By the end of 1971, two 150-man recruit courses had graduated. The Dubai Ruler wanted his force to be primarily made up of Dubai citizens or other Emiratis. Thus, the DDF's composition was radically different from that of the ADDF which had large numbers of Pakistanis, Sudanese, Jordanians, and other nationalities. In mid-1975, some 83 percent of the DDF's personnel were Emirati, with around 46 percent from Dubai and 37 percent from the rest of the UAE. Omanis made up just 13 percent and other countries were the source of only 4 percent.[72]

The consequence of this policy was that there was an ongoing shortage of experienced NCOs and officers in the DDF,[73] as it took time to grow these from within. To accelerate the development of Emirati officers, the ruler sent a number of Dubaians to foreign training establishments, notably in Britain.[74] While this was a medium-to-long-term solution, to address the lack of experience in the short-term, additional experienced seconded and contract British officers were engaged, starting in 1972. By February 1975, the DDF had five seconded and nine contract British personnel.[75] Most were British officers who initially commanded both combat and non-combat units, but by the mid-1970s, they had generally handed over their commands to Emiratis and had become advisors or Staff Officers. Small numbers of British NCOs were also engaged, mostly as specialists.

The DDF was initially organised into motorised infantry squadrons of about 150 men, with each structured into three troops. These were all lightly armed and equipped with Land Rovers. In 1972, the force had grown to three squadrons, thus creating the first regiment. Lacking any suitably experienced officer at regimental rank (i.e. a Lieutenant-Colonel), Dubai asked the British Government to locate a suitable regimental officer who could be seconded to the DDF. Lieutenant-Colonel A.B. (Tony) Wallerstein, an officer who had served with the TOS in 1959 and 1960, arrived in 1972 and became the DDF Commander. He was replaced in 1974 by another British seconded officer, Colonel M.L. (Michael) Barclay, who in turn was replaced in 1976 by the first local commander, Colonel Sheikh Ahmed bin Rashid Al Maktoum, the fourth son of the Ruler of Dubai.

70   Ibid.
71   Ibid.
72   TNA FCO 8/2371: Agar, 'Intelligence Report No 12', 3 June 1974.
73   TNA FCO 8/2371: Agar, 'Annual Report for 1973 by Defence Attaché United Arab Emirates', January 1974.
74   In early 1973, both Sheikh Ahmed bin Rashid and Sheikh Marwan Maktoum Al Maktoum graduated from Royal Military College at Sandhurst.
75   Wikileaks, US Embassy in London, 'Current Level of British Presence in Gulf States And Oman', 24 February 1975.

With the arrival of Saladin and Ferret armoured cars in 1972, the DDF stood up an armoured car squadron.[76] An Emiri Guard force was also established around this time, made up of both a plain-clothes mobile guard and uniformed static palace guards. By 1974, the Dubai Emiri Guard had a strength of 154, consisting of a 90-strong Special Guard and 64-strong Royal Guard.[77] By late 1973, the DDF consisted of 1,120 personnel with some 30 percent being civilians.[78] Most collective training was at section and troop level until 1973, whereupon training started at squadron level. In the following year, the first whole-of-force exercise was carried out.[79] By the end of 1974, the force's size had reached 1,733 which included 537 civilians.[80]

Although the DDF did not technically have an air force, it could access helicopters and light aircraft via the Dubai Air Wing. The Air Wing was administered by the police but was under the direct command of the Sheikh Mohammed bin Rashid in his capacity as head of Dubai Police and Security. Initially, the Air Wing's personnel, including pilots, were principally Western expatriates,[81] but from 1974 onwards, Dubai nationals began serving as pilots.[82]

In 1973, the Ruler of Dubai ordered the expansion and upgrading of the DDF. This decision was driven by his concern over the future cohesion of the UAE and tensions with Sharjah following the August 1973 Tawi Nizwa incident (see the Sharjah National Guard section below). Large volumes of new equipment started to arrive in 1974 and 1975, including Scorpion armoured reconnaissance tracked vehicles, 81mm mortars, GPMGs, 20mm Hispano-Suiza anti-aircraft weapons, Carl Gustaf 84mm anti-tank recoilless rifles, and Bedford and Scammel trucks. By the end of 1974, the DDF combat element of the force consisted of an infantry regiment of three squadrons, two armoured car squadrons,[83] and a support squadron equipped with 81mm mortars and 20mm AA/anti-APC cannons. The force also had a training squadron, ordnance section, workshops, and a boys' training squadron (see Figure 19).[84]

76   Lt Colonel J.J. Williams, founding Officer Commanding, Armoured Car Squadron, DDF, interview, London, 17 December 2015.
77   TNA FCO 8/2371: Agar, 'Intelligence Report No 12', 3 June 1974.
78   TNA FCO 8/2371: Agar, 'Annual Report for 1973 by Defence Attaché United Arab Emirates', January 1974.
79   Ibid.
80   Ibid.
81   The initial commander was the contract British officer, Major A. Tooth, who was succeeded by the Austrian, Major G. Trosch. Other pilots by 1974 were three Austrians, one US and one British contract officers. TNA FCO 8/2371: Agar, 'Intelligence Report No 12', 3 June 1974.
82   In 1974, there were four Dubai nationals were undergoing pilot training in Italy and three in the UK. Ibid.
83   One armoured car squadron was made up of 18 Saladins and four Ferret scout cars, and the other with 10 Scorpions and four Ferrets. Ibid.
84   Ibid., Appendix 1 to Annex A to DA/INT/51 of 3 June 1974.

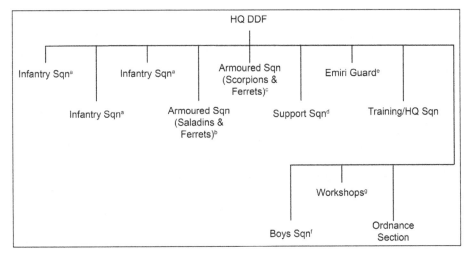

Figure 19: Organisation of the Dubai Defence Force, mid-1974.

Notes
a. A squadron consisted of 154 men, organised into the Land Rover-borne platoons. The squadrons did not have infantry support weapons.
b. Equipped with 18 Saladins and eight Ferrets which were subsequently reduced to four Ferrets; the squadron was then re-organised into an HQ (two Saladins), four Saladin Troops (each with four Saladins) and one Ferret Troop (with four Ferrets).
c. Raised in July/August 1974; the squadron then consisted of ten Scorpions and four Ferrets.
d. Support squadron eventually consisted of a mortar troop of ten 81mm mortars and a 20mm cannon troop of 18 20mm Hispano Suiza cannons of which 12 were mounted on long wheelbase Land Rovers.
e. At this point, 90 strong plain-clothes mobile guard for the ruling family.
f. Boys' Squadron was raised on 7 May 1974 with 54 boys.
g. A static workshop but planned to have a field capability.

In 1975, the total strength of the DDF was 1,733, made up of 61 officers, 1,135 Other Ranks and 537 civilians.[85] With the arrival of additional Scorpions in 1976, an armoured regiment was established. In addition, a second infantry regiment and an artillery squadron with 105mm light guns were formed.[86]

The Dubai Air Wing's capabilities also expanded with the arrival of additional helicopters and fixed wing training and observation aircraft in 1974 and 1975.[87] However, the most important advancement occured in 1975 when four Aeromacchi MB 326G jet trainers arrived. These new aircraft could also serve as light ground-attack

85   Ibid.
86   TNA FCO 8/2897: Bromage, 'Annual Report for 1976 on the United Arab Emirates Armed Forces', 30 January 1977.
87   The fleet in 1975 was two troop-transporting Augusta Bell 205A-1 and three light Augusta Bell 206B helicopters, in addition to one fixed-wing Cessna 182 and one Siai-Marchetti SF.260WD Warrior trainer. TNA FCO 8/2371: Agar, 'Intelligence Report No 12', 3 June 1974.

aircraft,[88] and resulted in the Air Wing achieving a level of military significance.[89] By this time, the DDF's key installations were the new DDF headquarters at Jumeirah, a training centre at Al Aweer, a training camp in Dubai's Wadi Hatta exclave on the Oman border, and a camp at Jebel Ali.

Sharjah National Guard (1972-76)

The Sharjah National Guard (SNG) was formed in 1972 as a direct result of the killing of the Ruler of Sharjah, Sheikh Khalid bin Mohammed Al Qasimi, by his cousin, Sheikh Saqr bin Sultan Al Qasimi. Sheikh Saqr had been Ruler of Sharjah until 1965 when he was deposed following a loss of support from the British and the ruler's own family.[90] Sheikh Khalid became his successor.

In an attempt to regain the rulership, Sheikh Saqr stormed the Ruler's fort palace in Sharjah township with around 20 armed supporters on 25 January 1972. During the attack, Sheikh Khalid and several palace servants were killed. Sheikh Saqr proclaimed himself the new ruler. This pronouncement was not accepted by the principal UAE rulers – and a combined military operation involving the UDF, ADDF and DDF forced the rebellious sheikh and his followers to surrender.[91]

Shortly after, Sheikh Sultan bin Mohammed Al Qasimi became the Ruler of Sharjah. Recognising that the ruler and his family were only protected by untrained armed retainers and police guards, and hence were vulnerable to a small, well-armed, well organised adversary, Sheikh Sultan decided to form Sharjah's own armed force.

The principal roles of the SNG were to ensure internal security and to protect the ruler and his close family.[92] Given Sharjah's limited financial resources – oil had yet to be discovered in its offshore territory – Sharjah approached Abu Dhabi for assistance. Abu Dhabi agreed to fund and equip a force of 14 officers and 230 men. However, it

88   Three were MB-326KD single-seat ground-attack aircraft and one was a MB-326LD two-seat advanced jet trainer. 'United Arab Emirates', *Flight International*, 13 March 1975, p. 431.
89   TNA FCO 8/2371: Agar, 'Intelligence Report No 12', 3 June 1974.
90   A key factor in his removal was the ruler's support for Nasserism. Davidson, *The United Arab Emirates: A Study in Survival*, p. 81; H. von Bismarck, '"A Watershed in our Relations with the Trucial States": Great Britain's Policy to Prevent the Opening of an Arab League Office in the Persian Gulf in 1965', *Middle Eastern Studies*, 47, 1 (2011), pp. 16-20.
91   For details on the military operation, see Commander UDF's report of the rebellion written the day after it ended. TNA FCO 8/1925: Lt Colonel H.E.R. Watson, Commander UDF, 'Report on Operations in the period 24/25 January 1972', 26 January 1972. See also a first-hand report written by Maj C.G.B.H. (Cameron) Mackie, OC 'C' Sqn, who led the tactical response until he was wounded. Cameron Mackie, 'Sharjah Battle, 24th January 1972', *Trucial Oman Officers Association Newsletter*, February (2012).
92   D. Neild, *A Soldier in Arabia* (London, 2016), p. 146.

insisted that the force should be known as a national guard,[93] probably because this reflected its role as a guard for the ruler and because to call it an armed force would have been perceived as contrary to Abu Dhabi's stated policy of bringing together the Emirati armed forces, not creating new ones.

Political control over the force was given to Sheikh Abdul Aziz bin Mohammad Al Qasimi, a former TOS captain and brother of the new ruler. To provide the force's professional military leadership, Sheikh Abdul Aziz contacted Lieutenant-Colonel David Neild, whom he had served under in the TOS. Neild, who had just retired as Commander of the Ras Al Khaimah Mobile Force, agreed to assist in setting up the SNG.[94] He became the Commander SNG in 1972.

The development of the SNG was rapid for by mid-March 1972, the SNG consisted of some 75 former palace guards in addition to another 55 men, who had completed basic training or were awaiting training in Sharjah by instructors loaned by the ADDF.[95] Within a few months of taking command, Neild had built up a 'reasonably well-trained' one-hundred strong company of light infantry which had taken over full responsibility for the security of the ruler and his family. The SNG Commander was confident that his force could also respond effectively to any civil unrest.[96]

Lieutenant-Colonel Neild resigned from the SNG in 1973, by which time the force had grown to 300. He was the only Briton to have served in this force. He handed over command to Sheikh Abdul Aziz, who by then had been promoted to Lieutenant-Colonel. The SNG's force's leadership were all former TOS officers, with most being Emirati. SNG's leadership in 1974 consisted of Sheikh Abdul Aziz, Commander; Major Hassan Said, Deputy Commander; Major Ali Sultan, OC Infantry Squadron; and Captain Nair (Pakistani) Adjutant (former TOS Records Officer). [97]

On 20 August 1973, an incident occurred at Tawi Nizwa on the Sharjah-Dubai border which had great significance for both the SNG and the Dubai Defence Force. Tawi Nizwa was a small inland settlement which both Sharjah and Dubai claimed was in their territory. Dubai had recently drilled a water well at the location. On 20 August, a DDF helicopter containing the head of Dubai Police and Security, Sheikh Mohammed bin Rashid Al Maktoum, who was also the Federal Minister of Defence, and the DDF's Commanding Officer, Lieutenant-Colonel A.B. Wallerstein, flew over the site to view developments on the ground. Sharjah forces on the ground fired at the helicopter. It was hit some 43 times and forced to

93 TNA DEFE 68/397: H.B. Walker, UK Ambassador in the UAE, 'Tel No. 69', 19 February 1972.
94 Neild, *A Soldier in Arabia*, p. 145.
95 TNA DEFE 68/397: Treadwell, 'Your Telno 15: British Loaned Officers in UDF and ADDF', 18 January 1972.
96 Neild, *A Soldier in Arabia*, p. 148.
97 TNA FCO 8/2371: Agar, 'Intelligence Report No 12', 3 June 1974.

land. No-one was injured, and the passengers retreated to safety before the SNG arrived.[98]

This incident could have escalated into a conflict between the two Emirates, but did not thanks to the personal intervention of Sheikh Zayed in his role as President of the UAE.[99] However, it did lead the Ruler of Sharjah to authorise a doubling of the SNG's manpower,[100] funded by the State's oil income which it had just started receiving. Lieutenant-Colonel Sheikh Abdul Aziz developed a plan for expansion which included forming an air wing. Before the expansion could be implemented, relations broke down between the Ruler of Sharjah and Sheikh Abdul Aziz. Consequently, the ruler did not provide the necessary funds for the expansion and, as a result, Lieutenant-Colonel Sheikh Abdul Aziz withdrew from active involvement in the force.[101] This was a significant blow to the armed force as he had been the impetus behind the SNG's continual improvement, according to the British Defence Attaché. The Attaché noted that as a result of Sheikh Abdul Aziz's departure, 'the Force is slipping downhill fast and the standard of discipline has quickly fallen away'.[102]

From this point until 1976, when it was integrated into the UAE Armed Forces, the SNG remained essentially unchanged. Over this period, its force structure was principally one motorised infantry squadron equipped with light weapons, an armoured car group made up of six Shorland armoured cars, one mortar troop equipped with four 81mm mortars, and an Emiri Guard of 60 men.[103] The 1976 unification of Emirati military forces saw the combat elements of the SNG being integrated into the Al Yarmouk Brigade, and the Emiri Guard element become administratively part of the Sharjah Police.

Central Military Command (1976-97)

As will be detailed in Chapter 9, the 1976 unification of Emirati armed forces saw the ruler-based forces becoming regional (i.e. geographic-based) commands of the UAE Armed Forces. In the case of Dubai, the Dubai Defence Force became Central Military Command (CMC). The 1978 integration of the UAE military dissolved

---

98   TNA FCO 8/2371: Agar, 'Annual Report for 1973 by Defence Attaché United Arab Emirates', January 1974.
99   This was noted by the British Defence Attaché who said that 'This incident which could have had such disastrous and far-reaching consequences for the UAE was fortunately well handled by the President of the Union and tempers were allowed to cool'. Ibid.
100 Ibid.
101 TNA FCO 8/2371: Agar, 'Intelligence Report No 12', 3 June 1974. With the ongoing absence of Sheikh Abdul Aziz, the force was led by its Deputy Commander, Major Hassan Said. Ibid.
102 Ibid.
103 Ibid.

these regional commands, with their land force elements becoming structured into brigades under the GHQ of the UAE Armed Forces. The CMC officially became 1st Brigade. However, Dubai immediately withdrew its force from the UAE Armed Forces due to concerns over the nature of the military decision-making process and, more broadly, the future political structure and powers of the Federal Government. As such, the force again became effectively a regional command, which is reflected in Dubai's ongoing use of its previous name – the CMC.[104] The CMC would continue to operate independently from the rest of the UAE Armed Forces until 1997 when it was officially reintegrated into the UAE Armed Forces.

Dubai funded the CMC itself. This gave it control over the force's administration, recruitment and weapons procurement rather than this residing with federal government. The CMC operated as an independent, single service force with land, air, Emiri Guard and special forces elements. It had no naval component (although it had a Royal Boat Squadron), as Dubai's inshore maritime domain was protected by the Dubai Police, with the UAE Navy providing security offshore. It had an air force called the Dubai Air Wing.

From its formation in 1976 to its dissolution in 1997, the CMC reported to Sheikh Mohammed bin Rashid Al Maktoum, in his roles as Dubai's Head of Police and Public Security and Minister of Defence. Sheikh Mohammed was the third son of Sheikh Rashid bin Saeed Al Maktoum, Ruler of Dubai (r. 1958-90). The force's Commander-in-Chief for most of this period was Major-General Sheikh Ahmed bin Rashid Al Maktoum, the fourth son of Sheikh Rashid, with operational control resting with his two Deputy Commanders, the brothers Sheikh Butti bin Maktoum bin Juma Al Maktoum and Sheikh Ahmed bin Maktoum bin Juma Al Maktoum, who were cousins of the Dubai Ruler.

In general, there was little cooperation between Central Military Command and the UAE Armed Forces from the late 1970s to the 1990s. Dubai's forces did not participate in the three year, 750-man contribution of UAE forces to the Arab Deterrent Force in Lebanon (1977-79). Nor did they participate in the first Gulf Cooperation Council military exercise in the UAE in October 1983.[105] The British Defence Attaché observed in 1984 that not only had the Chief of Staff of the UAE Armed Forces 'still not ventured into the CMC ... there is little integration likely to be seen in the foreseeable future.'[106] Nor did it collaborate in weapons procurement. This was clearly illustrated in Dubai's purchase of eight to 15 Scud ballistic missiles

104 TNA FCO 8/4385: Cameron, 'Annual Report for 1981 on the United Arab Emirates Armed Forces', 31 January 1982.
105 *Middle East and North Africia 1984-85*, 1984), p. 748.
106 TNA, FCO 8/5468, Cameron, 'Annual Report for 1983 on the United Arab Emirates Armed Forces', 25 January 1984.

from North Korea in 1988, a missile capability which was lacking in the rest of the UAE Armed Forces.[107]

An enduring reason for CMC's independence was that the Ruler of Dubai strongly opposed transferring control of his armed forces to Abu Dhabi. This was frequently reported in UK embassy correspondence. In 1982, when asked about the possibility of integrating the CMC and the UAE Armed Forces, Sheikh Butti, Deputy Commander of the CMC reportedly said, 'no, not whilst Shaikh Rashid remains alive, but we might have some change after he has gone.'[108]

However, when the UAE faced an imminent threat, the two forces did cooperate. On 25 November 1986, Iranian aircraft fired two missiles at Abu Dhabi's Abu Al Bukhoosh offshore oil complex which consisted of five connected platforms, manned by 230 workers. The attack caused serious damage to the oil rig and accommodation platform. The attack killed five people (two French, two Indians and one Pakistani) and injured 24. It was the second attack on the platform in a two-month period.[109] Dubai's military helped during the evacuation of personnel from Das Island following the attack through the provision of two C130 transport aircraft. While Abu Dhabi had medium transport aircraft, none were available at that time.[110] In addition to medical aid, Dubai provided a detachment equipped with RBS 70 man-portable air-defence systems. The detachment deployed to four rigs around Abu Al Bukhoosh, in addition to basing a reporter radar on the main Abu Al Bukhoosh platform.[111] A further example of Dubai providing aid in times of need was during the 1990-91 Gulf War. Dubai allocated a mechanised infantry company and support units to the coalition operation.[112]

In terms of capabilities, the CMC in 1977 had an approximate strength of 3,500.[113] By 1984 it had grown to around 8,500.[114] In 1976, it had an armoured regiment made up of wheeled light and medium armoured cars and tracked armoured reconnaissance vehicles,[115] and, by 1984, it was equipped with main battle tanks.[116] In 1976, its

107 National Foreign Intelligence Board US Central Intelligence Agency, *Prospects for Special Weapons Proliferation and Control, NIE 5-91C/11* (Washington DC, 1991).
108 TNA FCO 8/4973: A.F. Walker, UK Embassy in the UAE, 'Report from Col Anthony Walker', 29 March 1983.
109 Dara Kadva, 'Workers Recall Offshore Ordeal', *Khaleej Times*, 27 November 1986.
110 TNA FCO 8/6174: Michael Tait, UK Ambassador, Abu Dhabi to FCO, 'Attack on Abu Dhabi's Al Bukhoosh Oil Platform 25 Nov', 27 November 1986.
111 TNA FCO 8/6177: Kay, MoD to Embassy Abu Dhabi, 'Reaction to Attack on the UAE's Abu Al Bukhoosh (ABK) Oil Rig', 10 December 1986.
112 UAE Armed Forces, *The UAE Armed Forces History and Missions*, p. 53.
113 TNA FCO 8/3105: Colonel T.N. Bromage, UK Defence Attaché, 'Annual Report on the UAE Armed Forces for 1977', 2 February 1978.
114 TNA FCO 8/5468: Cameron, 'Annual Report for 1983 on the United Arab Emirates Armed Forces', 25 January 1984.
115 TNA FCO 8/2897: Bromage, 'Annual Report for 1976 on the United Arab Emirates Armed Forces', 30 January 1977.
116 These were 18 OF-40 Italian main battle tanks (delivered 1981-83).

infantry were mounted in Land Rovers and trucks and, by 1984, wheeled armoured personnel carriers had been introduced.[117] Moreover, in 1976 its artillery consisted of one squadron with 105mm light guns, as well as another with 20mm anti-aircraft guns.[118] And, by 1984, it had been expanded to two batteries of light guns and one anti-aircraft battery which including both surface-to-air missiles and guns.[119]

As of 1983, the CMC's land forces had bases at all key border areas in Dubai Emirate. CMC headquarters was in Dubai city, with a rifle squadron base near the Abu Dhabi/Dubai coastal border (Camp Mina Sayahi at Jebel Ali) and another on the Oman/Dubai border (Hatta),[120] an armoured camp near the Sharjah/Dubai border (Aqrab), and an artillery battery along the Abu Dhabi-Dubai road from Al Ain (Marmoum).[121] The CMC also had a special forces element (known as the Commandos) which included assault and sniper groups based at Wadi Shabak.[122]

In 1976, the Dubai Air Wing consisted of four Aeromacchi MB 326 jet trainers which also could serve as light ground-attack aircraft, in addition to helicopters and observation aircraft.[123] These were based at Dubai Airport. By 1984, the force had grown to some 30 aircraft organised into two fighter squadrons of jet ground attack/ trainers, a helicopter squadron and a transport squadron.[124] During the mid to late 1980s, these were augmented by five advanced Aermacchi MB-339 trainer and light attack aircraft. Around this time, the CMC's air force was relocated to its own air base (Al Minhad), 24km outside of Dubai city.

Dubai had established an Emiri Guard in the early 1970s, with its base at the ruler's Zabeel Palace. In 1983, it consisted of one squadron of plainclothes Special Guard

117 There were 60 wheeled EE-11 Urutu Brazilian amphibious APCs (delivered 1982-83).
118 TNA FCO 8/2897: Bromage, 'Annual Report for 1976 on the United Arab Emirates Armed Forces', 30 January 1977.
119 The anti-aircraft battery consisted of 13 Swedish RBS 70 launchers with 143 missiles (delivered 1980) and 20mm guns. TNA, FCO 8/4385, Cameron, 'Annual Report for 1981 on the United Arab Emirates Armed Forces', 31 January 1982; TNA, FCO 8/5468, Cameron, 'Annual Report for 1983 on the United Arab Emirates Armed Forces', 25 January 1984.
120 TNA FCO 8/4385: Cameron, 'Annual Report for 1981 on the United Arab Emirates Armed Forces', 31 January 1982.
121 TNA FCO 8/5468: Cameron, 'Annual Report for 1983 on the United Arab Emirates Armed Forces', 25 January 1984.
122 Ibid.
123 By 1976, Dubai's fleet consisted of three Bell 206/OH 58 light helicopters, one Cessna 182 Skylane light aircraft, two Bell 205/UH 1D helicopters, one SIAI-Marchetti SF.260W Warrior military trainer, an Aeritalia G 222 medium-sized STOL military transport aircraft, and four Macchi single-seat MB-326KD ground attack aircraft.
124 One squadron consisted of eight BAE Hawk 61 single-engine, jet-powered advanced trainer, and another of Aermacchi MB 326 trainer and light attack aircraft. The helicopter squadron consisted of six Bell 205, four Bell 214B, one Bell 206, and the transport squadron of one G222 and two 130H-30. TNA FCO 8/5468: Cameron, 'Annual Report for 1983 on the United Arab Emirates Armed Forces', 25 January 1984.

(*Harras Al Khas*) plus a second Special Guard squadron being formed, and a squadron of uniformed Royal Guard (*Harras Amiri*) plus two more Royal Guard squadrons being formed. The Emiri Guard was also responsible for the parachute school at Al Aweer.[125]

At the time of the 1990-91 Gulf War, the CMC's strength was reported as 11,000.[126] Like the rest of the UAE Armed Forces, the CMC underwent a programme of modernisation and expansion after the Gulf War. It purchased over 400 BMP-3 infantry fighting vehicles,[127] in addition to 136 Turkish armoured fighting vehicles and derivatives,[128] resulting in the full mechanisation of its infantry brigade. By the late 1990s, the Dubai Air Wing had also ordered several aircraft including four anti-ship helicopters equipped with air to surface missiles and 14 light, multipurpose military helicopters.[129]

In December 1997, a resolution was issued by Sheikh Mohammed bin Rashid Al Maktoum, the UAE Minister of Defence, and then the Crown Prince of Dubai, for the full amalgamation of the CMC into the UAE Armed Forces.[130]

The number of UAE Armed Forces members in Dubai today is far less than during the last decade of the CMC. The 2011 Dubai Statistical Handbook stated there were just 5,430 individuals (5,375 men and 55 women) employed in the UAE Armed Forces in Dubai Emirate.[131]

Umm Al Quwain National Guard (1976-2006)

The Umm Al Quwain National Guard was formed in 1976, but little accurate information is available about this small force. Planning for the force by the Ruler of Umm Al Quwain appears to have commenced in 1975 when the Ruler asked permission from the UAE Ministry of Defence to import around 50 rifles, 30 GPMGs, 30 mortars and 11 Carl Gustaf 84mm anti-tank recoilless rifles.[132] By late 1977, the force had a strength of about 180 and was equipped with 12 jeep-mounted 106mm recoilless rifles, ten Scorpion light tanks (previously owned by the Al Yarmouk Brigade)

125 Ibid.
126 Metz, *Persian Gulf States: Country Studies*, p. 362.
127 400 BMP-3 were delivered 1992-2000, and 136 AIFV-APCs were delivered 1999-2000.
128 These consist of ACV-350 AIFVs made up of 76 ALV and ACV-AFOV artillery fire control, 8 ARV and 52 ACV-ENG AEV versions.
129 These were four ASW AS565S Panther helicopters (delivered 2001-02) fitted with AS 15 TT missiles, and 14 AS-350/AS-550 Fennec light helicopters (delivered 2001-02).
130 'UAE Armed Forces Through the Years', *Gulf News*, 5 May 2016.
131 Dubai Statistics Center Government of Dubai, *Statistical Yearbook – Emirate of Dubai 2011* (Dubai, 2012), p. 77.
132 TNA FCO 8/2430: Colonel P.W.G. Seabrook, UK Defence Attaché to the UAE, 'Weapons for Umm al Qawain', 26 June 1975.

and around four mortars.[133] At this time, it was commanded by Colonel Sheikh Saud bin Rashid Al Mualla. He was the eldest son of the Crown Prince, Sheikh Rashid bin Ahmad Al Mualla, who was the son of the Ruler. Like other ruler-controlled forces, when they were established the professional head of the force was an expatriate. The force appears to have suffered from a high leadership turnover, for it had four different executive commanders (either British or Sudanese) in its early years. It was primarily manned by Pakistanis and officered in the main by expatriates.[134] Its headquarters was at Umm Al Quwain Camp with its training facilities in the Mehteb area.[135]

By the beginning of 1982, the Umm Al Quwain National Guard had a strength of just 200, organised into one infantry squadron, one reconnaissance squadron and one support unit.[136] The force's considerable quantity of equipment, coupled with its small number of personnel, probably resulted in it not being sustainable. It was formally integrated into the UAE Armed Forces in 2006.[137]

Re-established armed forces of Ras Al Khaimah and Sharjah (1984-1990s)

In the mid-1980s, both Sharjah and Ras Al Khaimah re-established armed forces. Details on these forces are quite limited. In 1984, the British Ambassador reported that the Ruler of Sharjah was 'trying to re-equip his national guard with such equip-ment as armoured cars and even missile-firing helicopters ... [and] the Ruler of Ras Al Khaimah followed suite with a less dramatic reinforcement of his guards'. The Ambassador attributed these attempts to a 'further slackening of the already loose ties holding the federation together', which resulted in the more independently minded rulers deciding to pursue policies that were at odds with the federalist agenda.[138] This situation was attributed to the disengagement in Federal issues by the Ruler of Dubai due to his ongoing illness, and a significant decline in Abu Dhabi's oil income, and hence the influence of the Capital over the nation.[139] In addition, the economies of both Sharjah and Ras Al Khaimah were growing, and hence these Emirates depended less on the Capital's financial support and were therefore less willing to acquiesce to its

133 TNA FCO 8/3105: Bromage, 'Annual Report on the UAE Armed Forces for 1977', 2 February 1978.
134 Ibid.
135 UAE Armed Forces, *The UAE Armed Forces History and Missions*, p. 23.
136 TNA FCO 8/4385: Cameron, 'Annual Report for 1981 on the United Arab Emirates Armed Forces', 31 January 1982.
137 UAE Armed Forces, *The UAE Armed Forces History and Missions*, p. 23.
138 TNA FCO 8/5826: Walker, 'United Arab Emirates: Annual Review for 1984', 20 January 1985.
139 This was due to a fall in the global oil price and a commitment to OPEC's output constraints.

views.[140] In the case of Sharjah, another probable motivating factor for re-equipping its forces was concern over a border dispute with Dubai.[141]

The re-established Ras Al Khaimah armed force was controlled by the Ruler's son, Sheikh Sultan bin Saqr Al Qasimi. He continued to exercise significant power until he retired in the mid-1990s. At this time, the force became integrated into the UAE Armed Forces.[142]

By 1986, Sharjah's armed force had grown to two infantry battalions, one 81mm mortar company and a rocket launcher battery, in addition to logistics and support companies. It also had several helicopters and transport planes, as well as some air defence capability.[143] The force's headquarters was in the Merghab Area, while Khodirah Camp in Al Dhaid was used for training.[144] In June 1987, when the Ruler of Sharjah, Sheikh Sultan bin Mohammed Al Qasimi, was out of the country, the force's Commander and the brother of the Ruler, Sheikh Abdal Aziz bin Mohammed Al Qasimi, claimed the rulership. To strengthen his position, he deployed his force across Sharjah city. At this time, the Sharjah force was reported to be 2,500 strong.[145] The crisis was resolved peacefully through the intervention of Sheikh Zayed and the other rulers. It resulted in Sheikh Sultan remaining as the Ruler of Sharjah, with Sheikh Abdal Aziz becoming the Deputy Ruler. Sheikh Abdal Aziz was subsequently dismissed. The Sharjah armed force was integrated into the UAE Armed Forces in 1990, although the Emiri Guard component became an autonomous element under administrative control of the Sharjah Police.

Looking forward

No ruler-controlled armed forces have existed in the UAE since 2006, however these could be established again providing they are not deemed to be a land, naval and/or air force, as constitutionally such forces can only be formed by the Federal Government. Reasons that a ruler would establish a ruler-controlled armed force could be: (1) to demonstrate his sovereignty to his citizens, (2) to mitigate the risk that he would be removed by federal forces or his local security forces, and (3) to build a capability which he considers has been neglected by the Federal Government.

---

140 For example, Sharjah was becoming economically more self-reliant. By mid-1985, it expected to be producing up to 70,000 barrels of oil a day. TNA FCO 8/5459: Sir D.F. Hawley, 'Meeting with Sheikh Sultan bin Mohammed al Qasimi, Ruler of Sharjah, 14 November 1983', 25 November 1983.
141 TNA FCO 8/5826: Walker, 'United Arab Emirates: Annual Review for 1984', 20 January 1985.
142 Sheikh Majid Abdulla Al Moalla, 'Analysis of the United Arab Emirates' National Security' (PhD thesis, Durham University, 2017), p. 51.
143 TNA FCO 8/6176: H.B. Walker, UK Ambassador in the UAE, 'Visit of CDS to the UAE, 14-16 January', 21 January 1986.
144 UAE Armed Forces, *The UAE Armed Forces History and Missions*, p. 19.
145 J. Phillips, 'Sheikh Rejects Pleas to Abandon Coup in United Arab Emirates', *UPI*, 18 June 1987.

9

Federally Controlled Armed Forces

Before the 1976 unification of all Emirati armed forces, there had been one federally controlled armed force. This was the Union Defence Force (UDF) which was formed in 1971 and renamed the Federal Armed Force (FAF) in 1974. The UDF was, in effect, the British-controlled Trucial Oman Scouts which had been transferred to the UAE Government upon Britain's departure from the Gulf.

The 1976 unification involved the merging of the FAF and the four ruler-controlled forces to create the UAE Armed Forces. In 1978, the UAE Armed Forces were reorganised – resulting in their so-called 'integration'. At this point it is important to differentiate between *unification* and *integration* as they have specific meanings when they are applied to the UAE Armed Forces. While both involved a degree of amalgamation and centralisation, unification denotes something less than integration.

When in 1976 all Emirati armed forces were brought together to form the UAE Armed Forces, a 'unified command' structure was created. This consisted of a single professional military head based in Abu Dhabi, supported by a small secretariat, plus some joint planning and intelligence staffs. While he could issue directions to his subordinate commanders, those outside of Abu Dhabi could choose whether to follow his guidance or not. This was because the subordinate commanders of forces in Dubai, Sharjah and Ras Al Khaimah had complete control of their command's operations and administration. The professional military head exercised direct control over just the commands in Abu Dhabi which then consisted of the Western Regional Command, the Navy and the Air Force.

In 1978, the UAE Armed Forces were reorganised to create an 'integrated command' structure. This continued the practice of having a single professional military head, but now he was supported by large staffs and exerted considerably more authority over all UAE Armed Forces' formations and units. Under this structure, the professional military head could direct all subordinate commanders on all matters, including operational and administrative questions. This gave him potentially the freedom to build a cohesive national force and enforce consistency across doctrine, equipment, training, and administration. However, as will be seen below, the level of integration varied over time due to political issues between the Emirates.

What follows is a historical account of the UDF/FAF (1971-76), the 1976 'unification' of the UAE armed forces, and the 1978 'integration' of the armed forces and its aftermath. The remainder of this chapter then seeks to provide a detailed history of the UAE Armed Forces and its combat commands following the 1978 'integration', taking in developments up to the present day.

Union Defence Force/Federal Armed Force (1971-76)

The Union Defence Force was the first federally controlled armed force in the UAE. It was formed in 1971, and in 1974 it was renamed the Federal Armed Force (FAF). In 1976, the land forces component of the FAF was renamed the Al Yarmouk Brigade.

The UDF was established on 22 December 1971.[1] This was the day after Britain had disbanded its armed force, the Trucial Oman Scouts (TOS) and discharged all of its members. Before disbandment, the approximately 2,000 officers and enlisted men of the TOS, which included some 35 serving British officers and NCOs, were invited to join the UDF. All but a handful did. The UDF reflected the TOS's command and manpower structure. That is, its higher ranks were filled by British officers. Britons would continue to command the force until 1976, although the number of British personnel declined significantly after 1974.

The UDF's force structure, as of the early 1970s, was the same as the TOS – that is the UDF comprised a headquarters at Murqaab Camp (near Sharjah town), and five motorised rifle squadrons, which rotated through bases at Murqaab Camp, Al Ain (Abu Dhabi), Manama (Ajman), Masafi and Ham Ham (Ras Al Khaimah). Manama also hosted the TOS/UDF's heavy weapons support element (originally called Support Group and then Support Squadron), and the training squadron, which included a boy's school.

In the early 1970s, the UDF established the Murbah Camp in Khor Fakkan so as to control tensions between rival groups claiming the same territory. Another significant development was the formation of a sixth rifle squadron, named 'E' Squadron. A final change was the formation of an armoured reconnaissance force which, by the end of 1973, consisted of 18 Ferret Scout cars and 10 Scorpion light tanks.

In the years immediately before 1971, Britain had advocated forming a Federal defence force in the UAE. It argued that it should be based on the TOS. This was not agreed to by the rulers due to disagreement over control of such a force. However in 1973, the UAE rulers commenced formal talks on the unification of the various armed forces in the UAE. But due to disagreement, a decision was postponed. Notwithstanding this, the UAE Minister of Defence took a step towards forming a truly national armed force when, in that year, he issued a decree changing the name of

1   Mann, *The Trucial Oman Scouts: The Story of a Bedouin Force*, p. 192.

the UDF to the FAF.[2] This reflected the Ruler of Dubai's position which was for the FAF to become the national armed force, rather than Abu Dhabi Ruler's position of basing it around the ADDF. To reinforce the perception of the FAF's national association, the force introduced a new device and head-dress badge, based on the newly created UAE Coat of Arms. This would become the head-dress badge of the UAE Armed Forces after it was formed in 1976.[3]

It is important to note that the use of 'Federal' in the FAF's name is best understood to mean that the force was federally provided, rather than being a force *for* the federation. Federally provided forces were not required in the wealthier Emirates of Abu Dhabi and Dubai who had their own substantial armed forces. This interpretation of the term 'federal' resonates to this day. For example, Federal Police members, Federal SWAT teams, and the Federal Police Air Wing exist primarily to support the northern Emirates, with the wealthier Emirates self-funding their own forces.

Along with the name change from UDF to FAF in 1973, the FAF's mission changed. No longer would it have an internal security role as this task was now the responsibility of the rapidly expanding police forces of each Emirate and the Federal Ministry of Interior. Instead, the FAF's primary mission became defence of the external borders of the six northern Emirates. This required the force to become a regular infantry, brigade-sized battle group. Some of the needed changes were already well underway in 1973, such as a heavy weapons troop being added to some rifle squadrons,[4] the force's support squadron being up-armed, and new weapons purchased.[5] Training was also changed to emphasise defensive warfare. By 1975, the FAF had an establishment strength of 3,250 (for the organisation structure, see Figure 20).[6] During 1975-76, a parachute squadron was formed in the FAF.[7] Despite the new mission, the force was involved in some internal security tasks, notably, rounding up illegal immigrants and intervening in tribal disputes.[8]

2   UAE Armed Forces, *The UAE Armed Forces History and Missions*, p. 11.
3   The changeover to the force's new name, devices, badges etc appears to have been inconsistent, resulting in the force still being referred as the UDF in official documents and on base signage etc until all Emirati forces were unified in 1976.
4   The increase in the size of the rifle squadron may not have been applied consistently across the force. In 1974, Culley wrote that a squadron was about 220 of all ranks, formed of four rifle troops (equivalent to a British infantry platoon), a motor transport group and a squadron HQ troop, which included a 15-man signal section. The squadron vehicles consisted of 22 Land Rovers, three Bedford 4-ton trucks and a water bowser. Lt. Colonel H.A. Culley, UDF/FAF, 1973-75, 'Serving with the Union Defence Force, United Arab Emirates', *The Wire: The Royal Signals Magazine*, November-December 1974, pp. 460-61.
5   These included 24 GMPGs, 50 light machine guns, six Carl Gustaf 84mm anti-tank recoilless rifles, 25 60mm mortars, and six 81mm mortars.
6   Lt. Colonel N.C.F. Weekes, UDF/FAF, 1974-76, email, 30 September 2018.
7   A. Noyes, 'Last Marines in the Trucial States', *Globe & Laurel*, May-June (1976), pp. 148-49.
8   Lt. Colonel H.A. Culley, UDF/FAF, 1973-75, email, 13 January 2018.

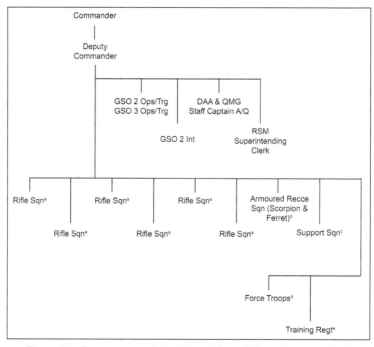

Figure 20: Organisation of the Federal Armed Force, January 1975.

Notes

a.   Rifle squadrons rotated through Sharjah and five outstations of Al Ain (Jahili Fort), Murbah, Ham Ham, Manama and Masafi. Rotations took place every six months. Each squadron comprised an HQ and three rifle troops, all mounted in Land Rovers and Bedford 3-ton trucks.

b.   The Armoured Reconnaissance Squadron was based at Sharjah, and it consisted of four Troops of Ferrets, two troops of Scorpions.

c.   The Support Squadron was based at Manama. It was armed with 81mm mortars and .5 calibre Browning machine guns mounted in Dodge Power Wagons.

d.   The force troops were located at Sharjah, with small detachments in outstations; consisted of the Signal Squadron, Air Wing (based in Dubai), Transport Squadron, Medical Squadron (including Hospital), Ordnance Squadron, Force Quartermaster, Workshop Squadron, Force Paymaster, Works Squadron, Education Squadron (including School), HQ Squadron (including a pipes and drums and mounted troop), Guard Squadron and messes.

e.   The training squadron was based at Manama and undertook recruit and infantry continuation training.

The original plans for the UDF were for it to possess both a sea wing and air wing. While UDF/FAF did not obtain any maritime craft, it did build up an air capability. By 1976, it consisted of around ten transport, liaison and reconnaissance aircraft.

In 1975, a new regiment-based structure was announced for the FAF. Its combat formations would now consist of two regiments, each made up of three rifle squadrons and a regimental HQ. This transformed the FAF into a regular infantry brigade, consisting of a Force HQ and two combat infantry regiments. It also had a training regiment. The changes were implemented over about a two-year period. In 1975, the

Training Regiment at Manama was inaugurated. In 1976 the two regiments were fully formed, both with three rifle squadrons respectively.[9]

In May 1976, as part of the unification of the UAE Armed Forces, the FAF and parts of the Sharjah National Guard were integrated to become the Al Yarmouk infantry brigade.

While Britain hoped that the UDF/FAF would become the basis for the UAE's Federal defence force, this was not to be the case. Instead, the ADDF provided the core of the new UAE Armed Forces. The UDF/FAF failed to become the Federal force primarily because it never received the political and financial support required to expand into a national force. Specifically, in the years immediately after the UAE's formation, sufficient funds were not provided to allow the UDF/FAF to grow and re-equip. This was because Abu Dhabi, as the principal source of funding for Federal Government entities, including the UDF/FAF, prioritised funding for its own force. Likewise, the Ruler of Dubai decided not to fund the force directly, also preferring to fund his own armed force. Another factor in the lack of desire to fund the UDF/FAF as the nucleus of the UAE's armed force was that Sheikh Zayed did not want to have high numbers of British personnel in leadership positions. On multiple occasions, he expressed his dissatisfaction with the large British presence in the UDF/FAF and its slow rate of Emiratisation.[10]

An illustration of the differences between the UDF/FAF and the ADDF was that, in early 1974, the former had 3,000 men while the latter had more than four times this number, with 13,000.[11] Another difference was the forces' capabilities, with the UDF/FAF having no sea wing and its small air wing had no offensive capabilities, while the ADDF's force had rapidly growing naval forces plus its air force had specialised ground attack and air defence aircraft. Given the ADDF's size, capabilities and political backing, it was inevitable that the UAE Armed Forces were built around it, and not the UDF.

The 1976 unification of Emirati armed forces

When the UAE came into existence in 1971, the country was better described as a union rather than united. While there was commitment by the rulers to work towards a federalist agenda, historic grievances and personality clashes meant achieving this end would be a slow process. Occasional setbacks were inevitable.[12] Support for federalism varied across Emirates in the early decades of the UAE. The rulers of Abu

9   Ibid.
10   A. Rossiter, 'Strength in Unity: The Road to the Integrated UAE Armed Forces', *Liwa: Journal of the National Archives*, 7, 13 (2015), p. 49.
11   TNA FCO 8/2371: Agar, 'Intelligence Report No 10', 4 April 1974.
12   B. Friedman, 'From Union ('ittihād) to United (muttahida): The United Arab Emirates, A Success Born of Failure', *Middle Eastern Studies*, 53, 1 (2017), p. 116.

Dhabi and Sharjah supported accelerated federalism while the rulers of Dubai and Ras Al Khaimah advocated a far more cautious implementation. The other smaller Emirates generally supported the first group due to their reliance on Abu Dhabi's financial support.

The cautiousness towards federalisation by some Emirates led to a clause being inserted in the UAE Constitution of 1971 that allowed each Emirate to have a security force under its control. These forces were in addition to the federally controlled force which came into being in December 1971. While it may have been hoped that the number of armed forces would be reduced after the formation of the UAE, the opposite occurred. In 1972, Sharjah established its own armed force and, in 1976, so too did Umm Al Quwain.

This speaks to an enduring characteristic of the post-1971 political system in the UAE – a strong independent streak in some Emirates. This arose because 'each Emirate joined the federation while continuing to embrace its own legacy of tribal loyalties and commitment to its individuality', according to the UAE's preeminent historian, Frauke Heard-Bey.[13] This has been manifested in rulers sometimes pursuing their own interests to the detriment of national interests. Examples of this include the construction in nearly all the Emirates of international airports, cement factories and ports regardless of their need, or the fact they duplicate what exists only a few dozen kilometres away in another Emirate.

This attitude explains why rulers prioritised their own forces and underfunded the UDF/FAF. Sheikh Zayed had long argued for the need to federalise the various armed forces as this would lead to a more effective and efficient mechanism for national defence. Finally, in May 1975, the Federal Supreme Council gave Sheikh Zayed consent to develop a plan for military unification. To do this, a military commission was formed, comprising military officers from neighbouring Arab countries. This had occurred because Sheikh Zayed had asked Saudi Arabia, Jordan and Kuwait to send military commissions to make recommendations for improving the UAE's armed forces, and, upon arrival, the three commissions were integrated into one joint committee.[14]

Known as the Arab Technical Military Committee, it was led by Major-General Othman Al Humaidi of Saudi Arabia. The committee was tasked with making recommendations on how armed force unification could be achieved and what the new force structure should be.[15] The committee's report completed in mid-1975, was considered by the rulers. However, a decision was delayed because the Ruler of Dubai wanted more information on the proposed command structure, force disposition and force numbers. He finally agreed to unification providing the Minister of Defence

13   Frauke Heard-Bey, 'Six Sovereign States: the Process of State Formation', in J.E. Peterson (eds.), *The Emergence of the Gulf States* (New York, 2016), p. 299.
14   Noor Ali Rashid, *Sheikh Mohammed – Life and Times* (Dubai, 2009), pp. 139-40.
15   'Study to Integrate Forces Finished', *Gulf Weekly Mirror*, 28 July 1975.

would have some authority over the post of Chief of Staff.[16] This was agreed to, and on 6 May 1976, the Supreme Defence Council, issued a directive to unify the armed forces of the Emirates.[17]

The directive saw the armed forces placed under the headquarters of the Command of General Headquarters (GHQ). GHQ was to be headed by a Chief of Staff (CoS),[18] the force's professional head. A seconded Jordanian officer, Major-General Awadh Mohammed Al Khalidi, was appointed as the first Chief of Staff. The appointment of a non-national probably not only reflected the lack of an Emirati with the required staff education and experience, but also indicated the concern of certain rulers that if a local from another Emirate was appointed, he would not act impartially. Sheikh Zayed, as UAE President, became the Supreme Commander, with his son, Lieutenant-General Sheikh Khalifa bin Zayed, becoming the Deputy Supreme Commander.[19] The Minister of Defence remained the same – Sheikh Mohammed bin Rashid of Dubai. In the chain of command, the Deputy Supreme Commander was superior to the Minister, and reporting to the Minister was the Chief of Staff. As seen in Chapter 3, the power of the Minister over the Chief of Staff has been very constrained both through law and convention. This meant that, in practice, the CoS effectively reported directly to the Deputy Supreme Commander.

The 1976 unification resulted in the armed forces of Abu Dhabi, Dubai and Ras Al Khaimah being reorganised into three regional commands – Western, Central and Northern respectively (see Table 18, Figure 21).[20] Sharjah's armed force merged with the federally-controlled FAF to create the Al Yarmouk infantry brigade, and, in December 1976, a relative of the Sharjah Ruler, Lieutenant-Colonel Sheikh Humaid bin Abdulla Al Qasimi, became its Commanding Officer.[21] The commanders of the three regional commands remained the same as before unification, that is, the sons of

16   TNA FCO 8/2660: H. St John B. Armitage, UK Embassy Abu Dhabi to Justin Nason, FCO, 'UAE Internal', 10 May 1976.
17   *UAE Supreme Defence Council Decision No. 1 'Regarding the Unification of the Armed Forces in the United Arab Emirates* (1976). The unification was to be effective from November 1976. TNA, FCO 8/4385, Cameron, 'Annual Report for 1981 on the United Arab Emirates Armed Forces', 31 January 1982.
18   UAE legislation names the professional head of the UAE Armed Forces as both the Chief of the General Staff and the Chief of Staff. In recent decades, only the title of Chief of Staff has been used.
19   This occurred in February 1976. TNA FCO 8/2897: Bromage, 'Annual Report for 1976 on the United Arab Emirates Armed Forces', 30 January 1977.
20   This organisational chart, as it appeared in the UK Defence Attaché's 1977 report, shows the envisaged relationships rather than the actual situation. It does not show that HQ Central Military Command and HQ Northern Military Command were more or less independent. It also shows that GHQ reports to the Ministry of Defence which was not the case. TNA FCO 8/2897: Colonel T.N. Bromage, UK Defence Attaché, 'Order of Battle United Arab Emirates Armed Forces', Annex B to DA/INT/28, 30 January 1977.
21   Ibid.

the respective rulers. The UAE Navy and Air Force (which was primarily that of Abu Dhabi) also came under GHQ control.

As part of the efforts to end the practice of ruler-controlled armed forces, on 6 November 1976 the Federal Supreme Council amended the Provisional Constitution and withdrew the right for each Emirate to have its own force.[22] The change involved rewriting Article 142, which was originally, 'The member Emirates shall have the right to set up local security forces ready and equipped to join the defensive machinery of the Union to defend, if need arises, the Union against any external aggression.' It now read, 'The state alone has the right to establish armed land, naval, and air forces.'

While the aim of unification was to create a unified command and force structure, the change was somewhat limited. This is reflected in the description by the British Defence Attaché who wrote that it was 'merely a cosmetic one as the regional commanders were still controlled by the individual Emirates'.[23] Nor did unification result in a rebalancing of the forces between the Emirates. Both before and after the unification, the forces in Abu Dhabi (i.e. Western Military Command, the Navy and the Air Force) were far larger than those of the rest of the country combined in terms of manpower, technology and capabilities.

Table 18: Force elements of the UAE Armed Forces following the 1976 unification

Force	Main constituent force	Headquarters location	Professional military commander (relationship to ruler)	Strength[24]	Key force characteristics as of 1977[25]
Army – Western Military Command	Abu Dhabi Defence Force	Abu Dhabi	Colonel Sheikh Sultan bin Zayed Al Nahyan (2nd son of the ruler)	15,000	One armoured brigade, two infantry brigades, a light Emiri Guard brigade, an artillery regiment, and a training regiment.

22   Al Abed, Vine, and Al Jabali, *Chronicle of Progress*, p. 104.
23   TNA FCO 8/4385: Cameron, 'Annual Report for 1981 on the United Arab Emirates Armed Forces', 31 January 1982.
24   TNA FCO 8/2897: Bromage, 'Annual Report for 1976 on the United Arab Emirates Armed Forces', 30 January 1977.
25   Committee on International Relations US House of Representatives, *United States Arms Policies in the Persian Gulf And Red Sea Areas: Past, Present, And Future – Report Of A Staff Survey Mission To Ethiopia, Iran and The Arabian Peninsula* (Washington DC, 1977), pp. 66-68.

Force	Main constituent force	Headquarters location	Professional military commander (relationship to ruler)	Strength[24]	Key force characteristics as of 1977[25]
Army – Central Military Command	Dubai Defence Force	Dubai	Colonel Sheikh Ahmed bin Rashid Al Maktoum (4th son of the ruler)	2,600	An armoured car squadron, three infantry squadrons, a support squadron, a training squadron, an Emiri Guard, and a small air force.[26]
Army – Northern Military Command	Ras Al Khaimah Mobile Force	Ras Al Khaimah	Colonel Sheikh Sultan bin Saqr bin Mohammed bin Salim Al Qasimi (2nd son of the ruler)	700	Three infantry companies, and a support company which included armoured cars.
Army – Al Yarmouk Brigade	Federal Armed Force	Sharjah	Colonel Shaikh Humaid Abdulla Al Qasimi (cousin of the ruler)	4,600	Two combat infantry regiments, a training regiment, and armoured and support squadrons.
Umm Al Quwain National Guard		Umm Al Quwain	Colonel Sheikh Saud bin Rashid Al Mualla (eldest son of the Crown Prince, Sheikh Rashid bin Ahmad Al Mualla, who was the son of the ruler)		Force being established.
Navy	UAE Navy	Abu Dhabi	Colonel Nabil Madhwar (Egyptian seconded officer)	300-400	Fleet of six 110ft Vosper, three 56ft and six 40ft patrol boats (based in Abu Dhabi).
Air Force	UAE Air Force	Abu Dhabi	Brigadier Ghulam Haider (Pakistani seconded officer)	550-1,200	Fleet of Mirage III and V fighter/ attack aircraft, helicopter squadron and communication flight (all based in Abu Dhabi), Hawker Hunter squadron (based at Sharjah).

26   Consisting of an Aeromacci flight and communication squadron as part of the Dubai Air Wing.

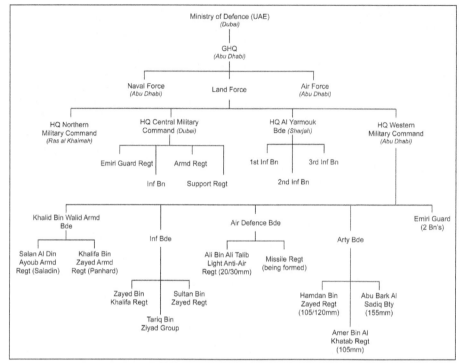

Figure 21: Organisation of the UAE Armed Forces, December 1976.

The 1978 integration and its aftermath

The introduction of regional commands did little to increase uniformity in standards, methods and equipment across the forces, nor did it reduce the duplication of forces and facilities. While Sheikh Zayed and several other leaders wanted to see greater federalism, the new military arrangements were a compromise between them and those who did not want to see authority centralised. The limited military reforms reflected a broader lack of consensus between the rulers over federalisation.

The unsatisfactory military command arrangements lasted until January/February 1978 when Sheikh Zayed unilaterally issued several decrees to restructure the armed forces. One decree cancelled the regional commands and introduced an integrated command structure which gave GHQ full control over all land, sea, and air forces. Another created the post of Commander-in-Chief as the immediate superior to the Chief of Staff. Sheikh Zayed filled this new post with his then 23-year-old second son, Sheikh Sultan bin Zayed, who was promoted from Colonel to Brigadier.[27] Thus

---

27   Al Abed, Vine, and Al Jabali, *Chronicle of Progress*, p. 126.

a new chain of command was created: Supreme Commander – Deputy Supreme Commander – Commander-in-Chief – Minister of Defence/Chief of Staff.

The decrees ordered that the land forces of the regional command be restructured into brigades, with each headed by a Lieutenant-Colonel or Colonel reporting directly to GHQ.[28] These arrangements can be seen in the UAE Armed Forces' structure in 1981 (Figure 22).[29] It shows the reintegration of Ras Al Khaimah's forces, but not that of Dubai's forces (Central Military Command). It also shows that the Ministry of Defence was simply responsible for CMC forces. This organisation diagram does not show the Umm Al Quwain National Guard, probably because its military capability was too limited to be included.

The integration decisions – and particularly the lack of consultation – greatly irritated the rulers of Dubai and Ras Al Khaimah, in particular. They viewed the integration as a way of centralising military power under Abu Dhabi's control, thus limiting their autonomy and ability to protect themselves.[30] In addition, the changes were seen by some Emirates as a loss of 'a totem of each Emirate's individual identity', as noted in an official biography of Sheikh Zayed.[31] Given that Abu Dhabi's forces were more than five times larger than all the others combined, the restructure would mean, in effect, that local armed forces would be subsumed into those of Abu Dhabi,[32] and Abu Dhabi officers would dominate in the forces on the territories of the other rulers. The affected rulers thought this would diminish their prestige as the master of their lands. Finally, they strongly opposed the appointment of Sheikh Sultan bin Zayed as Commander-in-Chief.[33] At a more strategic level, the Ruler of Dubai also objected to the size of the armed forces as he considered that what the UAE really needed was an efficient police force.[34] Animosity between the rulers may also have influenced the response to the integration; for example, the Ruler of Ras Al Khaimah felt that Ruler of Abu Dhabi had not supported him adequately during Ras Al Khaimah's 1978 border dispute with Oman.

Sheikh Zayed's decisions had negative military and political consequences. Both the rulers of Dubai and Ras Al Khaimah pulled their forces out of the new command structure, and re-established local control. Tensions between Abu Dhabi and Dubai increased, with the Ruler of Dubai at one point ordering his forces to be placed on

28   TNA FCO 8/4385: Cameron, 'Annual Report for 1981 on the United Arab Emirates Armed Forces', 31 January 1982.
29   Ibid., Annex A.
30   Ibid.
31   *Soft Power*, p. 224.
32   A.M. Khalifa, *The United Arab Emirates: Unity in Fragmentation* (Boulder, 1979), n. 19, p. 82.
33   TNA FCO 8/4385: Cameron, 'Annual Report for 1981 on the United Arab Emirates Armed Forces', 31 January 1982.
34   TNA FCO 8/3101; D.A. Roberts, UK Ambassador, Abu Dhabi to I.I.M. Lucas, MED, FCO, 'Arms for the UAE', 25 July 1978.

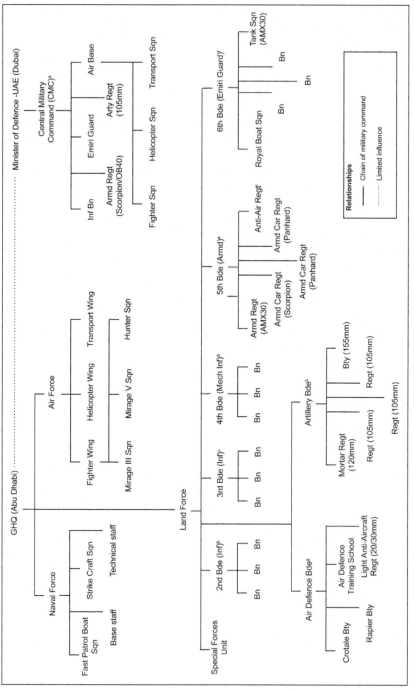

Figure 22: Organisation of the UAE Armed Forces, 1982.

Notes to Figure 22

a.   CMC land and air forces operated as one command; CMC land forces were technically named 1st Brigade, but the appellation was rarely used.

b.   2nd Bde (Al Badr) was previously Eastern Military Command (1976-78), and Ras Al Khaimah Mobile Force (1968-76).

c.   3rd Bde (Al Yarmouk) was previously the UDF/FAF (1971-76).

d.   4th Bde (Al Dhafra) was previously the ADDF's Al Dhafra Brigade (est. 1977).

e.   5th Bde (Khalid bin Al Waleed) was previously the Khalid bin Al Waleed Brigade (est. 1974).

f.   6th Bde (Emiri Guard) (est. 1980), descended from the ADDF's Emiri Guard (est. 1968).

g.   The Air Defence Bde was previously the ADDF's Air Defence unit (est. 1974).

h.   The Artillery Bde was previously the ADDF's Artillery Battery.

i.   Anti-aircraft regiment was being formed.

an hour's standby,[35] and, later in 1978, ordered the up-arming and mechanising his force.[36] The 1978 military restructuring decisions fed into some rulers' broader concerns over the direction of the federation. In particular, the restructure worsened the already strained relationship between Abu Dhabi and Dubai. Six months after the restructure, Dubai effectively 'washed its hand of Federal business ... [although] nominally remaining part of the Union', according to an assessment of the British Government.[37]

In February 1979, tensions between the rulers further increased following a full meeting of the Council of Ministers and Federal National Council to discuss federalisation. One outcome was a 10-point plan which included the unification of defence forces, the merging of revenues into a Federal budget, and the abolition of all internal borders which would end the control by individual Emirates over their natural resources.[38] The joint meeting also wanted an ending to wasteful arms purchases by individual Emirates and greater democracy, including giving the Federal National Council full legislative powers.[39] There was widespread public support for these initiatives and the intention was to submit this plan to the Federal Supreme Council for ratification. However, just as in 1976, the move towards greater federalisation was rejected by some rulers, led by the Ruler of Dubai, who did not want to cede authority over their states to the Federal Government. The rulers of both Dubai and Ras Al

35   F.M. de Butts, *Now the Dust Has Settled: Memories of War and Peace, 1939-1994* (Padstow, 1995), p. 237.

36   The British Ambassador wrote that 'Dubai is certainly arming itself against the risk of aggression from Abu Dhabi ... [and] when I saw Shaikh Rashid he more or less confirmed it outright'. TNA, FCO 8/3101, Roberts, 'Arms for the UAE', 25 July 1978. TNA, FCO 8/3101, UK Defence Attaché in the UAE, 'Arms Sales to Dubai. Ref My Z8G/Z8K/U2H', 10 August 1978.

37   TNA FCO 8/6171: S. Hadwick, MoD, 'United Arab Emirates – Debt Owed to MoD UK in respect of the Al Yarmouk Brigade', 1986.

38   TNA FCO 8/1814: G.G. Arthur, Political Resident, 1970-71, 'The Withdrawal of British Forces from the Gulf', 2 February 1972.

39   Heard-Bey, 'The United Arab Emirates: Statehood and Nation-Building in a Traditional Society', p. 364.

Khaimah boycotted subsequent Federal Supreme Council meetings over the issue, leading to a constitutional crisis which brought the future of the UAE as a federation into question.[40]

The crisis was overcome through convincing the Ruler of Dubai to accept the post of the Prime Minister, a post held previously by one of his sons (i.e. his Crown Prince and eldest son, Maktoum). This position gave him greater influence over the direction of the Federal Government. This was on top of his power as Vice President, and his ability to partially control Federal finances through both deciding how much Dubai would give towards the Federal Budget, and because his son Hamdan was Minister of Finance, a post he has held from 1971 to the present

To ameliorate concerns by him and some other rulers over Abu Dhabi's excessive influence in the Council of Ministers, the Council was reconstituted with ministerial posts being shared by all Emirates. Two other factors at this time also resulted in the advocates of greater federation putting aside their demand for an acceleration of efforts, and instead accepting the status quo during the 1980s: first, the Ruler of Dubai became very ill and it was considered inappropriate to push for change at such a time; and, second, the 1979 Iranian Revolution and the outbreak of the Iran-Iraq War in 1980 focused attention on the rising external threats which demanded internal disagreements to be set aside in order to confront the threats with a unified front.[41]

While Ras Al Khaimah withdrew its forces on its territory from GHQ control immediately after the 1978 military restructuring, in October 1979 the ruler reversed the decision.[42] However the Ruler of Dubai did not rescind his decision and his force continue to be effectively autonomous after the 1979 constitutional crisis.[43]

In the years after 1978, Sheikh Zayed continued to champion the establishment of a wholly unified armed force. However, he could not push it vigorously for he recognised that he needed to 'wait for the rulers of each Emirate to relinquish military independence voluntarily', according to his official biography.[44]

Following the death of the Dubai Ruler in 1990, and the growing friendly relations between the leadership of Dubai and Abu Dhabi, collaboration between the CMC and the UAE Armed Forces increased. Finally, in 1998, the CMC was formally integrated into the UAE Armed Forces.

40   TNA FCO 8/1814: Arthur, 'The Withdrawal of British Forces from the Gulf', 2 February 1972.
41   Heard-Bey, 'The United Arab Emirates: Statehood and Nation-Building in a Traditional Society', p. 365.
42   Al Abed, Vine, and Al Jabali, *Chronicle of Progress*, p. 151.
43   Tingay, 'Legions Galore'.
44   *Soft Power*, p. 225.

UAE Armed Forces (1976-present)

The UAE Armed Forces were formally established in 6 May 1976, a day now celebrated as the UAE Armed Forces Day. The evolution of the UAE Armed Forces' organisational structure from 1976 to the present, and its antecedent armed forces are shown in Figure 1. It identifies that the organisation structure as of 1976 was based around regional commands, plus a separate Navy and Air Force. In 1978, the regional commands were replaced by a brigade structure for land forces. The main change to the organisation structure of the UAE Armed Forces since 1978 has been the adoption of a functional command structure. This has involved the formation of separate commands based around a function that is unique and enduring, such as conventional land forces and special operations. Functional commands can be of any size; in the UAE, they have ranged from a heavy battalion to a division.

In general, a functional command structure will see the armed force's GHQ delegate significant responsibility to the GHQs of its commands. The armed force's GHQ will make policy, and a commands' GHQ will decide how to execute the policy. This generally means that a command's GHQ will determine its readiness levels, doctrine, capability requirements and sustainment needs. However, in the case of the UAE, this is not generally how the functional command structure has operated. Instead, GHQ's control extends well into what in the West would be considered the prerogative of functional commanders.[45] There are exceptions to this, such as the Emiri Guard where the HQ has had considerable autonomy. Commands are responsible for their own training as well as providing training in their specialities to other commands. All commands have their own training facilities.

The reason for establishing functional commands in the UAE appears to have been the same as in other countries – to manage the military's constituent elements more effectively and efficiently. The need for such improvements became apparent after the 1978 integration. This saw each of the eight brigades, plus navy, an air force, multiple corps, and numerous others organisations all reporting directly to GHQ. Control by GHQ over such a large and growing number of units was cumbersome. Furthermore, as no single unit was responsible for a complete functional activity across the armed forces, GHQ found it increasingly difficult to efficiently and effectively coordinate activities.

The first functional command to be established was the Special Forces Command in 1984. This was followed by Navy Command in 1985, Air Force and Air Defence Command in 1987, Land Forces Command in 1987 and Emiri Guard Command

---

45   There appears to be four factors which account for this situation. These are the Arab cultural tendency for centralisation, the small size of the UAE Armed Forces, the power of the Chiefs of Staff due to their personal and trusted relationship with rulers, and a general reluctance by officers to act without explicit orders from above.

in 1992.[46] The late 2010s saw major changes in commands with three new ones created – the Critical Infrastructure and Coastal Protection Authority in 2010, the Presidential Guard Command in 2011, and Joint Aviation Command in 2011. The outlier to the functional command structure during the 1980s and 1990s was Central Military Command. This was a regional command which covered Dubai Emirate. It was a unified command in that it had land and air assets. In 1997, the Central Military Command was disbanded, its establishment reduced significantly through mass retirement and dismissals, with some units ceasing to exist and most of its remaining units integrated into the functional command structure of the UAE Armed Forces.

Figure 23 shows the national command, and key combat commands and specialised branches of the UAE Armed Forces as of mid-2020. It does not include entities being stood up, such as the Electronic Warfare/Cyber Command, nor does it include support commands, such as Joint Logistics Command. It does not include operation centres, such as Joint Operations Centre and the Air Force Air Operation Centre, nor the numerous support entities which report directly to GHQ Command, such as the National Defence College, military police and the Space Reconnaissance Centre.

The key directorates of the Ministry of Defence include policy and strategic affairs, defence industry and capability development, and support services. The key directorates of the General Staff include operations, administration/manpower, supply, communications/IT, and military intelligence and security.

The future is likely to see increased integration of the Ministry of Defence and GHQ. This is because having two relatively independent organisations is inefficient and undermines cohesion. A potential option is to create an US-style Joint Chiefs of Staff who serves as the principal military adviser to the Supreme Commander but has no responsibility for combatant forces. In this model, the Joint Chiefs of Staff effectively replace the defence ministers as they stand today. Another option is to introduce a diarchy structure made up of a Chief of Staff and an Under Secretary who would jointly manage the military. This model would require the existing defence ministers to be replaced, and reforms made to the national command arrangements.

The remaining element in the history of the UAE Armed Forces, which takes the story up to the present day, is an account of the various combat commands as they have evolved since 1976. These are detailed below. In addition, a history of the National Service and Reserve Authority is presented due to the national and military significance of this command. It is one of the entities which reports to the Chief of Staff.

46   UAE Armed Forces, *The UAE Armed Forces History and Missions.*

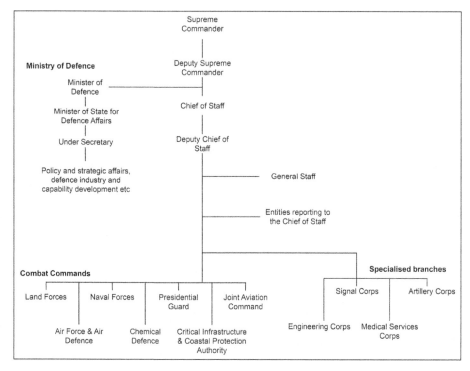

Figure 23: Key elements of the UAE Armed Forces, mid-2020.

Note
This chart was compiled from information from WAM, *Nation Shield* (the UAE Armed Forces' military professional magazine), and the Abu Dhabi Government's *Chart of Accounts*.[47]

Land Forces

The role of land forces in the UAE Armed Forces has always been territorial defence. Consequently, these forces prioritised tactical mobility, close air support, and heavy weapons support (e.g. armoured vehicles, artillery and mortars) for deterrence and defensive operations. From 1976 to the early 2010s, land forces have generally been organised into single service brigades, typically made up of three battalions, some of which had specialist skills, such as parachuting.

The brigade structure dates to the mid-1970s when the ADDF's expansion led to its regiments being grouped into brigades. Brigades of the ADDF consisted of 1st, 2nd, 3rd and 4th motorised infantry brigades, the Khalid bin Al Waleed armoured brigade, and both an artillery and air defence brigade. As part of the 1976 unification

47   Abu Dhabi Government, *Chart of Accounts* (Abu Dhabi, 2012).

of Emirati armed forces, another brigade was formed. This was the motorised infantry Yarmouk Brigade, and formed out of the Federal Armed Forces.

The 1976 unification saw Emirati armed forces renamed regional commands, but these were dissolved in 1978 and replaced by brigades: Central Military Command became 1st Brigade; Northern Command became 2nd Al Badr Brigade; and Western Command became 4th Al Dhafra Brigade. The Al Yarmouk Brigade was designated 3rd Brigade. As of 1978, 1st, 2nd and 3rd Brigades were essentially motorised light infantry forces supported by armoured reconnaissance elements. By 1978, the 4th Brigade was well on its way to becoming fully mechanised after receiving both armoured personnel carriers (APCs)[48] and infantry fighting vehicles.[49]

The late 1970s saw armoured and artillery brigades order and receive large amounts of new weaponry. Between 1976 and 1978, the armoured brigade[50] received 90 heavily armed, wheeled armoured cars.[51] Between 1980 and 1982, it also received some 64 main battle tanks.[52] During the 1970s, the brigades' anti-tank capabilities did not grow substantially,[53] however this occurred with the delivery in 1984 and 1985 of BGM-71 TOW anti-tank guided missiles.[54] The Artillery Brigade's capabilities improved significantly in the 1970s, firstly when it received towed 105mm guns and then starting in 1978, it received 155mm self-propelled guns.[55]

For most of the 1980s, the size and structure of the Land Forces remained unchanged – they consisted of two infantry brigades, one mechanised infantry brigade, one armoured brigade, one field artillery brigade, one air defence brigade in addition to the CMC brigade (see Figure 22). From a few years into the 1980s, the

---

48   APCs consisted of 11 tracked AMX-VCI (delivered 1975); 198 wheeled Panhard M3 VTT (delivered 1975-78); 20 wheeled VAB VTT (delivered 1980), and 82 wheeled VCR (delivered 1981-82).
49   IFVs consisted of 15 to 18 tracked AMX-10P (delivered 1977-79).
50   TNA FCO 8/3105: Bromage, 'Annual Report on the UAE Armed Forces for 1977', 2 February 1978. By 1982, the Armoured Brigade was made up of two armoured car regiments of Panhards, a regiment of Scorpions, a regiment of AMX 30, and an air defence regiment of M3 VDA fitted with twin 20mm cannons.
51   These were wheeled AML 60/90 (delivered 1976-78).
52   These were 64 AMX 30, which were ordered in 1978.
53   The main anti-tank capabilities of the ADDF were Vigilant missiles mounted on its Ferret Mk-2/6 'tank destroyer' armoured cars delivered from 1971. Around this time, several forces, notably the ADDF and RAKMF, started to receive the Carl Gustaf 84mm anti-tank recoilless rifle. In 1973, anti-tank weaponry increased with the receipt of 13 106mm recoilless rifles mounted on jeeps which arrived from Jordan. TNA FCO 8/2134: Agar, 'Intelligence Report No 3', 14 April 1973.
54   The TOWs were ordered in 1981, consisting of 54 launchers, 1,085 missiles and 101 training missiles.
55   Towed artillery in the late 1970s and during the 1980s consisted of 59 L-118 105mm (delivered 1975-77) and 36 Model-56 105mm (delivered 1981-82). Self-propelled artillery consisted of 20 AMX-Mk-F3 155mm (delivered 1978-82). The artillery brigade also had a 120mm mortar regiment.

decade saw only small quantities of new equipment arrive, notably additional Scorpion light tanks, self-propelled multiple rocket launchers, and anti-tank missiles.[56] This lack of investment reflected the priority placed instead on building up the UAE's air and naval forces. In terms of structural reform, the most significant organisational changes in this decade were the reorganisation of Land Forces' headquarters in 1982[57] and the establishment in 1989 of Land Forces Command.[58]

The 1990-91 Gulf War led to a massive re-equipment and improvement programme for Land Forces, which at that time was described by a CIA assessment as having 'limited capabilities and possess[ing] obsolete equipment'.[59]

Major equipment purchases in the early 1990s included nearly 400 main battle tanks, over 200 infantry fighting vehicles with some fitted with anti-tank missiles, and both self-propelled and towed artillery. The end of the 1990s saw a further purchase of some 400 infantry fighting vehicles, and additional self-propelled and multiple rocket launcher artillery.[60] The 2000s witnessed the continued purchase of additional equipment, but not on the scale of the 1990s.[61]

56   The only identified new equipment delivered between 1983 and 1990 was 48 FIROS 122mm, self-propelled multiple rocket launchers (delivered 1987-88), ten wheeled APC AT-105 Saxons (delivered 1989), Scorpion light tanks (36 delivered 1980-81 with 40 delivered 1984-86), BGM-71 TOW (delivered 1984-85) and MILAN (45 ordered in 1981, delivered 1984-85).
57   TNA, FCO 8/5468, Cameron, 'Annual Report for 1983 on the United Arab Emirates Armed Forces', 25 January 1984.
58   UAE Armed Forces, *The UAE Armed Forces History and Missions*, p. 37.
59   Office of Near East and South Asian Analysis US Central Intelligence Agency, *The United Arab Emirates: A Handbook* (Washington DC, 1992), p. 31. This claim is supported by the fact that during the UAE's peace keeping deployment to Somalia in January 1993 to April 1994, the transport vehicles taken were 1960-vintage Bedford 3-ton trucks. Author's collection, Abu Dhabi, Dawson files, D.A. Dawson, CENTCOM Historian, 'With Marine Forces Somalia, Appendix E', 1993.
60   Major equipment of the 1990s consisted of 20 Type-59-1 130mm towed guns (delivered 1993-94); 78 G-6 Rhino 155mm self-propelled guns (delivered 1991-93); 652 (250 for Abu Dhabi and 402 for Dubai) BMP-3 infantry fighting vehicles with some fitted with 9M117 Bastion/AT-10 anti-tank missiles (delivered 1992-2000); 390 Leclerc main battle tanks (delivered 1994-2006) plus some 46 Leclerc armoured recovery and engineering vehicles (delivered 1997-2010); 12 M-198 155mm towed gun (delivered 1995); 87 M-109A1 155mm self-propelled guns (delivered 1997-99); and 136 AIFV-APC (for Dubai) (delivered 1999-2000).
61   Major equipment ordered or delivered in the 2000s included 24 BTR-3U Guardian infantry fighting vehicles (delivered 2003); 48 T-122 122mm self-propelled multiple rocket launchers (delivered 2005-08); 124 RG-31 Nyala armoured personnel carriers (delivered 2006-2012, with a variant being known as Agrab-2 120mm Mobile Mortar System (72); 20 M-142 HIMARS self-propelled multiple rocket launchers (delivered 2011); three COBRA artillery locating radar (delivered 2010); and three T-300 300mm self-propelled multiple rocket launchers (delivered 2010).

Alongside procurement of new equipment, the 1990s witnessed efforts to modernise Land Forces by updating doctrine and improving training. This appears to have had limited success despite the emphasis given to it by the Sheikh Mohammed bin Zayed, who became the UAE Armed Forces' Chief of Staff in 1992. This disappointing lack of improvement seems to have driven him to initiate, in 2003, the Military Contract Officers (MCO) programme. This programme involved recruiting around 300 mostly British former service personnel to provide training and advice to assist in the modernisation of Land Forces and, subsequently, other parts of the UAE military. The MCO programme, over its roughly ten years of operation, facilitated some significant improvements in Land Forces, such as the application of the systems approach to training, and the formation of the Military Adventure Training Centre.

In 2012, the Commander of Land Forces, Major-General Juma bin Ahmed Al Bawardi Al Falasi, started a five-year, strategic plan to transform the entire force. The subsequent commander, Major-General Saleh Mohamed bin Saleh Al Ameri (2014-), describes the intent of this transformation 'to ground military operations in the six warfighting functions: mission command, movement and manoeuvre, intelligence, fires, sustainment, and protection'.[62] Known as the Building the Land Forces Strategy, it aimed to create a force capable of operating across the spectrum of conflicts in a complex environment.[63] These ranged from counter-insurgency to military support to civil authorities, and from peace enforcement to large scale conventional brigade-level assaults within a joint task force. The transformation was facilitated by a team of around 200 expatriate advisors, the vast majority of whom were US Army veterans.

At a conceptual level, the transformation involved building a doctrine-driven force aligned with US Army and Joint Service doctrine, and implementing a force generation cycle based around training, deployment, and regeneration. At a force structure level, the transformation strategy saw the single arm brigades being converted into what are in effect brigade combat teams. Brigade combat teams are the core deployable units in the US Army. They consist of a manoeuvre brigade, as well as assigned combat and support units, thus allowing the brigade team to operate independently for a period. Today Land Forces has four manoeuvre brigades – 1st Emirates, 3rd Zayed, 4th Al Dhafra and 5th Rashid. As of the mid-2010s, a Land Forces brigade group of the mid-2010s had 2,700 men and consisted of three manoeuvre battalions (i.e. infantry, cavalry or tanks) and one artillery battalion.[64] Collectively, these four

---

62   Harry Sarles, US Army Command and General Staff College. 'Emirati Land Forces Commander Inducted to U.S. Army CGSC International Hall of Fame', 2018 <www.usarcent.army.mil/News/Features/Article/1664709/emirati-land-forces-commander-inducted-to-us-army-cgsc-international-hall-of-fa/>

63   Some analysts, such as those at Jane's, have characterised this as building an expeditionary force, which is simplistic. Jane's Information Group, *Jane's World Armies* (Coulsdon, 2014), p. 2 of the United Arab Emirates section.

64   H. Kilgore, Brigade Training Team Deputy Lead, OPs/Fires, Land Forces (2014-15). 'User Profile', n.d., LinkedIn, <linkedin.com/in/haimes-andy-kilgore-ltc-r-mba-61b48770>.

manoeuvre brigades had a strength of around 12,000 men,[65] out of the Land Force's total establishment strength of between 40,000 and 45,000.[66]

To build effective brigade teams, the life of Land Force units needs to be organised around the force generation cycle. This cycle is a training and certification system which aims to produce forces certified as competent and ready for deployment. The cycle has three main stages: (1) 'reset', which sees personnel and equipment arriving, personnel undertaking individual training including career courses, and the start of collective training; (2) 'train', which involves the units undergoing an intense period of training and certification to ensure that they are ready to deploy; and (3) 'ready', which involves having forces ready for deployment.

The force generation cycle is linked with certification of competencies. At each stage, a unit needs to demonstrate competency, typically through exercises. Common exercise forms are command post, simulated, or field exercises. In terms of brigades, the ultimate demonstration of competence is done through mission readiness exercises, which in the US system are undertaken at a combat training centre. This type of exercise involves the brigade undertaking missions in a realistic and challenging environment, and facing an opposing force which thinks, acts and has capabilities of the expected enemy.

Introducing the force generation cycle to Land Forces required fundamental changes. For example, by the end of the first stage of 'reset', Land Forces needed to have built up the battalions to their full establishment strength. It was then critical that this body of men were kept together throughout the 'train' and 'ready' phases. Achieving these changes meant changing manpower planning as units were generally understrength and had continually suffered from large, unplanned absences of personnel. Another challenge was that during the 'reset' phase, individuals had the required individual basic competencies, such as weapon handling and small unit tactics, upon which more advanced individual and collective training could be built. Achieving this required that training move from an hours-based to competency-based training system.

An important element in improving training was to make it as realistic as possible. This was predicated on the idea that the closer the training is to operational experience, the fewer casualties are likely from a deployment. In addition, realistic training has greater learning power for the trainee. Expatriates championed more dynamic field training exercises, as well as building up the fledgling combat training facilities

65   M. Meredith, International Field Artillery and Operations Consultant, Land Forces (2012-18). 'User Profile', n.d., LinkedIn, <www.linkedin.com/in/michael-meredith-72a1285a/>.

66   Trayer stated 45,000. G. Trayer, Consultant and Courseware/Doctrine Development Officer, Land Forces (2013-15). 'User Profile', n.d., LinkedIn, <linkedin.com/in/gene-trayer-84020945>. Nevarez stated 40,000. H. Nevarez, Senior Instruction, Courseware & Doctrine Developer, Land Forces (2012-14). 'User Profile', n.d., LinkedIn, <www.linkedin.com/in/hector-nevarez-ba-2419b030/>.

into three advanced combat training centres and driving the creation of a Training Brigade to support exercises and other operations.

The UAE's largest combat training centre is at Al Hamra Military Base in Abu Dhabi Emirate. This facility serves the same purpose as Fort Irwin National Training Center does for the US Army. The Al Hamra Combat Training centre includes a sprawling model Middle Eastern city, complete with multistorey buildings, stand-alone houses, an unfinished gas station, an airport control tower, an oil refinery and a central mosque.[67] Its scale, variety of urban environments and obstacles such as a canal, has led to claims that it is the one of the most impressive urban operations training area in the Middle East.[68] The Centre provides areas not only for urban operations but also for amphibious landings, and expeditionary logistical support operations. Expatriates developed a plan for the facility based on Mission Essential Task List and provided the training support essential to develop the exercise objectives, scenarios, briefings and debriefings.

The Training Brigade is a hollow brigade in that it is heavy on officers and light on enlisted personnel. One of its functions is to serve as an opposing force, which would be tailored to the exercise requirements, and equipped and operated along the lines of an actual enemy. Another of its functions is to observe the exercising unit and mentor them. It also provides friendly force actors and infrastructure to run the command post and other exercises.

The Building the Land Forces Strategy also resulted in a standardisation of training and instruction across the four previously independent Land Forces training schools – Infantry, Armour, Artillery and Military Engineering – through the creation of the Land Forces Institute. This helped build consistency and develop a combined arms mentality. The institute is now also the home of doctrine development, making it equivalent to the US Army Training and Doctrine Command. The institute also established processes to synchronise training schedules between the institute and field units within the context of the force generation cycle.

The transformation strategy also focused on improving logistics, procurement and capability development. New equipment in the 2010s included mine-resistant infantry vehicles, multiple rocket launchers, and specialised armoured fighting vehicles (e.g. artillery forward observation, command post, ambulance, mortar and engineering).[69] A number of these armoured vehicles have been provided to local forces in Yemen.

---

67   J. Gambrell, 'US, UAE troops launch major exercise Native Fury', *Defense News*, 23 March 2020.

68   Y. Martin, US Army. 'USARCENT commander engages military leaders in UAE', 19 April 2016, <www.army.mil/article/166305/usarcent_commander_engages_military_leaders_in_uae>

69   Major equipment ordered or delivered in the 2010s included eight Canavr towed multiple rocket launchers (delivered 2012); 800 Oshkosh MRAP all-terrain vehicles (delivered 2011-13); six G-5 155mm towed guns (delivered 2014); 56 Mamba APCs (delivered 2013-15); 500 Caiman APCs (delivered 2016); 2,397 MaxxPro APCs (delivered 2016-

Air Force and Air Defence

When the first air force of the Emirates was established in 1968, its role was to support land forces through ground attack, reconnaissance and transport. Since the early 1970s, the air force's roles have been broadened to those of a modern air force – that is, air space awareness and control, bombing, and support to land and maritime forces. An additional component of air control is ground-based air defence: Emirati forces first obtained this capability in the mid-1970s. At that time, ground-based air defence was under the control of Land Forces. It remained so until 1987, when air defence and the air force were merged to create the Air Force and Air Defence (AFAD), a command which has continued to the present.[70]

Before the unification of the five Emirati armed forces in 1976, there were three separate air forces. The oldest, largest, and most technologically advanced at that time was the ADDF Air Wing. Established in 1968, by 1971 its fleet had grown to consist of sub-sonic ground attack aircraft fighter-bombers, light and troop transport helicopters, and tactical transport fixed wing aircraft. In 1972 it was renamed the Abu Dhabi Air Force and it became a functional command on 6 January 1974. In 1973, it received the first of its supersonic Mirage 5 fighter/ground attack aircraft.[71] The force was renamed the UAE Air Force on 14 July 1974.[72]

The second air force to be established was in Dubai in the early 1970s. Known as the Dubai Air Wing, it supported both the Dubai Defence Force and Dubai Police. Its first assets, ordered in 1971, were light helicopters and fixed wing aircraft. In 1974, it ordered light ground attack jet aircraft to support land forces. By 1976, it had also obtained a medium transport aircraft, giving it a tactical airlift capability.[73] The 1976 unification of the armed forces did not see the Dubai Air Wing placed under control

19); 100 N35 APCs (delivered 2016-19); 12 M-142 HIMARS Self-propelled multiple rocket launchers (delivered 2018); around 40 AMV APCs (delivered 2016); 6 Norinco AH4 155 mm/39 calibre lightweight gun-howitzers (delivered 2019); the Norinco SR5 multiple rocket launchers (delivered 2019); 400 Rabdan (deliveries commenced 2019); and four WISENT 2 Armoured Support Vehicle (delivered 2014).

70   UAE Armed Forces, *The UAE Armed Forces History and Missions*, p. 41.
71   By 1976, the ADDF's fleet consisted of four BN-2 Islanders (delivered 1968-72), one DHC-4 Caribou (delivered 1971), 12 Hawker Hunters fighter/ground attack aircraft (delivered 1970-71), five SA 316B Alouette 3 light helicopters (delivered 1972), and three SA 330 Puma helicopters (delivered 1972), and Mirages. The Mirages were delivered in two batches. The first batch consisted of ten 5AD fighter-bombers and two 5RAD reconnaissance version aircraft (delivered 1973-74), and second batch consisted of two 5AD fighter-bombers, one 5RAD reconnaissance version aircraft, one 5DAD (two seater) trainers and fourteen 5EAD radar-equipped fighter-bombers (delivered 1976-77).
72   UAE Armed Forces, *The UAE Armed Forces History and Missions*, p. 41.
73   By 1976, Dubai's fleet consisted of three Bell 206/OH 58 light helicopters (delivered 1972-73), one Cessna 182 Skylane light aircraft (delivered 1971), two Bell 205/UH 1D helicopters (delivered 1973), an one SIAI-Marchetti SF.260W Warrior military trainer (delivered 1974), an Aeritalia G 222 medium-sized STOL military transport aircraft

of GHQ; instead, it continued to be accountable to Dubai's Director of Police and Public Security, Sheikh Mohammed bin Rashid Al Maktoum, who was then, and remains today, the Minister of Defence. In 1978, the Dubai Air Wing was divided into two – the military component and the Police Section (later known as the Dubai Police Air Wing).

The third air force was the UDF/FAF's Air Wing. Formed in 1972 with three light observation helicopters, by around 1976 it also had seven medium utility helicopters and one medium-sized STOL military transport aircraft.[74] The UDF/FAF Air Wing was based at Dubai airport. The 1976 unification of the armed forces saw the UDF/FAF Air Wing dissolved and most of its helicopter assets used to form the Air Wing of the Ministry of Interior.[75]

In the second half of the 1970s, the UAE Air Force increased its ground attack capabilities by acquiring HOT second-generation, long-range, anti-tank missile for its helicopters.[76]

With the outbreak of the Iraq-Iran War in 1980, the UAE feared that it would be targeted by one or both sides for its alleged support of the other. Of concern was inadequate air defence fighters. The short range of the UAE's main air defence fighters, the Mirage-3/5, meant the northern Emirates could not be patrolled from the main fighter base in Abu Dhabi. This limitation led the UAE to order a new fleet of multirole fighters in 1983 – initially 18 and, eventually, a total of 36 fourth-generation Mirage 2000 aircraft. These arrived between 1989 and 1991; when fitted with short to medium-range air-to-air missiles, they enabled UAE aircraft to engage in air-to-air combat beyond visual range for the first time.[77] The Air Force also increased the number of nationals undertaking pilot training, so nationals could reach a pilot-to-aircraft ratio of 1:1. This enabled nationals to sustain combat operations continuously, or at least for a short period of time.[78]

(delivered 1976), and four Macchi single-seat MB-326KD ground attack aircraft, later supplemented by another one seater and two-seat MB-326LD advanced jet trainers.

74   By 1976, the FAF's fleet consisted of three light AB 206B JetRangers (donated by Abu Dhabi in 1972), four Bell 205A-1 troop lift helicopters (first arrived in 1975), three AB 212s and one Aeritalia Fiat G222 (delivered 1976). 'United Arab Emirates', *Flight International*, 2 July 1977, p. 81.

75   This Air Wing has continued to exist to the present. Since its formation, its main role has been to support police, search and rescue, transport, and observation tasks on behalf of other elements of the Ministry of Interior in the northern Emirates. From the mid-1970s to the early 2000s when the Border Guard and Coast Guard were part of the Ministry of Interior, the Air Wing also supported these operations.

76   The HOT anti-tank missiles arrived in 1979 and 1980 and carried by six SA-342 Gazelle helicopters.

77   These were Super 530D missiles (delivered 1989) and the AIM-9L/M Sidewinder (delivered 1989-90), both fitted to the Mirage 2000. Both had an operational range of about 35km.

78   US Central Intelligence Agency, *Military Capabilities of the Smaller Persian Gulf States*, p. iii.

The Air Force also expanded its airlift capability with the purchase of six C-130 Hercules and five turboprop-powered STOL medium transport aircraft.[79] The rotary fleet also expanded to some 26 light and medium helicopters and, for the first time, an anti-ship capability was introduced when sea-skimming Exocet missiles were fitted to some of its Puma helicopters.[80] Finally, the fixed wing trainer fleet was expanded with the purchase of numbers of turboprop aircraft, as well as advanced trainer/combat aircraft.[81] Other significant developments in the 1980s were the introduction into service of 13 light attack and trainer jet aircraft, in addition to some helicopters to Dubai's air force,[82] and the opening in 1983 of the Al Dhafra Air Base which became UAE Air Force's main air interception base.[83]

The first ground-based air defence system in the Emirates was established in the ADDF in 1974. It consisted of towed or vehicle-mounted 20mm anti-aircraft guns.[84] Additional anti-aircraft guns were ordered and by 1978, an Air Defence Brigade had been established, which consisted of a regiment of manually-laid, light anti-aircraft guns,[85] and a battery each of Rapier and Crotale SAMs.[86] These were supplemented by an armoured anti-aircraft regiment made up of some 60 armoured cars fitted with radar-controlled 20mm cannons.[87] This unit was part of the Armoured Brigade. To facilitate the introduction of the new equipment as well as building up air defence expertise, the Air Defence School was established in 1980.

79   Medium transport aircraft consisted of one C-130H-30 Hercules for Dubai (delivered 1981), two C-130H Hercules for Abu Dhabi (delivered 1981 and 1984), one C-130H-30 Hercules for Dubai (delivered 1983), one DHC-5 Buffalo for Abu Dhabi (delivered 1982), and four C-212-200 for Abu Dhabi (delivered 1982).
80   The AM-39 Exocet anti-ship missile arrived in 1983 and 1984.
81   The UAE Air Force received 16 BAE Hawk 63 (delivered 1984-85).
82   Dubai received eight BAE Hawk 61 single-engine, jet-powered advanced trainer (delivered 1983) in addition to five Aermacchi MB-339 trainer and light attack aircraft in two tranches in 1984 and 1987. It also received three Bo 105 helicopters around 1982.
83   Air interceptors were also based at Sharjah Airport at that time. TNA, FCO 8/5468, Cameron, 'Annual Report for 1983 on the United Arab Emirates Armed Forces', 25 January 1984.
84   These were 20mm Hispano Suiz cannons. TNA, FCO 8/2371, Agar, 'Intelligence Report No 12', 3 June 1974.
85   This was the Ali bin Abi Talib Regiment which was equipped with 36 20mm and 24 30mm light anti-aircraft guns. TNA, FCO 8/3105, Bromage, 'Annual Report on the UAE Armed Forces for 1977', 2 February 1978.
86   The Rapier system consisted of 12 launches and 12 Blindfire fire control radars (delivered 1976-78) and the Crotale R 440 system of three launchers (1977-78).
87   These were Panhard M-3 VDA with radar controlled twin AME 20mm cannon. TNA, FCO 8/3105, Bromage, 'Annual Report on the UAE Armed Forces for 1977', 2 February 1978.

By 1983, Dubai had also formed one air defence battery made of RBS-70 short-range SAMs[88] and 20mm anti-aircraft guns.[89] The following year, Dubai received Blowpipe man-portable SAMs.[90] In 1984, the UAE received the trailer-mounted 35mm twin anti-aircraft cannons coupled to a fire control radar,[91] and placed orders for five TRIAD (triangular air defence) batteries of I-Hawk SAMs.[92]

The UAE's continued use of anti-aircraft guns in the 1980s was unusual for armed forces at that time. This was because most forces were introducing efficient low-level SAM systems, like Rapier, which removed the need for anti-aircraft guns. While the UAE had the Rapier, it decided to also buy the US I-Hawk SAM. This SAM did provide a low-level capability, but only over the sea or flat desert and then only if there is a long exposure time. Consequently anti-aircraft guns were retained to compensate for the I-Hawk's inadequacies.[93]

At the start of the 1980s, the ability of the UAE Armed Forces to monitor UAE airspace was very limited. In 1980, the British Embassy reported significant gaps in radar coverage of the mainland with the oil-processing islands not covered at all. It also noted that the existing radar systems lacked the ability to detect low flying aircraft, and that the UAE also had a 'very small' maritime surveillance capability, limited to visual observations and three Mirage 5 RADS single-seat reconnaissance aircraft.[94] Another weakness was that the UAE had difficulty coordinating aircraft. In 1983 the United Kingdom Defence Attaché reported that the Dubai Air Wing's aircraft were 'not yet in direct radar contact with air traffic control and is therefore limited in its approach to unidentified aircraft entering its airspace'.[95]

These surveillance inadequacies were vividly revealed when aircraft attacked the Abu Al Bukhoosh offshore oil facility, about 140km northwest of Abu Dhabi, on

88   These were supplied via Singapore by the manufacturers which became part of the Bofors AB and Nobel Kemi AB scandal. This involved a number of business transactions in which Swedish arms manufacturing executives deliberately violated or circumvented prohibitions on arms sales to belligerents and on bribes to foreign officials. Directorate of Intelligence US Central Intelligence Agency, *Sweden's Bofors Arms Scandal: A Summary of the Diversions, Investigations, and Implications* (Washington DC, 1988).

89   TNA FCO 8/5468, Cameron: 'Annual Report for 1983 on the United Arab Emirates Armed Forces', 25 January 1984.

90   Dubai received 24 guns. Ibid.

91   These were 30 Oerlikon GDF 35mm twin aircraft cannons and 15 Skyguard fire control radars (delivered 1984). All were trailer mounted. A common configuration of the weapon is for one Skyguard unit to control two 35mm guns.

92   The I-Hawk purchased, fully delivered by 1987, consisted of 47 launches and 343 MIM-23B missiles.

93   TNA FCO 8/4356: Colonel K. Grantham-Wright, MoD, 'Air Defence in the Gulf', 30 September 1982.

94   TNA FCO 8/3453: D.A. Roberts, UK Ambassador, Abu Dhabi to FCO, 'Your visit. Ref Your Telno 338 of 15 Oct', 16 October 1980.

95   TNA FCO 8/5468: Cameron, 'Annual Report for 1983 on the United Arab Emirates Armed Forces', 25 January 1984.

25 November 1986.[96] The attack killed five people, including two French citizens, and injured 24.[97] Not only was the armed force unable to provide any early warning of the attack, it could not track the attacking aircraft after the attack which meant their origin could not be identified.[98] Both Iraq and Iran blamed the other for the attack, although both the United Kingdom and US believed the attacking aircraft were Iranian.[99] This incident saw some US$1.5 billion made immediately available for defence equipment;[100] likewise, it accelerated improvements in airspace monitoring and ground-to-air defence. The following two years saw the delivery of three air search radar systems,[101] while man-portable SAM systems were purchased in large numbers.[102]

The importance of the air force relative to the other services had been increasing in the 1980s due to the Iran-Iraq War. Its criticality was explicitly recognised by the Deputy Supreme Commander, Sheikh Khalifa bin Zayed, in the month following the Abu Al Bukhoosh attack, when he defined the goal of the UAE's defence policy. He stated there was a need 'to build a force capable of defending our country and securing the sovereignty of the state on its land, by achieving the supremacy of the air force in the UAE's skies, in full co-ordination with the land and sea forces'.[103]

In 1987 merger of the air force and air defence into AFAD was driven by the observation that during the early years of the Iran-Iraq War, the lack of integration of air forces and air defence in each country significantly weakened their national defensive and offensive capabilities.[104] Merging offensive air forces and air defence capability was seen as central to improving coordination between them.[105] One is not subservient

---

96 The attack was conducted in two phases by Iranian Phantom jets, according to a British Government summary. The first involved two missiles being fired at the storage tanker *World Trader* which was moored to the loading buoy. The missiles failed to hit. The second attack hit No 2 Living Quarters and a bridge on the AK East Platform. TNA FCO 8/6174: Tait, 'Attack on Abu Dhabi's Al Bukhoosh Oil Platform 25 Nov', 27 November 1986.

97 Rabinovich and Shaked, *Middle East Contemporary Survey, 1986*, p. 106.

98 TNA FCO 8/6177: Pratt, 'Call on Sh Mohammed bin Zaid – 10 Dec 1986', 16 December 1986. At that time, Abu Dhabi's only radar coverage of the offshore islands was from a French Tiger Radar on Sir Abu Nuayr island and a British-loaned Plessey Watchman on Zirku island. TNA FCO 8/6177: Michael Tait, UK Ambassador, Abu Dhabi to FCO, 'Your Telno 222 and MoD Telno 1818162', 23 December 1986.

99 TNA FCO 8/6177: Tait, 'Your Telno 222 and MoD Telno 1818162', 23 December 1986. Association for Diplomatic Studies and Training, *Country Reader: United Arab Emirates*, p. 77.

100 TNA FCO 8/6492: UK Foreign and Commonwealth Office, 'Mr Mellor's Visit to Oman and the UAE, 24-25 November 1987: Defence Sales Points to Make', 1987.

101 There was one Watchman radar system for surveillance and air traffic control out to 200km for Dubai (delivered 1986), 11 Tiger radar systems for Abu Dhabi (delivered 1989), and three TPS-70 radar systems for Abu Dhabi (delivered 1987-88).

102 These consisted of some 100 Soviet Strela-3 and 9K310 Igla-1 SAMs (delivered 1986-87).

103 'The Shield of the Nation', p. viii.

104 'The First Priority is Defending the UAE: Interview with Maj Gen Khaled Abdullah Al-Buainain, Commander of the UAE Air Force and Air Defence', *Military Technology*, November (2005), p. 14.

105 Metz, *Persian Gulf States: Country Studies*, p. 364.

to the other, as reflected in the fact that today the AFAD Chief has two deputies – one for the air force, the other for air defence.

In terms of human resource development, the 1980s saw a significant increase in the number of Emirati pilots, with Emiratis being appointed to all senior air staff posts. In the initial years of all the Emirati air forces, these positions were filled by expatriates, mainly British, Pakistani, Jordanian, and Sudanese. Pilot training for Emiratis commenced in the early 1970s, and in that decade, all were sent to foreign countries for training. Local training started in earnest in 1982 with the establishment of a pilot training school at Al Dhafra Air Base. It rapidly expanded into offering advanced training facility, and this was reflected when its name changed to the Air Academy in 1984. It subsequently moved to Al Ain and, in 1996, was renamed the Khalifa bin Zayed Air College. This facility enabled all basic pilot training to be done in-country and saw an immediate increase in the numbers of Emiratis being trained as pilots.[106] The priority pilot posts for nationals were combat aircraft, and soon entire squadrons would be made up solely of Emirati pilots, starting in 1983 with the Gazelle helicopter squadron. Pilot posts for transport and army liaison aircraft were slower to be 'Emiratised'.[107] It appears that nearly all air force pilots were Emirati by the 1990s, with expatriates serving only as pilot instructors, something that has continued to the present. In 1983, the first Emirati was appointed as Commander of the Air Force, replacing a seconded Pakistani officer.

Observations from the 1990-91 Gulf War reinforced the priority placed on improving the AFAD. The war made it clear that air superiority would be critical in all future conflicts. The war also highlighted the capability gap between the air forces of the West and Arab Middle East; it was noted that Iraq was considered to have the best Arab air force, but still lost the air war decisively. The gap existed not only in the quality of aircraft capabilities and weapons, but also in early warning, electronic warfare, and command, control and communication.

The defeat of Iraq in 1991 meant the threat that the country posed to the UAE diminished significantly. However, the threat from Iran started to increase, and countering this has been the ADAF's primary concern to the present.

Among the numerous AFAD developments initiated in the early 1990s, several stand out as the most critical. One was the development of network-enabled, integrated command and control capabilities which enhanced real-time situational awareness of the UAE's airspace, thus allowing decisions to be made far more quickly.[108]

---

106 TNA FCO 8/5468: Cameron, 'Annual Report for 1983 on the United Arab Emirates Armed Forces', 25 January 1984.

107 Ibid., Annex F.

108 Work started in 1995 to build the national fibre-optic military network, known as Al Sharyan, which served as the backbone of AFAD battle connectivity. It links all bases and commands and is part of the combined forces intranet. It has four elements – a whole-of-country fibre-optic military data network, a high-speed tactical datalink system and radio grid system, an air operations centre, and early warning and reconnaissance system. P. La

Central to this were improvements in: (1) ground-based, air-based (including balloon-based),[109] and space-based surveillance systems; (2) the networking of data between aircraft and the ground;[110] (3) fielding specialised maritime surveillance aircraft;[111] and (4) the purchase of Airborne Early Warning and Control System/Airborne Ground Surveillance aircraft.[112]

A second significant development was the enhancement of close support, ground attack capabilities. Between 1993 and 1996, the UAE took delivery of 30 AH-64A Apache helicopters which could carry anti-tank Hellfire missiles. All helicopters were initially under AFAD, but these were subsequently transferred to specialist helicopter units in Land Forces, Special Operations Command and Navy.

Probably the most noticeable development in AFAD's capabilities was the introduction of new generation combat aircraft. In the early 1990s, AFAD's air combat forces consisted of specialised fighters and ground attack aircraft. These were grouped into two fighter-ground attack squadrons (equipped with Mirage 3s and Hawks, with the latter having both a ground attack and training role), one air defence squadron (equipped with Mirage 5s and Mirage 2000s), in addition to one light attack aircraft and training squadron (equipped with the Aeromacchis and Hawks) controlled by Dubai.[113]

Rather than maintain separate types of combat aircraft, AFAD wanted multi-mission, all-weather, day/night capable combat aircraft. This change was driven both by the availability of such aircraft, and a desire to reduce manpower requirements

Franchi, 'UAE Air Force Lays Out Advanced Warfighting Plans', *Flight International*, 16 December 2005; David Donald, 'UAE Forces Focus on Net Warfare', *AINonline*, 11 December 2006.

109 Aerostats host low altitude surveillance radars which can detect low-flying aircraft out to several hundred kilometres. Aerostat mounted radars have significant advantages over ground-based radars which because of the Earth's curvature can only see low flying aircraft out to about 32km.

110 The UAE established a tactical datalink capability as part of the Mirage 2000 purchase in the mid-1980s, with its speed and security upgraded in 1992 where it become known as Link UAE 2. Complementing Link UAE 2 was the development of a UAE-wide high-speed tactical radio grid. This allowed airborne assets to obtain and contribute to the complete UAE airspace awareness (such as carrying information from aircrafts' electronic warfare systems and imaging sensors) and effectively undertake missions. In the 2000s, this was updated to provide Link 16 connectively with allied forces. The UAE first developed a high-speed, ground-to-air tactical radio (GATR) system in 1998, which allowed connection to ground stations and thus the information from the entire land, sea and air network. La Franchi, 'UAE Air Force Lays Out Advanced Warfighting Plans.'

111 These included two Dash-8 transport aircraft fitted with Ocean Master radar (delivered 2012) and two P-180MPA aircraft fitted with RDR-1700 radar.

112 These included two Saab-340AEW modernized to S-100D level, in addition to two Global-6000 and two Saab-2000 aircraft fitted with Erieye SRSS. Two additional Global-6000 were modified to become SIGINT aircraft.

113 Metz, *Persian Gulf States: Country Studies*, p. 364.

through possession of a smaller range of aircraft. New fighter fleets were ordered in 1999, with some 60 Mirage 2000-5 Mk 2 delivered between 2003 and 2007.[114] In 2000, 80 F-16E Block 60 were ordered; they were delivered between 2004 and 2008. The F-16 was particularly attractive because it was capable of configuration for both ground attack and interceptor missions.[115] In addition, some 30 Mirage 2000 already in AFAD's inventory were rebuilt to Mirage-2000-9 standard. A variety of new weapons for these aircraft were purchased, including guided bombs, air-launched cruise missile, and air-to-ground tactical missile and rockets.[116] The introduction of such a large number of new aircraft also saw AFAD undertake a massive expansion of its pilot training and the purchase of advanced trainers.

The 1990s also saw the initiation of an unmanned aerial vehicle (UAV) programme. The first UAVs obtained were the South African tactical reconnaissance Seeker in 1996. Recognising the utility of UAVs, AFAD established a UAV Research and Technology Centre in 2003. One of the first operational uses of UAVs by AFAD was the deployment of a squadron of Seeker II UAVs to Bagram Air Base in Afghanistan in 2004.[117] The UAE Armed Forces now has an extensive range of small[118] to large UAVs, with the larger ones controlled by ADAF. Non-AFAD units with UAVs include the Presidential Guard's reconnaissance group.[119] In 2017, the UAE Armed Forces awarded a contract to establish a training centre for UAVs, introducing a course for remote piloted aircraft at the Khalifa bin Zayed Air College.[120]

---

114 The Mirage-2000 was ordered by the UAE after USA refused the sale of F-16 combat aircraft because of its unwillingness to supply the source code for the F-16's radar and electronic warfare suites in addition to concern over the UAE potentially engaging 200 serving Pakistan Air Force pilots to fly them. 'Pakistani Pilot Deal Linked to US Block on UAE Technology Release', *Flight International*, 24 March 1999.

115 Katzman, *United Arab Emirates: U.S. Relations and F-16 Aircraft Sale*, p. 4.

116 To increase survivability, the aircraft are equipped with on-board self-defence suites. 'The First Priority is Defending the UAE: Interview with Maj Gen Khaled Abdullah Al-Buainain, Commander of the UAE Air Force and Air Defence', p. 14. Weaponry included PGM-500/PGM-2000 designated Al Hakim (delivered 1989-98), Al Tariq enhanced bombs (delivered 2015), Paveway laser-guided and GPS bombs, Storm Shadow/SCALP for Mirage-2000-9, AGM-65 Maverick for F-16E (delivered from 2003), and CIRIT rockets (delivered 2013-16).

117 Wikileaks, Marcelle M. Wahba, US Ambassador to the UAE, 'Scenesetter for General Abizaid's visit to the UAE', 2004.

118 Its smallest UAVs are the Black Hornets, weighing just 16 grams and used by individual soldiers to provide local situational awareness. Another tactical UAV is the 6kg Puma, fitted with electro-optical and infrared camera for medium-range maritime and land surveillance.

119 These include two Pterodactyl 1 (delivered 2013), ten RQ-1 Predator (delivered 2016) and eight P-1HH Hammerhead.

120 CAE, 'CAE Awarded Contract to Provide Comprehensive RPA Training Solution to UAE Air Force & Air Defence', news release, 8 May, 2017, <www.cae.com/CAE-awarded-contract-to-provide-comprehensive-RPA-training-solution-to-UAE-Air-Force-Air-Defence/>.

By the early 1990s, AFAD's Air Defence Brigade consisted of 18 batteries armed with Rapier, Crotale, I-Hawke, and RBS-70 SAMs.[121] The mid-1990s saw the introduction of several additional portable and short-range SAM systems.[122] The 1990s also witnessed the start of efforts to counter ballistic missiles. Of particular concern was the threat from Iran which had both locally manufactured missiles and imported longer range and more accurate missiles. This threat became more pronounced with reports in the early 2000s that Iran was studying ways to fit a nuclear device to missiles and was developing nuclear weapons.

In the early 2000s, the UAE contracted the development and delivery of a Russian vehicle-mounted combined missile and gun systems (Pantsir-S1) to enhance its short-to-medium range anti-aircraft and anti-missile protection. The Pantsir-S1 started arriving in 2009 and around 50 were delivered. In 2008, the UAE ordered the Patriot PAC-3 long-range SAM system, which has some anti-ballistic missile capabilities, as well as the ability to destroy aircraft, helicopters, UAVs, and cruise and other missiles. Delivery of these systems began in 2012. In 2015, the Patriots were supplemented with the first of two Terminal High Altitude Area Defence (THAAD) anti-ballistic missile batteries.[123] The THAAD is designed to intercept short and medium-range ballistic missiles during their terminal phase of flight when they are falling towards the target. Collectively these and the other air defence systems have resulted in the UAE being one of only a handful of countries worldwide to possess an integrated, defence-in-depth, anti-missile, and anti-aircraft shield.

To aid in the detection of unmanned aerial vehicles, missiles, artillery fire, mortars and rockets from very low to high altitudes, in 2013 the UAE ordered 17 truck-mounted anti-aircraft radar systems.[124] Remote observation was also enhanced from the early 2010s, with the purchase of two high-resolution Helios-type military reconnaissance satellites and ground facilities.[125] Organisationally, ADAF has two Air Defence Brigades, each made up of three battalions.

Additional capabilities AFAD obtained in the 2000s expanded its strategic and tactical airlift. It purchased eight C-17A Globemaster-3 heavy transports, as well as three 330 MRTT tanker/transports.[126] The latter aircraft also serve as air-to-air refu-

121 Metz, *Persian Gulf States: Country Studies*, p. 364.
122 These were Mistral systems (delivered 1993-94). They were augmented by numbers of SAM systems for Land Forces, notably 9K310 Igla-1 (delivered 1998-99).
123 Each THAAD battery consists of six truck-mounted M1075 launchers, 48 interceptors (8 per launcher), a THAAD Fire Control and Communications (TFCC) unit, and one Raytheon AN/TPY-2 radar. The truck platform used for THAAD is the Oshkosh M1120 HEMTT LHS.
124 These were Thales's Ground Master 200 (GM200) tactical air surveillance and weapon coordinating radar systems.
125 The satellites were manufactured by Astrium with Thales supplying the Falcon Eye imaging payloads.
126 Six of the Globemaster-3 were delivered in 2011 and 2012, with another two in 2015. The 330 MRTT tanker/transports were delivered in 2013.

elers, introducing a capability which in the past had been only available to the UAE via allies.

In the early 2000s, ADAF in partnership with the US Air Forces Central Command also established the Air Warfare Centre at Al Dhafra Air Base. It provides training that bridges the gap between pilot training and becoming a fighter pilot, as well as training in tactical electronic warfare; ballistic and other missile defence; joint terminal attack control; and combat search and rescue. Its first course ran in 2005, with attendees coming from the UAE, the United Kingdom and the US.[127] A high profile activity of the Centre is its six, annual joint training exercises which see participation by not only the UAE and US, but also from GCC states and major allies. In 2015, the Centre trained around 2,000 participants.[128] As of 2017, ADAF's Air Warfare Centre had over 100 staff from six nations, mainly UAE and US, who were augmented by smaller numbers of French, German, British and GCC nationals. The Air Warfare Centre has grown into a role similar to that of the US Air Force Warfare Centre at Nellis in Nevada, which is the nerve centre for US Air Force tactics and doctrine.

The Air Warfare Centre also provides support to the integrated air and missile defence battle lab created in 2010 at Al Bateen Air Base.[129] This is part of the UAE Integrated Air and Missile Defence Center. The center conducts command and control training with UAE and US Air Force Operation Centers and with partners within the Gulf Cooperation Council.[130] Its largest exercise is the multilateral, annual Falcon Shield Exercise which is designed to test and improve the synergy of air and missile defence capabilities. In 2019, the three-week exercise involved eight countries – UAE, Kuwait, Saudi Arabia, Bahrain, Jordan, United Kingdom, France, and the US with participation from both the US Air Force and US Army.[131]

The last decade has also seen an expansion in ADAF air bases, which for the 1990s and 2000s were primarily Al Dhafra Air Base (housing fighter squadrons), Al Bateen Air Base (housing transport and helicopter squadrons), and Al Minhad (housing helicopter, AWAC and air-to-air refuelling squadrons).[132] Two large new air bases were opened in the 2010s – Liwa (also known as Al Safran) Air Base in the oil rich western

127 Wikileaks, Wahba, 'Scenesetter for General Abizaid's visit to the UAE', 2004.
128 M.V. Schanz, 'Curtain Up at AFCENT's Air Warfare Center', *Air Force Magazine*, 12 January 2015.
129 Air Forces Central Command. 'Al Dhafra welcomes new Air Warfare Center commander', 19 June 2019, www.afcent.af.mil/Units/380th-Air-Expeditionary-Wing/News/Display/Article/1937190/al-dhafra-welcomes-new-air-warfare-center-commander/.
130 Valine, 'United Arab Emirates gets air defense boost from U.S.'.
131 Air Forces Central Command. 'Falcon Shield strengthens coalition's air defense', 8 October 2019, www.afcent.af.mil/Units/380th-Air-Expeditionary-Wing/News/Display/Article/1983278/falcon-shield-strengthens-coalitions-air-defense/.
132 There are a number of other less significant ADAF air bases such as Sweihan, Al Hamra and Al Ain, see Figure 4.

region of Abu Dhabi,[133] and the Qasawera Air Base in the Umm Al Zomool (also written as Umm Az Zamul) area, near the intersection of the UAE, Oman and Saudi Arabian borders.[134] Abu Dhabi International Airport is also used by strategic transport aircraft.

Navy

Since Emirati naval forces were established in 1967, their priority has always been protecting territorial waters, and offshore oil and gas facilities. This required that naval forces continually maintained a physical presence through patrolling in the 'brown waters' of the southern Arabian Gulf and along the littoral coast of the Gulf of Oman. Naval forces have also historically undertaken a range of secondary tasks, including the provision of support to the UAE's other military commands and security agencies, such as through sea lift, intercepting illegal migrants and contraband, surveillance of maritime air space, augmenting air defence, and undertaking maritime search and rescue. Since the 2000s, the UAE Navy has started undertaking activities outside the UAE's immediate maritime area, including protecting maritime freedom and safe passage, and expeditionary support. Over the history of the UAE Armed Forces, the Navy has always been the smallest of the three military services in terms of manpower.[135] Despite this, the force's platform count today is substantial, having over 70 vessels, although this figure includes vessels under 30m which many navies do not count when reporting their fleet size.

When the UAE Armed Forces were unified in 1976, the Navy consisted of six 110ft/33m large patrol craft (*Ardhana* class), three 56ft/17m patrol boats (*Kawkab* class), and six 40ft/12m small patrol boats (*Dhafeer* class), as well as a number of smaller and support vessels. Its main naval base was in the deep water Abu Dhabi

---

133 K. Shaheen, 'The New Air Base Extends the Reach of The Nation's Air Defence Facilities to the Oil-Rich Western Region', *The National*, 6 January 2011.

134 T. Osborne, 'UAE's Mysterious Airbase', *Aviation Week*, 2 April 2015. There has been for several decades an airstrip at Qasawera with a beacon as seen in TNA, FCO 8/6177, G. Howe, Secretary of State, FCO to Rt Hon Julian Amery MP, [untitled, NB 087/2], 26 January 1987. It is unclear if this airstrip was in the same location as one used in the 1950s by the British during tensions with the Saudis.

135 In 1976, land forces had a strength of about 23,000, air force, 550 and naval force 400 (i.e. 1.6 percent). TNA, FCO 8/2897, Bromage, 'Annual Report for 1976 on the United Arab Emirates Armed Forces', 30 January 1977. In 1982, land forces had a strength of 40,150, air force 2,500 and naval force 1,500. TNA, FCO 8/5468, Cameron, 'Annual Report for 1983 on the United Arab Emirates Armed Forces', 25 January 1984. In 2016, land forces had a strength of 44,000, Presidential Guard 12,000, Air Force and Air Defence 4,500, and Navy 2,500 (i.e. 5.6 percent). Cordesman and Toukan, *Iran and the Gulf Military Balance*, p. 61.

port.[136] It also had forward operating bases on Das Island (the main oil-processing island at that time), at Dohat Al Quwaisat on the far west of Abu Dhabi's coast,[137] and at Khor Fakkan on the Gulf of Oman in the UAE's far east.[138]

By 1976, the officer corps was dominated by Egyptians and Pakistani seconded officers, with ratings mostly Omani, and technical posts primarily filled by Pakistanis. Throughout the 1970s there was an emphasis on increasing the number of Emirati naval officers. While short courses and on-the-job training could be provided internally, the UAE Navy did not have the resources or capabilities to deliver more substantial education and training.[139] Hence, while basic naval training was done in Abu Dhabi, the training of naval cadets and officers was primarily carried out in foreign countries, as was much specialist training of ratings. Britain was initially a key source of the force's education and by the late 1970s the Navy had commenced a programme to train the bulk of its Emirati officers at Royal Navy establishments.[140] (This education, in addition to the strong involvement of British naval officers in the establishment of the UAE Navy, resulted in its doctrine reflecting that of Britain. This heritage is still reflected in key elements of the Navy's doctrine.[141]) Increasing amounts of training was done locally, which reflected in the 1977 establishment of a school for ratings and then in 1985, a new school for both naval officers and ratings. In the 1980s to the 2000s, Pakistan and Egypt were the main countries to which Emirati officer cadet and specialist ratings were sent. In more recent decades, the UAE Navy has provided the vast bulk of its own training needs.

Up until 1977, maritime border enforcement was the responsibility of naval forces in the UAE. This changed when, in that year, the UAE Coast Guard was formed under the control of the Federal Ministry of the Interior. To provide the Coast Guard with a nucleus of vessels, the Navy gave it all six of its 40ft/12m *Dhafeer* class patrol boats. With the creation of the Coast Guard, three separate forces were now responsible for the maritime domain in the UAE – the Emirate police maritime units (primarily operating in Abu Dhabi, Dubai, Sharjah and Ras Al Khaimah), the UAE Coast Guard (primarily operating in Dubai and the northern Emirates), and the UAE Navy

---

136 Naval HQ remained at the original naval fleet base near Al Nahyan military base on Abu Dhabi Island, until moving in the early 2010s to Abu Dhabi Port.

137 The naval base was later moved to a nearby island as the depth of water at Dohat Al Quwaisat was too shallow for larger patrol boats. Subject 382, interview, Al Ain, 7 July 2018. The island is now connected by a causeway to the headland Ras Ghumais.

138 Gregory, interview, Woodstock, UK, 30 May 2016.

139 A. Yates, 'Building a Navy From Scratch in Just a Decade: the Abu Dhabi Sea Wing and Navy (1966-1976)', in J. Dunn and D. Stoker (eds.), *Middle Eastern Naval History* (Solihull, 2021 (in press)).

140 TNA FCO 8/3105: Bromage, 'Annual Report on the UAE Armed Forces for 1977', 2 February 1978.

141 An example is tactical manoeuvring for air defence. Lt Colonel S. Thompson, Military Contract Officer, Fleet Sea Training Team, UAE Navy 2009-15, phone interview, 7 January 2018.

(primarily responsible for all of Abu Dhabi's non-port waters in addition to all the other Emirates' offshore waters). These arrangements continued until the early 2000s.

The need to up-arm the Navy became pressing with the massive expansion of the navies of both Iran and, to a lesser degree, Saudi Arabia in the 1970s. Given the UAE's limited manpower and naval skills, obtaining large conventional warships was impractical. Thus, around 1977, the UAE ordered a new type of vessel – the fast attack craft (FAC). These vessels were a radical naval innovation at that time; small vessels fitted with surface-to-surface missiles that could destroy conventional warships. FACs can be deployed individually to shadow hostile vessels and enforce blockades, or in swarms enabling them to threaten even the largest capital ships. This was clearly demonstrated in 1967 when a Soviet-built Egyptian FAC sank an Israeli destroyer. Since the 1960s, FACs have been purchased by multiple Middle Eastern nations due to their low cost (excluding weapon systems), maintenance and manpower requirements. Between 1980 and 1981, the UAE Navy received six 45m FACs (*Bani Yas* class) which had a maximum speed of 40 knots.[142] The vessels were equipped with four MM-40 Exocet anti-ship missiles which could target vessels over 70km away, providing the attacking craft had the ability to locate the position of an enemy vessel at this range.[143] The Exocets represented a major leap in capabilities as the heaviest naval weapon previously in the Navy's arsenal was the 30mm cannon carried by the *Ardhana* class boats, an ineffective gun against warships.

Unlike later FACs, the *Bani Yas* class had no air defence capabilities, nor electronic countermeasures. Instead, it relied on the vessel's high speed and manoeuvrability to avoid being destroyed by aircraft. Other limitations of the early FACs were that they lacked both the seakeeping necessary to operate in higher sea states and only had several days' endurance due to their small size and cramped quarters.

By 1981, the Navy was structured into two main squadrons – a Fast Patrol Boat Squadron made up of 33m *Ardhana* patrol boats, and a Strike Squadron made up of 45m *Bani Yas* FACs. The force's strength was 1,500. Its main base was at Abu Dhabi port, and it had three other mainland bases in Sharjah, Ras Al Khaimah and Khor Fakkan, as well as two island bases on Das and Arzanah Islands.[144]

---

142 The *Bani Yas* class boats (also known as the *Lurssen 45m* class vessels) are P151 Baniyas, P152 Marban, P153 Rodqum, P154 Shaheen, P155 Saqr, and P156 Tarif. Their armament was initially MM-40 Exocet anti-ship missiles, one 76mm and one 40mm/70 Bofors anti-aircraft gun. They had a crew of 40.

143 At that time and for many years afterwards, over the horizon targeting was a major challenge. The problem was that a vessel's radar is limited in range due to the curvature of the earth. To overcome this, a common solution used by the UAE Navy was to deploy a forward observation vessel which would radio back the coordinates of a target to the missile boat.

144 TNA FCO 8/4385: Cameron, 'Annual Report for 1981 on the United Arab Emirates Armed Forces', 31 January 1982.

Despite its equipment and infrastructure, the Navy's capabilities at that time were reported to be extremely limited. In 1982, the British Defence Attaché wrote that its vessels were 'under-crewed and spend most of their time alongside [the navy wharves]' and that the large patrol boats would not 'be at sea out of working hours'. He also noted that personnel had difficulty operating weapons systems, calculating ranges and using modern navigation methods.[145] This assessment reflected that of the CIA a few years later, as seen in the following extract from a declassified review of Gulf navies. It reported that the UAE:

> Navy's small size, heavy reliance on expatriate personnel, and inadequate training sharply limit its combat effectiveness ... operational planning and interservice cooperation were almost non-existent and [UAE officers] maintained that the Navy rarely conducted tactical maneuvers. The UAE officers also underscored the Navy's critical lack of native manpower. Sudanese, Egyptians, and Omanis serve in the Navy, primarily in the enlisted ranks.[146]

The quality of the Navy was obviously a concern in the early years of the Iran-Iraq War, for, in 1982, Sheikh Zayed instructed the new commander of the Navy, Brigadier Hamad Hilal Al Kuwaiti, to 'revitalise the Navy'.[147] His appointment seems to have had a dramatic impact on the Navy operationally, as the British Defence Attaché reported in 1983: 'The Navy has taken on a new role of importance due mainly to its "active" role in patrolling and protecting the offshore oil installations ... [and] for the first time in its short history, the Navy has been seen to be carrying out its proper role'.[148]

Significant new equipment introduced in the 1980s included 54m heavy landing craft (*Al Feyi* class), with each capable of transporting four medium tanks,[149] and offshore support ships and tugs.[150] The landing craft were primarily used to support

145 TNA FCO 8/4385: Lt Colonel J.P. Cameron, UK Defence Attaché, 'Quarterly Report 1 January – 31 March 1982', 14 April 1982.
146 Office of Near East and South Asian Analysis US Central Intelligence Agency, *The Growing Naval Power of the Arab Gulf States* (Washington DC, 1984), p. 17.
147 TNA FCO 8/4385: Lt Colonel J.P. Cameron, UK Defence Attaché, 'Quarterly Report 1 April – 31 June 1982', 10 July 1982. Brigadier Hamad Al Kuwaiti became the first Emirati to hold the post of Commander UAE Navy, and took formal command in June 1983. He had no naval background, however, he had a strong relationship with Sheikh Zayed due to his time both in the Emiri Guard and filling staff officer positions in GHQ.
148 TNA, FCO 8/5468, Cameron, 'Annual Report for 1983 on the United Arab Emirates Armed Forces', 25 January 1984.
149 The *Al Feyi* class heavy landing crafts were L5401 Al Feyi (introduced into service in 1989), L5402 Jananah, and L5403 Dayyinah. They had a crew of 10, 54m in length and a displacement of 650 tons full load.
150 These vessels included three *Barracuda* class offshore support ships (one delivered 1983 and two more in 1989), the A3501 Annad coastal tug (delivered 1989, and built for towing, firefighting, rescue and salvage) and the Marawah logistics ship (delivered 1990).

the civilian development and resupply of Abu Dhabi's islands which were a priority for Sheikh Zayed.[151] To support the larger fleet, in 1985 design work started on a new naval base at Al Taweelah, 35km north of Abu Dhabi.[152] It was designed to accommodate over 50 ships.[153] While part of the fleet was to be based there, Naval HQ as well as the training and workshops divisions remained in Abu Dhabi.[154] In 1985, the force was designated Navy Command.[155]

In 1986, the priority given to the Navy vis-à-vis the other Commands of the UAE Armed Forces increased markedly. That year saw an escalation of the 'tanker war' in which Iraq attacked Iranian tankers; Iran responded by attacking initially tankers carrying Iraqi oil and then the tankers of the Gulf States supporting Iraq. Several ships in international waters close to the UAE were attacked.[156] Iranian aircraft also attacked Abu Dhabi's Abu Al Bukhoosh offshore oil platforms. That year saw two more FACs (*Mubarraz* class) and two 65m corvettes (*Murayjib* class) ordered. A new small facility on the offshore island of Al Qaffay in the extreme west of the UAE was constructed around this period,[157] with the rationale for its establishment the demonstration of ownership of the island, rather than as a defensive base protecting the UAE's western waters.[158]

In the final few years of the Iran-Iraq war, the UAE suffered an attack on an oil rig in Dubai waters by fast attack craft,[159] and at least one civilian vessel in UAE waters was destroyed by Iranian mines.[160] This highlighted the limited deterrence offered by UAE naval forces; and, recognition of this seems to have been a driver behind the new naval capabilities acquired in the early 1990s.

Two new *Mubarraz* class FACs, delivered in 1991, were better protected than the Navy's previous FACs as they had electronic countermeasure equipment and a

151 Subject 382, interview, Al Ain, 7 July 2018.
152 Al Abed, Vine, and Al Jabali, *Chronicle of Progress*, p. 55.
153 The base was planned to be the major naval base and accommodate the bulk of the in-service or planned fleet which at that time was 8 frigates, 20 fast attack craft, 20 patrol boats, 8 minesweepers, 8 landing craft as well as auxiliary vessels. TNA FCO 8/6492: UK Foreign and Commonwealth Office, 'Mr Mellor's Visit to Oman and the UAE, 24-25 November 1987: Defence Sales Points to Make', 1987.
154 TNA FCO 8/5468: Cameron, 'Annual Report for 1983 on the United Arab Emirates Armed Forces', 25 January 1984.
155 UAE Armed Forces, *The UAE Armed Forces History and Missions*, p. 39.
156 Examples of attacks just outside UAE waters included one in May 1986 in which the Liberian-registered super-tanker, the *Aristotle Onassis*, was hit by a missile near Sir Abu Nuair, and one in June 1986 when the Liberian-registered tanker, *Koriana*, and Cypriot tanker, *Superior*, were each hit by missiles.
157 'The Shield of the Nation', p. viii.
158 Subject 382, interview, Al Ain, 7 July 2018.
159 On 17-18 April 1988, an Iranian helicopter and small boats attacked Mubarak oil field.
160 These mines floated into UAE waters, and in June 1988, one destroyed a fishing boat off Khor Fakkan, killing one person and injuring two others. 'Mine Blasts Fishing Boat Off Khor Fakkan; 1 Dead', *Emirates News*, 1 June 1988.

surface-to-air missile system.[161] The *Murayjib* corvettes, delivered 1990-91,[162] also introduced new capabilities not previously held by the Navy. They could operate in 'blue water' (i.e. open ocean) for extended periods and had a helicopter landing pad, enabling them to undertake surveillance 'over-the-horizon'. This last capability was one which most regional navies lacked at that time. But as corvettes lacked hangers, the helicopters had to return to their base at Al Bateen airport for operational support. This constrained the vessels' surveillance capabilities.[163] The corvettes were reported to be technically very capable for their size, as they carried weapon systems and sensor suites normally only found on destroyers and above. The vessels' radar detectability was reduced through stealthy design features, such as minimising their radar cross section. In terms of self-protection, the corvettes' defences were multi-layered and included a range of electronic warfare and decoy systems, surface-to-air missiles, and a seven-barrel gatling gun close-in weapon system (CIWS) designed to destroy incoming missiles, aircraft and fast-manoeuvere surface vessels.

Around the mid-1990s, Iran purchased three Russian Kilo class submarines and, in response, the UAE Navy expanded its anti-submarine capabilities. In 1995, the Navy modernised its fleet of ten utility helicopters to become anti-submarine and/or anti-ship capable. In the same year, seven anti-submarine helicopters were ordered, with the first arriving in 1998, and others delivered in subsequent years.[164] Additional maritime patrol aircraft were also purchased, which further enhanced the Navy's surveillance, search and rescue, and logistics capabilities.

161   The *Mubarraz* class boats (also known as German-made *Lurssen 44m* class vessels) were P141 Mubarraz and P142 Makasib. Their armament was four MM-40 Exocet, one 76mm OTO DP, and one 6-cell Sadral SAM (Mistral missiles). They had a range of 4000 nautical miles at 16 knots.

162   The *Murayjib* class boats (also known as the German-made *Lurssen 62m* class vessels) were Murayjib (FPB 65/PM161) and Das (FPB 65/PM162). Their armament was a 76/62 compact gun, eight MM-40 Exocet SSM, one 8-cell Crotale SAM, one 76mm OTO DP, one 30mm Goalkeeper CIWS and two Dagaie decoy launching systems. They had a crew of 43, and a range of 4,000 nautical miles at 16 knots, and a top speed of 35 knots.

163   The Navy's helicopter fleet consisted of ten AS-332 Super Puma medium-size utility helicopters as of the early 1990s. The first was introduced into service in August 1991. Some Super Pumas were equipped for an anti-surface ship role which included carrying Exocet anti-ship missiles. Others were equipped for the anti-submarine role, carrying active dipping sonar and possibly A244 324mm torpedoes. These helicopters now appear to be mainly used as transport helicopters. The anti-submarine helicopter fleet consisted of around seven to eleven AS565S/AS365 N3 Panthers (delivered 1999-2002) which have been fitted to carry AS-15TT anti-ship missiles.

164   Anti-ship capabilities were augmented with the introduction in 2005 of the RGM-84 Harpoon anti-ship missile fitted to the UAE's F-16s. It was further enhanced by the delivered in 2014 of DM2A4 SeaHake M4 long-range, heavyweight torpedo torpedoes which can target both submarines and surface ships.

The appearance of the Iranian submarine threat coincided with the UAE purchasing two modernised Dutch 130m anti-submarine frigates (*Kortenaer* class).[165] Arriving from 1997 to 1998, the frigates had over three times as many crew as the smaller *Murayjib* class of corvettes, rendering them difficult to man fully. The *Kortenaer* class had anti-ship and anti-submarine capabilities. The frigates appear to have rarely left their base at Abu Dhabi port,[166] probably due to insufficient manpower and operational challenges. In 2008, these vessels were decommissioned.

The late 1990s saw a modernisation programme commence for the six *Bani Yas* class and two *Mubarraz* class fast attack craft delivered in the early 1980s. Over the following decade, they would undergo a series of improvements to their weapon, air search, sea search and fire control systems.[167]

The 1990s and 2000s saw the Navy pursue several initiatives to improve individual and collective training. These included establishing a Naval College on Saadiyat Island in 1992, which generated cadres of officers and NCOs for the various branches of the Navy.[168] The College subsequently became the Naval Forces Institute, moving in 2006 to the Al Taweelah naval base. A naval officer cadet academy was opened in 1999, also on Saadiyat Island. It moved to Al Taweelah and, in 2012, was renamed the Rashid bin Saeed Al Maktoum Naval College. From around the mid-2000s, a concerted effort was made to improve individual instruction and course quality, primarily through the introduction of the systems approach to training (SAT) methodology, course redesign and new instructors. Another initiative was the revitalisation of the sea training group, whose aim was to bring ships up to a specified operational standard and then ensure they maintained this standard through ongoing training and exercising.

In 2001, the UAE Coast Guard, which had been under the control of the Ministry of the Interior since 1976, was transferred to the control of the Navy. This change in responsibility was likely to have been driven by increased concern over the possibility of terrorist attacks on critical infrastructure in the UAE's littoral zone and on its islands, and the effectiveness of the Coast Guard in countering this threat. To assist in building up the Coast Guard, naval officers and ratings were transferred to this

165 In the UAE, the *Kortenaer* class of frigates was renamed the *Abu Dhabi* class. However, to prevent confusion with the *Abu Dhabi* class of corvettes introduced in the late 2000s, this book refers to the frigates as *Kortenaer* class. The *Kortenaer* class ships are F01 Abu Dhabi (commissioned in 1983, formerly named Abraham Crijnssen) and F02 Al Amarat (commissioned in 1983, formerly named Piet Hein). Their armament includes four Harpoon SSM, one 8-cell AIM-7M Sea Sparrow launcher (24 missiles, manual reload), one 76mm OTO DP, one 30mm Goalkeeper CIWS, two 20mm guns, and four 12.75-inch torpedo tubes. They had a crew of 140, and a cruising speed of 20 knots.

166 Subject 262, contracted officer with UAE Navy, email, 5 February 2018.

167 In the 1990s, they were fitted with the Giraffe-75 air search radar, and Scout sea search radar, and in the late 2000s, their Exocet anti-ship missiles were upgraded to the more advanced MM-40 Block 3 version.

168 Al Dhaheri, *Roll of Honour: the Armed Forces of the United Arab Emirates*, p. 125.

function, and naval trainers and facilities were used to improve the competence of Coast Guard personnel. By the beginning of 2004, the Coast Guard had become a separate service within the UAE Armed Forces, and was no longer the responsibility of the Navy.[169] In general, the Coast Guard has been responsible for all law enforcement activities across the country's ports, as well as inshore and offshore waters, as far as this is within its capabilities.[170] In areas where the Coast Guard is unable to do this, the Navy is expected to assume the Coast Guard's responsibility.[171]

In the 2000s, a new vision for the Navy was developed which was based on it being able to operate within a multi-national task group, including assuming a command role both in a conventional war-fighting and in military operations other than war.[172] This was driven both by Iran's ongoing aggressive behaviour and other unconventional threats. The former saw Iran's Islamic Revolutionary Guard Corps (IRGC) Navy continue to harass vessels in the Gulf, including firing upon civilian vessels and undertaking provocative actions against US warships. IRGC vessels also penetrated UAE waters and fired upon UAE vessels. In addition, Iran continued to threaten the closure of the Strait of Hormuz. The new unconventional threats facing the Gulf were piracy and terrorism which arose in the 2000s and have continued to be of concern. One of the highest profile maritime terrorist attack close to the UAE in that decade was an attack by an Al Qaeda affiliated group on the oil-laden Japanese-owned MV M. Star as it was transiting the Strait of Hormuz.[173]

The new direction for the UAE Navy required a significant change to the Navy's force structure, according to Major-General Ibrahim Salem Al Musharakh, Chief of the Navy from 2010 to 2017. He described the then force-in-being as made up of vessels which were 'small enough to be used in shallow waters but large enough to hold weapons to maintain the security of the UAE and its offshore installations'.[174] Now what was needed were multi-mission vessels capable of operating in blue water, in addition to specialised vessels to support an expanded mission set and a fleet of support vessels to provide endurance for deployed platforms.

A step in building the new force was the decision in 2004 to replace the 1970s-era 33m *Ardhana* class large patrol boats with six 71m corvettes (*Baynunah* class).[175]

---

169 S. Duffy, Senior Advisor Coast Guard, 2004-10, email, 9 March 2018.
170 In the early 2010s, this was estimated to be roughly five nautical miles. Ibid.
171 There appears to have been historically a lack of clarity over the Coast Guard verses the Navy's areas of responsibility.
172 Nasir Alyafei, 'UAE is Politically and Diplomatically Key to GCC Maritime Aspirations', *National Defense*, 2014, p. 29.
173 R. Herbert-Burns, *Petroleum Trade Security in the Indo-Pacific Region: an Assessment of Australia's Crude Oil and Refined Product Import Security and Supply Resilience* (Canberra, 2015).
174 Mustafa, 'UAE Navy Goes High-tech to Thwart Pirates'.
175 The *Baynunah* class vessels are P171 Baynunah, P172 Al Hesen, P173 Al Dhafra, P174 Mezyad, P175 Al Jahili and P176 Al Hili. Their armament consists of eight Exocet MM-40 Block 3, one OTO Melara 76mm/62 gun, and two Rheinmetall MLG 27 27mm, as

The first was delivered in 2011 and the last in 2017. Unlike larger navies which have specialised corvettes, such as those focusing on mine laying/detection and anti-air capabilities, the UAE's *Baynunah* class are multi-mission corvettes, designed to undertake a range of tasks including patrolling, surveillance, minelaying, maritime interdiction and anti-surface warfare operations. Technically, they can operate both in shallow waters with their low draft and water jet propulsion,[176] and in blue water due to their good seakeeping design. However, the vessels' multiple weapon systems have added significant extra weight which may have compromised their in-shore and sea handling performance.

Another change in the Navy's force structure in the 2000s was the expansion of its amphibious capability. Since the 1980s, the Navy have possessed large landing craft, which enabled it to land large vehicles and company-sized formations. Between 1996 and 2000, it received an additional seven 64m landing craft. Around the mid-2000s, it introduced into service twelve 24m troop-carrying amphibious transport boats (*Ghannatha* class) which could ferry a platoon (around 40).[177] These vessels use waterjets, which gives them high manoeuvrability and the ability to operate in shallow water. This latter capability also aids their survivability as they can operate close to the shoreline, which confuses anti-ship missiles and makes radar detection harder. Initially, the amphibious transport boats were only fitted with heavy machine guns. In the late 2000s, they were re-armed with heavier weapons in order to provide close fire-support during amphibious operations. Six of these vessels became gun boats equipped with a rapid-firing 27mm cannon, while the other six became mortar boats carrying automated breech loading 120mm mortars.[178]

Another amphibious capability initiated in the first half of the 2000s was the formation of the Navy Marines. These grew into a light battalion equipped with some 90 amphibious armoured personnel carriers.[179] Since the late 2000s, the emphasis placed on amphibious operations has declined markedly. The marines have been transferred from the Navy to the Presidential Guard and have become an air-mobile, ranger-like force.

In 2006, the Navy obtained two specialist minelaying, mine-detection, avoidance, and disposal vessels (*Frankenthal* class). These were two former German mine hunters,

    well as anti-air missiles comprising of four Raytheon Mk 56 dual-pack VLS (8x RIM-162C ESSM missiles), one Mk49 mod 3 Guided Missile Launcher (21x RAM block A1 missiles). They have a crew of 55.

176 The use of water jet propulsion rather than propellers both improves the vessels' shallow water operations given that only their water jet propulsion inlet needs to be submerged and enhances their manoeuvrability as a steerable jet nozzle provides vectored thrust.

177 The *Ghannatha* class boats have a crew of three.

178 Several vessels were converted for use in the UAE Coast Guard.

179 These are 8×8-wheeled BTR 3U Guardians fitted with a 30mm dual-feed cannon in a Buran-N1 turret.

built in the early 1990s.[180] In 2009, it ordered 12 additional FACs, which were faster, stretched, 27m *Ghannatha* class vessels, fitted with medium-range surface-to-surface missiles.[181] These *Ghannatha* class FACs were delivered between 2013 and 2015.

In the late 2000s, work commenced on building a new 88m multi-mission corvette (*Abu Dhabi* class). Larger than the *Baynunah* class, the *Abu Dhabi* class has anti-submarine, anti-air and anti-surface capabilities. Each vessel is equipped with a helicopter pad and hanger.[182] The first of the class was delivered in 2013; no decision has yet been announced on the construction of a second vessel.

Around 2009, the Navy also ordered two stealth 55m patrol boats (*Falaj 2* class), which were delivered in 2013. The vessels' geometry is designed to minimise their radar detection, thus enhancing their ability to undertake the key roles of patrolling, surveillance, and both ship and land attack.[183] In addition to the above vessels, a number of support vessels were also purchased in the 2010s, thus enabling other vessels to remain on station for longer. These support vessels include two 58m vessels (*Rmah* class) delivered in 2014. In 2019, the Navy indicated it was likely to purchase at least two multi-mission French *Gowind* class corvettes. These are twice as large as the *Baynunah* class corvettes and augment the navy's existing anti-ship, anti-submarine and short-to-medium-range anti-air warfare operations.

In 2010, the Fujairah Naval Base on the UAE's east coast facing the Gulf of Oman was opened. A key reason for its establishment was to better protect Fujairah port following the completion of an oil pipeline from Abu Dhabi to Fujairah and, thus, to allow the UAE to continue to export oil if the Strait of Hormuz was closed. In 2018, the Navy also opened a new base, Ghantoot Naval Base, to the east of Al Taweelah.[184]

In the late 2000s, the Navy become involved in multi-country operations and in operations outside UAE waters. The first was in 2009 when the UAE held the six-month rotational command of Combined Task Force 152, a coalition of US, UK and

180 The *Frankenthal* class vessels are M02 Al Murjan (built in 1992, formerly Frankenthal) and M01 Al Hasbah (built in 1993, formerly Weiden). They are built with non-magnetic steel.
181 There were equipped with more powerful engines given them a maximum speed of 45 knots. The older *Ghannatha* class vessels had a maximum speed of 38 knots. The surface-to-surface missiles are four box launchers for MBDA Marte Mk 2/N which can strike targets at ranges in excess of 30km.
182 The *Abu Dhabi* class boat (based on the *Comandante* class corvettes) is P191 Abu Dhabi. Its armament consists of four MM-40 Block 3 Exocet anti-ship missiles, an Otobreda 76mm Super Rapid gun, and two remote controlled Marlin 30mm weapons stations. It carries one helicopter and has a helicopter hanger. It has a crew of about 70 and a range of more than 3,000 nautical miles at 14 knots.
183 The *Falaj 2* class boat are P251 Ganthoot and P252 Qarnen. Their armament consists of four MM40 Block 3 Exocet Anti-ship missiles (2 launchers with 2 missiles each), an Oto Melara 76/62 gun (Stealth Version), two Oto Melara Hitrole-G 12.7mm remote controlled naval turrets, and six MBDA VL Mica surface-to-air missiles (2x3 VLS cells at the stern). It has a crew of 29.
184 'Saif Attends Naval Forces Golden Jubilee Celebrations', *Gulf News*, 15 September 2018.

several GCC naval vessels that cover the waters of the Arabian Gulf, the Strait of Hormuz, and waters well into the Gulf of Oman. As well as fighting piracy, terrorism, drug-trafficking and human smuggling, one of the Task Force's aims is to assist in the training and building of regional navies.[185] Participation in this task force was the first time that the UAE Navy had ventured outside the Gulf in its fight against piracy and the protection of merchant vessels.[186]

Since 2015, the UAE Navy has been operating in the Yemen region. *Baynunah* class corvettes have been patrolling in the southern Red Sea area undertaking blockading and force protection operations. Transport vessels have been involved in moving equipment and personnel to Yemen and within the wider region, such as between Little Aden and the UAE's forward operating base in Assab, Eritrea.[187] The Navy has had to hire additional support vessels to help with its sea lift demands. The most well-known of these vessels is HSV-2 Swift, a wave-piercing, aluminium-hulled, commercial catamaran which was severely damaged by a surface-to-surface missile launched off the coast of Yemen in 2016. The Navy has undertaken a few operations, including supporting the capture of various coastal cities and islands. This has demonstrated its ability to support amphibious operations.

The second half of the 2010s saw Iran escalate its normal harassment of vessels in the Arabian Gulf and Gulf of Oman which typically involves multiple speedboat-type craft crossing the bows and sterns of foreign vessels at extremely close range and high speeds. On 12 May 2019, explosive charges were placed near the waterline on four oil tankers off Fujairah's coast in the Gulf of Oman. All were damaged. On 13 June 2019, two oil tankers near the Strait of Hormuz suffered attacks from 'limpet'-like mines or airborne-delivered explosives. The governments of the US, UK, Saudi Arabia and others blamed Iran, but it denied responsibility.

These attacks increased the need for the UAE Navy to improve the defence of UAE waters and the protection of vessels transiting through the surrounding waterways. This means countering both surface craft as well as underwater threats, whether they are mines or unmanned underwater vehicles. This will lead to an enduring need for close cooperation between the Navy, and other UAE military elements, notably Joint Aviation Command and special operations forces.

An ongoing priority will also be to improve intelligence, situational awareness, and interoperability with the naval forces of allied navies deployed in the region to build maritime stability and security. The recent and likely enduring increase in the number of friendly foreign naval vessels in the region, plus the addition of innovative naval platforms, such as the US's expeditionary sea based vessels which serve as

185 Loveday Morris, 'A Regional Solution to Gulf Naval Security', *The National*, 18 April 2010.
186 Mustafa, 'UAE Navy Goes High-tech to Thwart Pirates'.
187 Alex Mello and Michael Knights, 'West of Suez for the United Arab Emirates', *War on the Rocks*, 2 September 2016.

floating staging platforms, will see the UAE Navy increasingly focus more on building dynamic capability with partners.

Presidential Guard

The Presidential Guard was established in 2011 through the amalgamation of four units – the Emiri Guard, Special Operations Command, the Navy's Marine Battalion and the reconnaissance forces of the Directorate of Military Intelligence. It also originally included Group 18 for air support, but this was subsequently allocated to Joint Aviation Command. Bringing together these units has created a division-sized force, making it the second largest command after Land Forces. In 2016, its reported strength was 12,000.[188]

The mission of the Presidential Guard is to develop and maintain a high-readiness, multi-purpose, fighting capability that can operate across land, sea, and air domains.[189] Today it is organised into five combat groups. These are the: (1) Special Operations Command, which is responsible for special operations and counter-terrorism; (2) Presidential Special Guard, which is responsible for close personnel protection of the rulers, their family and visiting dignitaries, as well as static guarding for key palaces and offices; (3) Khalifa bin Zayed 2nd Brigade, which consists of combined-arms mechanised brigade similar in concept to the US's Marine Air-Ground Task Force; (4) Al Forsan Brigade, which is a light infantry unit designed for larger scale offensive and raiding operations, similar to the US's 75th Ranger Regiment; and (5) the Reconnaissance Group, which provides long-range, armoured and UAV reconnaissance forces to support other manoeuvre units.

The Presidential Guard maintains high readiness, short-notice, counterterrorism, and internal security teams. While the teams' prime role is to respond to security incidents involving the ruler and his family, they can augment specialist units within the police forces (e.g. Abu Dhabi Police's F7 SWAT) in areas such as counter-siege, explosive disposal and counter-sniping. The Presidential Guard also has support elements, including the Joint Fires Control Group which provides specialised teams to control artillery fire and close air support, the Presidential Guard Institute which provides individual training and supports collective training, a national service recruit school, and field hospital, transport and CBRN elements which can also be used to augment civil capabilities.

188 Cordesman and Toukan, *Iran and the Gulf Military Balance*, p. 61.
189 Presidential Guard, *Vision Statement [Wall Plaque]* (Majalis, Presidential Guard Building, 2012).

From Emiri Guard to Presidential Special Guard

In a traditional tribal society, a paramount sheikh would be protected by his armed retainers (*mutarizaya, mutarzi* (singular)) who would shield him from other members of his family seeking to usurp his position, protect him when he travelled, enforce his decisions, and guard his forts and checkpoints. These retainers would invariably come from tribes which had demonstrated long-term loyalty to the ruler. These guards would receive regular payments for their services, with the income being highly valued by their tribe, and which ensured both individual and collective loyalty to the sheikh.[190]

In the second half of the 1950s, both Dubai and Abu Dhabi established police forces, and these worked alongside the rulers' *mutarizaya*. The *mutarizaya* generally provided close personal protection while the police provided stationary guards at palaces and key points, as well as escorts and crowd control when the ruler travelled. With the formation of professional armed forces, responsibility for close personal protection, palace security and travel security became the responsibility of the Emiri Guard. Police continued their previous role in providing an outer cordon. Emiri Guard units were initially staffed with *mutarizaya* who underwent military training.

The first Emiri Guard unit was established in Abu Dhabi in January 1968.[191] Dubai, Ras Al Khaimah and Sharjah had all formed Emiri Guard units by the early 1970s. At different times and in each Emirate, the Emiri Guard carried different names, but the function has always existed and continues to exist today. Since 2011, the Emiri Guard of the UAE Armed Forces has been known as the Presidential Special Guard.

The Emiri Guard is usually divided into two elements – the plainclothes Special Guard (*Harras Al Khas)*, and the uniformed Royal Guard (*Harras Amiri*).

The Special Guard acts as bodyguard for the ruler and other key family members; it is made up of the most trusted individuals and invariably only those from the ruler's Emirate. The Special Guard units were initially trained by the British SAS. Around 1968/69, several SAS operators provided formative training and advice to

190 Heard-Bey, *From Trucial States to United Arab Emirates*, pp. 120-1, 205-6, and 430 (fn 92).
191 UAE Armed Forces, *The UAE Armed Forces History and Missions*, p. 43.

Abu Dhabi[192] and, in the early 1970s, to Dubai.[193] This assistance continued in subsequent decades.[194]

The Royal Guard typically has three roles. One is the static guarding at the ruler's and other close family members' palaces and work places, including their courts (*diwan*) and *majlis*.[195] The Royal Guard may maintain vessels to provide sea-side protection of palaces, or when the ruler travels by sea, and pilots and aircraft for flying around the ruler. The second role is to provide a small, high-readiness unit which could immediately respond to security incidents, such as bolstering the security around a palace in response to protests or a rebellion.[196] Historically, an element of this force operates on very short notice, typically less than an hour. The third role is to provide a small, independent, heavily armed combat force. This force's original rationale was to counter a rebellion by a military unit or another security force. This was a realistic concern in the past, for within the Middle East region some seven military coups occurred during the 1950s and 1960s.[197] Historically, the Royal Guard's combat force was structured around countering the threat from a land force.[198] Of principal concern was the threat of attacks by armoured units since, as noted by the British Ambassador to the UAE in 1980, 'tank regiments have often been used to carry out coups in the Middle East'.[199] This explains why the Royal Guard received anti-armour weapons, tanks and armoured personnel vehicles before land forces' units did.[200] By 1984, the UAE Armed Forces' Emiri Guard

---

192 T. Geraghty, *Who Dares Wins: The Story of the Special Air Service, 1950-1992* (London, 1992), pp. 122-123. The then SAS Commander, Colonel (later Brigadier) W.M. (Mike) Wingate Gray, visited Abu Dhabi several times around this period supervising the SAS element. Former SAS personnel providing training to Abu Dhabi's Special Guard are believed to be Captain Peter Bailey, Captain Welsh and Lieutenant Hook. Subject 383, Emirati Special Guard officer, late 1970s-early 1970s, interview, Al Ain, 7 July 2018.

193 Horniblow, *Oil, Sand and Politics*, p. 209.

194 For example, in 1984, two SAS teams came out to provide training for Dubai's Emiri Guard. TNA, FCO 8/5468, H.B. Walker, UK Ambassador in the UAE, 'Op Jasmin 2', 24 April 1984.

195 For palaces of lesser ruling family members, static guard functions are provided by the police, paramilitary forces and Gurkha veterans.

196 For example, the high-readiness unit in 1984 was a squadron (typically between 80 and 180 men) out of the 1,500-man UAE Armed Force's Emiri Guard Brigade. TNA, FCO 8/5468, Cameron, 'Annual Report for 1983 on the United Arab Emirates Armed Forces', 25 January 1984.

197 Egypt in 1952, Iraq in 1958, Tunisia in 1957, Libya in 1969, Yemen in 1962, Algeria in 1954, and Syria in 1963.

198 This was noted by the UK Ambassador when discussing the likelihood of potential coup against Sheikh Zayed in 1973, 'the air arm is almost entirely foreign and mercenary and would not act on its own. The sea arm would not be significant whatever it did'. TNA, FCO 8/2134, D.J. McCarthy, UK Ambassador to FCO, 'Abu Dhabi Forces', telno 335 of 3rd December 1973, 3 December 1973.

199 TNA FCO 8/3512: Roberts, 'Moroccan Troops in Abu Dhabi', 25 June 1980.

200 The first batch of some 70 AMX tanks and 25 AMX 10 command vehicles and armoured personnel carriers went to the Emiri Guard, at a time when the Armoured Brigade only

combat force had grown into an Independent Armoured Regiment made up of two squadrons of main battle tanks, armoured cars and armoured personnel carriers armed with anti-tank missiles.[201]

To provide an additional layer of protection against a rebellion by regular forces, the Emiri Guard in each Emirate has historically operated outside the main military chain of command.[202] Rather than reporting to the professional head of the armed force, they report directly to the ruler. The Emiri Guards have invariably received separate budgets from the rest of the armed forces, and had their own procurement processes and employment arrangements. A reflection of the independence of the Emiri Guard units can be seen in the case of Abu Dhabi, where the Emiri Guard was designated a Command in its own right on 1 January 1970, years before this occurred elsewhere in the armed forces.[203]

An additional regime-protection strategy has been for the Emiri Guards to be physically located close to the ruler's main palaces and areas of government, with land forces' combat units located at a distance. In the late 1960s, the Abu Dhabi Emiri Guard first had its headquarters at the ruler's official residence and *majlis*, then at Al Manhal Palace; and, since the mid-1970s, it has been the only land-based combat force on Abu Dhabi Island.

Like the *mutarizaya*, members of the Emiri Guard are selected on the basis of loyalty to the ruler. Ideally, members were selected from the most loyal tribes, and on the personal recommendations of tribal leaders, and were citizens from the respective ruler's Emirate.[204] In the case of Abu Dhabi's Emiri Guard, the ruler instructed as early as 1968 that the force should be manned by soldiers from Bani Yas, Awamir and Manasir tribes, which are Abu Dhabi tribes.[205] Building Emiri Guard units comprised only of locals took considerable time due to the large numbers and high skill required for this kind of force. In 1973, only 60 percent of the 1,100 men in Abu Dhabi's Emiri Guard were Abu Dhabi citizens.[206] Numbers of expatriates, notably Omanis and Moroccans, continued to serve in significant numbers in this force at least well into the 1980s.

had armoured cars. TNA FCO 8/3105: Bromage, 'Annual Report on the UAE Armed Forces for 1977', 2 February 1978.

201   The vehicles were AMX 30, AMX 90 and AMX 10. TNA, FCO 8/5468, Cameron, 'Annual Report for 1983 on the United Arab Emirates Armed Forces', 25 January 1984.

202   The UK Ambassador directly links the Emiri Guard's independence with its role of countering any military coup. TNA FCO 8/2134, McCarthy: 'Abu Dhabi Forces', telno 335 of 3rd December 1973, 3 December 1973.

203   UAE Armed Forces, *The UAE Armed Forces History and Missions*, p. 43.

204   TNA FCO 8/3512: Roberts, 'Moroccan Troops in Abu Dhabi', 25 June 1980.

205   *Colonel E.B. Wilson's Archives*, 1, Colonel Wilson, 'Notes on a Meeting with HH The Ruler on 31 Aug 68', p. 24.

206   In early 1973 the Emiri Guard was structured into two rifle squadrons, a Royal Boat Squadron and an Armoured Car Troop. TNA FCO 8/2134: Agar, 'Intelligence Report No 3', 14 April 1973.

Loyal and competent soldiers were also required as leaders of the Emiri Guard. At various times, commanders have been highly trusted Western and Arab expatriates, as well as royal family members and non-royal Emiratis. The initial commanders of the Emiri Guard of both Abu Dhabi and Dubai were Western expatriates. They possessed the advantage over Arab expatriates of not being able to build a support base from which to mount a challenge against the ruler. In the case of Abu Dhabi's Emiri Guard, the founding commander was the British officer, Captain C. (Charles) Wontner. He had served in the TOS since 1962, was temporarily attached by the TOS to the ADDF in 1965, serving first as the ADDF's Deputy Commander, and later as aide-de-camp to Sheikh Zayed. Dubai's Emiri Guard, which was formed in 1971, was initially commanded by the former SAS officer, Lieutenant D.L.H. (David) Bulleid.[207] The engagement of Westerners as the head of the Emiri Guard units continued at least into the early 1980s, as illustrated by the British contract officer, Major W.D. Millar, who served as the Officer Commanding Royal Guard Squadron in Abu Dhabi,[208] and the British contract officer, Major C. (Clive) Wilcox, who served as the Commander of the Ras Al Khaimah Emiri Guard.[209] As Emiratis gained the necessary skills and experience, and demonstrated their ability, they replaced the expatriates as commanders. In Dubai the cousin of the Ruler, Lieutenant-Colonel Sheikh Marwan bin Maktoum Al Maktoum, had become the head of its Emiri Guard by 1978.[210] By the 1990s, all of the Emiri Guards units were headed up by Emirati nationals, mostly by the rulers' close relatives.[211]

Despite the unification of Emirati armed forces in 1976, the Emiri Guards of individual Emirates remained somewhat independent of GHQ control. This occurred in different ways in different Emirates. In the case of Abu Dhabi, the force reported directly to the ruler rather than via GHQ. In Dubai, the separation of the Emiri Guard from GHQ reflected the broader CMC-GHQ separation. In Umm Al Qaiwain, its entire force (i.e. the Umm Al Qaiwain National Guard) was in effect an Emiri Guard and due to its small size and extremely limited capability, had little to do with GHQ. In Sharjah in the mid-1980s, the ruler established a locally controlled light regiment-sized force (i.e. the Sharjah National Guard), which included a sizeable Emiri Guard element. The Sharjah force was integrated into the UAE Armed Forces

207 Bulleid family, 'Bulleid News', 30 May 2011.
208 TNA FCO 8/4385, Cameron: 'Annual Report for 1981 on the United Arab Emirates Armed Forces', 31 January 1982.
209 TNA FCO 8/3925: P.R.M. Hinchcliffe, UK Embassy, Abu Dhabi, to K.J. Passmore, FCO, 'Arms Purchases by UAE Personalities', 10 December 1981.
210 TNA FCO 8/3105, Bromage, 'Annual Report on the UAE Armed Forces for 1977', 2 February 1978.
211 In 1997 Abu Dhabi's Emiri Guard was headed by one of the Ruler's son, Sheikh Nasser bin Zayed; Dubai's by the Ruler's cousin, Sheikh Marwan bin Maktoum bin Juma Al Maktoum; and Ras Al Khaimah's by the Ruler's seventh son, Sheikh Talib bin Saqr bin Mohammed Al Qasimi.

in 1990, although the Emiri Guard element was separated and today it is administered within the Sharjah Police.[212]

A significant step towards unification of the nation's Emiri Guard occurred in 1998, when the Emiri Guard of Dubai's Central Military Command, along with an Emiri Guard infantry battalion from Ras Al Khaimah's 2nd (Al Badr) Brigade, was integrated into the Emiri Guard Command of the UAE Armed Forces which was formed in 1992.[213] While certain Emiri Guard functions have been centralised, such as training, individual rulers still have a significant say in the personnel and command of Emiri Guard elements protecting them and their close family.

In 2011, the Emiri Guard Command of the UAE Armed Forces was integrated into the new Presidential Guard Command, and then restructured. Its Special Guard element was renamed the Presidential Special Guard, while the independent combat force of the Royal Guard became the Khalifa bin Zayed 2nd Brigade.

The evolution of special forces

The UAE's special forces trace their roots back to the ADDF's Force HQ Defence Squadron which was formed in early 1971. Originally formed as the ADDF's 9th rifle squadron based on Abu Dhabi Island, it functioned as an infantry squadron under the direct command of Force HQ.[214] In November 1971, this squadron was renamed the ADDF's Tariq bin Ziyad Group,[215] with a mission to become an elite, physically fit and aggressive infantry fighting force. To mark its difference from other infantry units, its members wore a camouflage uniform as well as a green beret, both unique to the Group at that time. The name change reflected the unit's shift from an infantry to a commando unit which could fight collectively or in small elements to undertake raids.[216] The founding Officer Commander (OC) of both the Defence Squadron and Tariq bin Ziyad Group was Major T.D. Cooper, a British contract officer. He was succeeded in 1973 by another British contract officer, Major Andrew Baker and, by early 1974, the first local, Major Ahmed Salem, was appointed OC for the Group.[217]

In its early years, the Tariq bin Ziyad Group's training focused on fitness and advanced infantry tactics. In 1973, a special forces school was established in Al Ain which offered SAS-like training for officers and NCOs who had already completed

212 The exception to this is Sharjah, for today its Emiri Guard is not a part of the UAE Armed Forces. Instead it is administered as part of the Sharjah Police. Sharjah Police. 'About Us', n.d. <www.shjpolice.gov.ae/en/about.aspx>
213 UAE Armed Forces, *The UAE Armed Forces History and Missions*, p. 43.
214 Major T.D. Cooper, ADDF Land Forces, 1970-73, email, 13 October 2017.
215 The unit was named after Tariq bin Ziyad, a famous Muslim commander from the AD 700s. The name of the unit is often mistakenly written as Tariq bin Zayed.
216 Cooper, email, 13 October 2017.
217 TNA FCO 8/2371: Agar, 'Intelligence Report No 10', 4 April 1974.

commando training. The instructors were Jordanian.[218] Later in the 1970s, parachute training was introduced.

From the mid to late-1970s, the Group grew in size, partly through the incorporation of the paratrooper company of the Al Yarmouk Brigade.[219] By the end of 1981, the UAE special forces consisted of some 850 personnel structured into one battalion, with camps in Abu Dhabi, Al Ain and Sharjah. A second battalion was being planned at that time.[220]

In 1982, the Tariq bin Ziyad Group was redesignated the Special Forces Group,[221] and in 1984 it was restructured into a functional command – Special Forces Command. Its role was to carry out 'conventional' special forces' missions, such as airborne operations, covert operations, long-range reconnaissance, deep target interdiction, internal security (e.g. riot control and vehicle check points) and raids on the enemy's supply lines. It did not carry out counter-terrorism missions, which was the responsibility of a separate unit – Anti-Terrorist Company 71. By 1986, the UAE had three battalions of special forces, all of which were parachute trained.[222] In addition to these special forces, Dubai maintained separate special forces, which by 1981 consisted of a Commando squadron at Wadi Shabak and a paratrooper school.[223]

In 1991, a new special forces group was established – the Special Operations Group – which focused on both land and maritime counter-terrorism activities. This group absorbed Anti-Terrorist Company 71.[224] In 1998, the two special forces elements – Special Forces Command and Special Operations Group – were combined to form the Special Operations Command.

The first overseas operational deployment of the UAE special forces is believed to have been in 1999 when they operated in Albania as part of the UAE relief operation for Kosovo refugees (Operation White Hands).[225] In 2003, UAE special forces started deploying to Afghanistan as part of the 40-plus country coalition to destroy Al Qaeda and stabilise the country. The initial deployment consisted of a 35-man contingent based at Bagram Air Base.[226] This contingent operated alongside US forces and, as they had no organic support, depended on the US for provision of food, water, shelter and emergency medical care.[227] Subsequent UAE contingents,

---

218 Ibid.
219 UAE Armed Forces, *The UAE Armed Forces History and Missions*, p. 45.
220 TNA FCO 8/4385: Cameron, 'Annual Report for 1981 on the United Arab Emirates Armed Forces', 31 January 1982.
221 UAE Armed Forces, *The UAE Armed Forces History and Missions*, p. 45.
222 TNA FCO 8/6176: Walker, 'Visit of CDS to the UAE, 14-16 January', 21 January 1986.
223 TNA FCO 8/4385: Cameron, 'Annual Report for 1981 on the United Arab Emirates Armed Forces', 31 January 1982.
224 UAE Armed Forces, *The UAE Armed Forces History and Missions*, p. 45.
225 This consisted of special operations platoon. Ibid., p. 65.
226 Wikileaks, Wahba, 'Scenesetter for General Abizaid's visit to the UAE', 2004.
227 Center For Law And Military Operations US Department of Defense, *Legal Lessons Learned From Afghanistan And Iraq: Volume I, Major Combat Operations (11 September 2001 To 1 May 2003)* (Washington DC, 2004), p. 153.

which rotated every six months, grew in both numbers and support; by 2005 the UAE's forces in Afghanistan comprised more than 200 personnel.[228] This deployment had three goals according to the UAE Chief of Staff, Lieutenant-General Hamad Mohammed Thani Al Rumaithi. These were to deter extremism, to demonstrate a commitment to the common cause of stopping terrorism and rebuilding Afghanistan, and to provide a means by which UAE forces could gain battlefield experience.[229] The importance the Deputy Supreme Commander, Sheikh Mohammed bin Zayed, placed on battle-hardening UAE forces was reflected in a 2005 conversation with General John Abizaid, US Central Command commander. During this conversation, Sheikh Mohammed 'expressed a strong desire to toughen his country's special forces ... [and noting that the current contingent] has not seen any action ... he asked Abizaid to consider allowing the UAE force closer to the Pak-Afghan border'.[230] The emphasis on building experience in the UAE special forces reflects a strong desire since the early 2000s to have a force that can effectively confront imported or domestic terrorism.

In 2011, Special Operations Command was incorporated into the Presidential Guard.

Special forces' roles in recent foreign operations have included reconnaissance and surveillance, counter-terrorism missions, and coordinating air force ground attack missions. In addition, special forces have undertaken a core mission of many foreign special forces – training, advising and sometimes leading local irregular military and security forces.

Joint Aviation Command

Joint Aviation Command (JAC) was formed in 2011 and is responsible for the rotary and fixed wing aircraft of several military commands, notably Land Forces, Presidential Guard and Navy. It also does this for the National Search and Rescue Centre.[231] JAC provides the aviation capabilities to undertake air assaults, ground attacks, reconnaissance, medical evacuation, search and rescue, VIP transport, and

---

228 Wikileaks, Michele J. Sison, US Ambassador to the UAE, 'Scenesetter for PDAS Cheney's visit to the UAE', 2005.
229 Wikileaks, Michele J. Sison, US Ambassador to the UAE, 'UAE Counterterrorism Efforts: Good Hardware, but Poor Coordination', 2005.
230 Ibid.
231 The National Search and Rescue Centre was established in 2013 under the supervision of the Supreme Council for National Security. Its Commander is the Commander Joint Aviation Command, and its pilots come from both this Command and Abu Dhabi Aviation which is an aviation support company. Its fleet consists of AgustaWestland AW139 search and rescue-equipped helicopters. These are to be augmented by three AgustaWestland AW609 tiltrotor aircraft.

transport of people and equipment. It appears to have today around 5,000 personnel and flies some 240 fixed and rotary wing aircraft.[232]

JAC was formed by bringing together two aviation units – the Presidential Guard's Group 18 and 10th Army Aviation Group. The naval helicopter fleet was also transferred to JAC. JAC also operates a VIP helicopter fleet, as well as helicopter trainers.[233] Currently, JAC collectively manages one of the region's largest military helicopter fleets.[234]

Group 18 provides aviation support primarily to special forces. The bulk of its assets are some 60 Black Hawk helicopters, but it also has numbers of other helicopters.[235] In addition, it has several fixed wing aircraft. In the 2000s, these were primarily light turboprop transport planes[236] used for training and covert missions.[237] In the 2010s, Group 18 purchased additional aircraft, including Air Tractors equipped for intelligence, surveillance and reconnaissance, and ground attack, and Twin Otters configured for paratrooper operations. Group 18's main bases are at Sas Al Nakhl Air Base, mainly for helicopters, and Al Ain Air Base (Falaj Hazza camp) for fixed wing aircraft. Sweihan Air Base is also home to JAC's fixed wing aircraft, and its school, the JAC Institute.

The 10th Army Aviation Group provides rotary wing support to Land Forces. It was formed in 2006 when the Air Force and Air Defence transferred its Apache ground attack helicopters, Eurocopter AS550 Fennec light helicopters and CH-47 Chinooks[238] to 10th Army Aviation Group. Some 30 AH-64A Apaches were acquired in the early 1990s, and these were upgraded with the AH-64D Longbow specification in the late 2000s, which has much superior capabilities, including target detection, tracking and acquisition. The Apache capability was subsequently doubled with the purchase of 37 advanced AH-64E Guardian in 2016. The 10th Army Aviation Group's main base is at Al Dhafra Airbase. The Group is modelled on a US combat

232 R. Ross, Senior Safety Advisor, JAC. 'User Profile', n.d., LinkedIn <www.linkedin.com/in/robert-ross-293b6a51/>

233 Its VIP fleet includes AgustaWestland AW139 and Dauphin AS.365N3 helicopter, and its trainers include Pilatus PC-7, PC-21 and Alenia Aeromacchi M-346.

234 B. Sweetman and T. Osborne, 'It's Open Season For Defense Sales To UAE', *Aviation Week & Space Technology*, 11 November 2013.

235 Its helicopter fleet includes UH-60L/M Black Hawk, AH-64A/D Apache, CH-47C/D/F Chinook, AS.365N3 Dauphin II, AS.550C3 Fennec, AgustaWestland AW139, EC 155B1, IAR/SA 330 Puma and NorthStar Aviation 407MRH.

236 Its fixed wing fleet includes eight Cessna 208B Grand Caravan II Light turboprop transport (delivered 2005-07) some 20 Air Tractors and nine Twin Otter Series 400 (delivered 2013-15).

237 A number of these aircraft were fitted with a FLIR Systems BRITE Star sensor turret, and underwing hardpoints for launching Hellfire missiles.

238 This consisted of about nine CH-47C Chinook of which eight were modernised to CH-47D level, arriving in 2006-10, in addition to four CH-47F Chinook arriving in 2010 and about another 12 CH-47F Chinook arriving in 2012-15.

aviation brigade concept which fields attack/reconnaissance helicopters and medium/ heavy-lift helicopters.

Coastal, border and infrastructure protection forces

Responsibility for protecting the Emirates' external borders and critical infrastructure has alternated between military and internal security entities over the last five decades. Today, this responsibility is centralised under the Critical Infrastructure and Coastal Protection Authority (CICPA), a division-sized command within the UAE Armed Forces. CICPA is made up of three operational groups – the Coast Guard, the Border Guard and the Critical Infrastructure Protection Guard.

While it is a Federal entity, the operational involvement of CICPA in each Emirate varies considerably. For example, while the Coast Guard operates in all UAE waters, the Critical Infrastructure Protection Guard appears to only operate within Abu Dhabi Emirate.[239]

CICPA was established in 2012. Its antecedent organisation was the Critical National Infrastructure Authority (CNIA),[240] which was an Abu Dhabi entity established in 2007 to protect the Emirate's maritime borders and critical infrastructure.[241] The CNIA was accountable to Abu Dhabi's Executive Council and consisted of Abu Dhabi's Coast Guard, as well as several units responsible for protecting critical infrastructure, and, after 2010, an air wing to support maritime security.[242] Like other Commands of the UAE Armed Forces, CICPA has its own training facilities. The CICPA Institute is made up of two schools – the Coast Guard Institute at Port Sadr and another for infrastructure and border protection at Sweihan.

Coast Guard

A coast guard is a maritime law enforcement force and, as such, is typically under the control of law enforcement bodies rather than armed forces. This was the case for many decades in the Emirates, but in 2001 it became a military responsibility.

The history of guarding the coast from a law enforcement perspective starts in the 1950s when Dubai Police established a maritime police unit. By the late 1960s, most other police forces had done likewise. These police maritime units operated in inshore waters and focused on port policing with the exception of Abu Dhabi's Police Coast

---

239 In the other Emirates, their role is undertaken by local police and private security.
240 *Abu Dhabi Law No. 14 of 2012 on the "Transferring CNIA Functions and Responsibilities to the Critical Infrastructure and Coastal Protection Authority"* (2012).
241 *Abu Dhabi Law No. 14 of 2007 on the "Establishment the Critical National Infrastructure Authority"* (2007).
242 K. Shaheen, 'New Naval Base to Guard "Life Vein" of Oil Industry', *The National*, 22 October 2010.

Guard. By the mid-1970s, it was operating from one offshore base, as well as out of five mainland bases.[243]

To provide law enforcement coverage for the UAE's brown water, in the first half of the 1970s a Federal Coast Guard was raised under the control of the Ministry of Interior. Its role, like that of Abu Dhabi's Coast Guard, was to stop illegal migration; end contraband movement and illegal fishing; protect maritime infrastructure (notably offshore and littoral oil and gas facilities, sea cables and pipes, ports and navigational equipment); and enforce maritime exclusion zones around critical infrastructure. It also had a maritime safety and environmental mandate which, in the case of the UAE Coast Guard today, includes search and rescue, vessel registration, environmental enforcement and response, and maritime safety education.

In the 1970s and for several more decades, the geographic division of responsibilities was that Abu Dhabi's Coast Guard was responsible for its waters, with the Federal Coast Guard patrolling in the Arabian Gulf from the Abu Dhabi/Dubai border to the Ras Al Khaimah/Oman border (Al Shams), and in the Gulf of Oman from the Dibba/Oman border to the Kalba/Oman border (Khatma Malaha). The Federal Coast Guard's headquarters was in Sharjah, with posts at Umm Al Qaiwain, Ras Al Khaimah and Khor Fakkan.[244]

The Federal Coast Guard's fleet in 1974 consisted of four 45ft/12m patrol boats, seven launches, with four Fairey Spear launches on order.[245] Around 1976 it received six lightly armed 40ft/12m *Dhafeer* class boats which previously were used by the Abu Dhabi Defence Force's Sea Wing/Navy. The Coast Guard supported local maritime police where they existed, such as in Ras Al Khaimah. By 1984, the Federal Coast Guard's fleet was reported to consist of 13 armed coastal patrol craft, 16 armed small patrol cutters, 26 light launches, one amphibious craft, two diving tenders, one water carrier and five tugs.[246] By 1991, the Federal Coast Guard had reportedly had grown to some 28 inshore patrol craft and some 30 smaller vessels.[247] Several larger vessels were purchased in late 1990s, such as two 33m (*Protector class*) patrol boats. In the mid-1980s, a new Federal Coast Guard operations headquarters was built in Umm Al Nar (now known as Sas Al Nakhl) in Abu Dhabi, and a training academy was established near Port Zayed.[248]

---

243 Abu Dhabi Police's Coast Guard posts in 1974 were at Jebel Dhanna, Port Zayed, Dabbiya, Al Silaa, Abu Dhabi and Das Island. TNA, FCO 8/2371, Agar, 'Intelligence Report No 12', 3 June 1974.

244 Ibid., Annex D to DA/INT/51.

245 TNA FCO 8/2371: Agar, 'Annual Report for 1973 by Defence Attaché United Arab Emirates', January 1974.

246 J. Paxton, 'United Arab Emirates', in *The Statesman's Year-Book 1984-85* (London, 1985), p. 1277.

247 B. Hunter, 'United Arab Emirates', in *The Statesman's Year-Book 1991-92* (New York, 1992), p. 1293.

248 TNA FCO 8/5468: Cameron, 'Annual Report for 1983 on the United Arab Emirates Armed Forces', 25 January 1984.

By 2001, the UAE Government had recognised that its maritime domain needed better protection than the Federal Coast Guard was able to provide. This led to that force being transferred from the Ministry of the Interior to the UAE Armed Forces; where it became a responsibility of the Navy.[249] This change was probably justified on the basis that it would improve coordination between the Navy and the Federal Coast Guard, as well as being the best mechanism for rapidly building up the Federal Coast Guard's capability, as it could draw upon the Navy's personnel, systems and resources. By this time, Abu Dhabi's Coast Guard had become part of the Federal Coast Guard, with the Abu Dhabi Police continuing to operate a close inshore maritime unit.

By 2004, the Federal Coast Guard became a separate command within the UAE Armed Forces, and no longer the responsibility of the Navy.[250] At this time, the Federal Coast Guard's operational concept under development was described as involving the use of as 'many as 200 small patrol craft in the future to conduct a picket line interdiction operation 12 miles outside the coast and around the exclusion zones to investigate any unregistered *dhows* or ships entering the patrol zone.'[251] This plan apparently drove a major re-equipment programme in the 2000s which included purchasing three 18m coastal patrol craft (*Baglietto* class), thirty 9.5m assault boats and twelve 34m fast patrol boats (*Al Saber* class).[252]

In 2007, the UAE Coast Guard was reorganised. The Abu Dhabi squadrons were transferred from the UAE Armed Forces to a newly established, stand-alone agency known as the Critical National Infrastructure Authority (CNIA). Vessels of the Abu Dhabi Police's Marine Police were also transferred to the CNIA, which now had a fleet of more than 70 vessels.[253] The CNIA also established a new Coast Guard school in 2009 at Al Taweelah, alongside the existing UAE Coast Guard school. The UAE Coast Guard's other squadrons, based in Dubai, Sharjah, Umm Al Quwain, Ras Al Khaimah and Fujairah, remained under the responsibility of the UAE Armed Forces.

When CICPA was formed as a command within the UAE Armed Forces in 2012, it absorbed both the UAE Coast Guard and the CNIA Coast Guard. Today, the Coast Guard is responsible for the UAE's 30 ports, and is structured into six squadrons – 1st Fujairah, 2nd Ras Al Khaimah, 3rd Sharjah, 4th Dubai, and 5th and 6th Abu Dhabi.

---

249 *UAE Federal Decree No 1 of 2001 "On the Guarding of Land and Sea Borders of the Country"* (2001).

250 Duffy, email, 9 March 2018.

251 Wikileaks, Sison, 'UAE Counterterrorism Efforts: Good Hardware, but Poor Coordination', 2005.

252 The *Al Saber* class vessels have a crew of seven and a range of 440 nautical miles. They have a stern ramp to accommodate a high-speed boat which can be launched at sea to enable fast interception.

253 Samir Salama, 'Strategic Assets to Come Under Protection Shield', *Gulf News*, 25 March 2010.

The Coast Guard Group continues to modernise its assets, such as acquiring two 'sea axe' design, militarised *Arialah* class offshore patrol vessels[254] and it is currently trialling the use of unmanned surface vessels (USVs).[255] From a security perspective, the key current challenge for the Coast Guard is dealing with Iranian fishing boats that enter into the UAE's territorial waters. Such instances can lead to boat seizures, arrests and occasionally deaths, resulting in escalating tensions between the two countries and tit-for-tat responses.[256]

Border Guard

A border guard is responsible for securing land borders in order to ensure only author-ised people and material are allowed to cross. For the Emirates, enduring border security concerns are illegal migrants, criminals and subversives, as well as weapons, ammunition and drugs. The work of a border guard has typically involved manning border crossing and observation posts, and patrolling borders to both deter and track illegal crossings.

The UAE Border Guard was created under the control of the Federal Ministry of the Interior in 1976. Before this, the border guarding role was shared between police and armed forces; the military patrolled contested borders (e.g. Buraimi Oasis and the western end of the Saudi-Abu Dhabi border) and stopped smugglers and illegal migrants (e.g. Buraimi Oasis and Oman-UAE Musandam border), while police manned international and some inter-Emirate border checkpoints and patrolled these borders.[257]

---

254   This is Arialah (P6701) (delivered 2017) and Hmeem (P6702) (delivered 2018). It carries one Bofors 57mm gun Mk3, two OTO Melara 30mm guns, and one Mark49 mod 2 11-cell Rolling Airframe Missile system.

255   Examples are the 11.5m *Tamin*-class vessels built by Al Seer Marine Technologies. The water jet powered vessels are remotely controlled through a portable command and control station manned by a navigator and a mission specialist. They have a maximum speed of 45 knots, and range of 350nm at 30 knots. Their armaments include sonic, directed electromagnetic and laser dazzler weapons.

256   A recent example of this was in August 2020 when the Coast Guard sought to intercept eight fishing boats carrying out prohibited fishing activities. WAM, 'CICPA: Eight violating fishing boats spotted in UAE's territorial waters carrying out prohibited fishing activities'. This apparently led to two Iranian fishermen being killed, and Iran seizing a UAE-registered vessel. Arab News. 'Iran detains UAE-registered ship, its crew', 21 August 2020 <https://www.arabnews.com/node/1722331/middle-east> It appears that since 2018, UAE and Iran have held every three months a joint coast guard meeting to deal with these types of issues. Al Arabiya. 'Iran, UAE hold routine coast guard meeting regarding fishing zones', 30 July 2019 <https://english.alarabiya.net/en/News/gulf/2019/07/30/Iran-UAE-renew-annual-coast-guard-meeting-regarding-fishing-zones.html>

257   Police-manned border checkpoints between Abu Dhabi and Dubai existed until 1974. 'Police Checks between Abu Dhabi and Dubai', *Gulf Weekly Mirror*, 24 November-1 December 1974.

At this time, the Commander of the UAE Border Guard also commanded both the Coast Guard and the guarding force responsible for protecting petroleum infrastructure.[258] Very little is known about the UAE Border Guard until 2001 when it became a force within Land Forces Command of the UAE Armed Forces.[259] This transfer of responsibility appears to have been driven by concern that porous land borders could allow the movement of extremists. There was also concern over illegal migrant workers crossing from Oman, but this was of secondary importance. The UAE Border Guard was expanded significantly in the early 2000s, with some 5,000 personnel (reportedly five battalions) [260] being transferred from Land Forces to the Border Guard.[261]

To improve border security, the mid-2000s saw the completion of both a physical and electronic border along the UAE's 867km of land borders.[262] In desert and flatter areas, this involved building a solid 3-4m high physical fence. On the UAE side of the fence, an asphalt or earth road was constructed for patrol vehicles. In mountainous and remote areas, a virtual fence was assembled consisting of unmanned observation posts equipped with sensors, notably electro-optical day and night cameras, infrared sensors and radar. In some mountainous regions, such as Jebel Hafeet which sits at the border of Abu Dhabi Emirate and Oman, fences have been built. In addition to patrols and cameras, observation of borders is augmented by manned helicopters, unmanned aerial vehicles, and mobile and stationary tethered balloons (i.e. aerostats).[263] Border crossings are only now possible at a small number of permanently manned border points, or through temporary points which are opened to allow camels to be herded across. In the early 2010s, the UAE Border Guard became part of CICPA.

Critical Infrastructure Guard

Since the early 1960s when Abu Dhabi Emirate started to export oil, ensuring a continued flow has been paramount to the state's economic and political survival. Originally, security for Abu Dhabi's oil fields was provided by posts manned by the Abu Dhabi Police near key oil development areas. When labour unrest at oil fields occurred, as it did in the early 1960s, the Trucial Oman Scouts would also deploy

---

258 *UAE Decision of the Federal Supreme Council No 1 "On the Establishment of Border Guards and the Control of Immigration"* (1976).

259 *UAE Federal Law No 6 of 2014 "on the National Military Service and Reserve Force"* (2014).

260 Wikileaks, Sison, 'UAE Counterterrorism Efforts: Good Hardware, but Poor Coordination', 2005.

261 Ibid.

262 The physical border was completed around 2005. Wikileaks, Sison, 'CENTCOM Deputy Commander General Smith Visits UAE', 2005.

263 Global Security. 'UAE Security Wall / Security Fence', n.d., <www.globalsecurity.org/military/ world/gulf/uae-security.htm>. In the 2000s, the UAE military has acquired at least one 420,000 ft3 aerostat for airspace surveillance. These carried cameras and air-to-surface radars. C. Pocock. 'Aerostats Rise Through the Ranks in Surveillance Service', 12 November 2011, <www.ainonline. com/aviation-news/defense/2011-11-12/aerostats-rise-through-ranks-surveillance-service>.

to re-establish stability and security. In 1969, the Ruler of Abu Dhabi authorised the Abu Dhabi Defence Force to form a 110-man Special Security Squadron. Its role was to guard oilfield infrastructure, principally in the area of the Bab and Bu Hasa oilfields (known as the Murban area),[264] alongside Abu Dhabi Police which also maintained dedicated oil protection elements.[265]

Recognising the growing threat to oil fields from both foreign states and terrorist groups in the early 2000s, Abu Dhabi Emirate established a specialist paramilitary force to take over this work from the police and armed forces. Known as the Critical Infrastructure Guard, its role has been to provide physical protection of critical infrastructure assets, and to maintain a rapid response force, although in recent years responding to terrorist attacks on critical infrastructure has also been a task of the Presidential Guard. The Critical Infrastructure Guard became part of CNIA when that organisation was established in 2007. Under the guard's supervision, infrastructure owners and operators have been required to introduce improved physical security measures. With the formation of CICPA in 2012, the guard became a group within this command.

A key focus of the Critical Infrastructure Guard over the last decade has been to build up its capabilities to protect the UAE's nuclear power plants at Barakah in Abu Dhabi Emirate. This is because CICPA has a mandate with respect to nuclear security to: (1) develop the threat assessment which forms the basis for designing safeguards to protect against acts of radiological sabotage; (2) prevent the theft of nuclear material; and (3) operate and support the implementation of physical protection at the plants.[266]

In addition to the nuclear plants, the Guard today defends around 30 other strategic infrastructure assets,[267] principally onshore/offshore oil and gas installations, water desalinisation plants, power stations, pipelines, seaports, airports and communications networks in Abu Dhabi.

Chemical Defence Command

The UAE Armed Forces' chemical, biological, radiological, and nuclear (CBRN) unit appear to date from around 1980[268] with its formation likely to have been driven by

---

264 *Colonel E.B. Wilson's Archives*, Vol. 6 (Abu Dhabi, n.d.), 'Report to His Highness the Ruler on the State of the Abu Dhabi Defence Force as of 1st May 1969', May 1969, p. 164.

265 In 1974 the Oil Protection Unit of the Abu Dhabi Police had detachments at the oil production centres at Bu Hasa, Jebel Dhanna, Habshan, Tarif and Shames. TNA FCO 8/2371: Agar, 'Intelligence Report No 12', 3 June 1974.

266 UAE Federal Authority for Nuclear Regulation, *Safety Evaluation Report of an Application for a Licence to Construct Barakah Units 1 and 2: Part 1: Summary* (Abu Dhabi, 2012), p. 6.

267 UK Trade and Investment Defence and Security Organisation, *Defence & Security Opportunities: The UAE* (London, 2016), p. 5.

268 The first identified reference to a chemical warfare element in the UAE military was in January 1980. 'News', *Emirates News*, 27 January 1980, p.2.

the start of the Iraq-Iran war in September 1980. Iraq had built up a small stockpile of chemical weapons which it started to use against Iran in late 1980. The UAE's chemical warfare unit was very active around this time, as illustrated by the fact that it had completed its tenth chemical defence course by July 1981.[269] By 1983, the unit was included in the UAE's order of battle as a battalion group with a training facility in Sweihan.[270] By 1987, it had become a command. From its inception, its unique capabilities meant it that civil authorities could turn to it for assistance. For example, in 1987, it provided advice which led to the impounding of highly radiation polluted livestock and foodstuffs from Turkey as the products entered the UAE.[271]

During the 1990-91 Gulf War, the possibility of Iraq using both chemical and biological weapons was a serious concern. To assist the UAE in improving its chemical defences, a US Mobile Training Team, made up of US Army Chemical Corps personnel, arrived in August 1990 in Abu Dhabi. This training team ran train-the-trainer courses for responding to chemical, biological and radiological attacks. It also reviewed 'the type, quality, condition and state of maintenance of the UAE chemical defence equipment, and recommended purchases to address the immediate short-falls'.[272] In addition, in late 1990, UAE doctors received chemical and biological training from the US Army's Medical Research Institute for Chemical Defense.[273] A chemical warfare platoon was part of the UAE's armed force contingent deployed during Operation Desert Storm.[274] A chemical warfare platoon would also be a feature of several future deployments such as the peacekeeping operations in Kosovo (1999-2001).[275]

Despite Iraq's defeat in the 1990-91 Gulf War, chemical and biological weapons remained a threat in the region. While Iraq's chemical and biological weapons program had effectively ended following the Gulf War,[276] Iran built up its chemical weapons capability. Concern over Iran's weapons capability escalated in 1995 when the US Secretary of Defense William Perry made public that Iran had deployed chemical weapons as part of its military build up to the UAE islands of Abu Musa and the two Tunb islands.[277]

---

269 'News', *Emirates News*, 10 July 1981, p. 3.
270 TNA, FCO 8/5468, Cameron, 'Annual Report for 1983 on the United Arab Emirates Armed Forces', 25 January 1984.
271 Leila Hijazi, 'Radiation-polluted Food and Livestock Impounded', *Emirates News*, 7 March 1987.
272 A.J. Mauroni, *Chemical-biological Defense: U.S. Military Policies and Decisions in the Gulf War* (Westport, 1998), p. 35.
273 S.K. Prasad, *Chemical Weapons* (New Delhi, 2009), p. 20.
274 UAE Armed Forces, *The UAE Armed Forces History and Missions*, p. 53.
275 Ibid., p. 69.
276 Nuclear Threat Initiative. 'Iraq', July 2017, <www.nti.org/learn/countries/iraq/>.
277 Michael Knights noted that Perry's statements probably referred to CS (tear) gas. M. Knights, *Rising to Iran's Challenge: GCC Military Capability and U.S. Security Cooperation*, Vol. 127, Policy Focus (Washington DC, 2013), p. 30.

While the UAE Armed Forces have long had personal protective equipment and unit decontamination equipment, their nuclear, biological and chemical (NBC) capabilities were enhanced enormously in 2007 with the arrival of 32 Fuchs 2 armoured and amphibious NBC detection vehicles.[278] These vehicles take samples from the air, water and ground while the crew remain safely within the vehicle. These samples are processed in the vehicles, allowing any contamination to be safely analysed with the results transmitted to higher command in real time.

Chemical Defence Command, also referred to as the Chemical Corps and CBRN Command, runs the Chemical Defence School which trains personnel to operate in a contaminated environment and in decontamination operations.[279] The command has undergone several significant changes in the 2010s. One such change has been to formerly adopt the new mission of military support to civil authorities for CBRN, rather than being solely focused on supporting the UAE Armed Forces. Another has been its adoption of an adapted version of the US CBRN doctrine, which has driven changes in the Chemical Defence Command's organisation and tactics.[280]

National Service and Reserve Authority

Given the small size of the Emirati population, and not infrequent periods of extreme insecurity, mandatory military service for nationals has been proposed multiple times over the last five decades. The first identified reference to conscription was in 1964 when Sheikh Sultan bin Shakhbut, the son of the Ruler of Abu Dhabi and nominated Commander-in-Chief of the proposed army for Abu Dhabi was reported to have said that, 'if necessary a form of national service might be introduced, [with] every Abu Dhabi youth having to serve for a year in the army', as a way of filling out the

---

278 The vehicles consist of 16 Fox NBC-RS vehicles for detecting and identifying nuclear and chemical contamination, eight Fox BIO-RS vehicles for detecting and identifying biological warfare agents, and eight Fox NBC-CPS command post vehicles. Rheinmetall Defence, 'Rheinmetall Unveils New Armoured Fuchs/Fox BIO Reconnaissance Systems for United Arab Emirates', news release, 20 February, 2011 <www.rheinmetall-defence.com/en/rheinmetall_defence/public_relations/news/detail_1348.php>

279 Camber Corporation, 'Operations Advisor, Chemical Defense Command – 13036', news release, n.d. <www.10minuteswith.com/external/operations-advisor-chemical-defense-command-13036>; TanQeeb, 'CBRNE Specialist, UAE Chemical Defense Command – 13999', (2016).

280 Details from job positions offered by Camber Corporation, 'Operations Advisor, Chemical Defense Command – 13036.' and TanQeeb, 'CBRNE Specialist, UAE Chemical Defense Command – 13999'. Like other Commands, it has sought to modernise its instruction, which was described by one instructor as shifting from a lecture and memorisation approach to a Western style of learning based hands-on practical exercises. J. Torgler, Curriculum Specialist, UAE Chemical Defense School, Abu Dhabi, for Camber Corporation, 'User Profile' (LinkedIn, n.d).

force's ranks.[281] This did not occur nor did the proposal in the late 1970s to introduce compulsory conscription as a means of increasing the numbers of nationals in the then expatriate-dominated UAE Armed Forces.[282]

Following the 1980 outbreak of the Iran-Iraq War,[283] and again after tensions escalated in 1986,[284] conscription bills were drafted by the Federal Government. In both cases the bills did not become law; however, a programme of paramilitary training for school children was introduced.[285] In 1990, after Iraq invaded Kuwait, a one-off six weeks of mandatory military training was ordered for all male nationals.[286] In the late 2000s, a law on national mobilisation was passed which included a clause that conscription could be introduced for all UAE citizens over 18 in times of extreme emergency.[287]

Finally, in 2014, the UAE actually introduced compulsory national service.[288] It requires male nationals aged between 18 to 30 to undergo military service, although there are a number of exceptions.[289] The length of service was initially two years for those without high school degrees, and nine months (extended to 12 months in 2016) for those who have graduated from high school.[290] In July 2018, the length of service

---

281 D. Slater, Political Agency, Abu Dhabi to T.F. Brenchley, FO, [untitled letter], 3 August 1964 in Burdett, *Records of the Emirates 1961-1965: 1964*, pp. 217-18.

282 Wikileaks, Dickman, 'Security Assistance Reporting – First Annual Integrated Assessment – UAE', 25 July 1978.

283 In May 1980, draft legislation for compulsory military service was discussed by the Federal National Council. It proposed mandatory 19-months service for all 18 to 35-year-old nationals, except for university graduates who would serve for 9 months. 'Draft Law for Military Service Finalised', *Khaleej Times*, 12 May 1980.

284 TNA FCO 8/6170: Tait, 'First Calls on the Rulers of the Northern Emirates', 19 May 1986.

285 School children 14 years and over undertook six-day a week training over their school holidays from 31 July to 9 September 1982. The training was provided by the UAE Armed Forces at three centres of Abu Dhabi, Al Ain and one in the northern Emirates. 'Military', *Gulf News*, 29 April 1982. Since the 1980s, there have been a variety of programs for military-linked education at schools. For example, in Al Ain, Emirati boys at government school have participated in what was in effect a British-style army cadet program. Another one was the Al Bayariq Student Citizenship Program, a combination of a military cadets and youth development programme. Designed for Grade 10 to 12 students and provided to government schools throughout the UAE, Al Bayariq operated from 2011 to 2014. This initiative was sponsored by Land Forces, Abu Dhabi Police and Abu Dhabi Education Council. Al Bayariq Student Citizenship Program. 'What is Al Bayariq?', ca. 2014, <noufandtufool.wordpress.com/al-bayariq-vision/>.

286 Rashid, *Sheikh Mohammed – Life and Times*, p. 40.

287 M. Habboush, 'If the UAE Came Under Attack…', *The National*, 16 June 2009.

288 *UAE Federal Law No. 6 of 2014 "on the National Military Service and Reserve Force"* (2014).

289 The sole sons of families and medically unfit citizens can be exempt.

290 Small numbers of individuals may do less than the standard programmes. Some may undertake just the 16-week recruit training, and then three months of specialised security education, thus making their total service only six months.

increased to three years for those who do not have a high school qualification, and 16 months for those who do. National service is optional for women aged between 18 and 30; it is also optional for men in the 30 to 40 years age range. A new military command – the National Service and Reserve Authority – was established to administer national service.

An individual's time in national service is divided into three phases – recruit training, specialisation training, and unit work. As of 2020, recruit training is a 16-week program which emphasises building physical fitness and basic military skills. This is undertaken at one of the country's five national service recruit training centres.[291] Four are for male recruits – two in Al Ain (Seih Hafair and Seih Al Hammah camps), and one each in Manama (Ajman Emirate) and Liwa (Al Dhafra region of Abu Dhabi).[292] Female recruits are trained at the Khawla Bint Al Azwar Military School in Abu Dhabi.

After completion of basic training, most service members are assigned to a command where they undertake specialisation training. This typically lasts for eight to 14 weeks. After this training, an individual will generally remain in their assigned unit for the rest of their national service requirement. Some national service personnel will also be assigned to non-military organisations such as the Ministry of Interior, Supreme Council for National Security or State Security. After basic training, the better performing national service personnel are offered the opportunity to become a National Service Officer or NCO. Becoming an officer involves attending a six-month officer training course at Zayed Military College, with an NCO undertaking a four-month course.[293]

Upon completing mandatory national service, national service personnel become part of the UAE Armed Forces reserve. The UAE's reserve, as it stands at the time of this book's writing, bears little resemblance to a typical reserve in a Western country. The UAE reserve does not provide reservists weekend camps, short courses nor opportunities to work alongside regular forces. Instead the only commitment of reservists is to attend annual refresher training, typically two weeks.

The decision in 2014 to introduce national service coincided with rising instability in the region, notably the aftermath of the 2011 Arab Spring, but also the threat posed by Iran. This has led to an assertion that the UAE introduced national service as a mechanism to build up its defences. Another assertion made to explain why national service was introduced is that it was to build a larger military so that the UAE could pursue a more activist foreign policy agenda. Both of these assertions should be treated with caution. Barany in his work on conscription in the Gulf notes that any

291 Gil Barndollar, national service researcher, Catholic University of America, interview, November 2019.
292 WAM. 'UAE Armed Forces' training centres welcome 10th group of recruits', 5 August 2018, <wam.ae/en/details/1395302702346>.
293 Barndollar, interview, November 2019.

link between 'proactive foreign policy and conscription should not be overplayed'.[294] The authors of the most comprehensive study of the UAE's national service noted that 'to look solely at the defence argument for conscription in the UAE is to miss much of what the country seeks to achieve' with national service.[295] They argue that there are three other reasons for establishing national service. These are to promote a strong sense of shared Emirati national identity, to 'harden' up young Emiratis who have become over-privileged and soft, and to create a buffer against the forces that contributed to the Arab Spring.[296]

These reasons can be found in the official statements about the programme. The National Service and Reserve Authority states in its vision for national service that it will help in 'preserving the elements of national identity, and promoting loyalty, belonging and sacrifice among young people and protecting them from the consequences of opening [up the UAE] to the outside world'.[297] The power of national service to build patriotism, discipline, vigilance, resilience, modesty, and other desired national values, was also identified at the launch of the 2015-17 Strategy for National Service. A spokesperson stated that 'while some of today's youths may be directionless, the service will give them a sense of purpose and identity'. The importance of national service in contributing to reduced unemployment and increased Emiratisation was also noted, stating that it will teach conscripts skills that would make them more competitive in the job market.[298]

There are several other reasons to question the asserted causal link between the need for a larger military/military adventurism and the introduction of national service. One is that after the completion of national service, personnel are not provided sufficient ongoing training for them to constitute a useful military reserve. Another is that the manpower in the UAE Armed Forces has been sufficient for foreign operations, and no national service personnel have been identified as serving in combat units (however, they have been identified as undertaking low risk support activities in areas adjacent to and within the area of operations). Finally, if there was an expectation that large numbers of national service personnel would transfer to the regular military, this has not occurred.[299]

---

294 Z. Barany, 'Why Have Three Gulf States Introduced the Draft?', *The RUSI Journal*, 162, 6 (2017), p. 5.

295 Alterman and Balboni, *Citizens in Training: Conscription and Nation-Building in the United Arab Emirates*, p. 2.

296 Ibid., p. v.

297 UAE National Service and Reserve Authority. 'The Strategy', 2015, UAE National Service and Reserve Authority <www.uaensr.ae/Pages/الاستراتيجية.aspx>

298 Salama, 'UAE National Service Draft Strategy Announced'.

299 In 2019, some 12 to 15 percent of national service personnel elected to join the regular armed forces. Barndollar, interview, November 2019.

Before national service started, the number expected to complete it each year was between 15,000 and 21,000.[300] The numbers were lower than this as between 2015 and 2017, when some 50,000 Emiratis were called up for service.[301] One reason for this was that around 20 percent of those who should have started were not fit for military service and were channelled into alternative service programmes designed to help civil and security forces in times of national crises.[302] In 2019, around 10,000 individuals passed through national service.[303]

300 Draft 2015-17 Strategy for the National Service stated that three batches of about 5,000 to 7,000 conscripts will be enrolled every year. Salama, 'UAE National Service Draft Strategy Announced'.
301 Alterman and Balboni, *Citizens in Training: Conscription and Nation-Building in the United Arab Emirates*, p. 16.
302 Ibid.
303 This consisted of two intakes of about 5,000 each. Each intake consisted of roughly 4,600 who undertook the standard 16-month course and 400 who undertook the three-year course. Attrition of the 5,000 cohort is very low, about 200 (i.e. 4 percent). Barndollar, interview, November 2019.

10

Conclusion

Today, the UAE Armed Forces are probably the most effective Arab armed force, with capabilities normally only possessed by advanced middle powers. This is, of course, a statement which might be disputed by some. To conclude this study, it is necessary to provide some reasoning as to why this characterisation of the UAE Armed Forces can be made with confidence. In doing so, it also offers an explanation as to how the UAE was able to develop a highly capable military force from humble beginnings, and within a relatively short period of time.

The most capable Arab armed force?

The last decade has seen an increasing number of public statements by non-UAE senior military leaders and analysts claiming that the UAE Armed Forces have advanced capabilities in comparison to the other armies in the region. Four comments underscore how widespread this view is. In 2016, the US Secretary of Defence, Ash Carter, stated that the UAE 'unquestionably has one of the most capable militaries in the Middle East'.[1] In the early 2010s, the Commander of the US Central Command, General James N. Mattis, started calling the UAE 'Little Sparta', inferring that it had considerable military prowess relative to its size.[2] In 2014, Frederic Wehrey, senior fellow in the Middle East Program at the Carnegie Endowment for International Peace, when referring to the Arab Gulf states participating in a 2014 aerial campaign against ISIS targets in Syria, wrote 'the UAE fields the most capable air force ... among Gulf countries, [and] the Emiratis likely carried out the most sophisticated of

---

1   Ash Carter, Secretary of Defense, *The Logic of American Strategy in the Middle East* (Washington DC, 2016).
2   Chandrasekaran, 'In the UAE, the United States Has a Quiet, Potent Ally Nicknamed "Little Sparta".

air strikes.'[3] In addition, he noted the UAE's superior capabilities compared to other regional forces, when he wrote, 'all of the Gulf States were heavily reliant on US intelligence, targeting data, and perhaps aerial refuelling although the Emiratis have their own capability'.[4] And, a 2016 report by the Center for Strategic and International Studies stated that, 'the UAE's military arguably has the highest capability and the best-trained forces among any of the GCC states.'[5]

What is the evidence for these assessments? Starting with the most obvious, the UAE Armed Forces deploys the most advanced military systems. As noted by the Editor of *Air Force Magazine* in 2012, the UAE 'fields some of the most modernized forces in the region'.[6] While the author was referring specifically to the UAE Air Force and Air Defence with their sophisticated F-16 E/F Block 60s, Patriot batteries etc, the statement is equally true for the other commands of the UAE Armed Forces. The UAE's Land Forces today are equipped with some of the world's best fighting vehicles, such as the South African G6 155mm self-propelled howitzers, French Leclerc tanks fitted with the AZUR urban warfare protection package, Finnish customised Patria AMV 8×8 armoured vehicles, and Russian Pantsir-S1 combined missile and cannon anti-air system.

The second body of evidence is that the UAE has been willing to actually deploy these capabilities. Or, as US Defence Secretary Carter puts it, the UAE 'puts skin in the game'.[7] This was seen in the campaign against ISIS in Syria and Iraq where the UAE was striking targets that were just as dangerous as those attacked by the US.[8] Given that the UAE has participated in six coalition actions with the US (Somalia, Bosnia-Kosovo, Afghanistan, Libya, and the anti-ISIS campaign in Syria and Iraq), this willingness to engage and enduring involvement has made the UAE 'the foremost US military partner in the Arab world', according to the Gulf scholar, Kristian Coates Ulrichsen.[9]

Further evidence which can be offered that the UAE is the most capable Arab armed force is that the US has allowed certain UAE elements to work alongside US forces in high-risk missions. For example, in the early 2010s, UAE F-16s provided close air support to US troops under attack in southern Afghanistan. Trusting a

3 This is reinforced by the observation that during the anti-ISIS campaign, the number of UAE sorties flown against ISIS was second only to the US. Eleonora Ardemagni, 'The Gulf Monarchies' Complex Fight Against Daesh', *NATO Review*, 2016.
4 Frederic Wehrey. 'Gulf Participation in the Anti–Islamic State Coalition: Limitations and Costs', 23 September 2014 <carnegie-mec.org/diwan/56710?lang=en>
5 A.H. Cordesman, with assistance from M. Markusen and Eric P. Jones, *Stability and Instability in the Gulf Region in 2016: A Strategic Net Assessment (Working Draft)* (Washington DC, 2016), p. 270.
6 M.V. Schanz, 'Allies in the Gulf', *Air Force Magazine*, 12 January 2013, p. 43.
7 Carter, *The Logic of American Strategy in the Middle East.*
8 Chandrasekaran, 'In the UAE, the United States Has a Quiet, Potent Ally Nicknamed "Little Sparta"'.
9 Ulrichsen, *The United Arab Emirates: Power, Politics and Policy-Making*, p. 146.

non-NATO partner to such missions was rare, with Australia being the only other such partner afforded this trust.[10]

However, the most convincing evidence of the UAE Armed Forces' considerable capability is its actual operational performance. Before 2015, its performance could be described variously as niche, a junior element of a coalition, lacking in key combat enablers, and dependent on foreign logistic support. This can be clearly seen in the UAE's involvement in the NATO-run Operation Unified Protector, which enforced a no-fly zone over Libya during its civil war in 2011. The UAE provided twelve fast jets to Operation Unified Protector; these were based at airfields in the Mediterranean Sea. These UAE aircraft undertook air patrols and bombing sorties. To deploy the aircraft to the theatre, the UAE relied on air refuelling by US tanker aircraft. The US also airlifted munitions, spare parts, communication equipment, etc. from the UAE to the Mediterranean because the UAE did not have strategic airlift assets.[11] In the theatre, the UAE aircraft lacked the communication systems needed to integrate into NATO's communication system; this meant pilots had to receive encrypted messages via an open channel and manually decrypt them while flying, something which took 15 to 20 minutes to do.[12] This operation illustrated that while the UAE could deploy combat aircraft away from home bases, it lacked organic support and maintenance abilities.

Since 2015, the UAE Armed Forces have shown a marked improvement in numerous dimensions. As noted by Michael Knights, a leading analyst on military operations in the region, who undertook four 'embedded' visits with UAE forces during 2018, this has occurred because the UAE has undertaken dozens of combat operations in Yemen, starting in March 2015 and continuing to the present. These operations have included 'urban warfare, amphibious landings, armoured pursuit operations, precision strike operations with NATO-standard consideration of humanitarian law and non-combatant immunity, stabilization and reconstruction operations, and unconventional warfare in support of local proxies.'[13]

To better understand the recent leap in the UAE Armed Forces' effectiveness and capabilities, it is instructive to examine details of the Yemen operations. The immediate background to the UAE's involvement in Yemen was the September 2014 'coup' which saw the then-government, headed by President Abdrabbuh Mansur Hadi, forced out by a northern Yemen-based political and armed movement with the help of

---

10   Chandrasekaran, 'In the UAE, the United States Has a Quiet, Potent Ally Nicknamed "Little Sparta".

11   Mueller, *Precision and Purpose: Airpower in the Libyan Civil War*, pp. 354-45.

12   S. Trimble, 'UAE Air Combat Debut Hit by Communications Issues', *Flight Daily News*, 12 November 2011.

13   M. Knights. 'Lessons From the UAE War in Yemen', 2019, Lawfare <www.lawfareblog.com/lessons-uae-war-yemen>

forces loyal to the former president Ali Abdullah Saleh.[14] (In the rest of this chapter, these forces will be collectively referred to as the Houthi-bloc forces).

Consequently, Hadi and his loyalist forces fled the capital, Sanaa, southwards to the country's second-largest city and major port, Aden. The Houthi-bloc forces advanced southwards in late 2014 and, by early 2015, were closing in on Aden. Entering southern Yemen, the Houthi-bloc forces met resistance from various tribal and regionally based groups. One collection of such groups, which became important in the defence of Aden and the future course of the war, was the Southern Resistance. The constituent groups of the Southern Resistance were united around a desire to re-establish the pre-1990 country of South Yemen, but little else. The Southern Resistance was made up of several groups which held quite diverse ideological positions including Salafist/Islamist, nationalist and leftist positions. They also had different visions for the future after the hoped-for separation of South Yemen. Southern Resistance forces worked with Hadi-aligned forces to counter the advance of the Houthi-bloc forces. However, Hadi did not support separatism. This divergence of opinion within the anti-Houthi-bloc forces – beyond wanting to keep the 'northerners' out – pointed to the challenging political environment in which the war would be waged.

By March 2015, the Houthi-bloc forces had started to enter Aden with the Southern Resistance and other allied forces being pushed back into two main pockets around Aden, both less than 10 miles wide.[15] Both were on Aden's coastal peninsulas – one at Crater, which is the site of Aden's main port, and the other at Little Aden, which is the site of the city's oil refinery and tanker port.

The southern advances of the Houthi-bloc forces were viewed with increasing concern by the Saudi Arabian leadership who considered that a Houthi-bloc victory would see an Iranian proxy on Saudi Arabia's southern border. Iran has supported the Houthi-bloc forces with materiel, advice and training.[16]

In early 2015, Saudi Arabia assembled a coalition with the aim of reversing the gains of the Houthi-bloc forces and reinstalling the 'legitimate government' in Yemen. Known as the Arab Coalition, it consisted of forces from nine Arab and Islamic countries – Egypt, Morocco, Jordan, Sudan, the UAE, Kuwait, Qatar, Bahrain, and Pakistan. In addition, the US and Britain provided support in the form of intelligence, logistics, air strike command/control and munitions, and Djibouti, Eritrea and

---

14   These included Al Islah, the Sunni Islamist Yemeni chapter of the Muslim Brotherhood. International Crisis Group, *Yemen: Is Peace Possible?* (Brussels, 2016), p. 15. In 2016, Al Islah renounced its links with the Muslim Brotherhood and is now aligned with Hadi. However, the UAE has not accepted that the organisation's links with the Muslim Brotherhood have been broken and continues to take action against Al Islah.

15   Alex Mello and Michael Knights, *The Saudi-UAE War Effort in Yemen (Part 1): Operation Golden Arrow in Aden* (Washington DC, 2015).

16   G. M. Feierstein. 'Iran's Role in Yemen and Prospects for Peace', 5 December 2018, United States Institute of Peace <iranprimer.usip.org/blog/2018/dec/05/iran%E2%80%99s-role-yemen-and-prospects-peace>

Somalia also made their airspace, territorial waters and military bases available. After Saudi Arabia, the UAE has made by far the greatest military contribution to the Arab Coalition's campaign. Most other partners provided limited military support,[17] with the Kuwaiti, Bahraini, Qatari, Jordanian and Moroccan contributions characterised as 'token'.[18] While formally the Arab Coalition is referred to as Saudi-led, the UAE has pursued its own agenda in its area of operations – southern Yemen – which has meant its operations have been 'largely planned and executed independently from Saudi oversight', as noted in a Chatham House study.[19]

The UAE's military involvement in Yemen started with the Arab Coalition's opening operation – Operation Decisive Storm. This was an air operation which commenced on 26 March 2015 and ended formally 29 days later. The operation saw 2,415 sorties being carried out against targets across Yemen.[20] The largest contributor to the operation was Saudi Arabia which provided 100 fast jets, followed by the UAE with 30 jets (F-16s and Mirage 2000s).[21]

The UAE also played a major role in land operations, and arguably the key role in land battles in southern Yemen. Two land operations are worth examining in detail as each demonstrates hitherto unseen capabilities of the UAE Armed Forces. These are the 2015 Battle for Aden and its immediate aftermath, and the stalemate years from 2016 to the UAE's official military drawdown in 2019.

The Battle for Aden and its immediate aftermath

Below is a description of the 2015 Battle for Aden from Mello and Knights:

> These two pockets, each less than ten miles wide, were held for three-and-a-half months with the help of Saudi and Egyptian naval gunfire, Saudi-led airstrikes, and resupply by sea- and air-dropped pallets. In addition, a team of

---

17   An exception was Sudan which has provided both regular and irregular forces for ground force operations. The *New York Times* reports that many as 14,000 Sudanese militiamen have been fighting in Yemen over the conflict to late 2018, while *Jane's Defence Weekly* reported that a senior Sudanese Government leader in mid-2019 stated that Sudan had contributed 30,000 to the Arab Coalition for operations in Yemen. David D. Kirkpatrick, 'On the Front Line of the Saudi War in Yemen: Child Soldiers From Darfur', *The New York Times*, 28 December 2018. Jeremy Binnie, 'Sudan has "Largest Force" in Arab Coalition' (London: Jane's Information Group, 2019).

18   International Crisis Group, *Yemen: Is Peace Possible?*, 167, pp. 3, 21.

19   Peter Salisbury, *Yemen's Southern Powder Keg* (London, 2018), p. 11.

20   Saudi Press Agency. 'Brig. Gen. Ahmed Asiri Announces Achievement of Determination Storm's Goals, Beginning of Operation Hope Restore 2 Riyadh', 2015 <www.spa.gov.sa/viewstory.php?newsid=1352534>

21   Bahrain, Jordan and Morocco also provided fast jets but in much smaller numbers. Alex Mello and Michael Knights, *The Saudi–UAE War Effort in Yemen (Part 2): The Air Campaign* (Washington DC, 2015).

around fifty ship-deployed special forces landed in Crater in early May. The team was composed of Yemenis serving in the Saudi armed forces and other Yemenis trained by the UAE, including army officers who served the former People's Democratic Republic of Yemen and younger tribal fighters. Embedded with the Yemenis were well-equipped special forces from the UAE Presidential Guard, armed with top-of-the-line weapons such as U.S.-supplied Javelin antitank guided missiles (ATGMs). These Emirati troops directly engaged in ground combat in Aden city from May 4 onward, while Pakistani and Saudi naval drones provided observation for naval gunfire support.

The two pockets repulsed major Houthi attacks on June 8 and June 24. During this period, a larger Saudi-supported and UAE-trained force of 1,500 Yemenis was inserted into the Little Aden pocket. These troops were provided with 170 mine-resistant ambush-protected vehicles (MRAPs) and mortar and anti-tank systems via a new purpose-built temporary port near the refinery.

The larger force was developed to spearhead Operation Golden Arrow, a joint Hadi-Southern Resistance offensive to recapture Aden. On July 14, seventy-five MRAPs with around 600 troops broke out of the western perimeter of Little Aden and captured a new berth, Ras Amran, then hooked northeast to capture the road systems north of Aden city. Another 95 MRAPs and 300 troops were ferried across Aden harbor to the Crater pocket to liberate Aden International Airport and the city. UAE and Saudi special forces and eight UAE Enigma fighting vehicles with quad-mounted remote-control missile systems accompanied attacking forces. By the end of the day, Southern Resistance forces recaptured the airport with support from a flying column of MRAPs operated by trained Yemenis and a small number of UAE special forces. One UAE special forces officer, Lt. Abdul Aziz Sarhan Saleh al-Kaabi, was reportedly killed during the offensive. Meanwhile, supporting air forces launched 136 strikes in Aden during the operation's first thirty-six hours.

The UAE and Saudi Arabia also increased the flow of military materiel into Aden's seaports using tank landing craft and amphibious warfare vessels, including the logistics ship *Swift*, a former U.S. Navy High-Speed Vessel 2 (HSV-2). By August 3, a UAE armored/mechanized brigade task force had landed at Aden with a battalion-size contingent of Leclerc main battle tanks and armored recovery vehicles, dozens of BMP-3M infantry fighting vehicles, Denel G6 155 mm self-propelled howitzers, RG-31 Agrab 120 mm mortar carriers, and Tatra T816 trucks. Altogether, the UAE and Saudi Arabia now have nearly 2,800 troops in Aden, including special forces and almost a brigade of UAE regular army troops and logistics personnel.[22]

22   Mello and Knights, *The Saudi-UAE War Effort in Yemen (Part 1): Operation Golden Arrow in Aden*, 2464.

The victory in the Battle for Aden led to a breakout of anti-Houthi forces from Aden which expanded radially across southern Yemen. The UAE's armoured elements and special forces, in concert with the anti-Houthi bloc forces, rapidly captured the country's biggest air base, the Al Anad Air Base, some 48 km to the northwest, then the nearby Labouza military base on 4 August 2015. The following weeks saw the anti-Houthi-bloc forces move northwards to Lahej and Dhala, to the east of Sanaa centred on Marib,[23] and eastwards along the coast towards Mukalla which was a centre of Al Qaeda in the Arabian Peninsula (AQAP).

The land battles involved three commands of the UAE Armed Forces – Land Forces, Presidential Guard, and Joint Aviation Command. The armour, mechanised infantry, artillery, and field engineering elements of the first two undertook conventional activities such as assault, direct fires, indirect fires, and defensive structure construction. UAE special operations forces of the Presidential Guard undertook high-value missions that spanned the counter-insurgency, counter-terrorism and unconventional warfare spectrum. Examples include reconnaissance, intelligence collection, sabotage and capturing or killing high-value targets. Much of the UAE special operations effort was directed against AQAP and ISIS members. These operations were sometimes undertaken in partnership with local forces and/or with US special forces.[24] Joint Aviation Command provided reconnaissance, ground attack and transport tasks.

The Battle for Aden points to the UAE Armed Forces' ability to plan successfully and execute several types of missions which they had not previously undertaken.

First, and at a strategic level, it demonstrated that the UAE Armed Forces could effectively lead a multi-country coalition. They successfully assembled and managed a coalition force off the coast of Aden, with all of the challenges, including different rules of engagement, difficulty in sharing information due to lack of interoperability, and the need to operate some 2,000km away from its home soil. They managed the transition of operations from the defence of pockets of territory to the breakout, which shows considerable planning skills and adaptability as circumstances changed. Equally importantly, the UAE Armed Forces were able to develop a logistics system which enabled forces, materiel, ammunition and supplies to be stockpiled in forward locations around the Red Sea and Gulf of Aden, and transported when needed. This points to new capabilities in logistics planning and execution, including strategic and tactical air and sea lift. It also demonstrates that the UAE can rapidly obtain transport

23 This was the governorate where on 4 September 2015, some 45 Emirati soldiers died following a Houthi-bloc ballistic missile. It struck an ammunition dump at the Arab Coalition base outside of Safer, to the east of Sanaa.

24 Other countries also supplied special forces including Bahrain. HRH Prince Salman bin Hamad Al Khalifa, Crown Prince, Deputy Supreme Commander and First Deputy Prime Minister. 'HRH CP visits Royal Guard; honours servicemen who participated in Taskforce 11', 20 June 2017 <crownprince.bh/en/media-centre/news/4268/2017/6/20/HRH-CP-visits-Royal-Guard;-honours-servicemen-who-participated-in-Taskforce-11>

vessels and aircraft through commercial hire arrangements and utilising civil assets controlled by the UAE.

The Battle for Aden also revealed that UAE senior military and political leaders had strategic flexibility, for each area of the Yemen campaign has different circumstances and requires a tailored approach. The chief concern in the east and around Aden has been AQAP and ISIS. This means the UAE's priorities have been countering terrorism training and support for intelligence collection, processing and dissemination; identification and targeting cells; and small-scale operations. Along the Red Sea, operations have been more conventional in nature which has meant that the UAE prioritises training and support of manoeuvre and defensive operations.

At the operational level, the Battle for Aden demonstrated the ability of the UAE Armed Forces to lead and execute joint operations involving all of its commands, as well as foreign units and local forces. Of particular note was the Emirati ability to mount a sustained defensive operation in partnership with anti-Houthi-bloc forces in the Aden pockets. This required the UAE Armed Forces to insert small-scale forces in a contested environment and undertake aggressive action to keep attacking forces from taking the initiative. The battle also demonstrated the ability to plan and execute what is probably the riskiest and most complex joint operation – an amphibious landing. These are particularly challenging as they require extensive preparations before they can be attempted; and the reach and lethality of modern weapons systems enables defenders to inflict heavy casualties on assaulting forces, despite being tens of kilometres away. The amphibious operation in Aden has been described as the largest in the Middle East since the liberation of Kuwait in 1991.[25] The success of the landings was a remarkable achievement given that the UAE had never before undertaken this type of operation. Other successful amphibious operations were subsequently carried out elsewhere, such as at Belhaf.

These operations also showed a rapid improvement in the level of 'jointness' across Commands. This was reflected in elements of Land Forces, Presidential Guard, and Joint Aviation Command working together. It was also seen in the tailoring of land formations to reflect the needs of each operation. The flexibility to build bespoke formations is perhaps not surprising, as historically, when a UAE Armed Forces deployment was needed rapidly, an ad-hoc task groups was assembled rather than sending an existing company or battalion.

In the breakout from Aden and its immediate aftermath, a significant success factor was the Emiratis' ability to raise, train, equip, support, co-opt and sometimes lead local forces. This approach is known as the doctrine of fighting 'by, with, and through' local forces.

This doctrine was applied by the US to take back ISIS territory in Iraq and Syria after ISIS had captured most of Syria and about a third of Iraq's territory by 2014. This

---

25   Jeremy Binnie, 'Emirati Armoured Brigade Spearheads Aden Breakout' (London: Jane's Information Group, 2015).

approach involved the US not using its own armed force in a direct combat role, but instead working with local forces which did the vast bulk of the fighting, such as Iraqi government forces or Kurdish Peshmerga. As well as fighting, the local forces took the lead in decision making. The US, along with other partners of the US-led coalition, essentially provided supporting functions, notably training, advising, intelligence, operational coordination, communications, air movement, logistics, air strikes and fire support.[26] Occasionally the US-led coalition forces would accompany local forces during combat operations and fight alongside them. A special case was high-value operations that were of great significance to members of the coalition. In such cases, coalition forces could undertake these missions without local force support.

The UAE's application of the 'by, with, and through' doctrine in Yemen was similar to that of the US-led coalition in Iraq and Syria – and equally successful. The UAE provided training, equipment and wages to existing local Yemeni forces, as well as helping to expand their numbers. The latter was done by encouraging tribal leaders to send in fighters under a levy, supporting the training and return of Yemeni expatriates from the Gulf (notably the UAE), and recruiting former Yemeni Government soldiers and activists. The UAE also established new forces which it directly or substantially controlled.[27] Examples of such forces are the Hadramawt Elite Force (Al Nukhba Al Hadramiyya) based in Hadramawt region, and the Shabwa Elite Force (Al Nukhba Al Chabwaniyya) in Shabwaani region.[28] The local forces undertook much of the frontline operations. The UAE Armed Forces supported them by providing special-ised combat forces (e.g. armoured and special forces), combat support (e.g. intelligence and staff work) and logistics (e.g. weapons, ammunition, medical supplies).

The adoption by the UAE of the doctrine of fighting 'by, with and through' local forces was a necessity due to both the manpower constraints of the UAE Armed Forces, and a desire to maintain a small footprint in Yemen. It had the key benefit of

---

26   Seth J. Frantzman, '"By, With, and Through": How The U.S.-Led Coalition Defeated The Islamic State In Iraq Using Tactics Without Coherent Strategy For Confronting Iranian Influence', *Middle East Review of International Affairs*, 21, 3 (Fall/Winter) (2017), p. 7.

27   A 2019 UN Security Council report referring to the Security Belt Forces (a key armed force of the Southern Transitional Council based in Aden) and the Shabwani elite forces (the counter-terrorism orientated force based in the AQAP stronghold of the Shabwah Governorate) wrote that the 'legitimate government of Yemen had no effective control over those forces ... rather, those forces, which were created by the United Arab Emirates in 2016, were being paid, armed and trained by the latter ... the United Arab Emirates was, in fact, in charge of organizing and coordinating the operations of those forces.' United Nations Security Council, *Final report of the Panel of Experts on Yemen* (New York, 2019), p. 55. For details on the actual UAE chain of command for local forces, see Salisbury, *Yemen's Southern Powder Keg*, p. 11.

28   Both of which were created by the UAE after the liberation of Mukalla from AQAP in April 2016 in order to continue the counter-terrorism fight. Franck Mermier. 'Southern Secessionists Divided by Regional Identities', 20 March 2018, Italian Institute for International Political Studies, www.ispionline.it/en/pubblicazione/yemens-southern-secessionists-divided-regional-identities-19930.

allowing the UAE to leverage its limited number of formations to achieve an outcome that was disproportionately large for such a small country. It needs to be remembered that Yemen has a land mass six times that of the UAE, and a population more than 20 times larger.[29]

For much of the campaign, the UAE's force in Yemen appears to have been made up of between 2,000 and 6,000 service members. Given that the UAE Armed Forces' strength is just 60,000, this means that between 3 and 10 percent of the country's military was deployed to Yemen at any one time. If only actual combat personnel of the UAE Armed Forces are considered, then this means about a sixth of the country's entire fighting force was at war at any given moment, according to Knights.[30] This is a considerable proportion rarely matched by other countries in recent wars.

In addition to using local forces to compensate for the lack of Emirati military personnel, the UAE has augmented its forces with other groups. These included using military contractors which provided combat support services and, in a few cases, undertook combat operations.[31] These contractors were both Emirati and foreign. The UAE also deployed small numbers of volunteers from its foreigner-manned paramilitary unit to Yemen.[32] In addition, it also embedded foreign forces personnel within its contingent, for example in 2015 these included some 400 Eritrean soldiers.[33] The UAE has also facilitated the provision of personnel from the other Arab Coalition states, such as Sudan, through training, logistics and financial support.

The UAE's application of the 'by, with and through' doctrine in Yemen has shown that the UAE has the ability to deploy teams that can teach local forces how to operate, maintain, and employ weapons and support systems, and how to develop a self-training capability. It also demonstrates that the UAE Armed Forces have built up expertise in political negotiations with local leaders, as well as coordinating often disparate groups to achieve a desired outcome. However, it is important to note that the UAE's approach has not always been successful. An example of the difficulties involved in raising and maintaining local forces which aligned with the UAE's goals was seen in Mahra province which abuts the Yemen-Oman border.[34]

29   This figure is based on UAE nationals who make up the vast majority of those in the UAE Armed Forces.
30   Knights, 'Lessons From the UAE War in Yemen'.
31   Aram Roston, 'American Mercenaries', *BuzzFeed*, 16 October 2018.
32   Hager and Mazzetti, 'Emirates Secretly Sends Colombian Mercenaries to Yemen Fight.'
33   United Nations Security Council, *Letter Dated 9 October 2015 From the Chair of the Security Council Committee Pursuant to Resolutions 751 (1992) and 1907 (2009) Concerning Somalia and Eritrea Addressed to the President of the Security Council* (New York, 2015).
34   For details, see B.M. Perkins, 'Saudi Arabia and the UAE in al-Mahra: Securing Interests, Disrupting Local Order, and Shaping a Southern Military', *Terrorism Monitor*, 17, 4 (2019).

The stalemate years

Despite the early successes, Houthi-bloc forces were not rapidly defeated in Yemen. As noted by the military analysis consultancy, Force Analysis, after years of conflict, 'even though gains have been made on the ground, no decisive ground movements towards the capital Sanaa, or towards breaking the back of the Houthi militancy have materialized ... [despite even] a perpetual air campaign has been striking Houthi rebels and their allies on a daily basis since the start of the intervention'.[35]

In June 2019, the UAE started a 'drawdown' of its armed forces in Yemen. This was not a complete withdrawal as operations against ISIS and AQAP would continue. Officially, the withdrawal was driven by a desire to advance a political settlement.[36] It was also intended to 'restore international support for the UAE's foreign policy amid widespread opposition to its involvement in Yemen', according to the International Institute for Strategic Studies.[37] More broadly, the withdrawal was probably motivated by both increasing concern about Iranian hostilities in the UAE's immediate neighbourhood, limited ability to influence Saudi Arabia's approach, and the recognition that defeating the Houthi-bloc forces would take many more years, billions of dirham and lives. This withdrawal saw the UAE reduce its two major battle groups around Aden and on the western coast, as well as its many smaller detachments, such as at Marib. Before this, there were an estimated 3,500 UAE troops in Yemen supported by 3,000 UAE Armed Forces' personnel, operating offshore and in the region.[38]

The lack of a decisive military victory points to some limitations of the UAE Armed Forces. One is that its relatively small size has meant that it has not been able to insert large forces and win a military victory using its own resources alone. In numbers alone, the UAE Armed Forces have demonstrated it can field at any one time only several thousand troops in manoeuvre and special forces formations. Likewise, despite the large number of aircraft the UAE has, it only fielded what is in effect a 'heavy' squadron. It is also worth noting that despite the fact that the UAE's air elements, along with those of the other Arab Coalition members, dominated the airspace, they could not stem the southward advance of Houthi-bloc forces in 2015, nor facilitate rapid and deep advances by anti-Houthi forces.

Another limitation highlighted in the Yemen campaign is that there are tradeoffs when relying on local forces. Firstly, military action moves at a slower pace than if it was being undertaken by UAE forces alone. Secondly, these operations will only continue for as long as the local forces agree. And finally, significant amounts of time

---

35   Force Analysis, *Yemen: War Amongst Divided Alliances* (Belguim, 2018), p. 3.
36   'What the UAE Drawdown Means for the Yemen Conflict', *The National*, 6 August 2019.
37   Virginia Comolli, Francesca Grandi, and International Institute for Strategic Studies, *The Armed Conflict Survey 2020* (Oxon, 2020), p. 229.
38   Knights, 'Lessons From the UAE War in Yemen'.

and energy must go into managing the politics within and between local forces, which reduces effort spent on military operations.

The implication of these limitations is that the UAE's capabilities are significantly bounded. Specifically, the UAE does not yet have the ability to project military power abroad in the way that a significant military power would, such as Britain did in the Falkland Islands in 1982, Israel in the various campaigns in Lebanon/Gaza, and Russia in Georgia and Chechnya. In other words, the UAE cannot intervene using its forces alone to defeat an enemy or impose its will on another country.

In summary, today the UAE Armed Forces are a remarkably effective force given their small size; they can punch well above their weight. They have conventional and non-conventional capabilities not possessed by other regional powers. They can undertake joint, sustained and expeditionary operations both independently and with partners. They also have a proven ability to work with and influence local forces: noting that this approach also imposes significant constraints which reduce the UAE's ability to control military operations.

However, the UAE Armed Forces are constrained currently by their manpower strength. While currently the 'military burden' in the UAE as detailed in Chapter 6 is the highest in the world based on the country's national population (i.e. around 28 percent of all Emiratis in the labour force serve in the military), there is some ability to increase force numbers. This could be done by engaging the large pool of nationals who are entering the labour market over the next decade, and by increasing the proportion of women in the military. Additional manpower for the UAE Armed Forces could also be generated through engaging expatriates with strong ties to the country, notably those born and raised in the UAE but having foreign citizenship. (This path would not have to lead to the expatriates' citizenship via naturalisation, as most would be satisfied with permanent residency.) Another approach to mitigating the UAE Armed Forces' relatively small size is to accelerate their use of automation and autonomous systems, thus generating more capability per soldier.

The UAE's route to military effectiveness

An obvious but superficial answer to the question of how the UAE Armed Forces were able to build their current high level of capability is that they have spent huge sums on purchasing large quantities of the world's best weaponry. The UAE's defence spending has been considerable in both absolute and global terms as seen in Chapter 5. However, while materiel and technology are an important component of a country's armed force capability, they are insufficient to explain the UAE's present position. If this were all that were required, then Saudi Arabia should also be able to field and sustain highly effective armed forces as its military spending has long been double that of the UAE's.[39] However, Saudi Arabia does not have an equivalent military capability.[40]

Materiel preponderance (i.e. quantity) as well as the equipment's technology state (i.e. quality) have been commonly used as indicators of a nation's military capability. However, as noted by Stephen Biddle in his landmark book, *Military Power: Explaining Victory and Defeat in Modern Battle*, 'threat assessments based on the numbers and types of hostile weapons are likely to overestimate real capabilities for enemies with modern equipment but limited skills, and underestimate militaries with older equipment but high skills.'[41]

Biddle advances another method for determining military capability – the degree to which the employment of force reflects mastery of what he terms the 'modern system of warfare'. He defines this system as 'a tightly interrelated complex of cover, concealment, dispersion, suppression, small-unit independent manoeuvre, and combined arms at the tactical level, and depth, reserves and differential concentration at the operational level of war'.[42] He argues that mastery of the modern system requires proficiency in certain technical-military practices, and of secondary importance is the quality and quantity of materiel, technology and manpower. He claims, convincingly, that his theory explains why less well-resourced armed forces can achieve greater military success over better resourced ones.

Mastery of technical-military practices requires not only being technically proficient in specific military-related skills, techniques etc, it also depends on the armed forces having a culture which is supportive of the behaviours that underpin these practices. These behaviours include leadership, initiative, flexibility, and acceptance of

---

39   In 2019, Saudi Arabia was the world's fifth largest defence spender with expenditure estimated at US $61.9 billion. SIPRI has not provided estimate of military spending by the UAE since 2014 when it was $22.8 billion. SIPRI, *Trends in World Military Expenditure, 2019* (2020), p. 9.

40   This is demonstrated by Saudi Arabia's limited ability to mount significant ground operations in northern Yemen, despite its forces having over 200,000 personnel. The conduct of operations under the control of Saudi Arabia in northern Yemen also points to significant military weaknesses. An example of this was the inability to plan, train and concentrate forces to take Midi; and this only occurred after multiple failed attempts and high casualties. For details of this battle, see Force Analysis, *Yemen: War Amongst Divided Alliances*, p. 10; Force Analysis. 'After Year of Failure, Coalition Takes Midi', 2018, <force-analysis.com/438-2/>. Another illustration of the difference between the UAE and Saudi Arabia was seen in the Arab Gulf States contribution to the campaign against ISIS in Syria and Iraq. The *NATO Review* reported that the UAE Air Force conducted 'strikes against dynamic targets, such as armoured vehicles and troop transports' while Saudi Arabia predominantly struck just 'fixed and static targets such as military headquarters, training camps and facilities'. This reflected Saudi Arabia's lessor capabilities. Ardemagni, 'The Gulf Monarchies' Complex Fight Against Daesh.'

41   S. Biddle, *Military Power: Explaining Victory and Defeat in Modern Battle* (Princeton, 2010), p. 5.

42   Ibid., p. 3.

uncertainty. This can be seen in the cultural attributes embedded in Biddle's description of what is required for a force to exploit a breakthrough:

> [A breakthrough] requires quick, independent decision making by local commanders in lead units, and an ability to cope with the unexpected on the fly without detailed guidance from higher command ... Events move too quickly for extensive staff analysis or promulgation of detailed formal orders; an ability to improvise from partial instructions is critical to success. Such operations put a premium on judgement, mental agility, and individual initiative at all levels of command.[43]

Caitlin Talmadge in her book *The Dictator's Army: Effectiveness in Authoritarian Regime* also identifies behaviours of military culture which are linked to battlefield effectiveness. However, in her case these are ones which undermine effectiveness. She notes that the militaries of authoritarian regimes, which have often done poorly in conventional conflicts, commonly display the following traits: promotion based on loyalty not skill; training regimes which do not provide military skills because these could be used against the state's leadership; excessively centralised and convoluted command arrangements designed to make it difficult for an army to plot a coup or turn on the government; limiting the ability of officers to exercise initiative; and information management arrangements under which information is centralised at the top with minimal lateral sharing.[44]

If the technical-military practices of military effectiveness are known, why don't all armed forces adopt them? Kenneth M. Pollack has tackled this question in the context of the Middle East. His enduring question across his writings has been why Arab militaries, when fighting against Western forces, have generally not performed as well as would have been expected given their often very significant materiel, expenditure and manpower.[45] In his 2019 book *Armies of Sand,* he concludes that 'the greatest problems that Arab armed forces suffered during the modern era (and continue to suffer to the present day) have been driven by patterns of behaviour derived from the dominant Arab culture'.[46]

Pollack is not the first to consider culture as a key factor in understanding military effectiveness in the Arab world. Participants in Arab conflicts of the early and mid-twentieth century, such as T.E. Lawrence and Lieutenant-General Sir John Bagot

---

43 Ibid., p. 44.
44 C. Talmadge, *The Dictator's Army: Battlefield Effectiveness in Authoritarian Regimes* (Ithaca, 2015).
45 These include K.M. Pollack, 'The Influence of Arab Culture on Arab Military Effectiveness' (Massachusetts Institute of Technology, 1996). K.M. Pollack, *Arabs at War: Military Effectiveness, 1948-1991*, 2004); K.M. Pollack, *Armies of Sand: The Past, Present, and Future of Arab Military Effectiveness*, 2019).
46 Pollack, *Armies of Sand: The Past, Present, and Future of Arab Military Effectiveness*, p. 511.

Glubb (Glubb Pasha), have highlighted the centrality of culture and the need to adapt a Western military approach when dealing with Arab forces.[47] A more recent participant with Arab forces has been Norvell B. DeAtkine. In his widely quoted 1999 paper 'Why Arabs Lose Wars', he reinforces Pollack's conclusions and notes that while there are 'many factors — economic, ideological, technical — but perhaps the most important has to do with culture and certain societal attributes which inhibit Arabs from producing an effective military force'.[48]

Pollack et al. argue that, in general, military culture is a reflection of national culture, and if national culture does not support certain behaviours (e.g. risk acceptance, agility and delegation), then nor will the military culture.

It is important to note that Pollack et al. do not argue that a nation cannot master the modern system of warfare just because its national culture does not display the behaviours associated with effective technical-military practices. They argue that national-military cultural misalignment can be overcome through building a new culture within the armed forces. However, doing so is challenging as there is a natural tendency for the constructed culture in the military to always move back towards the national culture.

Both DeAtkine and Pollack identify a range of positive and negative cultural traits that can affect Arab military effectiveness. Traits which play a positive role include 'strong bonds of loyalty and cohesion found in Arab in-groups',[49] personal bravery,[50] and in the context of irregular Arab forces, a belief in psychological warfare and a way of fighting that are consistent with traditional Bedouin methods of waging war.[51] Negative traits include information hoarding; an education system predicated on rote memorisation and avoidance of hands-on learning; a highly centralized system of control with authority hardly ever delegated; a failure to use the non-commissioned officer corps; a lack of cooperation which means combined arms operations cannot occur effectively; passive and unimaginative tactical leadership; badly distorted flows of information across chains of command; and poor equipment maintenance.[52]

It needs to be noted that the link between Arab cultural traits and military effectiveness is not universally accepted. It has been criticised as echoing 'Orientalist tropes of the Imperial era',[53] and is contested due to a lack of qualitative analysis to support

47   T.E. Lawrence, *Seven Pillars of Wisdom: A Triumph* (London, 1935); J.B. Glubb, *The Story of the Arab Legion* (London, 1948).
48   Norvell B. DeAtkine, 'Why Arabs Lose Wars', *The Middle East Quarterly*, 7, 4 (1999).
49   Pollack, *Armies of Sand: The Past, Present, and Future of Arab Military Effectiveness*, p. 508.
50   Ibid., p. 505.
51   Norvell B. DeAtkine, 'The Arab as Insurgent', *American Diplomacy*, September (2009).
52   Pollack, *Armies of Sand: The Past, Present, and Future of Arab Military Effectiveness*, p. 511.
53   James Spencer. 'Pollack Book on Arab Militaries Misses Mark', 17 February 2019, LobeLog <lobelog.com/pollack-book-on-arab-militaries-misses-mark/>; Ahmed Salah Hashim, 'Military Orientalism: Middle East Ways of War', *Middle East Policy*, 26, 2 (2019).

the arguments.[54] Putting aside the first as it is not germane to identifying a causal relationship, the second argument has validity. This is because measuring culture, and the link between culture and military effectiveness, is problematic. While both authors use valid research approaches, either case studies or personal observation, these approaches have limitations caused by case selection, data analysis, and the generalisation of the findings. However, the research and observations of the author have led to the conclusion that their cultural argument is compelling. That is, there are some characteristics of Arab societies that make it more difficult to achieve a military culture consistent with the modern system of warfare.

In Chapters 2 and 3 of this book, cultural characteristics of Arab society were identified as they are manifested in Emirati society. These include the centralisation of power and influence under the ruler, the rulers' close supervision of armed forces, and strong bonds of loyalty and cohesion found in Arab in-groups. In addition, the rulers' decision-making style has and continues to be direct and personal, reaching down into relatively low levels in the organisation. A final important characteristic is that Emirati society is hierarchical, patriarchal and collectivist, which creates wide-ranging and powerful mutual obligations.

What do these cultural characteristics mean for the military? One is that if a ruler wants to form, expand or modernise his armed forces, change can occur rapidly, because there is a genuine desire by his subordinates to implement his instructions. In addition, by the ruler being closely involved in the military and able to reach down into the organisation, obstacles which typically slow or stop change are rapidly overcome.

There are, however, downsides to a ruler's ability to make rapid decisions and give instructions. One of these is that due to a top-down culture, information about the wider implications of a decision under consideration is rarely pushed up. Thus a decision may not be fully informed, which can lead to administrative conflicts, waste of resources and duplication of activity. The top-down approach also means that instructions can be given before an implementation plan has been developed. If an issue is complex, the lack of implementation planning can result in the outcome not being achieved on time or as envisaged by the ruler.

Another downside is that if an instruction is unclear in terms of what the ruler wants, there will be confusion about what needs to be done. This is particular the case if the instruction is based on outcomes, rather than either inputs or outputs. An example of an input-based instruction is 'purchase a set number of a certain aircraft', and an output-based instruction would be 'complete a certain number of training hours'. Examples of outcome-based instructions are 'transform land forces into a full-spectrum force' and 'ensure accurate battlefield intelligence is shared upwards and horizontally across commands'. In the case of outcome-based instructions, as there

---

54   Dov S. Zakheim. 'Kenneth Pollack's New History of Arab Armies', 10 February 2019, The National Interest, <nationalinterest.org/feature/kenneth-pollack%E2%80%99s-new-history-arab-armies-44092?page=0%2C3>

are numerous alternatives for achieving the outcome, the people expected to implement the instruction may seek to avoid risk by prevaricating and pushing decisions upwards. If the ruler is not actively engaged in this process, implementation can again be significantly delayed and be at variance with his objectives.

The influence of cultural traits can be seen in the history of the Emirati armed forces and formations described previously in Chapters 7, 8 and 9. Instances in which the ruler made a decision and it rapidly resulted in the establishment of a functioning and arguably effective armed force include the creation of the Abu Dhabi Defence Force, Ras Al Khaimah Mobile Force, Dubai Defence Force and Sharjah National Guard. Instances of rapid improvement in an existing force associated with decisions by the ruler or the political head of the military can be found in the UAE Navy in the early to mid-1980s, the Air Force in the mid to late-1980s, the Critical National Infrastructure Authority/Critical Infrastructure and Coastal Protection Authority in the late 2000s, and the National Service and Reserve Authority in the mid-2010s.

Conversely, these cultural characteristics also mean that without the direct engagement of a ruler, significant organically driven change rarely occurs and military effectiveness may even decline. Manifestations of such decline observed over the history of Emirati militaries include the decay of combat-orientated collective training; loss of cooperation, trust and information sharing across the organisations; risk-aversion in decision making; and discouragement of leadership at the junior officer and NCO levels. This kind of deterioration occurred during the post-1972 period of the Ras Al Khaimah Mobile Force, the post-1973 period of the Sharjah National Guard, and in several commands in the late 1990s.

The importance of implementing both appropriate technical-military practices and a supportive culture appears to have been recognised by the most militarily influential ruler in the UAE – Sheikh Mohammed bin Zayed Al Nahyan. An illustration of this was the promulgation of the 2012 founding Vision Statement for the Presidential Guard. Given the command's importance, it is inconceivable that Sheikh Mohammed did not approve its vision statement personally. The italicised words highlight examples of technical-military practices or cultural behaviours.

> It is our vision to become within three years the best military organisation in conventional and unconventional operations in the region, globally recognised as such and known and respected for an exceptional and enduring *operational focus*.
>
> To achieve this ambitious objective we will become *more selective* in our recruiting; we will produce *tougher, smarter and more skilful soldiers* through the conduct of more *intense and realistic basic and advanced training*; we will become effective at *combined arms operations* in the *joint environment*; we will establish *close and trusting relationships* with all our stakeholders both military and civil; we will develop an *integrated and sophisticated command and control system* based on world's best practice; we will develop a *leadership culture* which encourages and rewards individual *initiative* and *decision making at every level*, particularly amongst *our junior leaders*; we will *empower our NCOs* giving them

increased *authority and responsibility*; we will ensure our soldiers are amongst the best equipped in the world and we will provide them with the best living and training facilities possible; we will achieve this through carefully prioritized and managed development and procurement processes; we will manage our spending prudently, reduce bureaucracy and increase the effectiveness and efficiency of our management and logistic procedures.

We will learn to do all this ourselves by becoming progressively less reliant on embedded foreign advice. Most importantly our vision will be achieved and built upon a foundation of *energy, integrity, trust and teamwork*, an unwavering care and *respect for our soldiers* and loyalty to our senior leadership and to our nation.[55]

Combining the history of Emirati military forces, the work of Biddle and Pollack et al. and the author's research, the following succinct explanation of how the UAE Armed Forces have become so capable can be advanced:

The advanced capability of the UAE Armed Forces is due to the ruler instigating and overseeing the adoption of both: (1) conflict-winning modern technical-military practices; and (2) a military culture which encourages behaviours that support these practices, even when those behaviours are at odds with traditional culture.

Building an effective military force

The final question this book seeks to answer — what mechanisms has the ruler used to accelerate the adoption of technical-military practices and build a supportive culture in the UAE Armed Forces?

The author argues that Sheikh Mohammed bin Zayed has utilised three mechanisms: (1) sending Emiratis to Western military institutions; (2) building up operational experience; and (3) exploiting the knowledge of foreign military professionals.

Emirati attendance at Western military institutions is not new, as noted in Chapter 6. What has changed in recent years has been that far more Emiratis have been sent to gain knowledge and experience of technical-military practices rather than military education alone. Another change has been that far larger numbers of enlisted personnel have attended foreign institutions, rather than just officers as occurred in the past. And for the first time, large numbers have participated in collective training compared to the past when the vast majority of training was individual training. Collective training at foreign combat centres has been particularly effective in transformation as participants can readily see what proficiency looks like and, thus, what needs to change.

---

55   Presidential Guard, *Vision Statement* [Wall Plaque].

These changes have enabled far more Emiratis to not only learn and exercise modern technical-military practices but also, to some degree, to absorb the behaviours that underpin these practices. This absorption of supportive culture appears to be more pronounced for Emiratis with English language ability, those who are more reflective, and those who have been exposed to a foreign military culture for an extended period.

The second mechanism – building up operational experience – started in effect with the UAE's involvement in Afghanistan and has accelerated in the 2010s as the country has become increasingly engaged in foreign military operations (see Annex 7). These experiences have clearly led to improvements in military effectiveness. Several instances illustrate this. During the 2011 operation in Libya, it was found that the UAE's combat aircraft could not integrate into NATO's communications systems. Changing this situation became a priority after the campaign.[56] During the Yemen campaign, officers whose formations did not perform well were removed, with their replacements given instructions to make improvements.

The third mechanism – exploiting the knowledge of foreign military professionals – has seen significant numbers of foreign personnel engaged in the military. These expatriates have come primarily from Western nations, notably the US and the United Kingdom, with smaller numbers from Australia, South Africa, New Zealand, and France.[57]

The role of the foreign personnel has been to transfer knowledge on technical-military practices, specifically what the most effective practices are in what context, and how to build proficiency. Their work has ranged from writing combined arms doctrine to teaching small squad tactics, and from developing the strategic plans to modernise commands to mentoring brigade commanders in transformation implementation. As well as transferring knowledge on technical-military practices, expatriates have also helped to model supporting cultural behaviours. They may not have been explicitly aware that they were doing this, just as the Emiratis who benefited from this modelling may not have been consciously aware of it.[58]

The future

What of the future? If this analysis is correct, then one needs to observe three issues to forecast the future of the UAE's military capability.

---

56 Trimble, 'UAE Air Combat Debut Hit by Communications Issues.'
57 Since the early 1990s, the number of expatriates engaged grew steadily. They peaked around 1,300 in the early 2010s. These served primarily as advisors, trainers, and specialists. The figure does not those in maintenance and sustainment, nor those in non-military roles such as doctors in the military hospitals. A. Yates, *Invisible Expatriates: Western Military Professionals and the Development of the UAE Armed Forces.*
58 For details on the experiences, advantages, disadvantages and limitations of using foreign personnel in advancing the UAE Armed Forces, see ibid.

The first is the level of engagement by the militarily influential ruler in the affairs of the UAE Armed Forces. A necessary condition for the UAE's continued military effectiveness is the ruler's active direction, oversight and intervention to drive proficiency in technical-military practices and to maintain a supportive military culture.

The second is the emphasis placed on continuing mastery of the current technical-military practices. As practices change due to developments in technology, the capabilities and intents of adversaries, and international norms, it is essential that only relevant practices are identified. This requires ongoing strategic assessment, testing in battle laboratories, and applying lessons learned. It also requires continually modifying existing practices and standing up new capabilities, as well as the very challenging need to abandon long-standing tactics, processes etc that no longer serve the force.

The final issue is the degree to which the UAE Armed Forces' culture supports the technical-military practices. A supportive culture needs to be sustained and it also needs to change as technical-military practices evolve. This will be harder when the desired military culture is misaligned with national culture, and easier when it converges.

If these three conditions are met, then it is likely that the UAE Armed Forces will continue to be the most capable Arab military force for the foreseeable future.

Appendix I

Militarily Influential Rulers

A notably element in the Emirati political system is the preeminent, direct and personalised control that a ruler has had over his armed force. This involvement stems from the tribal tradition where a sheikh's first priority was to provide safety and security for his family, tribe and allies. If the sheikh fails to do so, he loses his family's and tribes' support, and is replaced.

Of all the rulers, Sheikh Zayed bin Sultan Al Nahyan (b. 1918, d. 2004) was the most influential in the history of the UAE Armed Forces. He was involved in key decisions to form the Abu Dhabi army under his brother, Sheikh Shakhbut, in the early 1960s,[1] and upon becoming Ruler of Abu Dhabi in 1966, he ordered the expansion of the Abu Dhabi Defence Force (ADDF) into a large, modern armed force. He was the principal advocate for the unification of the Emirati armed forces, which occurred in 1976 but technically was finally completed in 2006. Over his lifetime, he ensured that the armed forces were very well funded, with the vast bulk of this funding coming from Abu Dhabi's coffers.

The other key ruler during the early decades of Emirati military history was Sheikh Rashid bin Saeed Al Maktoum, Ruler of Dubai from 1958 to 1990, Vice President of the UAE from 1971 to 1990, and Prime Minister of the UAE from 1979 to 1990. He ordered the formation of the Dubai Defence Force in 1970, which while much smaller than Abu Dhabi's force, was considered efficient and very capable for its size.

Both of these rulers delegated much responsibility for their armed forces to their sons. Given their importance to the evolution of the armed forces, the biographies of the four key sons are below. Of these sons, currently the most significant are Sheikh Mohammed bin Zayed of Abu Dhabi and Sheikh Mohammed bin Rashid of Dubai, who together 'have long been considered the key strategists of UAE foreign and defence policy', according to Kenneth Katzman, a specialist in Middle Eastern Affairs

---

1   *Soft Power*, pp. 220, 339n8-10.

who has long written the US Congressional Research Services' yearly summary paper on the UAE.[2]

Sheikh Khalifa bin Zayed bin Sultan Al Nahyan

Sheikh Khalifa bin Zayed (b. 1948) is the oldest son of Sheikh Zayed. In February 1969 at the age of 21, he was appointed to his first military post – Chairman of the Department of Defence of Abu Dhabi. (That month also saw Sheikh Khalifa become the Crown Prince of Abu Dhabi). He was given the rank of Lieutenant-General, which reflected the position's status rather than his military education or experience, as he did not have either.[3] In 1971, the Department of Defence of Abu Dhabi was renamed the Ministry of Defence of Abu Dhabi, and Sheikh Khalifa was appointed by his father as Minister of Defence. He continued to hold this post until the Abu Dhabi Government restructure of 1973 when the Abu Dhabi ministries were renamed departments and their responsibilities split between Abu Dhabi departments and Federal Government ministries. New governance arrangements were also introduced at this time which included creating the post of Commander-in-Chief of the ADDF. This post was filled by Sheikh Khalifa.[4]

In 1976, as part of the unification of the Emirati armed forces to form the UAE Armed Forces, the posts of Supreme Commander and Deputy Supreme Commander were created. These posts were filled by Sheikh Zayed and Sheikh Khalifa respectively. Each would continue to hold their position until Sheikh Zayed's death in 2004. Then Sheikh Khalifa became President and thus, Supreme Commander. In 2014, the Sheikh Khalifa had a stroke.[5] Since then he has been inactive, with Sheikh Mohammed bin Zayed exercising Sheikh Khalifa's powers as Supreme Commander of the UAE Armed Forces, as well as his other national security responsibilities.

Over his life, Sheikh Khalifa's involvement in the armed forces appears to have been focused on political-military, strategic and ceremonial issues, rather than detailed force development or executive command. Reasons for this are likely to have been time constraints due to holding multiple positions in the Abu Dhabi and Federal Governments,[6] recognition that decisions were better exercised by professional military officers, and his attitude to the armed forces.

---

2   K. Katzman, *The United Arab Emirates (UAE): Issues for U.S. Policy* (Washington DC, 2017), p. 2.
3   Wilson, *Khalifa: Journey Into the Future*, p. 18.
4   On 14 January 1974, Sheikh Zayed appointed Sheikh Khalifa as the Commander-in-Chief of the ADDF. Al Abed, Vine, and Al Jabali, *Chronicle of Progress*, p. 55.
5   'UAE President Recovering From Stroke, Abu Dhabi Crown Prince Tweets', *The National*, 3 February 2014.
6   In his early years when he was Abu Dhabi's Minister of Defence, he was also the Emirate's Crown Prince (from 1969 to 2004), its Minister of Finance (from 1971), and the UAE's Deputy Prime Minister (from 1973 to 1977).

The official biography of Sheikh Khalifa characterises his attitude to the armed forces as preferring 'infrastructure to arms' and that 'big ticket military items equated … to lost roads, hospitals and schools'. However, he is also described as a pragmatist and recognised that 'an effective military [was] a deterrent to others, and one that could support the nation's foreign policy agenda was costly'. The biography goes on to state that when he started serving as the Deputy Supreme Commander of the UAE Armed Forces in 1976, he 'oversaw [that the force] operated from a defensive posture',[7] with the implication being that he was less supportive of a large, costly armed force that possessed capabilities beyond defensive ones. This was reinforced by a confidential report by the US Ambassador to the UAE in the mid-2000s which noted that some of the Ambassador's contacts in the UAE government considered that Sheikh Khalifa 'reportedly questions large expenditures on defense … [and is] skeptical of the utility of a robust defense network' because he 'feels the UAE has no prospects to 'win' a military engagement with the big regional (let alone the larger international) players'.[8] This may explain his emphasis on building personal and strategic relationships with key allies as reflected in such actions as personally informing US President Bill Clinton in the White House in 1998 that the UAE had decided to purchase 80 F-16 fighter-bombers.[9]

Sheikh Sultan bin Zayed bin Sultan Al Nahyan

Sheikh Sultan bin Zayed (b. 1955, d. 2020) is the second son of Sheikh Zayed. He attended Sandhurst in 1973, and his subsequent military training included a Platoon Commander's course, a field intelligence course in Pakistan, and a Company Commander's course in Egypt around 1975.[10] He was appointed Deputy Commander-in-Chief of the ADDF around 1973, and following the formation of the UAE Armed Forces in 1976, became Commander of the Western Military Command, one of the three regional commands. His rank was then Colonel. In early 1978 when the UAE Armed Forces were restructured, he was promoted to Brigadier at the age of 23, and became the forces' Commander-in-Chief.[11] This was a new position which he filled until 1982.[12] While he subsequently held a number of UAE government positions including Deputy Prime Minister (1997-2009), he never again assumed any military ones.

---

7   Wilson, *Khalifa: Journey Into the Future*, pp. 187-88.
8   Wikileaks, Sison, [untitled cable Abu Dhabi 00003851 001.2 of 006], 2 October 2006.
9   Wilson, *Khalifa: Journey Into the Future*, p. 213.
10   TNA FCO 8/2660: D.J. McCarthy, UK Ambassador to Sir Anthony Parsons, UK Ambassador to Tehran, 'The Shah's Worries over the UAE', 5 April 1976.
11   Al Abed, Vine, and Al Jabali, *Chronicle of Progress*, p. 126.
12   The was partly because of a personal scandal. H.R. Sindelar and J.E. Peterson, *Crosscurrents in the Gulf: Arab Regional and Global Interests* (London, 1988), p. 204.

Sheikh Mohammed bin Zayed bin Sultan Al Nahyan

Sheikh Mohammed bin Zayed (b. 1960) is the third son of Sheikh Zayed. He graduated from Sandhurst in 1979, and received further training in armoured warfare, piloting helicopters and in the paratroops. In 1979, he attended an Officers' Training Course in Sharjah. During the 1980s, he served primarily in the Air Force. In 1981, at the rank of captain, he became OC Helicopter Squadron.[13] By late 1985, he had become a Major and Commander of the Air School (which later became the Khalifa bin Zayed Air College) and in June 1986 was promoted to Colonel and appointed Commander of the Air Force. On 29 May 1990, he was promoted to Lieutenant-General and appointed Deputy Chief of Staff. In December 1992 at the age of 32, he was appointed Chief of Staff,[14] a post he held until his father's death in November 2004. In December 2003, Sheikh Mohammed became the Deputy Crown Prince of Abu Dhabi, thus confirming his precedence over Sheikh Zayed's second son, Sheikh Sultan, and preventing any potential inter-family dispute. Following his father's death, Sheikh Mohammed became Crown Prince of Abu Dhabi, and was appointed Deputy Supreme Commander of the UAE Armed Forces by his brother, President Sheikh Khalifa.

Sheikh Mohammed is viewed as engaged, influential and central to the modernisation of the UAE Air Force and Air Defence in the second-half of the 1980s, and the entire UAE Armed Forces after 1991. Writing in 1997, the Director of the Political and Military Affairs Section at the US Embassy in Abu Dhabi reported that Sheikh Mohammed had become known for his 'energetic pursuit of large-scale improvements in the UAE military, [and] is the key decision-maker in the multi-billion dollar UAE Armed Forces procurement and modernisation programme which began after Iraqi forces were expelled from Kuwait in March 1991'.[15] A 2000 Congressional Research Service report stated that Sheikh Mohammed is a 'pivotal figure on all major UAE arms purchase and defense cooperation decisions'.[16] Additionally, the UAE researcher Kristian Ulrichsen wrote in 2016 that Sheikh Mohammed had 'developed early on a reputation as an arch modernizer and highly capable administrator'. Examples given to support this assessment were his leadership in creating the defence offset programme designed to facilitate UAE armed forces industrial development, and deepening the security partnerships with key Western countries, notably the US, the United Kingdom and France.[17]

---

13   TNA, FCO 8/4385, Cameron, 'Annual Report for 1981 on the United Arab Emirates Armed Forces', 31 January 1982.
14   *UAE Federal Decree No. 83 of 1992* (1992).
15   van der Meulen, 'The Role of Tribal and Kinship Ties in the Politics of the United Arab Emirates', p. 122.
16   Katzman, *United Arab Emirates: U.S. Relations and F-16 Aircraft Sale*, p. 1.
17   Ulrichsen, *The United Arab Emirates: Power, Politics and Policy-Making*, p. 145.

Even though the only Federal title he holds is Deputy Supreme Commander of the Armed Forces, Sheikh Mohammed has long been recognised as the UAE's most influential security policy maker.[18] This recognition is seen in a leaked briefing note from the US Ambassador in the UAE to the US President which stated that 'in fact he is the key decision maker on national security issues … we assess that he has authority in all matters except for final decisions on oil policy and major state expenditures'.[19]

Sheikh Mohammed bin Rashid bin Saeed Al Maktoum

Sheikh Mohammed bin Rashid Al Maktoum (b. 1949) is the third son of Sheikh Rashid. Sheikh Mohammed passed out from Mons Officer Cadet School in 1969, receiving the sword of honour as the top Commonwealth student. He subsequently trained as a pilot in Italy.

In November 1968, he was appointed head of Dubai's Police and Public Security.[20] In this role, he worked closely with the Dubai Police Commandant, Jack Briggs, to plan and oversee the development of his father's armed force – the Dubai Defence Force (DDF). Upon the formation of the UAE in late 1971, in addition to his Dubai security position, he was appointed the Federal Minister of Defence. These positions gave him effective command of both the fully functioning Union Defence Force and the nascent Dubai Defence Force. He was actively involved in both strategic and operational decisions with these forces. Despite remaining the Federal Minister of Defence following the 1976 unification of the UAE's armed forces, his involvement with the UAE Armed Forces from then until the present has been limited, which is a product of both legislation governing the armed forces and convention as described in Chapter 3.

In January 1995, Sheikh Mohammed bin Rashid was appointed Crown Prince of Dubai by his elder brother, Sheikh Maktoum bin Rashid Al Maktoum, Ruler of Dubai (r. 1990 to 2006). Following Sheikh Maktoum's death in 2006, Sheikh Mohammed became Dubai's new Ruler, and immediately afterwards, he became the UAE's Vice President and Prime Minister.

18   Yates, 'Challenging the accepted understanding of the executive branch of the UAE's Federal Government'.
19   Wikileaks, Richard Olson, US Ambassador to the UAE, 'Mohammed bin Zayed', 31 August 2009.
20   O'Sullivan, *The New Gulf*, 279. P. Gupte, *Dubai: The Making of a Megapolis* (New Delhi, 2011), pp. 128, 132.

Appendix II

General Headquarters Structure

The structure of the General Headquarters of all commands of the Emirati armed forces has essentially reflected the structure of the British/Commonwealth army before the 1980s. While there appears to have been a recent shift to introducing the continental staff system in some commands,[1] this appears to have not yet occurred across the UAE Armed Forces.

The pre-1980s British/Commonwealth army structure has a Chief of Staff (CoS) at its apex. The CoS is supported by several Deputy/Assistant Chiefs of Staff. The typical General Staff structure has three-branches: General (G) Branch responsible for planning and directing operations, intelligence and training; Administration (A) Branch[2] responsible for personnel management; and Quartermaster (Q) Branch responsible for logistics and equipment support.

The influence of the British/Commonwealth armed forces structure can be seen across the history of the UAE Armed Forces structure. The 1977 structure as seen Figure 24[3] depicts that the professional head was the CoS and it had three Assistant Chiefs of Staff who headed up the three branches – Operations (i.e. G Branch), Administration Department, and Supply Department. The structure today, as seen in Figure 23, continues these arrangements. Specifically, at the core of GHQ today remains the three branches, now known as: Operations Authority, Administration and Manpower, and Supply Department. The more senior branch is Operations Authority and historically, the titles of its head were the Deputy Chief of Staff or Chief of Staff (Operations). The other branches were headed by Assistant Chiefs of Staff.

---

1   The continental staff numbering system is: 0 for command, 1 for personnel, 2 for intelligence, 3 for operations, 4 for logistics, 5 for planning, 6 for communications and information systems, 7 for individual training, 8 for finance, and 9 civil-military.
2   Originally, this was named the Adjutant General's Branch.
3   TNA FCO 8/3105: Bromage: 'Annual Report on the UAE Armed Forces for 1977', 2 February 1978.

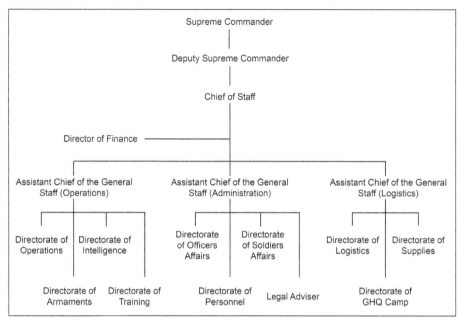

Figure 24: General Headquarters staff structure of the UAE Armed Forces, 1977.

Appendix III

Rank Structure

Since the first Emirati armed force was established in 1965 to the present, all armed forces and their land, sea and air forces have used the British Army's rank structure with only a few exceptions.[1] Table 19 lists the current UAE military rank structure in addition to its British/US equivalents for reference. While the TOL/TOS also used British Army ranks, the Arabic terms for them were slightly different from the terms used in Emirati forces. The TOL/TOS ranks and their Arabic equivalent were Commandant (*Qa'id*), Lieutenant-Colonel (*Qaimaqam*), Major (*Muqaddam*), Captain (*Rais*), Lieutenant (*Mulazim*), 2nd Lieutenant (*Mulazim thani*), Warrant Officer Class I (*Wakil Al qwa*), Warrant Officer Class II (*Wakil Al sarie*), Staff-sergeant (*Naqeeb*), Sergeant (*Shawish*), Corporal (*Areef*), Lance-corporal (*Jundi awal*) and Private (*Jundi*).[2]

While the prefix of 'Staff' is carried by Emirati officers who have graduated from a Staff College, this convention is not used in this book for simplicity. Staff College graduates wear a red tab on their rank epaulettes.

1   In the early years of the ADDF's Air Wing and Sea Wing, these forces used the British ranks of their respective Service.
2   Clayton, *Two Alpha Lima*, p. 188.

Table 19: Rank structure of the UAE Armed Forces and its British/US equivalents

UAE Rank	Arabic	Transliterated Arabic	British Army	Royal Navy	Royal Air Force	US Army
Field-Marshal[a]	المشير أو المشير	almushir 'aw almarshal	Field-Marshal	Admiral of the Fleet	Marshal of the Royal Air Force	General of the Army
General[a]	فريق أول	feriq awwal	General	Admiral	Air Chief Marshal	General
Lieutenant-General	فريق	feriq	Lieutenant-General	Vice-Admiral	Air Marshal	Lieutenant-General
Major-General	لواء	liwa	Major-General	Rear-Admiral	Air Vice Marshal	Major-General
Brigadier-General	عميد	amid	Brigadier	Commodore	Air Commodore	Brigadier-General
Colonel	عقيد	aqid	Colonel	Captain	Group Captain	Colonel
Lieutenant-Colonel	مقدم	muqaddam	Lieutenant-Colonel	Commander	Wing Commander	Lieutenant-Colonel
Major	رائد	raid	Major	Lieutenant-Commander	Squadron Leader	Major
Captain	نقيب	naqib	Captain	Lieutenant	Flight Lieutenant	Captain
1st Lieutenant	ملازم أول	mulazim awwal	Lieutenant	Sub-Lieutenant	Flying Officer	1st Lieutenant
Lieutenant	ملازم	mulazim	2nd Lieutenant	Midshipman	Pilot Officer	2nd Lieutenant
Warrant Officer Class I	وكيل أول	wakeel awwal	Warrant Officer Class I	Warrant Officer 1	Warrant Officer	Command Sergeant Major or Sergeant Major
Warrant Officer Class II	وكيل	wakeel	Warrant Officer Class II	N/A	N/A	1st Sergeant or Sergeant Major
Staff-Sergeant	رقيب أول	raqib awwal	Staff-Sergeant	Chief Petty Officer	Flight Sergeant	Sergeant 1st Class
Sergeant	رقيب	raqib	Sergeant	Petty Officer	Sergeant	Master Sergeant/ Staff-Sergeant/Sergeant
Corporal 1st class	عريف أول	areef awwal	N/A	N/A	N/A	N/A
Corporal	عريف	areef	Corporal	Leading Rate	Corporal	Corporal
Lance-Corporal	جندي أول	jundi awwal	Lance-Corporal	na	Senior Aircraftman or Leading Aircraftman	Private 1st Class
Private	جندي	jundi	Private	Able Seaman or Marine	Airman	Private

Note

a.   This rank appears to never have been held in any Emirati forces.

Appendix IV

Emirati Armed Forces Nomenclature

Emirati forces have generally used the British Army nomenclature for when referring to their formations and units. The tables 18 to 20 list the names historically used by Emirati land, air and sea forces.[1]

Formation and unit names are generally used for administrative, training, and ceremonial purposes. During operations by Emirati armed forces, elements of multiple formations/units are normally combined into a taskforce structure. Terminologically, taskforce nomenclature from the smallest to largest is *elements*, *groups* and *taskforces*, although these are not applied consistently.

Table 20: Nomenclature of Emirati land forces

Formations/units	Commanded by	Personnel	Made up of
Division	Major-General	10,000 to 20,000	2 or more brigades, and supporting elements
Brigade	Brigadier or Colonel	3,000 to 5,000	2 to 6 battalions, and supporting elements
Battalion or regiment	Lieutenant-Colonel	300 to 800	2 to 6 companies/squadrons
Company or squadron	Major or Captain	80 to 250	3 to 5 platoons/troops
Platoon or troop	Lieutenant	30 to 40	3 sections
Section	Non-Commissioned Officer	8 to 11	3 teams

---

1   Formations and units can carry names as well as numbers. For example, 4th Brigade is Al Dhafra Brigade, and in its early history, consisted of three battalions – Zayed bin Khalifa 1st Battalion, Sultan bin Zayed 2nd Battalion and Hazza bin Zayed 3rd Battalion.

Table 21: Nomenclature of Emirati air forces

Formations/units	Commanded by	Made up of
Group	Major-General or Brigadier	Entire airforce
Wing	Colonel or Lieutenant-Colonel	2 to 4 squadrons
Squadron	Lieutenant-Colonel, Major or Captain	15 to 20 aircraft
Flight	Captain	3 to 6 aircraft

Table 22: Nomenclature of Emirati naval forces

Formations/units	Commanded by	Made up of
Flotilla	Colonel or Brigadier	Several squadrons
Squadron[a]	Major or Lieutenant-Colonel	3 to 10 ships, or 2 or more divisions
Division	Captain	Up to 3 ships

Note
a. Naval squadrons can also be made up of non-ship assets, such as clearance diving teams and naval helicopters.

Appendix V

Emirates Armed Forces Leaders (1951-76)

Table 23 lists the names of the political and professional heads of the armed forces of the Emirates from 1951-76.

Table 23: Leaders of the armed forces of the Emirates, 1951-76

Force (formation and disestablishment dates)	Political head[a]	Professional military head (i.e. force commander)[a]
Trucial Oman Levies 1951-56 / Trucial Oman Scouts 1956-71	**Bahrain** Political Resident Gulf 1946-53: W.R. (William) Rupert Hay 1953-58: B.A.B. (Bernard) Burrows 1958-61: G.H. (George) Middleton 1961-66: W.H.T. (William) Luce 1966-70: R.S. (Robert) Crawford 1970-71: G. (Geoffrey) Arthur Delegated to: Political Officer Sharjah 1949-51: P.D. (Patrick) Stobart 1951-52: A.J. (John) Wilton 1952-53: M.S. (Michael) Weir 1952: M.S. (Martin) Buckmaster (attached) **Dubai** Political Agent in Dubai 1953: M.S. (Michael) Weir[1] 1954-55: C.M. (Christopher) Pirie-Gordon 1954-55: J. (Julian) Walker temporarily attached 1955-58: J.P. (John) Tripp 1958-59: D.F. (Donald) Hawley	**Commandant/Commander TOL/ TOS** 1951-53: Major J.M. (Michael) Hankin-Turvin[b] 1953-54: Lieutenant-Colonel W.J. (William) Martin[c] 1954-57: Colonel E.F. Johnston[c] 1957-61: Colonel S.L.A. (Stewart) Carter[c] 1961-64: Colonel H.J. (Bart) Bartholome[c] 1964-67: Colonel F.M. (Freddie) de Butts[c] 1967-70: Colonel K.P.G. (Pat) Ive[c] 1970-71: Colonel H.E.R. (Roy) Watson[c]

1   Post raised to the status of a Political Agency on 20 May 1953.

Force (formation and disestablishment dates)	Political head[a]	Professional military head (i.e. force commander)[a]
	1959-61: E.R. (Edric) Worsnop (acting) 1961-64: A.J.M. (Alfred) Craig 1964-66: H.G. (Glencairn) Balfour-Paul 1966-68: D.A. (David) Roberts 1968-70: J.L. (Julian) Bullard 1970-71: J.F. (Julian) Walker Assistant Political Agent: 1953-54: M.S. Weir 1954-56: J. (Julian) Walker 1956-57: J.M. Edes 1957: M.R. Melhuish (acting) 1957-58: W.J. Adams 1958-60 H.B. (Hooky) Walker 1960-62: I.S. Winchester 1962-?: M.St.E. Burton 1964?-66: M.L. (Michael) Tait 1966-68: T.J. (Terence) Clark 1968-71: A.J. Coles 1971: A. Ibbott **Abu Dhabi** Political Officer in Abu Dhabi 1955-58: M.S. (Martin) Buckmaster 1958-59: E.R. (Edric) Worsnop 1959: A.R. Wood (acting) 1959-61: E.F. (Edward) Henderson 1961: O. (Oliver) Miles (acting) Political Agent in Abu Dhabi 1961-65: Colonel B.F. (Hugh) Boustead 1965: D. Slater (acting) 1965-68: A.T. (Archie) Lamb 1968-71: C.J. (James) Treadwell Assistant Political Agent: 1961-63: A.J Johnson 1963-66: D. Slater 1966-68: S.J. Nuttall 1968-70: A. Reeve 1970-71: A.F. Green	
Union Defence Force (UDF) / Federal Armed Force (FAF) 1971-76	**UAE President** Sheikh Zayed bin Sultan Al Nahyan (1971-2004) **Delegated to:** Sheikh Mohammed bin Rashid Al Maktoum as Minister of Defence (1971-present)	**Commander UDF/FAF** 1971-74: Colonel H.E.R. (Roy) Watson[c] 1974-74: Lieutenant-Colonel K. (Ken) Wilson[c, b] 1974-76: Lieutenant-Colonel R.H. (Richard) Robinson[c]

Force (formation and disestablishment dates)	Political head[a]	Professional military head (i.e. force commander)[a]
Abu Dhabi Defence Force (ADDF) 1965-76	**Abu Dhabi Ruler before August 1966** Sheikh Shakhbut bin Sultan Al Nahyan, Ruler of Abu Dhabi (r. 1928-66) **Delegated to:** Sheikh Sultan bin Shakhbut Al Nahyan as Abu Dhabi Chairman of the Department Defence/Assistant to the Commander (1965-66) **Abu Dhabi Ruler after August 1966** Sheikh Zayed bin Sultan Al Nahyan, Ruler of Abu Dhabi (r. 1966-2001) **Delegated to:** Sheikh Khalifa bin Zayed Al Nahyan as Abu Dhabi Minister of Defence (1969-73), and as ADDF Commander-in-Chief (1974-76)	**Commander ADDF** 1965-69: Colonel E.B. (Tug) Wilson[c] 1969-71: Colonel J.T. (John) Paley[c] 1971-73: Brigadier J.R.D. (Jake) Sharpe[c] 1973: Colonel P. (Peter) MacDonald[b] **Chief of Staff ADDF** 1970-73: Lieutenant-Colonel J.D. (Tim) Wellings[c] 1973-?: Brigadier Sheikh Faisal bin Sultan Al Qasimi[d] **Commander[g]/CoS ADDF Land Forces** 1973-75: Lieutenant-Colonel I.D.B. (Ian) Mennell (CoS)[c] 1973-76: Brigadier R.J. (Ronald) Pope (Commander)[c, h] **Commander ADDF Air Wing/Air Force** 1969-72: Lieutenant-Colonel G.J. (Twinkle) Storey[b] 1972-74?: Colonel M. Sadruddin[e] **Commander ADDF Sea Wing/ Navy** 1968-72: Lieutenant-Colonel G.St.G. (Giles) Poole[b] 1972-75: Lieutenant-Colonel E.E. (Peter) Pain[b] 1975-83: Brigadier Mohammed Nabil Madhwar[f] **Commander ADDF Emiri Guard** 1968-?: Colonel C.W. (Charles) Wontner[c] 1970s?: Lieutenant-Colonel Obeid Rashid Al Arti[d]
Ras Al Khaimah Mobile Force (RAKMF) 1968-76	**Ras Al Khaimah Ruler** Sheikh Saqr bin Mohammed Al Qasimi (r. 1948-2010)	1969-72: Lieutenant-Colonel D. (David) Neild[b] 1972: Major Mifta bin Abdulla Al Khatiri[d] 1972-76: Sheikh Sultan bin Saqr Al Qassami[d]
Dubai Defence Force (DDF) 1971-76	**Dubai Ruler** Sheikh Rashid bin Saeed Al Maktoum (r. 1958-90) **Delegated to:** Sheikh Mohammed bin Rashid Al Maktoum as Head of Police and Public Security	1970-72: Major K. (Keith) Steel[c] 1972-74: Lieutenant-Colonel A.B. (Tony) Wallerstein[c] 1974-76: Colonel M.L. (Michael) Barclay[c] 1976-?: Lt Col G.F.B. (Guy) Temple (acting) 1976-?: Colonel Sheikh Ahmed bin Rashid Al Maktoum[d]

Force (formation and disestablishment dates)	Political head[a]	Professional military head (i.e. force commander)[a]
Sharjah National Guard (SNG) 1972-76	**Sharjah Ruler** Dr Sheikh Sultan bin Mohammed Al Qasimi (r. 1972-present)	1972-73: Lieutenant-Colonel D. (David) Neild[c] 1973-76: Sheikh Abdul Aziz bin Mohammad Al Qasimi[d]
Umm Al Quwain National Guard (UAQNG) 1975-2006	**Umm Al Quwain Ruler** Sheikh Ahmed bin Rashid Al Mualla (r. 1928-81) Delegated to: Colonel Sheikh Saud bin Rashid Al Mualla	Unknown

Notes

a. The listed rank is that held by the person the end of their service filling the specified post.
b. Contract British officer.
c. Serving or seconded British officer.[2]
d. Emirati officer.
e. Seconded Pakistani officer.
f. Seconded Egyptian officer.
g. The position title in 1973 was technically the ADDF Land Forces Commander as the post of Commander ADDF was eliminated and replaced by four Commanders, each in charge of either the Land Forces, Air Force, Navy and Emiri Guard. However, in practice, the term Commander ADDF continued to be used until the unification of the Emirati armed forces in 1976.
h. Brigadier Pope was killed in an aircraft crash in April 1976, and the position remained vacant until the unification of Emirati armed forces in 1976.
i. The operational head of the Ministry of Defence from January 1972 to April 1973 was Brigadier F.M. de Butts as Chief of Staff. He had direct oversight of the UDF.

2   The presence of British seconded officers both before and after 1971 is explained in Yates, 'The Use of British Seconded and Contracted Military Personnel to Advance Britain's Interests: A Case Study from the United Arab Emirates from 1965-2010'.

Appendix VI

Leaders of the UAE Armed Forces (1976-2020)

Table 24 lists the names of the political and professional military heads of the UAE Armed Forces from 1976 to 2018.

Table 24: Leaders of the UAE Armed Forces, 1976-2020

Command	Commander[a]
Political leadership	**Supreme Commander** 1976-2004: Sheikh Zayed bin Sultan Al Nahyan 2004-present: Sheikh Khalifa bin Zayed Al Nahyan **Deputy Supreme Commander** 1976-2004: Lieutenant-General Sheikh Khalifa bin Zayed Al Nahyan 2004-present: Lieutenant-General Sheikh Mohammed bin Zayed Al Nahyan[b] **Minister of Defence** 1971-present: Sheikh Mohammed bin Rashid Al Maktoum[b] **Minister of State for Defence Affairs** 2016-present: Mohammed Ahmad Al Bawardi Al Falasi **Commander-in-Chief** 1978-82: Brigadier Sheikh Sultan bin Zayed Al Nahyan[b]
GHQ Command (est. 1976)	**Chief of Staff** 1976-80: Major-General Awadh Mohammed Al Khalidi[c] 1980-81: Brigadier Aqueed Mohammed Said[b] 1981-82: vacant 1982-92: Brigadier Dr Mohammed Saeed Al Badi[b] 1992-2004: Lieutenant-General Sheikh Mohammed bin Zayed Al Nahyan[b] 2004-present: Lieutenant-General Hamad Mohammed Thani Al Rumaithi[b]
Land Forces Command (est. 1989)	**Commander Land Forces** 1994-96: Major-General Saif Sultan Mubarak Al Aryani[b] Early-2000s: Major-General Butti Sultan Mubarak Al Aryani[b] Mid-2000s: Major-General Saeed Mohammed Khalaf Al Rumaithi[b] Late-2000s: Major-General Ali Mohammed Subaih Al Ka'abi[b] 2008-11: Major-General Mubarak Salem Al Rida Al Mazrouei[b] 2011-14: Major-General Juma Ahmed Al Bawardi Al Falasi[b] 2014-present: Major-General Saleh Mohamed bin Saleh Al Ameri[b]

Command	Commander[a]
Air Force and Air Defence Command (est. 1987)	**Commander Air Force / Air Force and Air Defence Command** ?-1986: Colonel Abdullah Abd-ul-Jalin[f] 1986-90: Colonel Sheikh Mohammed bin Zayed Al Nahyan[b] 1990-2006: Major-General Khaled Abdullah Mubarak Al Buainain Al Mazroue[b] 2006-14: Major-General Mohamed Suwaidan Saeed Al Qamzi[b] 2014-present: Major-General Ibrahim Nasser Al Alawi[b]
Navy Command (est. 1985)	**Commander Navy** 1983-87: Brigadier Hamad Hilal Thabit Al Kuwaiti[b] 1987-93: Brigadier Haza Sultan Al Darmaki[b] 1993-96: Brigadier Muhamamd Khalfan Mohammed Al Muhairy[b] 1996-2006: Brigadier Suhail Mohammed Khalifa Shaheen Al Murar[b] 2006-07: Major-General Mohammed Mahmood Ahmed Al Madani[b] 2007-10: Major-General Ahmed Al Sabab Al Teneiji[b] 2010-17: Major-General Ibrahim Salim Mohammad Al Musharrakh[b] 2017-present: Major-General Pilot Sheikh Saeed bin Hamdan bin Mohammed Al Nahyan[b]
Central Military District Command (est. 1976, fully integrated 1997)	**Commander Central Military Command** 1976-90s: Brigadier Sheikh Ahmed bin Rashid Al Maktoum[b]
Emiri Guard Command (est 1992)	**Commander Emiri Guard** ?: Khalfan Matar Al Rumaithi[b] Late 1990s-2004: Brigadier Sheikh Nasser bin Zayed Al Nahyan[b] Mid-2000s: Abdullah Saeed Khalifa Al Musafri[b] Mid-2000s: Brigadier Salem Al Hameli[b] 2008-11: Brigadier Salem Helal Suroor Al Kaabi[b]
Special Operations Command (est 1984	**Special Operations Group/Command** Late 1970s-1980s: Lieutenant-Colonel Saif Obeid Saif, OC Tariq ibn Ziyad Commando Group[b] 1980s-98: Lieutenant-Colonel Juma Ahmed Al Bawardi Al Falasi, OC Special Operations Group[b] 1998-2011: Major-General Juma Ahmed Al Bawardi Al Falasi, Commander Special Operations Command[b]
Presidential Guard Command (est 2011)	**Commander Presidential Guard** 2011-present: Major-General M. (Mike) Hindmarsh[d]
Joint Aviation Command (est. 2011)	**Commander Joint Aviation Command** 2011-present: Major-General S.A. (Steve) Toumajan[e]
Critical National Infrastructure Authority (est. 2007)/ Critical Infrastructure and Coastal Protection Authority (est. 2012)	**Chairman CNIA/CICPA** 2007-10: Brigadier Sheikh Ahmed bin Tahnoun bin Mohammed Al Nahyan[b] 2010-19: Major-General Faris Khalaf Khalfan Al Mazrouei[b] 2019-present: Major-General Ali Mohamed Musleh Al Ahbabi[b] **Director General CNIA/CICPA** 2007-late 2000s: Brigadier Muhair Ali Al Khateri[b] Early 2010s-16: Brigadier Abdullah Saeed Mubarak Al Shamsi[b] 2016-present: Major-General Abdullah Mohammed Al Neyadi[b]
National Service and Reserve Authority (est. 2014)	**Chairman** 2014-present: Major-General Sheikh Ahmed bin Tahnoun bin Mohammed Al Nahyan[b]

Notes
a.   The listed rank is that held by the person the end of their service filling the specified post.
b.   Emirati officer.
c.   Jordanian seconded officer.
d.   Dual Australian/Emirati contract officer.
e.   Dual American/Emirati contract officer.
f.   Pakistani seconded officer.

Appendix VII

Foreign Deployments of Emirati Armed Forces

Table 25 lists the main foreign deployments of Emirati armed forces. It does not include teams deployed for the training of foreign forces, to assist allied forces, and to undertake de-mining operations, nor does the list contain deployments unconfirmed by the UAE.

Table 25: Foreign deployments of Emirati armed forces

Date	Country	Purpose	Descriptiona
1973-1975	Oman	Peace keeping	An ADDF infantry squadron was based in Sohar, Oman, from October 1973 to January 1974, and from November 1974 to April 1975. Its role was to relieve the Oman Gendarmerie unit in Sohar so it could deploy to the Dohar province in order to combat rebel activity.
1976-1979	Lebanon	Peace keeping	The UAE Armed Forces participated in the Arab League's peace keeping mission known as the Arab Deterrent Force. Five UAE contingents were deployed over the 1976 to 1979 period in the Bikaa Valley, Lebanon. The deployment generally consisted of a 700-man battle group made up of two infantry companies, one armoured company, fire support units, a field hospital, and administrative support. Three UAE Armed Forces personnel were killed in action, and eight injured.
1990-1991	Kuwait	Protection & combat operations	The UAE Armed Forces participated in both phases of the 1990-91 Gulf War – Operation Desert Shield (2 August 1990-17 January 1991) which involved the defence of Saudi Arabia and build-up of forces, and Operation Desert Storm (17 January 1991-28 February 1991) which involved combat operations to evict Iraqi forces from Kuwait. During Operation Desert Shield, land forces elements consisting of the 2nd (infantry) Battalion of the Ras Al Khaimah-based Second Badir Brigade were based in Hafr Al Batin, Saudi Arabia.

Date	Country	Purpose	Descriptiona
			During Operation Desert Storm, the land forces involved were the 3rd (infantry) Battalion of Second Badir Brigade; a mechanised infantry company and support company from the Dubai-based Central Military Command; as well as Abu Dhabi-based elements consisting of an AMX-30 tank company from Fifth Khalid bin Al Waleed Armoured Brigade, 105mm artillery company, and platoons from field engineering, air defence, chemical warfare, signals, transport medical and maintenance. They were deployed and advanced from the Ras Mishab area of Saudi Arabia. UAE Air Force's warplanes undertook 173 sorties over occupied Kuwait. Ten UAE Armed Forces personnel were killed in action and 15 wounded.
1993-1994	Somalia	Security & humanitarian assistance	From January 1993 to April 1994, the UAE Armed Forces participated in humanitarian operations in Somalia. UAE land forces supplied four rotations over this period. The UAE operated under the Unified Task Force (UNITAF) US-led, UN-sanctioned multinational force which ran from December 1992 until May 1993 (the activity was known as Operation Restore Hope). During this phase, the UAE supplied a 640-man group, starting in January 1993, known as the Al Wajeb Battalion, which consisted of three mechanised infantry and two light infantry companies. It was under the operational control of the 3rd Battalion, 11th Marine Regiment.[1] The UAE also operated under the UN Operation in Somalia II (UNOSOM II) which ran from March 1993 until March 1995. The UAE participated in this until April 1994. The deployed forces included two mechanised infantry companies, one reconnaissance company, one 81mm mortar platoon, one field engineering platoon and a field hospital. The force was equipped with Panhard M3 armoured personnel carriers. Aviation assets used included Puma SA330C/F helicopters. Three UAE Armed Forces personnel were killed in action.
1999-2001	Kosovo & Albania	Peace keeping & protection	The UAE Armed Forces participated in two missions in the Balkans over the 1991-2001 period. Almost 1,500 Emirati troops served in the two missions. The first mission was as part of the NATO-led international peacekeeping force known as the Kosovo Force (KFOR). The UAE participated in this mission from 29 July 1999 to late 2001, and during this time, the deployment involved six combat groups and five logistics unit contingents. The combat group which operated in the French zone consisted of the following land forces elements; a BMP-equipped mechanised

1   The UAE supplied a 640-man group from 11 January 1993 – 13 April 1993 known as the Al Wajeb Battalion. The name, meaning obligation, was chosen to reflect that the UAE had long held close ties with Somalia and an obligation to assist the nation. Author's collection, Abu Dhabi, Dawson files, Dawson, 'With Marine Forces Somalia, Appendix E', 1993.

Date	Country	Purpose	Description[a]
			infantry company, a Leclerc-equipped tank company, a light reconnaissance company, a 155mm artillery battery, a field hospital in addition to platoons of field engineering, air defence, chemical warfare, signal and maintenance. A UAE special operations company and a company of Apache helicopters (known as the 'Emirates Falcons') operated in the southern American sector. The second mission was Operation White Hands, which was a humanitarian mission at Kukes, Albania. Operations started on 10 April 1999 and ended on 29 July 1999. The UAE deployed a safeguarding and protection detachment which consisted of a special operations platoon, reconnaissance platoon, military police platoon, field engineering group, signals group, a military works group; a chemical warfare group; an air detachment; a field hospital; and support elements, including stores, transport and maintenance elements.
2002	Kuwait	Protection	The UAE Armed Forces deployed a mechanised brigade group to Kuwait from 9 February to 15 February 2002 to deter Iraq from hostilities against Kuwait. The mission was named Operation Steadfastness. The deployed force elements consisted of mechanised regiments, a field engineering company, a reconnaissance element, a supply element and an air detachment of Apache helicopters. The deployment was supported by a naval element consisting of a frigate and supply ships.
2003-2012	Afghanistan	Combat operations, reconstruction & humanitarian assistance	The UAE participated in the NATO-led International Security Assistance Force (ISAF) mission (2001 to 2014). In 2018, the UAE committed to contribute to the follow-on mission of ISAF; the NATO-led Operation Resolute Support (2015-). Multiple contingents of UAE Armed Forces personnel have been involved in both. UAE personnel have undertaken combat operations, train/advise/assist missions, reconstruction, and humanitarian work. Special Operations Command has deployed elements since 2003.[2] Land Forces and the Air Force have also deployed elements. For example, the latter deployed six F-16s between 2012 and 2014.[3] Another contribution made starting in mid-2018, was that the UAE Armed Forces started training recruits enlisted by the Afghan elite forces and UAE personnel have accompanied them on operations.[4]

2   Alex Gardiner, 'On the Frontline with UAE Forces in Helmand', *The National*, 22 July 2011.
3   Chandrasekaran, 'In the UAE, the United States Has a Quiet, Potent Ally Nicknamed "Little Sparta"'.
4   'UAE to Boost Troop Presence in Afghanistan for Training: Officials', *Reuters*, 8 June 2018.

Date	Country	Purpose	Descriptiona
2011-	Libya	Combat operations	The UAE Air Force participated in NATO's Operation Unified Protector from February to October 2011. Six F-16s and six Mirage 2000s were deployed.[5] The UAE's involvement in the Second Libyan Civil War (2014-present) has not been disclosed.
2014	Syria	Combat operations	The UAE was part of the Combined Joint Task Force – Operation Inherent Resolve (CJTF-OIR). The UAE Air Force's F-16s, from its deployed base in Jordan, attacked ISIS targets in Syria as part of a multinational coalition.
2015-	Yemen	Combat operations	See Chapter 10: Conclusion.

Note

The source was *The UAE Armed Forces History and Missions* unless otherwise stated.[6]

---

5   K Shaheen, 'UAE Fighter Jets on the Way to Libya', *The National*, 26 March 2011.
6   UAE Armed Forces, *The UAE Armed Forces History and Missions*.

Appendix VIII

British Armed Forces Policy and Military Command in the Trucial States (1951-71)

The policy and military command of all British armed forces was a shared responsibility between the British foreign affairs and military establishments. How this means of control was organised is depicted in Figure 25. It shows two distinct chains of command, with coordination within the Gulf carried out via joint committees. There were obviously additional means of coordination above the Gulf level, but these are not referred to here as they are not particularly relevant for the military history of the Emirates. Taken together, these political and security structures enabled Britain to exercise control over what officials at the time saw was an important part of their 'informal Empire'.[1]

Notes to Figure 25

a. The official titles were: (1) Secretary of State for Foreign Affairs (1782–1968), (2) Secretary of State for Foreign and Commonwealth Affairs (1968-2020).
b. The official titles were: (1) Foreign Office (1948-66), (2) Foreign and Commonwealth Office (FCO) (1968-2020).
c. Since the 1800s, the Residency had a representation in Sharjah provided by an Arab/Persian Muslim Agent (1823-1949). From 1939-47 during the winter months, the head of the representation was a British Officer. After 1947, its head was a full-time British Officer. In May 1953, the representation was upgraded to a Political Agency.
d. The Political Agency was moved from Sharjah to Dubai in 1953. The Dubai-based Political Agent would be responsible for all the Trucial States until 1961.
e. From 1957, the post was headed by a Political Officer who reported to the Political Agent in Dubai. From 1961, the post was upgraded to a Political Agency with the post's head becoming a Political Agent who reported directly to the Political Resident.
f. Up until 1964, political command was vested in the Single Service political heads. These were the: (1) First Lord of the Admiralty (1628-1964), (2) Secretary of State for War (1854-1964), (3) Secretary of State for Air (1919-64) and (4) Minister of Defence (1940-64). In 1964, the position of Secretary of State for Defence was established. The post has become recognised as the senior political head for the British Armed Forces.

---

1   The 'informal Empire' is today a contested term. On this, see Smith, *Britain and the Arab Gulf after Empire: Kuwait, Bahrain, Qatar, and the United Arab Emirates, 1971-1981.*

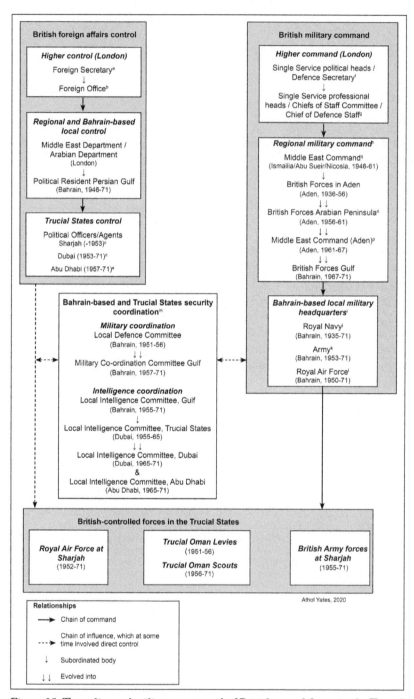

Figure 25: The policy and military command of British armed forces in the Trucial States, 1951-71.

g. The Single Service Heads were the professional heads of their respective services. They were, for the Royal Navy, the First Sea Lord and Chief of Naval Staff; for the British Army, the Chief of the Imperial General Staff, which was renamed in 1964 as the Chief of the General Staff; and for the RAF, the Chief of the Air Staff. The collective forum for operational and other military matters was the Chiefs of Staff Committee. Before 1955, there was no permanent chair for this committee with the Service Chiefs holding it in rotation. In 1955, a permanent post of Chairman of the Chiefs of Staff Committee was created and, in 1959, the post of Chief of the Defence Staff was also created, with the holder also being the chairman of the Chiefs of Staff Committee. The Chief of the Defence Staff has become recognised as the professional head of the British Armed Forces.

h. The Middle East regional command structure changed considerably over the two decades and is not covered here due to its lack of relevance.[2]

i. In 1967, with the withdrawal from Aden, all British forces in the region came under the command of the British Forces Gulf in Bahrain. It assumed command of the extant British Army, RAF and Royal Navy headquarters in Bahrain.

j. In 1935, the Royal Navy moved its headquarters and the base for its Persian Gulf Division of the East Indies Station to HMS *Jufair* in Bahrain, from Iran's Hengam Island located at near the Strait of Hormuz. The East Indies Station was a formation and command of the Royal Navy which was created in 1744: it was responsible for much of the Indian Ocean and included the Gulf and the Red Sea. Its head was the Commander-in-Chief, East Indies. The Persian Gulf Division was headed by the Senior Naval Officer Persian Gulf, based in Bahrain. In 1958, the headquarters of the East Indies Station was relocated to Bahrain, and the Senior Naval Officer Persian Gulf became an independent commander with the title Commodore, Arabian Seas and Persian Gulf. That same year, the East Indies Station was disbanded, and a new station was established with its headquarters in Bahrain – the Arabian Seas and Persian Gulf Station. This most senior Bahrain-based naval officer now carried the title of Flag Officer, Arabian Seas and Persian Gulf. In 1962, the status of the station was raised: it became Middle East Command, through the creation of the Flag Officer, Middle East. Following the British armed forces reorganisation following the Aden withdrawal, in 1967 the post was renamed Commander Naval Forces Gulf (1967-71).

k. After the end of the Second World War, the British Army was not represented in the Gulf until 1953. Following a visit of the Commander-in-Chief, Middle East Land Forces to Bahrain, a Brigadier was appointed as Military Advisor to the Political Resident. He served as the representative to the Commander-in-Chief, Middle East Land Forces in the Gulf, and as such was responsible only for British Army input. His duty was to advice the Political Resident on: (1) all Army matters; (2) the development employment of the TOL; and (3) local defence.[3] In 1952, a British Army command, Local Land Forces Persian Gulf, was established which reported to HQ Middle East Land Forces, the Brigadier who had previously been designated the Military Advisor to the Political Resident was accordingly appointed the Senior Army Officer, Persian Gulf, and concurrently Commander Local Land Forces Persian Gulf. The duties of the Commander Local Land Forces Persian Gulf were: (1) to supervise the training and administration of those land forces in the Gulf for which Britain was responsibility; (2) to coordinate the supply of equipment, instructors etc to the various police and armed forces in the small Arab Gulf States including Oman; and (3) in general, to maintain communications and cooperation in all military matters between the Political Residency, the senior officer of the Royal Navy and RAF in the Gulf, and the British Military Authorities in the Middle East. Local Land Forces Persian Gulf was relatively small, initially having an established strength of no more than four officers and 15 enlisted people.[4] Its name was changed in 1958 to Land Forces Gulf; it now reported to British Forces Arabian Peninsula (1958-61) and its successor, Middle East Command (Aden) (1961-67). After 1967, and until all British Army elements were withdrawn from the Gulf in 1971, the senior land forces officer was known as the Command British Army Gulf.

2   For details, see David Lee, *Flight from the Middle East: A History of the Royal Air Force in the Arabian Peninsula and Adjacent Territories, 1945-72* (London, 1981), pp. 25-34.

3   UK Foreign Office, *Historical Summary of Events in the Persian Gulf Shaikhdoms and the Sultanate of Muscat and Oman, 1928-1953*, PG 53, pp. 2-3, 48-9.

4   Ibid., Chapter 2: Bahrain, pp. 48-49.

l. In 1950, the post of Senior RAF Officer Persian Gulf was created, located in Bahrain. This officer was responsible to the Air Officer Commanding at Habbaniyah in Iraq for all RAF matters in the Gulf area, with the exception of airfields at Salalah and Masirah in Oman which were the responsibility of Air Officer Commanding in Aden.[5] With the closure of Habbaniya in 1956, the Senior RAF Officer Persian Gulf now reported to British Forces Aden (1956) and then to British Forces Arabian Peninsula (1956-59).

m. From 1958 to 1960, the Military Advisor held jointly the post of Commander Land Forces Gulf.

n. The position of Military Liaison Officer lapsed after 1967, with its function being undertaken by Commander British Forces Gulf.

o. British Forces Arabian Peninsula was created through splitting Middle East Command. It became fully autonomous on 1 April 1958. The new command was a separate, independent, and integrated command for the Arabian Peninsula and the Gulf, with its headquarters in Aden. The Army and RAF subordinate commanders were located together in Aden, but the Naval subordinate commander remained temporarily in Bahrain (HMS *Jufair*), subsequently moving to Aden.

p. In 1961, British Forces Arabian Peninsula was re-designated Middle East Command (Aden), with a remit which went beyond the Arabian Peninsula including down to Kenya.

q. In 1961, Middle East Command based in Cyprus was renamed Near East Command. Confusingly, at the same time, British Forces Arabian Peninsula was renamed Middle East Command (Aden).

Foreign affairs chain of command

The foreign affairs chain of command had at its apex the Foreign Secretary (i.e. the Foreign Minister), who headed the Foreign Office/Foreign and Commonwealth Office. The bureaucratic element responsible for policy in the region was the Middle East Department. It was to this department that Britain's diplomatic representative in the Gulf reported, whose title was Political Resident Persian Gulf and, after 1967, the Political Resident Gulf.[6] He was based in Bahrain and oversaw the political representatives who were posted to states around the Gulf. In terms of the Foreign Office hierarchy, subordinate posts were headed by Political Agents and, under these, were Political Officers and, before the early 1950s, Native Agents.

As of 1951, the Resident's local representative in the Trucial States was a British Political Officer. From his base in Sharjah, and supported by a handful of staff, he was responsible for all the Trucial States. The Trucial States Political Office moved to Dubai in 1953, with the post subsequently upgraded to that of a Political Agency and, hence, a Political Agent in charge. Due to the growing importance of Abu Dhabi for the British, a Political Office was established there in 1957. It was initially subordinate to Dubai and, in 1961, was upgraded to a Political Agency, with its head reporting directly to the Political Resident in Bahrain. This meant, organisationally, that from

---

5   Ibid., Chapter 2: Bahrain, pp. 47-48.

6   The Political Residency system originated at a time when British representatives resided at the courts of foreign heads. A resident was a diplomatic agent of the third class (later Consul-General), lesser in rank than an ambassador and envoy Minister. J. Onley, *The Arabian Frontier of the British Raj: Merchants, Rulers, and the British in the Nineteenth-Century Gulf* (Oxford, 2007), p. 12.

1961 the Political Agency Dubai was responsible for all of the Emirates except Abu Dhabi, with the Political Agency Abu Dhabi only responsible for that one Emirate.

The military chain of command

The military chain of command for British forces was far more complex and changed more frequently than that of the British foreign affairs establishment. The description of military command is divided into two parts – higher command and Bahrain-based local military command.

Higher command

Starting at the higher command level in London, before 1964 the political command of the British Armed Forces was not unified, rather it rested with the 'political heads' of the three military services – Royal Navy, RAF and British Army. Each of the political heads reported separately and directly to the Prime Minister; under each was a professional head.

In 1964, the political head positions were abolished and replaced by a single Defence Secretary (i.e. Defence Minister). Each of the three military services continued to have a professional head and continue to do so to the present day. In 1959, an additional post of Chief of the Defence Staff (CDS) was established and, over time, he became the professional head of the British Armed Forces, with the heads of the military services reporting to him.

The modern history of British regional military command, including the Gulf region, began at the end of the Second World War. At that time, Britain's military control of the Middle East was principally managed through Middle East Command based in Egypt. After the failed 1956 Suez intervention, British forces from the western Middle East were withdrawn from Egypt, with the command moving to the Mediterranean. From this location, it proved difficult to command British forces in the Arabian Peninsula, so the command was divided into two commands in 1961. One was Middle East Command (Aden), based in today's Yemen, with the remainder of the command based in Cyprus.[7] Middle East Command (Aden)[8] was responsible for British interests stretching from Kenya to the Arabian Gulf.[9]

---

7   This command was renamed Near East Command in 1961.
8   Middle East Command (Aden) had two subordinate, single Service formations – HQ Air Forces Middle East and HQ Land Forces Middle East. Command of British naval forces was the responsibility of Flag Officer Middle East, based in Bahrain. The Flag Officer Middle East remained there until 1963. Herrington, 'Operation Vantage – Kuwait 1961', p. 93.
9   Ibid.

Aden had long been a major military centre for the British. At the end of the Second World War, command of British forces in the Arabian Peninsula (then known as British Forces in Aden) had been a RAF responsibility; its chain of command was via HQ Middle East Air Force and Middle East Command, based in Egypt. In 1956, British Forces in Aden were renamed British Forces Arabian Peninsula.[10] In 1959, British Forces Arabian Peninsula became a unified command which meant that all three military services were controlled operationally by an inter-service headquarters in Aden. This was the first British Armed Forces' unified command established in peacetime; and this joint command model would be adopted for the British Forces Gulf command when it was established in 1967.

From the early 1960s to 1967, the British Government progressively withdrew its forces which were based in the Indian Ocean and Asia, including Aden, a policy which became known as withdrawing 'East of Suez'. An exception to this was the Arabian Gulf area. In July 1961, Britain increased its armed forces in the Gulf in response to the threat from Iraq to invade the oil-rich Kuwait. The historian Helene von Bismarck argues that this threat convinced British policy-makers of the necessity of a continuing British presence in the Gulf.[11] Furthermore, in 1967, British forces were further increased as some of the forces withdrawn from Aden were relocated to Bahrain and Sharjah.

On 28 November 1967, the Middle East Command (Aden) was disbanded as the last British forces were being evacuated from Aden. To provide command of British forces in the Arabian Gulf a new command – British Forces Gulf – was established, based in Bahrain, around September 1967. This command absorbed the pre-existing local British Army, RAF and Royal Navy headquarters in Bahrain. In January 1968, the British Government announced it would withdraw its forces 'East of Suez' which included Malaysia and Singapore, as well as from the Arabian Gulf. British forces in Sharjah, as of early 1968, consisted of 1,900 British Army personnel, and 800 RAF and RAF Regiment personnel.[12]

A description of the military developments between 1967-71, as reported by the last British Political Resident, Sir Geoffrey Arthur, is instructive as a summary of this period:

10   HQ British Forces Arabian Peninsula (BFAP) became autonomous on 1 April 1958. As BFAP was an operational HQ, not a GHQ, all non-operational work was handled by the War Office. TNA WO 32/17123: GHQ Middle East Land Forces, 'Transfer of Army Responsibilities to The War Office and Headquarters British Forces Arabian Peninsula', 5 March 1958.
11   von Bismarck, *British Policy in the Persian Gulf, 1961-1968.*
12   The Center for Strategic and International Studies, *The Gulf: Implications of British Withdrawal* (Washington DC, 1969). The main elements in Sharjah in October 1969 were one battalion of infantry, one squadron of Shackleton aircraft, and one squadron of Andover aircraft. National Archives of Australia, A1838, 181/1/15, Office of the High Commissioner for Australia in London to the Secretary Department of External Affairs, [untitled letter], 28 October 1969.

By the end of 1967, British Forces Gulf consisted of two frigates (one of which was usually away), a squadron of minesweepers, two infantry battalions and an armoured car squadron, two squadrons of Hunter fighters/ground attack aircraft, a squadron of Wessex helicopters and some transports (Argosies and Andovers) and a maritime patrol (Shackleton) aircraft. These forces, based in Bahrain and Sharjah, numbered about 7,000 men and were commanded from a joint head-quarters in Bahrain by an officer of two-star rank.

Following the decision by the British Government in January 1968 to with-draw its protection by 1971, planning started for the military evacuation. In the Gulf, the first battalion left in autumn 1970, the armoured car squadron in spring 1971, the Hunter squadron started its run down in May 1971, the minesweepers left in autumn 1971, the second battalion at the end of November, and the last transport and maritime reconnaissance aircraft and helicopters in December. By mid-December, HMS *Jufair* [Britain's main naval base in the Gulf] and the RAF Stations at Muharraq and Sharjah had closed. Headquarters British Forces Gulf ceased to function on 16 December ... HMS *Intrepid* and the last frigate, HMS *Achilles*, sailed on 19 December 1971.[13]

After the disbandment of British Forces Gulf in 1971, the control of Britain's residual military activities in the region passed to the Ministry of Defence in London.[14] The deployment of local forces would in future be exercised by the Ministry of Defence, with orders communicated directly to the in-theatre commander.

Bahrain-based local military command

The Bahrain-based local military command consisted of the commands and military headquarters in Bahrain which provided direction to British forces in the Emirates. Before 1950, the only British Service to have a permanent representative located in the Gulf was the Royal Navy. The Senior Naval Officer Persian Gulf was based in Bahrain which was the location of a British naval base. But with the establishment of the TOL in 1951, as well as the growing role for the British Army in the region and the need to provide the Political Resident with army advice, in 1952 a Military Advisor with the rank of Brigadier was appointed to the Political Resident's staff. The following year, a British Army post – the Senior Army Officer Persian Gulf (SAOPG) – was established

13   TNA FCO 8/1814: Arthur, 'The Withdrawal of British Forces from the Gulf', 2 February 1972.
14   These activities included the secondment of British personnel to the ruler-controlled and federally-controlled militaries, in addition to providing the Military Advisory Team, which operated in Sharjah from 1971 to 1975. Naval visits to the UAE would also occur, as would exercises for British Army and special forces units.

and co-located at the Political Residency in Bahrain.[15] The Brigadier, who had previously been the Military Advisor, now became the SAOPG. The SAOPG's role was to advise local land forces on training and equipment, serve as the Military Adviser to the Political Resident, and to be directly responsible for the operations of the TOL.

Following Saudi Arabia's occupation of parts of the Buraimi Oasis in August 1952, British land forces in the Trucial States expanded from just the TOL to include units of the RAF Regiment and RAF Aden Protectorate Levies. During the Buraimi Oasis operation, control over all British land forces rested with the RAF. On the day that the final RAF forces were withdrawn from the Trucial States, control and administration of all local land forces (then just the TOL) passed to the British Army's HQ Local Land Forces Persian Gulf (LLFPG). HQ LLFPG was established on the same day and headed by the SAOPG. HQ LLFPG reported to GHQ Land Forces Middle East.

Reflecting the growing army involvement in the Gulf, in 1958 the Land Forces Persian Gulf Command was established in Bahrain, replacing the LLFPG, with the post of SAOPG being replaced by Commander Land Forces Persian Gulf. The Commander would remain the immediate superior to the Commander TOS until British forces withdrew from the region. British Army presence in the region increased considerably with the establishment of a base in Bahrain in July 1961. This followed the threat by Iraq to invade Kuwait. This base would remain until the British withdrawal in 1971.

Local control over the Royal Air Force was vested initially in the Senior Royal Air Force Officer Persian Gulf, which was a post established in late 1953.[16] In 1959, HQ RAF Persian Gulf in Bahrain was established, headed by the Commander RAF Persian Gulf. This became Air Forces Gulf (1967-71), headed up by the Commander Air Forces Gulf.[17] During this time, the RAF had staging posts and bases in Sharjah, Bahrain and in Oman, at Salalah and on Masirah Island.

British military and security coordination

Coordination of Britain's military and security interests in the Gulf region was managed through a combination of the Political Resident, Agents and Officers working with their British military counterparts, Foreign Office funding of the military, and coordination committees. As already noted above, the British political representatives had considerable influence over the TOL/TOS and Gulf-based British armed forces. This was reinforced by the fact that the Foreign Office bore a significant

---

15   UK Foreign Office, *Historical Summary of Events in the Persian Gulf Shaikhdoms and the Sultanate of Muscat and Oman, 1928-1953*, PG 53, p. 150.

16   TNA FO 371/109881: Local Defence Committee (Persian Gulf), 'Directive to Senior Royal Air Force Officer Persian Gulf', 7 October 1953.

17   Warwick, *In Every Place*, p. 552; Lee, *Flight from the Middle East: A History of the Royal Air Force in the Arabian Peninsula and Adjacent Territories, 1945-72*, pp. 25-34.

part of the costs of both the HQ LFG[18] and the TOL/TOS. Two committees existed to help the political representatives coordinate political, military and security affairs – the Local Defence Committee/ Military Co-ordination Committee Gulf, and the Local Intelligence Committee.

The Local Defence Committee was formed in 1951, chaired by the British Political Resident, and its members included the senior British officers of all three armed services. Political and intelligence staff attended. The Committee met usually in the Residency in Bahrain on a regular schedule.[19] Its functions were to plan for: (1) all matters affecting the internal security of the Gulf area, whether in normal times, or in a general emergency; and (2) all those measures which in a general war emergency would primarily be the responsibility of the civil power.[20] In 1957, it was replaced by the Military Co-ordination Committee Gulf. The Military Co-ordination Committee Gulf was responsible for: (1) coordinating policy on all matters affecting the security of Kuwait, Bahrain, Qatar, the Trucial Oman States and Muscat/Oman; (2) preparing to implement general war measures in these territories; and (3) maintaining liaison on the Anglo/US defence cooperation in the area with the appropriate US service and civilian authorities.[21] The chair of it continued to be the Political Resident.

A committee structure to coordinate intelligence including political and military matters was established in 1955. The key committee was the Local Intelligence Committee Gulf (LIC Gulf) in Bahrain and reporting to it was the Local Intelligence Committee Trucial States (LIC Trucial States). In 1966, the LIC Trucial States were divided in two – LIC Abu Dhabi covering Abu Dhabi Emirate, with LIC Dubai covering all the other Emirates. The LICs supported the British political representatives in executing their responsibility by ensuring they had the best available intelligence upon which to base their decisions whether they were political, military, or commercial. The committee was invariably chaired by the senior British political representative, or his deputy, and attended by intelligence personnel, including those

18   As of 1961, the Foreign Office paid one third the cost of HQ LFPG (71,300 pounds). TNA FO 371/157038: D.W.T. Smithies, 'Requests Approval for Transfer of Army and RAF Desert and Field Intelligence Officers in Persian Gulf to TOS Establishment', 31 July 1961. The Foreign Office would continue to partly pay for the cost of HQ LFG to 1971, specifically £139,000 which was the cost of HQ LFG attributable to the TOS. TNA FCO 8/886: Working Party on the Trucial Oman Scouts, 'Report of the Working Party on the Future of the Trucial Oman Scouts', ca. June 1968.
19   Clayton, *Two Alpha Lima*, p. 3.
20   UK Foreign Office, *Historical Summary of Events in the Persian Gulf Shaikhdoms and the Sultanate of Muscat and Oman, 1928-1953*, PG 53, pp. 2-3.
21   TNA CAB 148/97: P.J. Bayne, Secretary, Chiefs of Staff Committee, to Commander British Forces Gulf, 'Directive for the Commander, British Forces Gulf', 20 March 1969.

from the military intelligence directorates of the three Service, the TOS and the Secret Intelligence Service.[22]

LICs were generally administered by a secretary who received all source intelligence for processing and distribution to LIC members, and others. LIC meetings were held weekly, with special meetings occurring where and when required. The primary role of the LIC was to advise the senior British political representative on matters of policy and organisation concerning internal and external intelligence and security intelligence. Other roles of the LIC were to oversee the operations of the local intelligence system to ensure its efficiency and focus, and define intelligence targets,[23] likewise to allocate priorities. It also prepared intelligence reports and assessments. LICs were accountable ultimately to the Joint Intelligence Committee in London.

22   For details on the LIC and British intelligence arrangements in the Trucial States, see A. Yates and A. Rossiter, 'Intelligence Collection in Arabia: Britain's Roaming Information-Gathers in the Trucial States, 1956-1971', *Intelligence and National Security*, 35, 6 (2020).

23   This control by the LIC over the TOS is seen in the 1961 *Directive* to the Commander. It states that intelligence 'priorities and specific targets will be laid down from time to time by LIC Gulf in consultation with LIC Trucial States'. TNA FO 371/156692: Military Co-ordination Committee (Persian Gulf), 'Directive to the Commander Trucial Oman Scouts', 7 October 1961.

Bibliography

I. Primary Sources – Archival

Author's Collection, Abu Dhabi
Abu Dhabi Defence Force, Intelligence Section. 'Abu Dhabi Town. Present And Expected Population to the Year 2,000', 1971.
Abu Dhabi Defence Force, 'Tribes of Abu Dhabi', 1970.
Abu Dhabi Defence Force, Records Office Force Headquarters. 'A Statistical Survey of Records Office Information Covering the Period 1 April 1968 to 31 March 1969', 1969.
Ash, Capt Tim. 'The Trucial Oman Scouts', n.d.
Dawson, D.A., CENTCOM Historian. 'With Marine Forces Somalia, Appendix E', 1993.
Helms, US Ambassador in Tehran to General Brent Scowcroft, White House. 'Paragraph 4 of WH 31209, May 16, 1973'.

British Library, London
IOR/R/15/4/3: File 0255 Boundaries, 1939-49.

Imperial War Museum, London
Documents.4105 Private Papers of Lieutenant Colonel W J Martin, 'Just a British Soldier [unpublished autobiography]', c.a. 1986.

Middle East Centre Archive, St Antony's College, Oxford
Abu Dhabi Defence Force, Induction Booklet for New British Officers with an Introduction by Col E.B. Wilson, 1968.

National Archives of Australia, Canberra
A1838, 181/1/15: Middle East – British Defence Plans for South Arabian Federation & Persian Gulf, 1966-75.

The National Archives of the United Kingdom, Kew

AIR 8/1888: Role of British Forces in Persian Gulf, 1954-56.

CAB 148/97: Defence Review Working Party: Meetings 1-2, 1969.

CAB 163/116: Intelligence organisation in the Persian Gulf: structure and intelligence gathering facilities, 1965-69.

DEFE 11/880: Persian Gulf and Arabian Peninsula: withdrawal planning; reinforcements of Bahrain and Sharjah to maintain essential services; meetings of Military Co-ordination Committee; Kuwait Liaison Team, 1969.

DEFE 68/397: United Arab Emirates: military relations with UK; Trucial Oman Scouts (TOS) / Union Defence Force (UDF); loan of UK personnel, 1971-73.

FCO 8/886: Trucial Oman Scouts: rulers should be asked to bear greater burden of cost, 1968.

FCO 8/900: Local intelligence committee reports for Abu Dhabi, 1967-68.

FCO 8/910: Assistance to police, 1968.

FCO 8/1241: Abu Dhabi Defence Force: general, 1969.

FCO 8/1245: Ras al Khaimah Defence Force, 1969.

FCO 8/1255: Intelligence reports, 1969.

FCO 8/1779: Conditions of service in Trucial Oman Scouts, 1971.

FCO 8/1925: Assassination of Shaikh Khalid, Ruler of Sharjah, 24 January 1971, 1972.

FCO 8/2134: Abu Dhabi Defence Force, 1972-73.

FCO 8/2371: Defence Attache's report for 1973 and intelligence reports on United Arab Emirates, 1974.

FCO 8/2430: Sale of military equipment from UK to United Arab Emirates, 1975.

FCO 8/2660: Internal political situation in United Arab Emirates, 1976.

FCO 8/2897: Defence Attache's annual review and other military reports on United Arab Emirates, 1977.

FCO 8/3101: Defence visits from United Arab Emirates (UAE) to UK, 1978.

FCO 8/3105: Defence Attache, Abu Dhabi: annual report on armed forces of United Arab Emirates (UAE) for 1977 and other military reports, 1978.

FCO 8/3453: Reactions of Gulf states to the Iran-Iraq War, 1980.

FCO 8/3461: Proposed visit by Francis Pym, Secretary of State for Defence, to Oman, United Arab Emirates, Qatar and Bahrain, January 1981, with briefing, 1980.

FCO 8/3512: Relations between the United Arab Emirates and Morocco, including Moroccan troops in Abu Dhabi, 1980.

FCO 8/3908: United Arab Emirates: annual review for 1980, 1981.

FCO 8/3909: Internal political affairs in the United Arab Emirates, 1981.

FCO 8/3925: Arms purchases by personalities of the United Arab Emirates, 1981.

FCO 8/4356: Gulf military cooperation, 1982.

FCO 8/4385: Defence Attache's annual report on the armed forces of the United Arab Emirates (UAE) for 1981, 1982.

FCO 8/4973: British loan service personnel for the United Arab Emirates (UAE), 1983.

FCO 8/5459: United Arab Emirates (UAE): annual review for 1983, 1984.

FCO 8/5468: UK training assistance to the United Arab Emirates (UAE): including annual report on the UAE armed forces for 1983, 1984.

FCO 8/5826: United Arab Emirates (UAE): annual review for 1984, 1985.

FCO 8/6170: Internal political affairs in the United Arab Emirates (UAE), 1986.

FCO 8/6171: UK/UAE Joint Committee, 1986.

FCO 8/6174: United Arab Emirates (UAE) and the Iran-Iraq War, 1986.

FCO 8/6176: UK military assistance to the United Arab Emirates (UAE), 1986.

FCO 8/6177: UK defence sales to the United Arab Emirates (UAE), 1986.

FCO 8/6181: Women in the United Arab Emirates (UAE), 1986.

FCO 8/6492: Visit by David Mellor, Minister of State for Foreign and Commonwealth Affairs, to Oman and the United Arab Emirates (UAE), November 1987, 1987.

FCO 18/792: Northern emirates of the United Arab Emirates (UAE), with internal boundaries and area in active dispute at Ras al-Khaimah-Oman border, 1978.

FCO 31/4053: Gift of Hawker Hunter and Islander aircraft by the United Arab Emirates (UAE) to Somalia, 1983.

FO 371/75018: Protection of British oil company personnel in Persian Gulf States. Boundary disputes between States. Proposed formation of a Levy Force, 1949.

FO 371/82175: Persian Gulf Levy Force: suppression of the slave trade in the Persian Gulf; formation of The Trucial Oman Levies, 1950.

FO 371/104268: Recommendations on HMG policy contained in a report by Sir Roger Makins on the Persian Gulf, 1953.

FO 371/109881: British Forces in the Persian Gulf States: protection of British interests; directive to senior RAF officer, 1954.

FO 371/114589: Internal political situation in Dubai and Trucial States: exile of Shekh Juma and family for flouting authority of the State, 1955.

FO 371/114680: Trucial Oman Levies; proposal to change name to Trucial Oman Scouts; financial responsibility for maintaining forces, 1955.

FO 371/120627: Trucial Oman Levies and Scouts, 1956.

FO 371/126951: Armed forces of UK in Persian Gulf, 1957.

FO 370/149048: Trucial Oman Scouts, 1960.

FO 371/156692: Military co-ordination Committee for Persian Gulf, 1961.

FO 371/157038: Trucial Oman Scouts (TOS), 1961.

FO 371/174718: Trucial Oman Scouts, 1964.

FO 371/179929: Abu Dhabi army, 1965.

FO 371/185551: Abu Dhabi army, 1966.

FO 464/58: Arabia: report on Trucial Coast frontier settlement, by Julian Fortay Walker, Assistant Political Agent, Trucial States, March 1955, 1955.

FO 1016/193: Trucial Oman Levies movements and progress report, 1952.

FO 1016/624: Internal political situation in Trucial States, 1958.

FO 1016/736: Trucial Oman Scouts: possible retention in Abu Dhabi, 1966.

WO 32/16413: Trucial Oman Levies: change of title to Trucial Oman Scouts and granting of colours, 1956-57.

WO 32/17123: Reorganisation of Headquarters British Forces Arabian Gulf and transfer of responsibilities and disciplinary powers, 1957-63.

WO 337/11: HQ intelligence summaries: nos 204-261 and 1-29, 1962-64.

WO 337/13: Security reports, 1959-71.

WO 337/14: Desert Intelligence Officer's reports for North East area of Trucial States, 1963-67.

WO 337/15: Intelligence summaries, 1965-67.

Royal Society for Asian Affairs, London

Barnes, Colin. A Short History of the Trucial Oman Levies, Trucial Oman Scouts and the Union Defence Force of the Trucial States (later United Arab Emirates) of the Arabian Gulf, 1951 to 1972, ca. 1976.

University of Exeter, Special Collections, Exeter

Trucial States Council. 'Trucial States Census Figures 1968', 1968. Exeter University.

National Archives of the UAE, Abu Dhabi

Colonel E.B. Wilson's Archives, Volumes 1, 2, 5 and 7, n.d.

II. Primary Sources – Published

Abu Dhabi Government

Abu Dhabi Emiri Decree No 8 of 1969 "Establishment of a Department of Defense to Be Responsible of Abu Dhabi Defense Force Matters at the Borders", 1 February 1969.

Abu Dhabi Law No. 14 of 2007 on the "Establishment the Critical National Infrastructure Authority", May 2007.

Abu Dhabi Law No. 14 of 2012 on the "Transferring CNIA Functions and Responsibilities to the Critical Infrastructure and Coastal Protection Authority", June 2012.

Chart of Accounts, 2012.

Statistical Yearbook of Abu Dhabi, 2017.

The Abu Dhabi Economic Vision 2030, 2008.

Cambridge Archive Editions

Burdett, A., ed. *Annual Records of the Gulf: 1961*, Volume 4: United Arab Emirates and Oman, 1991.

——. ed. *Defence 1920-1960* Vol. 10, The GCC States: National Development Records, 1994.

——. ed. Records of the Emirates 1961-1965: 1962, 1964 and 1965, 1997.

——. ed. Records of the Emirates 1966-1971: 1966, 1967, 1968 and 1969, 2002.

Priestland, J., ed. *The Buraimi Dispute: Contemporary Documents 1950-1961, Volume 5: 1954-1955*, 1992.

Trench, R., ed. *Arab Gulf Cities*. Slough: Archive Editions, 1994.

UK Foreign Office. *Foreign Office Annual Reports from Arabia, 1930-1960*, 1993.

——. Foreign Office Annual Reports from Arabia, 1930-1960: 1938-1953. Slough: Cambridge Archive Editions, 1993.

Dubai Government

Dubai Statistics Center. Statistical Yearbook – Emirate of Dubai 2010, 2011.

Dubai Statistics Center. Statistical Yearbook – Emirate of Dubai 2011, 2012.

Fujairah Government

Statistical Yearbook Nineteen Issue 2015, 2016.

UAE Government

Center for Higher Education Data and Statistics. Indicators of the UAE Higher Education Sector Students and the Learning Environment 2012-13, 2012

Constitution of the United Arab Emirates (Provisional), 1971

Study on the Educational Level of the Staff of the Federal Government in 2014, 2014

UAE Federal Authority for Nuclear Regulation. Safety Evaluation Report of an Application for a Licence to Construct Barakah Units 1 and 2: Part 1: Summary, 2012

UAE Federal Decreee No 1 of 2001 "On the Guarding of Land and Sea Borders of the Country", 30 September 2011 2001.

UAE Federal Decreee No 83 of 1992, 1992.

UAE Federal Law No 17 of 1972 "On Nationality, Passports and Amendments thereof", 1972.

UAE Federal Law No 17 of 2006 "On The Establishment Of The Supreme Council for National Security", 2006.

UAE Federal Law No 3 of 1971 "Regarding the Union Defence Force", 1971.

UAE Federal Law No 6 of 2014 "The National Military Service and Reserve Force", 2014.

UAE Ministry of Economy. *Annual Economic Report 2016*, 2016.

UAE Ministry of Environment and Water. *State of Environment 2015*, 2016.

UAE National Bureau of Statistics. *Census Population by Emirates 1975-2005*, n.d.

UAE National Bureau of Statistics. *UAE in Figures, 2009*, 2009.

UAE National Media Council. *UAE Annual Book 2016*, 2017.

UAE Supreme Defence Council Decision No. 1 'Regarding the Unification of the Armed Forces in the United Arab Emirates, 1976.

WAM media releases.

UK Government

UK Foreign Office. Historical Summary of Events in the Persian Gulf Shaikhdoms and the Sultanate of Muscat and Oman, 1928-1953, 1953.

UK Ministry of Defence. Defence: Outline of Future Policy, 1957.

UK Trade and Investment Defence and Security Organisation. *Defence & Security Opportunities: The UAE*, 2016.

UK Trade and Investment Defence and Security Organisation. Defence & Security Opportunities: The UAE. London, 2016.

UK Foreign Office. Historical Summary of Events in the Persian Gulf Shaikhdoms and the Sultanate of Muscat and Oman, 1928-1953. London: Foreign Office, 1953.

——. Historical Summary of Events in the Persian Gulf Shaikhdoms and the Sultanate of Muscat and Oman, 1928-1953, Appendices, Genealogical Tables. London: Foreign Office, 1953.

United States Government

Central Intelligence Agency. Military Capabilities of the Smaller Persian Gulf States, 1984.

Central Intelligence Agency. Prospects for Special Weapons Proliferation and Control, 1991.

Central Intelligence Agency. Sweden's Bofors Arms Scandal: A Summary of the Diversions, Investigations, and Implications, 1988.

Central Intelligence Agency. The Growing Naval Power of the Arab Gulf States, 1984.

Central Intelligence Agency. The Persian Gulf Amirates: Economic Assets and Prospects, 1970.

Central Intelligence Agency. The Terrorist Threat to the Gulf Cooperation Council States: The Next 18 Months. Washington, DC: CIA, 1986.

Central Intelligence Agency. *The United Arab Emirates: A Handbook*, 1992.

Central Intelligence Agency. *Tilting Toward Baghdad: Gulf States' Aid to Iraq.* Washington DC: CIA, 1981.

Department of Commence. 2016 Defense Markets Report Regional and Country Case Study: Middle East, 2016.

Department of Defense, Center For Law And Military Operations. Legal Lessons Learned From Afghanistan And Iraq: Volume I, Major Combat Operations (11 September 2001 To 1 May 2003), 2004.

Department of Defense. Foreign Military Training Fiscal Year: Joint Report to Congress, 2012/3, 2013/4, 2013/4 and 2014/5.

Department of State, Bureau of Arms Control, Verification and Compliance. *World Military Expenditures and Arms Transfers, 2005*, 2005.

Department of State, Bureau of Arms Control, Verification and Compliance. *World Military Expenditures and Arms Transfers, 2018*, 2018.

Department of State, Bureau of Democracy, Human Rights and Labor. *2018 Report on International Religious Freedom – United Arab Emirates*, 2019.

Department of State, Bureau of Democracy, Human Rights, and Labor. *2015 Report on International Religious Freedom – United Arab Emirates*, 2016.

Katzman, K., R.F. Grimmett, US Congressional Research Services. *United Arab Emirates: U.S. Relations and F-16 Aircraft Sale*, 2000.

Katzman, K., US Congressional Research Services. *The United Arab Emirates (UAE): Issues for U.S. Policy*, 2017.

Katzman, K., US Congressional Research Services. *The United Arab Emirates (UAE): Issues for U.S. Policy*, 2019.

US Arms Control and Disarmament Agency. World Military Expenditures and Arms Transfers 1972-1982, 1984.

US Central Intelligence Agency. Iranian Threats to the Persian Gulf States, 1987.

US Central Intelligence Agency. Persian Gulf Security: The Iranian Threat, 1982.

US House of Representatives, Committee on International Relations. United States Arms Policies in the Persian Gulf And Red Sea Areas: Past, Present, And Future – Report Of A Staff Survey Mission To Ethiopia, Iran and The Arabian Peninsula, 1977.

US Senate, Committee on Armed Services. Department of Defense Authorization for Appropriations for Fiscal Year 1989: Hearings Before the Committee on Armed Services, United States Senate, One Hundredth Congress, Second Session, on S. 2355, 1988.

III. Newspapers

Al Arabiya
Arab News
Emirates News
Financial Times
Gulf News
Gulf Weekly Mirror
Haaretz
Khaleej Times
Sunday Mirror
The Korea Times
The National
The New York Times
The News International
The Telegraph
The Times of India
The Wall Street Journal
Washington Post

IV. Primary Sources – Interviews and Correspondence

Al Suwaidi, Ahmed Madloum
Barndollar, Gil, national service researcher, Catholic University of America
Butler, M., ADDF 1968, & Special Branch Al Ain, 1968-70

Cooper, T.D., ADDF Land Forces, 1970-73

Culley, H.A., UDF/FAF, 1973-75

Curtis, J.M., A Squadron, TOS, 1966-68

Duffy, S., Senior Advisor Coast Guard, 2004-10

Gregory, D.J., ADDF Sea Wing Officer, 1969-75

Hellyer, P., UAE historian.

Hitchcock, R., OC A Squadron & subsequently founding officer 2nd Infantry Regiment, ADDF, 1967-70

Pillar, Brigadier A., Senior Military Contract Officer, UAE Armed Forces, 2002-11

Sheridan, R., ADDF Air Wing pilot

Steel, K., Commander DDF, 1971-72

Subject 262, contract officer with UAE Navy

Subject 382, Emirati Senior Naval Officer, 1980s

Subject 383, Emirati Special Guard officer, late 1970s-early 1970s

Subject 543, foreign academic researching the UAE national service, 2019

Subject 699, expatriate serving in a training institute from the late 2000s to mid-2010s

Thompson, S., Military Contract Officer, Fleet Sea Training Team, UAE Navy 2009-15

Weekes, N.C.F., UDF/FAF, 1974-76

Williams, J.J., founding Officer Commanding, Armoured Car Squadron, DDF

V. Primary Sources – Autobiographies

Balfour-Paul, G. T. *Bagpipes in Babylon: A Lifetime in the Arab World and Beyond.* London: I.B. Tauris, 2006.

Boustead, H. *The Wind of Morning: The Autobiography of Hugh Boustead.* Linden Pub., 2002.

Cawston, A., and M. Curtis. *Arabian Days: Memoirs of Two Trucial Oman Scouts.* Hampshire: Privately published, 2010.

Clayton, P. *Two Alpha Lima: The First Ten Years of the Trucial Oman Levies and Trucial Oman Scouts (1950 to 1960).* London: Janus Publishing Company, 1999.

de Butts, F.M. *Now the Dust Has Settled: Memories of War and Peace, 1939-1994.* Padstow: Tabb House, 1995.

Hawley, D. *The Emirates: Witness to a Metamorphosis.* Michael Russell, 2007.

Henderson, E.F. *This Strange Eventful History: Memoirs of Earlier Days in the UAE and the Sultanate of Oman.* Dubai: Motivate Publishing, 1993.

Holden, D. *Farewell to Arabia.* London: Faber & Faber, 1966.

Horniblow, P. *Oil, Sand and Politics: Memoirs of a Middle East Doctor, Mercenary and Mountaineer.* Cumbria: Hayloft, 2003.

Lamb, A.T., and J. Callaghan. *A Long Way from Swansea: A Memoir.* Clunderwen, UK: Starborn Books, 2003.

Lawrence, T.E. *Seven Pillars of Wisdom: A Triumph.* David Rehak, 2016.

Neild, D. *A Soldier in Arabia.* London: Medina Publishing, 2016.

Phillips, H. Envoy Extraordinary: A Most Unlikely Ambassador. London: Radcliffe Press, 1995.

Shepherd, A. *Arabian Adventure*. London: Collins, 1961.

Walker, J. *Tyro on the Trucial Coast*. Durham, UK: Memoir Club, 1999.

VI. Secondary Sources – Books, Articles, Chapters and Theses

Abdullah, M.M. *The United Arab Emirates: A Modern History*. London: Croom Helm, 1978.

Air Forces Central Command. *Al Dhafra welcomes new Air Warfare Center commander*, 19 June 2019, from <www.afcent.af.mil/Units/380th-Air-Expeditionary-Wing/ News/Display/Article/1937190/al-dhafra-welcomes-new-air-warfare-center-commander/>

——. *Falcon Shield strengthens coalition's air defense*, 8 October 2019, from

Ajjaj, A. 'Social Development of the Pirate Coast'. *Middle East Forum* XXXVIII Summer (1962).

Al-Dhaheri, Khalid. 'An Arabian Approach To Politics: Environment, Tradition and Leadership in the United Arab Emirates'. PhD thesis, University of Exeter, 2007.

Al-Khalifa, Shaikh Abdullah bin Khalid, and M. Rice, eds. *Bahrain Through The Ages – The History*. London: Taylor & Francis, 1993. Reprint, 2014.

Al-Sayegh, Fatma. 'Merchants' Role in a Changing Society: The Case of Dubai, 1900-90'. *Middle Eastern Studies* 34, 1 (1998).

Al-Ulama, Hesam Mohammed Jalil Sultan. 'The Federal Boundaries of the United Arab Emirates'. PhD thesis, University of Durham, 1994.

Al Abed, I., and P. Hellyer, eds. *United Arab Emirates: A New Perspective*. London: Trident Press, 2001.

Al Abed, I., P. Vine, and A. Al Jabali. *Chronicle of Progress: 25 Years of Development in the United Arab Emirates*. London: Trident Press, 1996.

Al Dhaheri, Nasser. *Roll of Honour: the Armed Forces of the United Arab Emirates*. Abu Dhabi: Directorate of Moral Guidance, The Armed Forces of the UAE, ca. 2006.

Al Mazrouei, N.S. *The UAE and Saudi Arabia: Border Disputes and International Relations in the Gulf*. London: I.B. Tauris, 2016.

Al Moalla, Sheikh Majid Abdulla. 'Analysis of the United Arab Emirates' National Security'. PhD thesis, Durham University, 2017.

Al Muhairi, Butti Sultan Butti Ali. 'The Islamisation of Laws in the UAE: The Case of the Penal Code'. *Arab Law Quarterly* 11, 4 (1996).

Al Nuaimi, Surour Ali Surour. 'The Relationship between Expatriates and Security in the UAE as Perceived by Emiratis and Expatriates'. Master's thesis, Khalifa University of Science and Technology, 2015.

Alkim, Hassan. *The Foreign Policy of the United Arab Emirates*. London: Saqi, 1989.

Allen, M. *Arabs*. New York: Bloomsbury Academic, 2006.

Almahasheer, H. *Environmental Monitoring and Assessment* 190, 85 (2018).

Almezaini, K.S. *The UAE and Foreign Policy: Foreign Aid, Identities and Interests*. London: Taylor & Francis, 2012.

Alneaimi, Mohamed Rashed. 'Population Growth and Water Resources in the United Arab Emirates, 1975 to 2025: A ArcGIS Approach'. PhD thesis, University of Arkansas, 2003.

Alterman, J.B., and M. Balboni. 'Citizens in Training: Conscription and Nation-Building in the United Arab Emirates'. Washington DC: Center for Strategic & International Studies, 2017.

Alyafei, Nasir. 'UAE is Politically and Diplomatically Key to GCC Maritime Aspirations'. *National Defense*, 2014.

APID-55 VTOL Minature UAV. Airforce Technology, n.d., from <www.airforce-technology.com/projects/cybaero-apid55-uav/>

Ardemagni, Eleonora. 'The Gulf Monarchies' Complex Fight Against Daesh'. *NATO Review*, 2016.

'The Armed Forces: An Active Role in Strengthening UAE'. *Nation Shield* 486, July (2012).

Army Recognition. 'IDEX 2013 Jobaria Defense Systems Multiple Cradle Launcher', 2013.

Association for Diplomatic Studies and Training. *Country Reader: United Arab Emirates*. Arlington: Association for Diplomatic Studies and Training, 2019.

Ayalon, A., and H. Shaked, eds. *Middle East Contemporary Survey, 1988* Vol. XII. Boulder: Westview Press, 1990.

Ayubi, N.N. *Over-stating the Arab State: Politics and Society in the Middle East*. London: I.B. Tauris, 1996.

Balfour Paul, G. *The End of Empire in the Middle East: Britain's Relinquishment of Power in Her Last Three Arab Dependencies*. Cambridge: Cambridge University Press, 1994.

Barakat, H. *The Arab World: Society, Culture, and State*. Berkeley: University of California Press, 1993.

Barany, Z. 'Why Have Three Gulf States Introduced the Draft?'. *The RUSI Journal* 162, 6 (2017): 16-26.

——. 'Military Officers in the Gulf: Career Trajectories and Determinants'. Center for Strategic & International Studies, 2019.

Barratt, R.H. 'British Influence on Arab Military Forces in the Gulf: The Trucial Oman Scouts'. MA thesis, American University of Beirut, 1972.

Belarus Government. *UAE Testing Belarusian Combat Tank Transporters*, 15 December 2016, from <www.belarus.by/en/business/business-news/uae-testing-belarusian-combat-tank-transporters_i_50298.html>

Below The Turret Ring. *Up-Armored Leclerc Operational with UAE Army*, 16 December 2017, from <below-the-turret-ring.blogspot.ae/2017/12/up-armored-leclerc-operational-with-uae.html>

Biddle, S. *Military Power: Explaining Victory and Defeat in Modern Battle*. Princeton: Princeton University Press, 2010.

Binnie, Jeremy. 'Emirati Armoured Brigade Spearheads Aden Breakout', In *Jane's Defence Weekly*. London: Jane's Information Group, 2015.

——. 'Sudan has "Largest Force" in Arab Coalition', In *Jane's Defence Weekly*. London: Jane's Information Group, 2019.

Bradshaw, T. 'Book Review – British Policy in the Persian Gulf, 1961-1968: Conceptions of Informal Empire, Helene von Bismarck'. *Britain & the World* 9, 1 (Jul 2016): 146-48.

——. 'The Hand of Glubb: the Origins of the Trucial Oman Scouts, 1948-1956'. *Middle Eastern Studies* 53, 4 (Jul 2017): 656-672.

——. 'Security forces and the end of empire in the Trucial States, 1960–1971'. *Middle Eastern Studies* (2020): 1-15.

Brown, R.J. *U.S Marines in the Persian Gulf, 1990-1991: With Marine Forces Afloat in Desert Shield and Desert Storm*. DIANE Publishing Company, 2000.

Bulleid family. 'Bulleid News', 30 May 2011.

CAE. 'CAE Awarded Contract to Provide Comprehensive RPA Training Solution to UAE Air Force & Air Defence'. news release, 8 May, 2017 <www.cae.com/CAE-awarded-contract-to-provide-comprehensive-RPA-training-solution-to-UAE-Air-Force-Air-Defence/>

Camber Corporation. 'Operations Advisor, Chemical Defense Command–13036'. news release, n.d., <www.10minuteswith.com/external/operations-advisor-chemical-defense-command-13036>

Carmi, Samir Anton. 'Administrative Development of the United Arab Emirates'. PhD thesis, American University of Beirut, 1983.

Carter, Ash, Secretary of Defense. *The Logic of American Strategy in the Middle East*. Washington DC: US Department of Defense, 2016.

Chubin, S. *Security in the Persian Gulf: Domestic Political Factors*. Vol. 1, Farnborough: Gower for the International Institute for Strategic Studies, 1981.

Comolli, Virginia, Francesca Grandi, and International Institute for Strategic Studies. 'The Armed Conflict Survey 2020'. Oxon: Routledge, 2020.

Cordesman, A.H. *The Gulf and the Search for Strategic Stability: Saudi Arabia, the Military Balance in the Gulf, and Trends in the Arab-Israeli Military Balance*. Boulder: Westview Press, 1984.

——. *USCENTCOM and its Area of Operations: Cooperation, Burden Sharing, Arms Sales, and Centcom's Analysis by Country and Subregion*. Washington DC: Center for Strategic & International Studies, 1998.

——. *The Military Balance in the Middle East – An Analytic Overview*. Washington DC: Center for Strategic & International Studies, 2004.

Cordesman, A.H., and A. Toukan. *Iran and the Gulf Military Balance*. Washington DC: Center for Strategic & International Studies, 2016.

Cordesman, A.H., and A. Wilner. *The Gulf Military Balance in 2012*. Washington DC: Center for Strategic & International Studies, 2012.

Cordesman, A.H., with assistance from M. Markusen and Eric P. Jones. *Stability and Instability in the Gulf Region in 2016: A Strategic Net Assessment (Working Draft)*. Washington DC: Center for Strategic & International Studies, 2016.

Crist, D.B. 'Operation Earnest Will: The United States in the Persian Gulf, 1986-1989'. PhD thesis, Florida State University, 1998.

Culley, Lt. Colonel H.A., UDF/FAF, 1973-75. 'Serving with the Union Defence Force, United Arab Emirates'. *The Wire: The Royal Signals Magazine*, November-December 1974.

Curtis, M. 'On Secondment with the Trucial Oman Scouts 1966-1968'. *Liwa: Journal of the National Center for Documentation & Research*, December 2:4 (2010).

Davidson, C.M. *The United Arab Emirates: A Study in Survival*. Boulder: Lynne Rienner Publishers, 2005.

——. *Abu Dhabi: Oil and Beyond*. Oxford: Oxford University Press, 2011.

——. 'Government in the United Arab Emirates: Progress and pathologies'. In *Governance in the Middle East and North Africa: A Handbook*, edited by A. Kadhim, 270-288. London: Taylor & Francis Group, 2013.

——. *After the Sheikhs: The Coming Collapse of the Gulf Monarchies*. Oxford: Oxford University Press, 2015.

Davis, Ian, and Steve Schofield. 'Upgrades and Surplus Weapons: Lessons From the UK Disposal Sales Agency': Bonn International Centre for Conversion, 1997.

DeAtkine, Norvell B. 'Why Arabs Lose Wars'. *The Middle East Quarterly* 7, 4 (December 1999).

——. 'The Arab as Insurgent'. *American Diplomacy* September (2009).

Dickman, F., US Ambassador Extraordinary in Abu Dhabi. 'Security Assistance Reporting – First Annual Integrated Assessment – UAE', 25 July 1978. Wikileaks.

Donald, David. 'UAE Forces Focus on Net Warfare'. *AINonline*, 11 December 2006.

Dresch, P., and J.P. Piscatori. *Monarchies and Nations: Globalization and Identity in the Arab States of the Gulf*. London: I.B. Tauris, 2005.

Duke Anthony, John, and John A. Hearty. 'Eastern Arabian States: Kuwait, Bahrain, Qatar, the United Arab Emirates, and Oman'. In *The Government and Politics of the Middle East and North Africa*, edited by D.E. Long and B. Reich. Boulder: Westview Press, 1980.

Edwards, F. *The Gaysh: A History of the Aden Protectorate Levies 1927-61 and the Federal Regular Army of South Arabia 1961-67*. Solihull: Helion & Co, 2004.

Eickelman, Dale. 'Tribes and Tribal Identity in the Arab Gulf States'. In *The Emergence of the Gulf States*, edited by J. E. Peterson. New York: Bloomsbury Publishing, 2016.

Embassy of the UAE in Berlin. *UAE Economic Bulletin*: Abu Dhabi, 2018.

Embassy of the UAE in Washington DC. *The UAE and Global Oil Supply*, n.d., from <www.uae-embassy.org/about-uae/energy/uae-and-global-oil-supply>

Europa Publications. *Middle East and North Africia 1984-85*. 1984.

Fawcett, L. *International Relations of the Middle East*. Oxford: Oxford University Press, 2016.

Feierstein, G. M. *Iran's Role in Yemen and Prospects for Peace*, United States Institute of Peace, 5 December 2018, from <iranprimer.usip.org/blog/2018/dec/05/iran%E2%80%99s-role-yemen-and-prospects-peace>

'The First Priority is Defending the UAE: Interview with Maj Gen Khaled Abdullah Al-Buainain, Commander of the UAE Air Force and Air Defence'. *Military Technology* November (2005).

Forbes, V.L. *The Maritime Boundaries of the Indian Ocean Region*. Singapore: Singapore University Press, National University of Singapore, 1995.

Force Analysis. *After Year of Failure, Coalition Takes Midi*, 2018, from <force-analysis.com/438-2/>

———. 'Yemen: War Amongst Divided Alliances'. Belguim: Force Analysis, 2018.

Forstenlechner, Ingo, and Emilie Jane Rutledge. 'The GCC's "Demographic Imbalance": Perceptions, Realities and Policy Options'. *Middle East Policy* XVIII, 4 (2011).

Frantzman, Seth J. '"By, With, and Through": How The U.S.-Led Coalition Defeated The Islamic State In Iraq Using Tactics Without Coherent Strategy For Confronting Iranian Influence'. *Middle East Review of International Affairs* 21, 3 (Fall/Winter) (2017).

Frenken, K. *Irrigation in the Middle East Region in Figures: AQUASTAT Survey – 2008*. Food and Agriculture Organization of the United Nations, 2009.

Friedman, B. 'From Union ('ittihād) to United (muttahida): The United Arab Emirates, A Success Born of Failure'. *Middle Eastern Studies* 53, 1 (2017): 112-135.

Gambrell, J. 'US, UAE troops launch major exercise Native Fury'. *Defense News*, 23 March 2020.

Geraghty, T. *Who Dares Wins: The Story of the Special Air Service, 1950-1992*. London: Little, Brown, 1992.

Global Security. *UAE Security Wall / Security Fence*, n.d., from <www.globalsecurity.org/military/world/gulf/uae-security.htm>

Glubb, J.B. *The Story of the Arab Legion*. London: Hodder and Stoughton, 1948.

Government of France. *The European mission is now operational in the Arabian-Persian Gulf*, 5 February 2020, from <www.gouvernement.fr/en/the-european-mission-is-now-operational-in-the-arabian-persian-gulf>

Granier, Bruno, Ahmed Al Suwaidi, Robert Busnardo, Sabah Aziz, and Rolf Schroeder. 'New Insight on the Stratigraphy of the "Upper Thamama" in Offshore Abu Dhabi (UAE)', 1-17: Carnets de Geologie, 2003.

Gulf Research Center and Migration Policy Centre. *UAE: Estimates of Total Population by Sex, Sex Ratios and Annual Demographic Growth Rates (1970-2010)*, 2014, from <gulfmigration.eu/uae-estimates-of-total-population-by-sex-sex-ratios-and-annual-demographic-growth-rates-1970-2010/>

———. *UAE: Estimates of Population Residing in the UAE by Country of Citizenship (Selected Countries, 2014)*, n.d., from <gulfmigration.eu/uae-estimates-of-population-residing-in-the-uae-by-country-of-citizenship-selected-countries-2014/>

Gupte, P. *Dubai: The Making of a Megapolis*. New Delhi: Penguin, 2011.

Harb, Imad K. 'Arab Gulf Military Institutions: Professionalism and National Development'. In *The Arms Trade, Military Services and the Security Market in the Gulf States: Trends and Implications*, edited by D.B.D. Roches and D. Thafer. Berlin & London: Gerlach Press, 2016.

Hashim, A.R.B. *Planning Abu Dhabi: An Urban History*. London: Taylor & Francis, 2018.

Hashim, Ahmed Salah. 'Military Orientalism: Middle East Ways of War'. *Middle East Policy* 26, 2 (2019): 31-47.

Hawley, D.F. *The Trucial States*. London: Allen & Unwin, 1970.

Hay, R. *The Persian Gulf States*. Washington DC: Middle East Institute, 1959.

Heard-Bey, Frauke. *From Trucial States to United Arab Emirates: A Society in Transition*. London: Longman, 1982.

——. 'The Tribal Society of the UAE and Its Traditional Economy'. In *United Arab Emirates: A New Perspective*, edited by I. Abed and P. Hellyer. London: Trident Press, 2001.

——. 'The United Arab Emirates: Statehood and Nation-Building in a Traditional Society'. *Middle East Journal* 59, 3 (2005): 357-75.

——. 'Six Sovereign States: the Process of State Formation'. In *The Emergence of the Gulf States*, edited by J.E. Peterson. New York: Bloomsbury Publishing, 2016.

Helms, US Ambassador in Tehran to General Brent Scowcroft, White House. 'Paragraph 4 of WH 31209, May 16, 1973', 16 May 1973. Author's collection, Abu Dhabi.

Henderson, E.F. *This Strange Eventful History: Memoirs of Earlier Days in the UAE and the Sultanate of Oman*. Dubai: Motivate Publishing, 1993.

Herbert-Burns, R. 'Petroleum Trade Security in the Indo-Pacific Region: an Assessment of Australia's Crude Oil and Refined Product Import Security and Supply Resilience', In *Soundings*. Canberra: Sea Power Centre, 2015.

Herr, W.E. 'Operation Vigilant Warrior: Conventional Deterrence Theory, Doctrine and Practice'. Air University, Maxwell Air Force Base, 1996.

Herrington, Air Vice-Marshal John. 'Operation Vantage – Kuwait 1961'. *Journal of the Royal Air Force Historical Society* 21 (2000).

Hoyland, R.G. *Arabia and the Arabs: From the Bronze Age to the Coming of Islam*. London: Taylor & Francis, 2002.

HRH Prince Salman bin Hamad Al Khalifa, Crown Prince, Deputy Supreme Commander and First Deputy Prime Minister. *HRH CP visits Royal Guard; honours servicemen who participated in Taskforce 11*, 20 June 2017, from <crown-prince.bh/en/media-centre/news/4268/2017/6/20/HRH-CP-visits-Royal-Guard;-honours-servicemen-who-participated-in-Taskforce-11>

Hunter, B. 'United Arab Emirates'. In *The Statesman's Year-Book 1991-92*. New York: Palgrave Macmillan, 1992.

Hurriez, S.H. *Folklore and Folklife in the United Arab Emirates*. London: Taylor & Francis, 2013.

Ibish, Hussein. 'The UAE's Evolving National Security Strategy'. Washington DC: The Arab Gulf States Institute in Washington, 2017.

International Crisis Group. 'Yemen: Is Peace Possible?', In *Middle East Report*. Brussels, 2016.

International Monetary Fund. *United Arab Emirates: IMF Country Report No. 09/120*. Washington DC, 2009.

———. *United Arab Emirate Selected Issues: IMF Country Report No. 17/219*. Washington DC, 2017.

Iqbal, A., and P. Hellyer. 'The UAE in World War Two: The War at Sea'. *Tribulus* 25 (2017).

Iqbal, A., P. Hellyer, and L. Garey. 'The UAE in World War Two: A Forgotten Fatal Air Crash in Sharjah'. *Tribulus* 25 (2017): 25-32.

Jane's Information Group. *Jane's World Armies*. Coulsdon: Jane's Information Group, 2014.

Juneau, Thomas. 'The UAE and the War in Yemen: From Surge to Recalibration'. *Survival* 62, 4 (2020): 157-186.

Kamrava, M. *Troubled Waters: Insecurity in the Persian Gulf*. Cornell: Cornell University Press, 2018.

Kay, Shirley. *Wings Over the Gulf*. Dubai: Motivate, 1995.

Kelly, J.B. *Britain and the Persian Gulf: 1795-1880*. 1968.

———. *Arabia, the Gulf and the West*. London: Weidenfeld and Nicolson, 1980.

Khalifa, A.M. *The United Arab Emirates: Unity in Fragmentation*. Boulder: Westview Press, 1979.

Kilgore, H., Brigade Training Team Deputy Lead, OPs/Fires, Land Forces (2014-15). *User Profile*, LinkedIn, n.d., from <linkedin.com/in/haimes-andy-kilgore-ltc-r-mba-61b48770>

Knights, M. *Troubled Waters: Future U.S. Security Assistance in the Persian Gulf*. Washington DC: Washington Institute for Near East Policy, 2006.

———. *Rising to Iran's Challenge: GCC Military Capability and U.S. Security Cooperation*. Policy Focus. Vol. 127, Washington DC: Washington Institute for Near East Policy, 2013.

———. *Lessons From the UAE War in Yemen*, Lawfare, 2019, from <www.lawfareblog.com/lessons-uae-war-yemen>

Kuwait News Agency. *Sheikh Zayed Ratifies Border Agreement With Oman*, 27 January 2003, from <www.kuna.net.kw/ArticlePrintPage.aspx?id=1315340&language=en>

La Franchi, P. 'UAE Air Force Lays Out Advanced Warfighting Plans'. *Flight International*, 16 December 2005.

Lacey, R. *Inside the Kingdom: Kings, Clerics, Modernists, Terrorists, and the Struggle for Saudi Arabia*. New York: Penguin Books, 2009.

Lawrence, T.E. *Seven Pillars of Wisdom: A Triumph*. London: Doubleday, Doran & Company, 1935.

Lee, David. *Flight from the Middle East: A History of the Royal Air Force in the Arabian Peninsula and Adjacent Territories, 1945-72*. London: HM Stationery Office, 1981.

Liebl, V. 'Oil War: Iran and the Military Balance in the Persian Gulf'. *Modern War*, Nov-Dec 2012.

Lienhardt, P., with A. Al-Shahi (ed.). *Shaikhdoms of Eastern Arabia*. London: Palgrave Macmillan, 2001.

Litwak, R. *Security in the Persian Gulf: Sources of Inter-state conflict*. Vol. 2, Farnborough: Gower for the International Institute for Strategic Studies, 1981.

Lorenz, Joseph P. 'Egypt and the New Arab Coalition', 1989. edited by National Defense University Institute for National Stragetic Studies. Washington, DC.

Louis, W.R., and S.R. Ashton. *East of Suez and the Commonwealth 1964-1971*. London: HM Stationery Office, 2004.

Lutterbeck, D. 'Change and Opportunities in the Emerging Mediterranean'. Chap. The Role of Armed Forces in the Arab Uprisings, edited by Stephen Calleya and Monika Wohlfeld. Malta: Mediterranean Academy of Diplomatic Studies, University of Malta, 2012.

Mackie, Cameron. 'Sharjah Battle 24th January 1972'. *Trucial Oman Officers Association Newsletter*, February (2012).

Macris, J.R. *The Politics and Security of the Gulf: Anglo-American Hegemony and the Shaping of a Region*. London: Taylor & Francis, 2010.

———. *Population and Economic Activities in the Arab Trucial States: A 1901 Accounting*. Vol. 6: 2015.

Maitra, J. *Zayed: From Challenges to Union*. Abu Dhabi: Centre for Documentation and Research, 2007.

Maitra, J., and A. Ḥajjī. *Qasr Al Hosn: The History of the Rulers of Abu Dhabi, 1793-1966*. Abu Dhabi: Centre for Documentation and Research, 2001.

Mallakh, R. *The Economic Development of the United Arab Emirates (RLE Economy of Middle East)*. London: Taylor & Francis, 2014.

Mann, M. *The Trucial Oman Scouts: The Story of a Bedouin Force*. Wilby, Norwich: Michael Russell, 1994.

Martin, Vice-Admiral Sir John. 'The Last Year in Aden – The Royal Navy'. *Journal of the Royal Air Force Historical Society* 18 (1998).

Martin, Y., US Army. *USARCENT commander engages military leaders in UAE*, 19 April 2016, from <www.army.mil/article/166305/usarcent_commander_engages_military_leaders_in_uae>

Mason, Robert. 'Breaking the Mold of Small State Classification? The Broadening Influence of United Arab Emirates Foreign Policy Through Effective Military and Bandwagoning Strategies'. *Canadian Foreign Policy Journal* 24, 1.

Mauroni, A.J. *Chemical-biological Defense: U.S. Military Policies and Decisions in the Gulf War*. Westport: Praeger, 1998.

Mawby, S. *British Policy in Aden and the Protectorates 1955-67: Last Outpost of a Middle East Empire*. London: Taylor & Francis, 2006.

Mello, Alex, and Michael Knights. 'The Saudi-UAE War Effort in Yemen (Part 1): Operation Golden Arrow in Aden', In *Policy Watch*. Washington DC: The Washington Institute, 2015.

———. 'The Saudi-UAE War Effort in Yemen (Part 2): The Air Campaign', In *Policy Watch*. Washington DC: The Washington Institute, 2015.

——. 'West of Suez for the United Arab Emirates'. *War on the Rocks*, 2 September 2016.

Meredith, M., International Field Artillery and Operations Consultant, Land Forces (2012-18). *User Profile*, LinkedIn, n.d., from <www.linkedin.com/in/michael-meredith-72a1285a/>

Mermier, Franck. *Southern Secessionists Divided by Regional Identities*, Italian Institute for International Political Studies, 20 March 2018, from <www.ispionline.it/en/pubblicazione/yemens-southern-secessionists-divided-regional-identities-19930>

Metz, Helen Chapin. *Persian Gulf States: Country Studies*. Washington DC: US GPO, 1994.

Middle East Research Institute. *United Arab Emirates*. London: Routledge Revival, 1984.

Miles, S.B. *The Countries and Tribes of the Persian Gulf*. London: Harrison and Sons, 1919.

Military-Today. *MZKT-74135 Tank Transporter*, n.d., from <www.military-today.com/trucks/mzkt_74135.htm>

Morton, M.Q. *Buraimi: The Struggle for Power, Influence and Oil in Arabia*. London: I.B. Tauris, 2013.

——. *Keepers of the Golden Shore: A History of the United Arab Emirates*. London: Reaktion Books, 2016.

Motohiro, Ono. 'Reconsideration of the Meanings of the Tribal Ties in the United Arab Emirates: Abu Dhabi Emirate in Early '90s'. *Kyoto Bulletin of Islamic Area Studies* 4, 1 & 2 (2011).

Mueller, Karl P. 'Precision and Purpose: Airpower in the Libyan Civil War'. Santa Monica: RAND Corporation, 2015.

Mühlböck, Monika Fatima. 'Rules and Regulations of the Federal National Council of the United Arab Emirates and the National Consultative Council of the Emirate of Abu Dhabi and their Functions within the Country's Socio-political Sphere'. *Verfassung und Recht in Übersee / Law and Politics Overseas* 31, 4 (1998): 483-522.

'Muslim Expatriates in Al Ain Rioted on 6 December 1992 – Pakistani Deportation'. *APS Diplomat Recorder – Arab Press Service Organization (ASPR)*, 26 December, 37: 26 1992.

Naylor, M. *Among Friends: The Scots Guards 1956-1993*. Havertown: Pen & Sword, 1995.

Nevarez, H., Senior Instruction, Courseware & Doctrine Developer, Land Forces (2012-14). *User Profile*, LinkedIn, n.d., from <www.linkedin.com/in/hector-nevarez-ba-2419b030/>

Noyes, A. 'Last Marines in the Trucial States'. *Globe & Laurel* May-June (1976).

Nuclear Threat Initiative. *Iraq*, July 2017, from <www.nti.org/learn/countries/iraq/>

Nye, J.S. *Soft Power: The Means To Success In World Politics*. New York: PublicAffairs, 2004.

——. *The Future of Power*. New York: PublicAffairs, 2011.

O'Sullivan, E. *The New Gulf: How Modern Arabia Is Changing the World for Good.* Dubai: Motivate Publishing, 2009.

Oliver, K.M. *Through Adversity: The History of the Royal Air Force Regiment, 1942-1992.* Rushden: Forces & Corporate, 1997.

Olsen, J.M. 'Norway Suspends Arms Exports to UAE Amid War in Yemen'. *AP*, 3 January 2018.

Olson, Richard, US Ambassador to the UAE. 'A Long Hot Summer for UAE-Saudi relations', 15 October 2009. Wikileaks.

——. 'Mohammed bin Zayed', 31 August 2009. Wikileaks.

Onley, J. *The Arabian Frontier of the British Raj: Merchants, Rulers, and the British in the Nineteenth-Century Gulf.* Oxford: Oxford University Press, 2007.

——. *Britain and the Gulf Shaikhdoms, 1820-1971: The Politics of Protection.* Washington DC: Center for International and Regional Studies, Georgetown University School of Foreign Service in Qatar, 2009.

Opall-Rome, B. 'Trump Could Let the UAE Buy F-35 jets'. *Defense News*, 4 November 2017.

Organization of the Petroleum Exporting Countries. '2020 OPEC Annual Statistical Bulletin'. Vienna, Austria: OPEC, 2020.

Osborne, T. 'UAE's Mysterious Airbase'. *Aviation Week*, 2 April 2015.

'Pakistani Pilot Deal Linked to US Block on UAE Technology Release'. *Flight International*, 24 March 1999.

Paxton, J. 'United Arab Emirates'. In *The Statesman's Year-Book 1984-85*. London: Palgrave Macmillan, 1985.

Perkins, B.M. 'Saudi Arabia and the UAE in al-Mahra: Securing Interests, Disrupting Local Order, and Shaping a Southern Military'. *Terrorism Monitor* 17, 4 (2019).

Petersen, T.T. *Richard Nixon, Great Britain and the Anglo–American Alignment in the Persian Gulf and Arabian Peninsula: Making Allies Out of Clients.* Sussex Academic Press, 2011.

Peterson, J.E. *Defending Arabia.* London: Croom Helm, 1986.

Phillips, J. 'Sheikh Rejects Pleas to Abandon Coup in United Arab Emirates'. *UPI*, 18 June 1987.

Plotkin Boghardt, Lori. *The Muslim Brotherhood on Trial in the UAE*, The Washington Institute, 2013, from <www.washingtoninstitute.org/policy-analysis/view/the-muslim-brotherhood-on-trial-in-the-uae>

Pocock, C. *Aerostats Rise Through the Ranks in Surveillance Service*, 12 November 2011, from <www.ainonline.com/aviation-news/defense/2011-11-12/aerostats-rise-through-ranks-surveillance-service>

Podeh, E., and O. Winckler. 'The Boycott That Never Was: Egypt and the Arab System, 1979-1989', In *Working Paper.* Durham: Centre for Middle Eastern and Islamic Studies, University of Durham, 2002.

Pollack, K.M. 'The Influence of Arab Culture on Arab Military Effectiveness'. Massachusetts Institute of Technology, 1996.

———. *Arabs at War: Military Effectiveness, 1948-1991*. University of Nebraska Press, 2004.

———. *Armies of Sand: The Past, Present, and Future of Arab Military Effectiveness*. Oxford University Press, 2019.

Porter, R. 'The Trucial Oman Scouts (TOS) 1951-1971'. *The Bulletin: Journal of the Military Historical Society* 41, 163 (1991).

Prasad, S.K. *Chemical Weapons*. New Delhi: Discovery Publishing House, 2009.

Presidential Guard. *Vision Statement [Wall Plaque]*. Majalis, Presidential Guard Building: Al Manhal Palace, Abu Dhabi, 2012.

Program, Al Bayariq Student Citizenship. *What is Al Bayariq?*, ca. 2014, from <noufandtufool.wordpress.com/al-bayariq-vision/>

Rabi, Uzi. 'Britain's "Special Position" in the Gulf: Its Origins, Dynamics and Legacy'. *Middle Eastern Studies* 42, 3 (2006): 351-364.

Rabinovich, I., and H. Shaked, eds. *Middle East Contemporary Survey, 1986* Vol. X. New York: Avalon Publishing, 1988.

Rashid, Noor Ali. *Sheikh Mohammed – Life and Times*. Dubai: Motivate Publishing, 2009.

Rheinmetall Defence. 'Rheinmetall Unveils New Armoured Fuchs/Fox BIO Reconnaissance Systems for United Arab Emirates'. news release, 20 February, 2011 <www.rheinmetall-defence.com/en/rheinmetall_defence/public_relations/news/detail_1348.php>

Rickli, J.M. 'The Political Rationale and Implications of the United Arab Emirates' Military Involvement in Libya'. In *Political Rationale and International Consequences of the War in Libya*, edited by D. Henriksen and A.K. Larssen. Oxford: Oxford University Press, 2016.

Ridge, N., S. Farah, and S. Shami. 'Patterns and Perceptions in Male Secondary School Dropouts in the United Arab Emirates', In *Working Paper 03*: Sheikh Saud bin Saqr Al Qasimi Foundation for Policy Research, 2013.

Ridge, N., S. Kippels, and B.J. Chung. *The Challenges and Implications of a Global Decline in the Educational Attainment and Retention of Boys*. Vol. RR 2.2017, Qatar: Wold Innovation Summit For Education, 2017.

Ross, R., Senior Safety Advisor, JAC. *User Profile*, LinkedIn, n.d., from <www.linkedin.com/in/robert-ross-293b6a51/>

Rossiter, A. 'Strength in Unity: The Road to the Integrated UAE Armed Forces'. *Liwa: Journal of the National Archives* 7, 13 (2015).

———. *Security in the Gulf: Local Militaries before British Withdrawal*. Cambridge: Cambridge University Press, 2020.

Roston, Aram. 'American Mercenaries'. *BuzzFeed*, 16 October 2018.

Rubin, B.M. *Guide to Islamist Movements*. Armonk: Sharpe, 2010.

Rugh, William A. 'The Foreign Policy of the United Arab Emirates'. *Middle East Journal* 50, 1 (1996): 57-70.

Saab, Bilal Y. 'The Gulf Rising: Defense Industrialization in Saudi Arabia and the UAE', 2014. edited by Atlantic Council.

Salisbury, Peter. 'Yemen's Southern Powder Keg'. London: Chatham House: The Royal Institute of International Affairs, 2018.

——. 'Risk Perception and Appetite in UAE Foreign and National Security Policy'. London: Chatham House: The Royal Institute of International Affairs, 2020.

Sarles, Harry, US Army Command and General Staff College. *Emirati Land Forces Commander Inducted to U.S. Army CGSC International Hall of Fame*, 2018, from <www.usarcent.army.mil/News/Features/Article/1664709/emirati-land-forces-commander-inducted-to-us-army-cgsc-international-hall-of-fa/>

Saudi Arabia and United Arab Emirates. 'Agreement Of the Delimitation of Boundaries (With Exchange of Letters and Map.) Signed at Jeddah, Saudi Arabia on 21 August 1974.', 1974.

Saudi Press Agency. *Brig. Gen. Ahmed Asiri Announces Achievement of Determination Storm's Goals, Beginning of Operation Hope Restore 2 Riyadh*, 2015, from <www.spa.gov.sa/viewstory.php?newsid=1352534>

Schanz, M.V. 'Allies in the Gulf'. *Air Force Magazine*, 12 January 2013.

——. 'Curtain Up at AFCENT's Air Warfare Center'. *Air Force Magazine*, 12 January 2015.

Seo, Jeongmin. 'South Korea–Gulf relations and the Iran factor'. In *External Powers and the Gulf Monarchies*, edited by J. Fulton and L.C. Sim. London: Taylor & Francis, 2019.

Shaikh, A.R. *The Story of the Pakistan Air Force, 1988-1998: A Battle Against Odds*. Islamabad: Shaheen Foundation, 2000.

Sharjah Police. *About Us*, n.d., from <www.shjpolice.gov.ae/en/about.aspx>

Shcherbakov, V. 'Pantsir: Guarding the Skies'. *Army & Navy Review (Russia)*, 2017.

Sherwood, L. 'Risk Diversification and the United Arab Emirates' Foreign Policy'. In *The Small Gulf States*, edited by K.S. Almezaini and J.M. Rickli. London: Routledge, 2017.

Sindelar, H.R., and J.E. Peterson. *Crosscurrents in the Gulf: Arab Regional and Global Interests*. London: Routledge, 1988.

Sison, Michele J., US Ambassador to the UAE. 'UAE Minimizing Influence of Islamic Extremists', 2004. Wikileaks.

——. 'CENTCOM Deputy Commander General Smith Visits UAE', 2005. Wikileaks.

——. 'General Abizaid Meeting with Abu Dhabi Crown Prince', 2005. Wikileaks.

——. 'Points for A/USTR Novelli's FTA BILATS', 2005. Wikileaks.

——. 'Scenesetter for PDAS Cheney's visit to the UAE', 2005. Wikileaks.

——. 'UAE Counterterrorism Efforts: Good Hardware, but Poor Coordination', 2005. Wikileaks.

——. '[untitled cable Abu Dhabi 00003851 001.2 of 006]', 2 October 2006. Wikileaks.

——. 'U/S Burns' January 22 Meeting with Abu Dhabi Crown Prince and UAE Foreign Minister', 2007. Wikileaks.

Smith, S.C. *Britain and the Arab Gulf after Empire: Kuwait, Bahrain, Qatar, and the United Arab Emirates, 1971-1981*. Oxon, UK: Taylor & Francis, 2019.

Soto, R. *Education in Dubai from Quantity to Quality*. Dubai: Government of Dubai, 2012.

Spencer, James. *Pollack Book on Arab Militaries Misses Mark*, LobeLog, 17 February 2019, from <lobelog.com/pollack-book-on-arab-militaries-misses-mark/>.

Stanley-Price, N. *Imperial Outpost in the Gulf: The Airfield at Sharjah (UAE) 1932-1952*. Sussex: Book Guild, 2012.

Stansfield, G., and S. Kelly. 'A Return to East of Suez? UK Military Deployment to the Gulf', In *Briefing Paper*. London: Royal United Services Institute, 2013.

Stewart, Phil. 'U.S. Signs New Defense Accord With Gulf Ally UAE'. *Reuters*, 16 May 2017.

Stockholm International Peace Research Institute. *Trends in International Arms Transfers*. 2011.

——. *Arms Transfers Database (recipient/supplier)*, 2018, from <www.sipri.org/databases/armstransfers>

——. *SIPRI Arms Transfers Database – Methodology*, 2018, from <www.sipri.org/databases/armstransfers/background>

——. *Arms Transfers Database (weapons category)*, 2019, from <www.sipri.org/databases/armstransfers>

——. *Military Expenditure Data: 1988–2018*, 2019, from <www.sipri.org/databases/milex>

——. 'Trends in World Military Expenditure, 2019', In *SIPRI Fact Sheet*, 2020.

Sweetman, B., and T. Osborne. 'It's Open Season For Defense Sales To UAE'. *Aviation Week & Space Technology*, 11 November 2013.

Talmadge, C. *The Dictator's Army: Battlefield Effectiveness in Authoritarian Regimes*. Ithaca: Cornell University Press, 2015.

TanQeeb. 'CBRNE Specialist, UAE Chemical Defense Command – 13999'. (2016).

The Center for Strategic and International Studies. *The Gulf: Implications of British Withdrawal*. Washington DC: Georgetown University, 1969.

The International Institute of Strategic Studies. *The Military Balance 2017*. London: Routledge, 2017.

The World Bank. *Armed Forces Personnel, Total 1985-2015*, n.d., from <data.world-bank.org/indicator/MS.MIL.TOTL.P1?end=2015&start=1985>

Thomas, B., and J. Lake. 'Innovation for and From the UAE'. *Military Technology* 2 (2017).

Torgler, J., Curriculum Specialist, UAE Chemical Defense School, Abu Dhabi, for Camber Corporation. 'User Profile': LinkedIn, n.d.

Toronto, N.W. *How Militaries Learn: Human Capital, Military Education, and Battlefield Effectiveness*. Lanham, Maryland: Lexington Books, 2018.

Trayer, G., Consultant and Courseware/Doctrine Development Officer, Land Forces (2013-15). *User Profile*, LinkedIn, n.d., from <linkedin.com/in/gene-trayer-84020945>

Trevithick, J. 'UAE Could Become the First Middle Eastern Country After Israel to Get the F-35'. *The Drive*, 6 November 2017.

Trimble, S. 'UAE Air Combat Debut Hit by Communications Issues'. *Flight Daily News*, 12 November 2011.

Type, M. 'TOL'. *Soldier Magazine* January (1956).

'UAE'. *Middle East Economic Digest* December 21 (1979).

UAE Armed Forces. *The UAE Armed Forces History and Missions*. Abu Dhabi: Museum and Military History Center, 2011.

UAE Ministry of Foreign Affairs and International Cooperation. *Embassy of the UAE in London: Bilateral Relations*, n.d., from <www.mofa.gov.ae/EN/Diplomatic Missions/Embassies/London/AboutEmbassy/Pages/BilateralRelations.aspx>

——. *Census Population by Emirates 1975-2005 (excel sheet)*. Abu Dhabi, n.d.

UAE National Service and Reserve Authority. *The Strategy*, UAE National Service and Reserve Authority, 2015, from <www.uaensr.ae/Pages/الأسترتاتيجية.aspx>

'UAE to Boost Troop Presence in Afghanistan for Training: Officials'. *Reuters*, 8 June 2018.

Ulrichsen, K.C. *Insecure Gulf: The End of Certainty and the Transition to the Post-Oil Era*. Oxford: Oxford University Press, 2015.

——. *The United Arab Emirates: Power, Politics and Policy-Making*. Basingstoke: Taylor & Francis, 2016.

'United Arab Emirates'. *Flight International*, 13 March 1975.

'United Arab Emirates'. *Flight International*, 2 July 1977.

United Nations Security Council. 'Letter Dated 9 October 2015 From the Chair of the Security Council Committee Pursuant to Resolutions 751 (1992) and 1907 (2009) Concerning Somalia and Eritrea Addressed to the President of the Security Council'. New York, 2015.

——. 'Letter Dated 4 March 2016 From the Panel of Experts on Libya Established Pursuant to Resolution 1973 (2011) Addressed to the President of the Security Council', 2016.

——. 'Final report of the Panel of Experts on Yemen'. New York, 2019.

University of Modern Sciences. *Umm Al Quwain*, n.d., from <ums.ae/data.aspx?Id=1111>

US Embassy in Abu Dhabi. 'UAE Establishes National Security Council', 14 June 2006. Wikileaks.

US Embassy in London. 'Current Level of British Presence in Gulf States And Oman', 24 February 1975. Wikileaks.

Valine, Debra, US Army. *United Arab Emirates gets air defense boost from U.S.*, 2019, from <www.army.mil/article/218898/united_arab_emirates_gets_air_defense_boost_from_u_s_>

van der Bijl, N. *Sharing the Secret: The History of the Intelligence Corps 1940-2010*. Havertown: Pen & Sword Books, 2013.

van der Meulen, Hendrik. 'The Role of Tribal and Kinship Ties in the Politics of the United Arab Emirates'. PhD thesis, Fletcher School of Law and Diplomacy, 1997.

von Bismarck, H. "'A Watershed in our Relations with the Trucial States": Great Britain's Policy to Prevent the Opening of an Arab League Office in the Persian Gulf in 1965'. *Middle Eastern Studies* 47, 1 (2011): 1-24.

——. *British Policy in the Persian Gulf, 1961-1968: Conceptions of Informal Empire.* Basingstoke: Palgrave Macmillan, 2013.

Wahba, Marcelle M., US Ambassador to the UAE. 'Scenesetter for General Abizaid's visit to the UAE', 2004. Wikileaks.

Walcot, Tom. 'The Trucial Oman Scouts 1955 to 1971: An Overview'. *Asian Affairs* 37, 1 (2006): 17-30.

Wallin, M. 'U.S. Military Bases and Facilities in the Middle East: Fact Sheet'. American Security Project, 2018.

Warwick, N.W.M. *In Every Place: The RAF Armoured Cars in the Middle East 1921-1953.* Rushden: Forces & Corporate Publishing, 2014.

Wehrey, Frederic. *Gulf Participation in the Anti–Islamic State Coalition: Limitations and Costs*, 23 September 2014, from <carnegie-mec.org/diwan/56710?lang=en>

Wilson, G.H. *Zayed, Man Who Built a Nation.* Abu Dhabi: Ministry of Information & Culture, 2013.

——. *Khalifa: Journey Into the Future.* Abu Dhabi: Media Prima, 2015.

Winger, Gregory. 'The Velvet Gauntlet: A Theory of Defense Diplomacy', In *VIWM Junior Visiting Fellows' Conferences*: Institute for Human Services, 2014.

Wittes, T.C. *Freedom's Unsteady March: America's Role in Building Arab Democracy.* Washington DC: Brookings Institution Press, 2008.

Yates, A. 'Challenging the accepted understanding of the executive branch of the UAE's Federal Government'. *Middle Eastern Studies*, 2020.

——. 'The Use of British Seconded and Contracted Military Personnel to Advance Britain's Interests: A Case Study from the United Arab Emirates from 1965-2010'. In *Defense Engagement since 1900: Global Lessons in Soft Power*, edited by G. Kennedy. Kansas: University Press of Kansas, 2020.

——. 'The Formation of Military Intelligence in the United Arab Emirates: 1965-1974'. *Journal of Intelligence History* (October 2020).

——. 'Building a Navy From Scratch in Just a Decade: the Abu Dhabi Sea Wing and Navy (1966-1976)'. In *Middle Eastern Naval History*, edited by J. Dunn and D. Stoker. Solihull: Helion & Co, 2021 (in press).

——. *Invisible Expatriates: Western Military Professionals and the Development of the UAE Armed Forces.* (forthcoming).

Yates, A., and C. Lord. *The Military and Polices Forces of the Gulf States: Trucial States & United Arab Emirates, 1951-1980.* Solihull: Helion & Co, 2019.

——. *The Naval Force of Abu Dhabi 1967 – 1976.* Canberra: C-Pubs, 2019.

Yates, A., and A. Rossiter. 'Intelligence Collection in Arabia: Britain's Roaming Information-Gathers in the Trucial States, 1956-1971'. *Intelligence and National Security*, 35, 6 (2020).

——. 'Military Assistance as Political Gimmickry? The Case of Britain and the Newly Federated UAE'. *Diplomacy & Statecraft* (2020 (in press)).

——. 'Forging a force: rulers, professional expatriates, and the creation of Abu Dhabi's Police'. *Middle Eastern Studies*, 56, 6 (2020).

Yetiv, Steve A. 'The Outcomes of Operations Desert Shield and Desert Storm: Some Antecedent Causes'. *Political Science Quarterly* 107, 2 (1992): 195-212.

Young, K.E. *The Political Economy of Energy, Finance and Security in the United Arab Emirates: Between the Majilis and the Market.* Houndmills: Palgrave Macmillan, 2014.

Young, K.E., and M Elleman. *Unlocking Growth: How the Gulf Security Sector Can Lead Economic Diversification.* Washington DC: The Arab Gulf States Institute in Washington, 2017.

Zahlan, Rosemarie Said. *The Origins of the United Arab Emirates: A Political and Social History of the Trucial States.* London: Macmillan, 1978.

Zakheim, Dov S. *Kenneth Pollack's New History of Arab Armies*, The National Interest, 10 February 2019, from <nationalinterest.org/feature/kenneth-pollack%E2%80%99s-new-history-arab-armies-44092?page=0%2C3>

Ziolkowski, M.C., Ziolkowski, L.T. 'The Bridges of Wadi Ham, Fujairah, U.A.E.'. *Liwa: Journal of the National Archives* 7, 16 (2016).

Index

Note: *t* following the page number for tables, an *f* following the page number for figures, and an *n* following the page number for footnotes